Level Design

Level Design

Concept, Theory, and Practice

Rudolf Kremers

CRC Press
Taylor & Francis Group
Boca Raton London New York

CRC Press is an imprint of the
Taylor & Francis Group, an **informa** business

AN A K PETERS BOOK

A K Peters/CRC Press
Taylor & Francis Group
6000 Broken Sound Parkway NW, Suite 300
Boca Raton, FL 33487-2742

© 2010 by Taylor and Francis Group, LLC
CRC Press is an imprint of Taylor & Francis Group, an Informa business

No claim to original U.S. Government works

ISBN 13: 978-1-56881-338-7 (pbk)

Visit the Taylor & Francis Web site at
http://www.taylorandfrancis.com

and the A K Peters Web site at
http://www.akpeters.com

For Kate

Contents

Preface

I hope that in finishing this tutorial you will be well on your way to creating worlds of your wildest dreams . . . or nightmares.[1]

As in many endeavors of this kind, much of this book comes from personal motivation and circumstances. I have tried to keep reference to those out of the main text but I would like to acknowledge them somewhere in the book. I guess that is why the preface was invented. Here, then, are some of the personal aspects of why and how this book came to be.

On Level Design

One of the many beautiful things about level design is that it is an almost all-encompassing field. There aren't many creative interests and expressions that cannot find a home in level design, yet it remains a unique profession with its own rules and quirks, and there are few jobs in games as satisfying or important as that of a level designer.

It is, however, a very young profession, and because of its youth, it is often misunderstood or misrepresented, which is regrettable. A good level designer can have as much impact as a good screenwriter or director, a great artist or musician. Those are vocations that people aspire to and recognize as being beneficial to society as a whole.

Video games have not yet come this far. Many people still look surprised to even hear video games mentioned in conjunction with other, more established art forms, although this is slowly changing. Perhaps one day this mistrust of video games as a medium that can compare to other art forms will be quaint and slightly amusing. Hopefully on that day this book will still be in print and the words you have just read will seem odd and out of place.

---

[1] *Worldcraft 1.6 Tutorial*, available at http://hosted.planetquake.gamespy.com/worldcraft/tutorial/index.shtm, 1997.

Either way, regardless of being greeted with a cheer or a puzzled face, being able to work or have a career as a level designer should be something to be immensely proud of. I certainly am.

Why This Book?

Working as a game designer or level designer for a substantial amount of time has shown me there is a lack of understanding of how level design works at a fundamental level. There are many very basic questions that go unasked:

- What fundamental concepts matter to this field?
- How do they translate into level design theory?
- How do we translate theory into practice?

Level design is an incredibly exciting and important field. Good or bad level design can make or break any game, so it is surprising how little reference material there is available for level designers to give them a deeper understanding of what exactly their field is about. Level designers have a limited understanding of what tools and techniques they can use to achieve their goals, or even define them. This is perhaps, considering the youth of the profession, (15–20 years or so[2]) not entirely surprising.

This is, however, a completely different situation from comparable professions in other industries; there are countless sage-like tomes available on topics as diverse as direction, production, set design, camera work, acting, lighting, writing and so on. In those disciplines, in stark contrast to level design, an enormous amount of knowledge has been collected and made available to others. Even within the game industry, there is a large amount of high-quality literature and other material available to programmers and artists, but not so much for designers.

Therefore, most people who work in the field of *level design* either learn through apprenticeship on the job, or are self-taught. This is less than ideal because, due to the high-pressure work environment of the game industry, it is very difficult for people to take a step back and incorporate a more formalized approach to their profession. Nor, as mentioned already, is relevant knowledge and reference readily available. Instead, a lot of level design isn't actually *designed*. Often it is a derivative of other successful work, implemented without a full understanding of why the original work was successful. Other times it is just reactionary, quickly improvised to vague parameters, sometimes based on nothing more than some nebulous sense of "fun." This is not meant as a harsh criticism

---

[2] At the time of writing.

of other people; I certainly have done it many times myself. It is just a logical consequence of working in a creative field where there is not enough support at a core level for people who already have limited time and are under much pressure to perform. This is one of many reasons why I believe there is a great need for a book that provides strong conceptual foundations, formulates working theories and, crucially, shows how to apply these in practice.

After learning about my craft the hard way, like other level designers, through self-training on the job, I realized that most of the hard-earned lessons in our field stay isolated from other level designers. The people most likely to hold the right answers to difficult level design questions posed in practice are often too busy working on their next game, while people outside of games don't have enough exposure to the hard reality of commercial or practical game development. This is why I have set out to write a book that bridges this gap between theory and practice, useful to people on either side of the spectrum—a book that will still be relevant as a work of reference or as a practical guide many years after being published. I wanted to write a book that uses a conceptual and theoretical foundation to build a set of practical tools and techniques that can be universally applied within the field of level design. Or, to put it more simply, I have tried to write the book that wasn't available to me when I first started as a level designer.

Hopefully it will fill that role for some of the readers.

Thanks and Dedications

While writing this book, I have gone through a number of events that have affected me in one way or another. I bought a house with my partner, sat through two earthquakes (yes, *two*), added two rescue dogs to our menagerie, started my own business making independent games and became a full-fledged vegetarian.

All of the above provided major distractions, as you can imagine; yet, in all that time, I was lucky enough to receive the love and unwavering support of my wonderful partner, Kate, without whom I would have been lost several times over. This book is therefore firmly dedicated to her.

Additional thanks go to my publisher, A K Peters, and the people there that have helped me get the book into a readable state: Alice and Charlotte, especially. And boy did I need the help!

I have also been lucky to receive the support of family and friends and all the people who have helped me with proofreading and advice all throughout the project. Thank you all very much! Special thanks go to Alex May for his work on Dyson. Extra special thanks go to Colin and Diana for their unfaltering support and belief in me.

I must also mention Neemo the courageous dog, Tom the wonder dog, and Billy the naughtypuss.

Finally, thanks to all the people who create the levels that inspire me every day.

Introduction

M̲ake things as simple as possible, but not simpler.

—Albert Einstein

This book is a hefty affair; there are many ideas, concepts theories, practical examples, tangents, and footnotes to read. I have done my best to present it in a way that makes sense to most readers. But, to really get the most of the book, I give you this introduction that explains how it all hangs together.

How to Use This Book

Ultimately it is up to you, the reader, to use this book in any way you see fit. However, the book has been written within a certain logical structure and flow that made sense to me while writing it. Wherever possible I have tried to introduce concepts and theories before I start showing their practical applications. This not only applies to the later chapters that are actually divided into concept, theory, and practice sections but also applies to much of the preceding content. A good example of this is the chapter on "Teaching Mechanisms" (Chapter 2), which explores ideas that are so fundamental to what level design is about that it made sense to cover it early on. I do advise people to read this chapter before the following ones.

This kind of hierarchy is applied throughout the bulk of the book—where understanding of certain ideas paves the way to understanding of others. Since later sections often refer to earlier ones, the book may be harder to use if read out of sequence, though I have tried to facilitate this by referring to related material in later chapter when I thought it appropriate. Nonetheless, there is plenty of material in the book that can be read in its own right. Indeed, it is almost impossible within the framework of such a wide field to adhere to strict linearity.

It is my hope that I have made a book that is useful to people with a general interest in the subject of games as well as to people with a more specific interest in level design.

Who Is This Book For?

Although this book can be read (and hopefully understood) by anybody who picks up a copy out of curiosity, I would like to highlight some potential readers who may be more interested than others.

Level Designers

Naturally, it is important that this book is useful to level designers. The book is written in such a way that it should prove useful to both inexperienced and veteran designers alike. I made a conscious choice to mainly focus on level *design* as opposed to level *construction*.[1] It is important to make that distinction, as level design is a universal field, whereas level construction is *technology dependent*. Too often have I come across texts that claim to be about level design but read more like a technical instruction manual for some 3D software application. This is only a useful approach for those people who will be using the same technology as the author of that text.

Instead, I have done my best to make the book as much about level design as possible, ignoring platform- or technology- or level-construction-specific issues. The book is based on the assumption that *design* knowledge has to come first. The way in which vertices are manipulated in a 3D mesh or how entities are placed in a level editor is so dependent on unpredictable technical factors that they are best tackled outside of the context of this book.

What this book *will* do, however, is cover material that teaches and informs level designers of all levels of expertise *what* to aim for in their designs, *why* they should do so, and *how* to achieve those goals in as many diverse situations as possible.

Students and Teachers

Similarly, the book is aimed at *future* level designers and their teachers. There should be much useful content for students and teachers to work with. Due to the fact that there are no insurmountable technical barriers barring readers from engaging with the text, it is ideal for general academic use.

There is a large amount of theory and high-level conceptual content to be found in this book. Much of it is supported by information derived from other fields of interest.

---

[1] Or production.

Nonetheless, this still only scratches the surface of the vast amount of knowledge that is relevant to level design. The book, therefore, could be used as a stand-alone text as well as a base for even more detailed course material.

The practical[2] aspect of the book provides an invaluable tool for assessing the progress made within a course. Since the material covered always has a final practical application, it is always possible to test the knowledge acquired against the harsh realities of real-world level design scenarios. This provides scope for benchmarking as well as the added advantage of providing real training and preparation for actual industry work.

Other Interested Parties

There are, of course, many other reasons why somebody could be interested in the field of level design. Just as I have throughout the book found inspiration and knowledge applicable to level design through the study of other creative disciplines, the same can be imagined of people in other disciplines in regards to level design. A certain amount of cross-pollination between art forms is to be expected and encouraged.

Furthermore, the book can be enjoyed on a non-professional level. Anybody who has an interest in level design or video games should find more than enough to keep them occupied for quite a while. Due to the fact that level design is such a wide-ranging discipline, it can easily spark off or feed other existing interests as well. Indeed, many of the chapters can function as short introductions and springboards to entire fields of related knowledge. This is one of the beautiful things about level design in general, and hopefully this multi-connected aspect will speak to people reading about it. It still does to me.

Organization

Whichever way you choose to read the book, it may be useful to understand the way the book has been structured. For this purpose a short summary of the chapters and parts of the book follows.

The main body of the book is organized into parts, then chapters, and then sections. Parts are thematically related: they handle areas of interest that can be seen through the filter of a general theme. The chapters handle more distinct areas of interest and cover specific subjects. The sections break the subjects down into three important aspects: concept, theory, and practice.

---

[2] The sections dealing with level design *practice* especially.

Part I: Introduction to Level Design

Before we can even begin to look at either high-level concepts or more practical aspects, we have to understand at a basic level exactly what it is that we are doing.

These chapters are about level design itself. It covers the nature of the beast all the way from examining its function within the field of game design to explaining what level design *is*—and, more importantly, what *good* level design is.

Furthermore, the text goes into a fair amount of detail regarding methodology and structure. This section of the book is fundamental to understanding the point of level design and the ability to define sensible goals and tasks springing from that knowledge. The section provides, among other things, much interesting information about the psychology of *play*, without which it is difficult to really grasp the impact of the techniques at our disposal. It also gives a first example of the concept-theory-practice breakdown used more extensively in later parts of the book.

Part II: Emotional Feedback Systems

This part of the book examines how game levels work as feedback systems. That is to say that game levels can provide players with emotional feedback—fun, tension, immersion and so on—based on their actions within the game world.

Part III: Game Environments

Part III looks at some of the senses through which we experience levels as game environments. Specifically, the visual and audio aspects of level design are studied in a fair amount of detail.

Part IV: Game Stories

Narrative and story are very controversial subjects within the framework of game studies. Yet, there is no escaping the fact that level designers have to deal with the subject on a regular basis and will be better able to do their work if they have an informed opinion or understanding of what factors are at play. I decided that due to the somewhat specific focus of the subject, it should be covered in a separate part of the book.

Part V: Designing Gameplay

This is a central part of the text, where many of the diverse parts about actually *designing* levels come together. Or, to paraphrase one famous level designer, Jay Wilbur; this is *"where the rubber hits the road."*

Many of the bread and butter issues of level design like puzzles, challenge levels, or item placement are examined in detail.

Part VI: Final Thoughts

In this final part of the book, matters are wrapped up by a taking a look at what may lie in the future of level design. There is also a small list of recommended material, reading or otherwise, that may be of interest to those readers who want to study more on the subject in the future, as well as a glossary and the book's index.

Notes on Concept, Theory, and Practice Sections

A large portion of the text is presented in chapters that each, in a fairly linear manner, cover a topic by addressing a basic *concept*, incorporating it in level design *theory*, and finally apply it in *practice* through examples and case studies. This structure—where *concept* leads to *theory* leads to *practice*—is the only way I could conceive to collate this much diverse information in one coherent text.

Concept

In these sections I will identify a large number of concepts, by which I mean any topics and areas of interest *related to* fundamental elements of level design. These are topics that anybody involved in level design will encounter at one point or another and are worth exploring. The *concept* section of a chapter presents the reader with a short essay or exploration that examines a specific topic that in some way matters to level design. These essays will mainly deal with high-level principles and ideas that take inspiration from sources as diverse as general psychology, language studies, other art forms like film or literature, or anything else that is relevant to the topic.

Through examination and analysis that goes beyond the limited framework of video games, the concept section will lead to a number of *general findings*.

Theory

The *theory* sections will take the general findings from the previous section and show what relevance they have when they are applied directly to the field of level design. It will show that, through this process and through general extrapolation, it is possible to arrive at a number of logical conclusions that can be useful and relevant to specific level design theory.

These sections will demonstrate that these theories can be applied to all kinds of different level design situations, largely irrespective of genre. In other words, they are fundamental to level design.

Practice

Finally, in the *practice* sections of the book, the level design *theory* of the previous section will get exposed to real-world *practical examples*. At this stage the subject matter becomes one of practical application and will be much more specific than before.

These sections will document numerous examples of typical level design situations or scenarios and show how they benefit from the conclusions of the previous sections. By using a wide and diverse range of examples, they will show how useful it is to be able to apply universal techniques and theories to real-world level design situations.

I will give practical examples on many level design situations, some of which will be drawn from existing levels, sometimes my own work, or will be completely new scenarios. We will look at examples from as many diverse genres as possible, including puzzle games, 3D action adventures, first-person shooters, 2D platform games, and many more.

The key point is that by using the lessons learned in the *concept* and *theory* parts of the books, it is possible to apply solutions to level design questions in almost any game genre or situation.

Goals

Finally, I would like to explain something about my general philosophy on books like this one. I do not expect the reader to agree with all my assertions and opinion in this book. I think it is futile to even try to do this, especially in a field like level design where there is still so little consensus in some of the key areas of interest.

What I am trying to offer instead is a book that gives the reader a number of useful tools to work with. This includes tools for examining the subject itself, tools to form or study theories, and tools for applying knowledge in practical and tangible situations. I firmly believe that an informative approach, rather than a dogmatic one, works best.

Within that spirit I hope that the reader will find it a useful and empowering work, and that it will open doors or avenues that may have been left unexplored otherwise.Giamcon henim do ex ecte facin volum vulputatum iriurer aesendi

Introduction to Level Design

"Gleicharmige Waage", *Wikipedia*, http://commons.wikimedia.org/wiki/File:Gleichar mige_Waage.png, 2009.

Game Design vs. Level Design

I t is often asserted that level design is a *subset* of game design. This is mirrored in the game industry, where, at the time of writing this book, level design does not have the same status as game design, and often, level designers have to aspire to game design roles to progress in their career. The pay grades within the industry enforce this bias, as well; a game designer will typically earn more money than a level designer. This situation is very unfortunate and based on a number of misunderstandings or misconceptions. Among these are that game design "trumps" level design, or that level design work is somehow subordinate to, or simpler than, game design. This assertion misses an important aspect of level design: it should not be underestimated how much of an impact level design has on a game. It is a well-known truism that:

> Bad level design can ruin a good game.

If this is true (it is), the impact of a game's level design is as strong as that of the game design. Conversely, we can therefore say:

> A bad game cannot be saved by good level design.[1]

The two statements seem to put level design and game design on somewhat equal footing, at least in terms of impact on the development of the game itself. It is clear that game design and level design are not the same discipline. However, they clearly cannot exist without each other. There is an interrelationship at work that operates on a deep and fundamental level. It is useful to try to find a way to interpret both fields and show how they are interconnected and what sort of relationship they form. To make this possible, we must have a look at the basic function that both fields perform.

---

[1] Although it can be argued that good level design can make a mediocre game enjoyable.

The Function of Game Design

There are many differing interpretations of what game design actually is; some are derived from detailed academic studies, while others come from experienced game designers who have gained their knowledge through practical application. The sheer amount of differing definitions almost inevitably leads to as many disagreements and arguments, although many disagreements seem to arise as much out of semantic differences as out of interpretive ones. The various game design definitions can arise from origins including ideology, commercial function, or practical analysis.

Because of this lack of consensus, and because of the sheer number of proposed definitions, there is currently no easily identifiable unifying concept of what constitutes *gameplay*, let alone *game design*. There are many sizeable books and academic studies devoted to games and gameplay but they often contradict each other and in some cases even attack each other. This presents a problem, since game design and level design are interrelated, and we need to agree upon a certain amount of theoretical common ground to formulate workable universal (or at least wide ranging) theories and techniques. So despite the lack of a universally accepted view on games and gameplay, we should nonetheless examine the diversity of opinion more closely. Even if no definitive consensus can be agreed upon by *everybody* in the field, we should still aim to find commonalities and individual defining features that can be used for the purpose of this book. Perhaps by looking at all the differing ideas on what constitutes a game or gameplay, we can derive a useful set of descriptions that can be used to characterize the *function* of game design.

Definitions

One of the most famous definitions of game design is the one from Sid Meier that states that:

A game is a series of interesting choices.

Further explanation of "interesting" often includes the following qualifiers:

- No choice should be consistently better than the others. (Or it would make the other choices uninteresting or redundant.)
- The choices shouldn't be the same. (It becomes meaningless to differentiate between choices.)
- Choices must be informed. (Lest they become arbitrary or random.)

On the surface, this rings true. People are easily engaged in gameplay when they are mentally challenged in an interesting way, especially if this is done in such a way that the player stays engaged. Chess, for example, keeps the player engaged by the multitude of options available, made interesting by the far-reaching strategic and tactical consequences within the game. Unfortunately, this description of a game or gameplay is not all-encompassing; it simply doesn't always apply, something that I am sure Sid Meier himself would agree with.

Jesper Juul offers this:

> But some games do away with interesting choices altogether. The object of the music/rhythm games Dance Dance Revolution and Vib-Ribbon is simply to hit the right buttons on the PlayStation controller or dance mat at the correct time. These games do in fact not contain any interesting choices whatsoever - but performing the non-interesting choices is marked by some other form of enjoyment, namely that of being in time with the music. They are still enjoyable games, which goes to prove that interesting choices is not all there is to it.[2]

Unfortunately, within the field of game design, both in a practical professional sense, as well as within the academic realm, there is no clear consensus on the nature of game design, partially because it is hard enough to find agreement on what it is that constitutes a *game*! To illustrate this point further, when I started to research game definitions for this book in the hope to shed some light on the topic, I found, much to my irritation, that I couldn't find much overlap between differing viewpoints. Instead, many views were contradictory, even when they tried to incorporate as many "accepted" elements as possible. Several people who have spent more time than me trying to define games have commented on this.

Katie Salen and Eric Zimmerman, in their book "Rules of Play," formally compared eight notable definitions or descriptions of games and put the defining characteristics in a comparative grid. This is one of their conclusions:

> All of the authors except Costikyan include rules as a key component. *Beyond this there is no clear consensus.*[3] Although 10 of the 15 elements are shared by more than one author, apart from rules and goals, there is no majority agreement on any one of them. (*Emphasis mine.*)[4]

---

[2] Jesper Juul, "Just What Is It That Makes Computer Games So Different, So Appealing?" *IGDA The Ivory Tower*, April 2003, available at http://www.igda.org/columns/ivory-tower/ivory_Apr03.php.

[3] Nonetheless, the authors then proceed to create a definition of games that is easy to disagree with.

[4] Katie Salen and Eric Zimmerman, *Rules of Play: Game Design Fundamentals*, MIT Press, Cambridge, MA, 2004, p. 93.

Perhaps a definition of games is too much to ask for, as it is clear that it cannot be unambiguously captured within a single concept. The same is true for the concept of *play*, which is very much related, of course. It is, however, a topic that is unsurprisingly, discussed as fiercely as that of game definition. Unsurprisingly, because gameplay is the logical consequence of a game, and therefore they seem to be aspects of the same thing, leading to the same disagreements. Isn't it fair to say that games cannot exist without gameplay? It is clear that play is central to the experience. But is it the defining element? It is, according to some game researchers who argue that exact point. But what of other elements often represented within games? For example, what of the narrative elements present in many game types? Once again, disagreements or lack of consensus come to the fore.

Ludologist vs. narrativist perspectives

As much as is the case of practical game development or commercial game funding, some disagreements within academic circles are quite profound. A good example of this can be found in the differing viewpoints often attributed to the *ludologists* and the *narrativists*.[5] Theirs is a disagreement that stems from a different interpretation of what games are, and within which context to place the play experience, a disagreement that has led to many articles and books, impassioned speeches, and even heated arguments. Although their defining features are often contested, they seem to be most clearly understood as follows.

Ludology is: A branch of game studies that approaches the subject through the prism of *play*.

While narrativism is: A branch of game studies that approach the subject through the prism of *narrative*.

This sounds straightforward enough, yet it has led to many, sometimes ill-tempered disputes. Let's look at the opinion of Michael Mateas,[6] who offers the following on narrativism:

> The narrativists generally come out of literary theory, take hypertext as the paradigmatic interactive form, and use narrative and literary theory as the foundation upon which to build a theory of interactive media.

And on ludologists:

> Ludologists generally come out of game studies [e.g., Avedon and Sutton-Smith 1971], take the computer game as the paradigmatic

---

[5] Narrativism is also often referred to as *narratologism*.

[6] A scholar active in the field of artificial intelligence, among other things, and one of the authors of *Façade*, an experimental interactive drama (*Façade* can be downloaded here: http://www.interactivestory.net/).

interactive form, and seek to build an autonomous theory of inter-activity. [7]

In some instances, ludologists have placed themselves in direct opposition to narrativist thinking, and vice versa. Differences between ludologist and narrativist thinking have produced so much friction that some even started attacking each other's viewpoints in public. (I am not going to go into specific examples, but things got quite heated.)

Ultimately, in the eyes of many, neither view is correct, or rather, they are both right and wrong at the same time, insofar as they both focus on legitimate aspects of the equation but try to invalidate other equally appropriate ones. (I am old and wise enough, however, to leave this debate to those willing to spend their time on it.)

Far from being the only positions available, the narrativist vs. ludologist standpoints illustrate how deeply entrenched people can become in their very particular beliefs about games and gameplay. It is notable that in many ways, both parties to some degree perpetuate a false dichotomy. Most narrativists, for example, don't deny the relevance of play, just the weight and importance given to it by some ludologists. We can still agree that play is fundamental to games, while also acknowledging the importance of narrative within a gaming experience. Narrative, however, will be discussed in detail in its own section of the book: Part IV, Chapter 12.

To be fair, much of this debate is suspect insofar as that often, when pressed, it seems there is only limited disagreement, which often stems from method-ological issues more than from anything else.

Gonzalo Frasca states in the abstract of one of his articles:

> During the last few years, a debate took place within the game scholars' community. A debate that, it seems, opposed two groups: ludologists and narratologists. Ludologists are supposed to focus on game mechanics and reject any room in the field for analyzing games as narrative, while narratologists argue that games are closely connected to stories. This article aims at showing that this description of the participants is erroneous. What is more, this debate as presented never really took place because it was cluttered with a series of misunderstandings and misconceptions that need to be clarified if we want to seriously discuss the role of narrative in video games. [8]

---

[7] Michael Mateas, "Michael Mateas Responds in Turn." *Electronic Book Review*, http://www.electronicbookreview.com/thread/firstperson/bestyled, 2004.

[8] Gonzalo Frasca, "Ludologists Love Stories, Too: Notes from a Debate That Never Took Place," *Ludology.org*, http://ludology.org/articles/Frasca_LevelUp2003.pdf, 2003.

Even though the dust has now settled a bit, it is worth reflecting on how difficult matters of definition can be, and game-related definitions are notoriously hard, by any standard.

External Goals

Since we are looking at matters of *function* and *purpose*, we should look at game design's external goals. If we know what game design is supposed to *achieve*, we have a much better idea of game design function. External goals are as fundamental as describing what something is *for*, and *how* this is achieved. Let's take a real world example: a *chair's* design, and use it as a simple test case.

A chair's design is subject to many requirements, but the main identifiable goal is to allow a person to sit on it. An observation that may be banal in its simplicity, but one that needs to be noted, nonetheless.

This basic goal leads to other related requirements that describe what the chair has to be:

- strong enough to take the weight of most people,
- stable,
- affordable,
- moveable,
- aesthetically pleasing.

At this point, a designer comes in and starts to formulate these external goals and requirements in a number of functional designs. Regardless of the content of those designs, the design's *function* or purpose is partly described by these external rules.

The same principle occurs in game design. The basic function of a game determines the *game design's* function. So a first step in game design is to correctly identify the game's external goals and to interpret those in such a way that they get represented well in the game's rules.

This means, for example, that a game whose defining external goals are of a commercial nature will end up radically different from a game whose external goals are centered on delivering, for example, a disturbing artistic narrative.

If we decide that the main defining external goals are simply aimed at gameplay and profit, and if we apply the chair analogy to a game, we could state that the game exists in order to *provide a fun and profitable gameplay experience.*

This then leads to other related requirements that describe what the game has to be:

- pretty,
- easy to learn,

- hard to master,
- of sufficient quality,
- showcase high production values,

and so on.

It is important, however, not to confuse these with the game's internal or intrinsic goals.

Gameplay Goals

It has been noted earlier that a defining feature of most games is that they have goals. These are the level design or general gameplay objectives that the game itself presents to the user. We encounter these all the time, and it is easy to name typical examples. Take the following list of player objectives:

- Attain the high score.
- Unlock the dungeon.
- Defeat the boss character.
- Win the race.
- Score more goals than your opponent.
- Explore the environment.
- Shoot the enemy soldiers.

Most gameplay is driven by these kinds of explicit objectives and motivations for the player, a fact that is hardly controversial. To the level designer, however these goals must be *designed*. And in order for them to be designed, they need to have a logical source or reason to be included in the levels. This reason is generally found in the game's internal or intrinsic goals.

Internal goals

These are similar to a game's external goals, insofar as they describe high level goals from which we can derive gameplay requirements. The difference with external goals lies in the fact that internal goals govern the high level goals that are directly related to aspects of the game and gameplay itself, as opposed to external factors. They tend to cover things like the following:

- Empower the player.
- Teach the player how to have fun with the game.
- Don't break the player's suspension of disbelief.
- Give the player a sense of achievement.
- Reward the player for exploration.
- Provide addictive, fun gameplay.

We will look in more detail at these kinds of goals and how they fit in a development and level design hierarchy in Chapter 3.

Defining Goals and Designing Rules

What all this tells us is that both internal and external goals are part of game design *function*. It describes functional necessity related to gameplay AND related to the game's more existential[9] goals, like turning a profit or making a particular artistic statement.[10] Goals like these are useless by themselves unless they get translated into actions. How do we achieve these goals? In the case of game design, this means that once the external or *meta* goals have been defined, the designer needs to design the actual game, which means designing the game's *rules* in such a way that they best support the external goals.

Rules

A fundamental aspect shared by most, although not all, video games, is that they adhere to a formal set of rules. Games without rules can exist, but they are either very abstract in form, or function more on the level of toys. Nonetheless, it cannot be denied that by far the majority of all games, not just video games, are based on or reliant on a *formal set of rules*, often predetermined, that the player has to follow in order to successfully play the game.

Some people go even further and argue that games cannot exist without rules:

> Rules are what differentiate games from other kinds of play. Probably the most basic definition of a game is that it is organized play, that is to say rule-based. If you don't have rules you have free play, not a game. Why are rules so important to games? Rules impose limits—they force us to take specific paths to reach goals and ensure that all players take the same paths. They put us inside the game world by letting us know what is in and out of bounds.[11]

However, this construction of formal game rules is completely abstract until executed in *play*. This is similar to theater, where the actual *play* does not exist until the *performance* takes place. The text of the play can be read in its own right, of

---

[9] Suggestions for a less pompous term are welcome.

[10] Chapter 3, "Level Design Goals and Hierarchies," will cover these subjects in much more detail, focusing both on external and internal goals and how they relate to level design.

[11] Marc Prensky, *Digital Game-Based Learning*, McGraw-Hill, New York, 2001, p. 14.

course, but the actual *theatrical play* only takes place during the performance. The same is true for games. Although a game's design may be able to formalize the rules of the game, until actual play occurs, this design is unfulfilled, and in many ways the game itself is *incomplete*. Game design facilitates play by designing rules under which play can *occur*.[12]

A quick word on toys

Toys are often excluded from definitions of games because they don't have a set of formalized rules associated with them. This is true to a degree but is somewhat misleading. It is more accurate to say that toys don't have a set of *predetermined rules* associated with them. This does not stop those who play with toys from formulating their own rules spontaneously at the time of play. The end result is the same as in other games: the player is actively engaged in gameplay. The newly formalized rules may be simple, for example a game of catch between two, such as parent and child, but they are gameplay rules nonetheless.

The conclusion that follows from this is that toys are *facilitators of games that ask players to define their own rule set*. Crucially, the player(s) temporarily take on the guise of game designer and level designer.

Game Design Function Summary

It appears to be difficult to agree on a definitive view on what games are. There are countless definitions of games and their associated viewpoints, and they often are in disagreement with each other. But study of games, gameplay, and game rules shows that there are a number of commonalities that can be highlighted:

- Play is central to games.
- Diverse and unrelated goals can motivate the production of games.
- Most games rely on rules, or facilitate the definition of them.

If seen in this light, we can describe a game as featuring: *an often predetermined, agreed-upon set of rules, which are designed to facilitate gameplay. The motivation behind the creation of a game itself can be diverse, for example including commercial, educational, artistic, or other elements.*

All of these elements are individually fairly obvious; yet taken as a whole, they spell out something fairly useful with regards to finding a workable concept of the function of game design. Within all of these observations lies an answer to the question about game design's *function* or *purpose*, because they describe what a designer needs to *achieve*.

---

[12] It is also good to note that just *facilitating* play is not enough to guarantee a *good* game.

Ultimately, a game designer is the person who determines the rules by which a game is formulated, in order to achieve the goals for which it is created. And in some ways, a *good* game designer is one who is good at determining what rules are appropriate for the desired gameplay.

A game design is a coherent set of rules that formalizes a game's content in such a way that it facilitates appropriate gameplay, in order to achieve the game's fundamental goals.

The Function of Level Design

Now that we have spent considerable time looking at game design function, we need to compare this with *level design function*. We have seen that in game design it is very important to define what the game's external goals are and design rules of play that correctly support them. Questions about level design in many ways seem to start from a completely opposite position. The rules of play are a *known*. How else can we construct a level if we don't already know what rules it has to facilitate?[13]

On closer inspection, however, we are left with a similar definitional problem as we had at the beginning of this chapter with regard to game design. Where *does* the rubber hit the road? How do we define this? Instead of trying to find an ultimate definition of level design, I would like to focus, just as we did with game design, on finding a useful description of the *function* of level design. The reason for trying to formulate an overall function or purpose for level design is that it should give us a way to determine what is within the level designer's responsibilities. This will give us more than a job description; it gives us a conceptual framework within which we can do our work. This is something that may sound unimportant on paper, but is nonetheless of vital importance in practice when we need to defend or explain our professional or artistic choices. (Even in those cases when we have to justify them to ourselves.) Or to put it in less dramatic terms; it gives us a practical framework through which we can approach level design.

A useful start to this endeavor is to look at level design in a historic context.

Level Design in a Historic Context

It is beyond the scope of this book to provide a complete history of level design, although it would be a fascinating project to attempt to do so. Instead, a short

---

[13] Scarily, in commercial level design, one is often asked to design levels without a clear understanding of the final gameplay parameters.

look at a number of historically interesting examples of level design or related fields will have to do.[14] Even this limited focus should produce some insights, as there is much to be learned. At the least, it should provide us with some historic context in which we can place level design.

Sports

Almost all sports take place within defined spaces. And, more importantly, most sports take place in *designed* spaces. At some point in time, somebody actually decided on the dimensions of a soccer field, the size of a hockey goal, or the placement of hurdles in an equestrian[15] course. How these original decisions by proto-level designers were made we don't always know, but it is clear that they allow for an important function of sports: competition. In order to compete under fair terms, their design allows a level *playing field*. (A term that sounds much like a video game *level* to me.) A sporting field or environment usually cannot be altered or bypassed by the participants of the sport. It is literally *against the rules*, and the offender typically gets punished heavily or even disqualified from participating further.

Board-game layouts

Board-game design is even closer to level design for video games, partly because it allows the creation of an *abstract representation* of an environment. There is not always a need to create a field of even grassland with play zones demarcated by chalk lines, or to run divisions of soldiers through complex tactics and strategy drills out in some field, if a similar effect can be created by an approximation or an abstraction in the form of a board game. Chess, for example, is a good case; the game portrays warfare and enhances strategic thinking, despite using a playing area that is rather abstract.

Furthermore, board games provide scope to introduce elements of the fantastic into play. In the context of a board game, it is fine to teleport players through the world, or to introduce mythical monsters as adversaries. A board game can introduce elements of chance (pick a card) and encourage the use of avatars.[16] Many of these choices are affected by the board's layout, which had to be *designed* at one point in time. Literally thousands of board games have been designed through the years, and the inherent level design choices that were made provide a rich source of information. They are especially interesting from a historic point of view, because they go back many hundreds of years.

---

[14] I do encourage people to do some of their own research in this area.

[15] Am I the only person who thinks of a platform game when these horses jump?

[16] A game piece that represents the player.

A good exercise for budding level designers would be to choose any board game, try to find out why the board was designed the way it was, and try to improve on its design. This is a guaranteed way to improve as a level designer[17] and as a byproduct is likely to teach some appreciation of board game designers, as well.

Pinball machines

Another beautiful example of proto-level design can be found in pinball games. The basic rules of pinball games can be summed up on the back of a napkin. As a set of rules describing a game, there really isn't much to it. Yet many hundreds of iterations of such games have successfully persuaded players all over the world to feed them coins. There are a huge number of pinball tables whose layout and content design, or in other words, their *level design*, showcases new and successful interpretations of those old and basic rules. The player still controls flippers, the table is still slanted so the ball rolls down, and the game offers three "lives" to earn a maximum amount of points.

Yet there is no shortage of unique and wildly differing pinball tables. Together, they provide an interesting and enduring example of an *interactive* game type that predates video games.

Dungeons and Dragons

In 1974, Gary Gygax and Dave Arneson designed a new type of game still enjoyed proudly by the geek tribes of the world. They created one of the first successful pen-and-paper roleplaying games and called it *Dungeons and Dragons*. The basic setup of the game consists of a group of players sitting around a table and enacting the roles of diverse *player characters* within a virtual *fantasy setting*, designed and described by the *dungeon master*. The dungeon master literally describes this virtual world to the other players in such a way that the players can imagine themselves to be there in their own imagination. The dungeon master tells the players what they encounter within this world, and the players describe their actions and reactions to the dungeon master, role-playing (play acting) their player characters. The physics and mechanics of this world are documented in complex and extensive rule books sold by the publisher, the adventures (modules) that the players experience within this virtual setting are designed beforehand, either by the dungeon master or by an independent designer. A skilled dungeon master can take the somewhat impersonal, systematic rules on how the world and its inhabitants or processes behave, and through the use of a well

---

[17] Game designers should try creating better rules or even design the board games themselves.

designed adventure, really bring it to life, providing the other players with an extremely compelling play experience.

Key to this, though, is the earlier prepared adventure, which functions as a perfect example of a level design outside of video games. The dungeon master or independent designer takes on the role of level designer because he or she ends designing the in-game encounters and dramatic occurrences that define the player reactions in the game. Although often maligned as an activity, *Dungeons and Dragons* pioneered a fascinating new way of playing deeply immersive games. This was borne out by the huge number of players who since have bought the games and associated products, the countless other similar games that have since become successful, and the countless tie-in products sold. But ultimately for the purpose of this book, this provides an interesting example of alternative level design.

Lessons from history

What these historic examples show us is that level design is not exclusive to video games, but instead can be found throughout very diverse other types of games. Level design never exists purely on its own terms. But what the above examples have shown is that most game designs also don't exist within a vacuum; instead, they can only work together, in unison. This so far shows us that there is indeed a very close link between game design and level design, but it does not explicitly tell us what level design's main function is.

Unfortunately, due to the very young age of level design as a profession, there is not much recourse to be found in professional literature. Hardly any serious texts exist on the subject, and many of those are relatively old or cover the mechanics of level production more than anything else. Even so, some opinions and views have been expressed in the past that provide unique insights.

Various Views on Level Design

Throughout the limited history of level design as a unique discipline, various people have tried to describe or define the field, often based on nothing but their own hard-won professional experience. These definitions are fascinating in many ways. It is always wise to heed the words of pioneers in any creative genre, as typically these early works were the result of completely original thought processes led by novel problems, and not led by existing conventions or styles. And especially since many of these early designers have demonstrated their skills and abilities by providing high-quality examples of their craft. Let's take a look at a number of notable examples.

Example 1: Jay Wilbur

> Level design is where the rubber hits the road.[18]

Much of level design is about making sure the player is taught[19] the rules of play. An important part of the act of level design is taking all the diverse game elements, teaching the player the associated rules, and using the means available to put them together into one coherent whole. This is what Jay Wilbur meant by his quotation. The game design at one point has to be put into practice, and to do so, the level designer needs to be able to put all the diverse elements of a game together in such a way that it doesn't fall apart when tested in the real world.

Example 2: Sam Sharami

> Level designers, or map designers, are the individuals responsible for constructing the game spaces in which the player competes. As such, the level designer is largely responsible for the implementation of the game play in a title.[20]

This is an interesting view of level design insofar as it talks about its goals and the level designer's responsibility. It touches upon the important fact that level design is responsible for gameplay implementation.

Example: John Romero

> A level designer has a very responsible position, because maps are where the game takes place.[21]

Again, this is an interesting observation because it makes a comment on what maps (levels) are. If they are "where the game takes place," it follows that levels allow the game to exist, or at least to be played. An obvious point perhaps, but it tells us something about the strong link between game and game levels.

---

[18] Jay Wilbur in conversation with Cliff Bleszinski, as reported in *Game Design: Secrets of the Sages*, MacMillan, New York, 1999, Ch. 6. Wilbur is a very famous designer who worked on titles like *Doom* and *Quake*, or more recently, *Gears of War*.

[19] See also Chapter 2, which discusses level design as a "teaching mechanic."

[20] Sam Shahrani, "Educational Feature: A History and Analysis of Level Design in 3D Computer Games—Pt. 1," *Gamasutra - Features*, http://www.gamasutra.com/view/feature/2674/educational_feature_a_history_and_.php, 1999.

[21] John Romero, notorious level designer, programmer, and game designer, who has been involved in many famous and even controversial games. In John Romero, "ION Storm," Chapter 6 of *Game Design: Secrets of the Sages*, Macmillan, New York, 1999; also available at *Gamasutra - Features*, http://www.gamasutra.com/features/19990723/levdesign_chapter_05.htm.

Summary of Views

We have heard that level design has to take all the disparate elements in a game and make them gel, that level designers are responsible for the implementation of the game, and that levels are where the game takes place. These observations, combined with what we have learned from historic examples of level design, provide us with something we can draw some initial conclusions from, and give us some guidance into what to examine next.

Level Design Function Summary

There seems to be no shortage of opinion and ideas on the topic of level design. It is disturbing, therefore, to note that, just as with game design, there is no clear underlying *theme* to these observations or definitions. This chapter has touched on a large number of diverse subjects, and throughout, we have reached a number of general conclusions. Many of these conclusions aren't individually that revelatory, but if taken together and placed in a shared context, they *do* provide useful results. Let's summarize and see where that takes us.

Codependency

It should be clear by now that level design and game design are not the same thing. It has also become clear that they are codependent and interrelated: one is useless without the other. Most games are unfulfilled without some kind of level design, while level design is an interpretation of a game's rules. Because of this codependency, it is very important to realize that we shouldn't study one without studying the other. To understand level design we have to understand game design. How can we interpret a game design without knowledge of it? And conversely, how can we define rules for an experience we do not understand?

Game and Level Design *Function*

This book is about level design, but if we take into account the findings of this chapter, this means that, at least to some degree, it is also about game design. If a game designer designs the gameplay *rules,* the level designer designs *how* the player is confronted with those rules. Looking at it from that angle, a level designer and a game designer have completely different jobs. A game designer *formulates* the game's rules, while a level designer *interprets* them for maximum results. To some degree, one represents theory while the other represents practice. This is the basic *function* of level design.

Play and Application of Game Rules

Just as a theatrical play needs a performance to be complete, a video game's rules need *gameplay* to occur. This is a basic *purpose* of level design, to interpret the game rules, and to translate them into a construct (a level) that best facilitates play. Another way of expressing this is by stating that "level design is applied game design." Not the most impressive definition of level design out there, but it is suitable for the needs of this book. It describes much of the function and purpose of level design, and therefore, much of the work of a level designer.

So, for the purpose of this book, level design will be defined as applied game design, not as a separate function subordinate in a game design hierarchy,[22] but as a description of its main function and purpose. This does not mean that I will focus overly on game design issues in this book to the exclusion of level design issues; far from it. Rather, it means that in order to understand certain level design issues, we have to understand certain game design issues. They are different sides of the same coin.

Area of Responsibility

These observations on level design's function or matters of definition are not unimportant or abstract. If we ourselves don't understand the nature of our work it will be impossible to confidently defend it. This isn't always achieved by the content we create, although that is obviously of the utmost importance. We need to be able to explain to others (as much as to explain to ourselves) why we made those choices in the first place. As often as not, we need to be able to make clear and defensible choices from the get-go; to do this; we need to know within what *area of responsibility* we work. It is helpful to be able to work from within a clear framework and to be able to say what the *function* of our work is and what areas it covers. This furthermore allows us to create clearly defined goals for ourselves, a theme that will be further explored in the imaginatively named Chapter 3, "Level Design Goals and Hierarchies."

---

[22] Is a written play superior to its theatrical performance?

Teaching Mechanisms

2

We have established in the previous chapter that: "level design is applied game design." This tells us something about the function of level design, but it does not give us enough information on the core content that a level designer needs to provide. This leaves important questions unanswered. What are the intrinsic internal workings of level design, as opposed to its external goals? *What is it that we are trying to do in the context of the game?*

We already know how closely game design and level design are intertwined. If we examine both at the point where they overlap the most, we start to take a look at fundaments of gameplay. In order to define the *nature of level design,* we will have to define the *nature of gameplay,* and how it relates to level design.

The following three sections provide a detailed examination of these matters. They also provide a preview of the methodology used later in this book, where a given subject is examined through chapters covering the subject's basic *concept,* how it applies to level design *theory,* and what applications it has in *practice.*

Concept

The Nature of Gameplay

Anybody who has spent any time around animals, perhaps a pet dog or a cat, knows that they are very *playful* creatures. It is very easy to start playing a game with them on the basis of rules that are surprisingly easily understood.

- Catch the ball.
- Retrieve the stick.
- Let's pretend my hand is prey!
- Obstacle course!

It is clear when we watch the behavior of animals of a certain level of intelligence, that play comes *naturally* to them. This becomes even clearer when we watch them at play when they are young. When young animals at play are observed, it is clear that almost anything in their environment can be an excuse to initiate gameplay. To a puppy, for example, almost anything can be incorporated into gameplay, and that is true without anybody teaching the animal how to engage in this behavior. It is easy to observe that *gameplay comes naturally to animals* of sufficient intelligence, which hints at the possibility of play being fundamental to their well-being, due to evolutionary reasons. It may be linked to the animal's survival. This is as true for animals as it is for human beings.

Survival Skills and Make-Believe

Play is a relatively well-understood phenomenon. People from fields as diverse as behaviorism, anthropology, and biology have studied it, and a number of general findings can be agreed upon. First and foremost, it has to be understood that it is clear that there is very serious reason for this innate ability to be playful; it helps maximize the animal's chances of survival. Through play, valuable lessons are taught that clearly demonstrate this point. Through play, the young animal's skills are honed that are necessary in order to *hunt, fight, mate, hide,* or one of many other activities that are key to survival as an adult. Games provide a *safe context* in which these lessons can be learned through *play*. With this in mind, it is not controversial to state that *"Gameplay teaches skills that are important and necessary in order to survive in real life."*

This seems a straightforward-enough statement, but upon examination, a number of startling further conclusions can be reached. Not the least of which is the realization that animals are capable of grasping abstract concepts like *games* or *make-believe* It is irrefutable, however, because to engage in this kind of safe play, human beings (or animals that are capable of gameplay) need to be able to accept imposed boundaries and rules to their behavior. They need to understand that the gameplay experience is an artificial one. This means that fairly complex and abstract concepts are at play. We are, after all, talking about the understanding of something that is by definition an *abstract construct*, governed by a set of formalized rules.

Or to put it in other terms, when engaged in gameplay, we need to understand the difference between the rules that govern our *reality*, and those that govern the make-believe, or virtual, world of a *game*. This is quite an amazing skill, and the fact that we as human beings are adept at constructing and manipulating our experiences within these parameters is nothing less than remarkable.

Our propensity towards gameplay has far-reaching and interesting consequences. We see this ability to accept artificial, invented realities reach into areas beyond gameplay. For example, it is easily identifiable as crucial to the enjoyment of film, literature, art, music, and countless other forms of art and entertainment.

I will go into further detail with regard to this ability in Chapter 8, on immersion.

"Fun" as a Reward for Gameplay

It is safe to say that *good games are rewarding*. A good game is *fun*, or makes us *feel good*. But what is it exactly that creates this reward for us, and how does it work on a biological level? It needs no explanation that the answers to these questions are valuable to any level designer.

From studying gameplay in animals, we have learned that engaging in gameplay makes the animals feel good. They *want* to play games from a very young age on and need no prompting by external factors. In fact, they often do their best to initiate gameplay tendencies in others. Some of this behavior may originate from the fact that engaging in gameplay causes chemicals to be released in the bloodstream that act as a reward for playful behavior. This in turn makes animals *feel encouraged* to engage in this behavior. This is no accident, as the rewarding aspect of gameplay is *biologically necessary*. (This necessity stems from the need to learn survival skills within the safe context of a game, as we established previously.)

It only requires a small step to take this information and extrapolate to human behavior, which is basically the same. In fact, as already noted at the beginning of this chapter, our ability to understand games crosses the *species boundary*,[1] which is a strong indicator that comparable processes are at work. Much of human gameplay, when examined, bears striking similarities with gameplay in some advanced animals. *Hide and seek* or *tag* come to mind. We also are rewarded when we engage in gameplay, and in the case of humans, the chemical award is the release of certain pheromones, which make us feel good, or in other words, we experience "fun."[2] Our large brains enable us to engage in games that are much more complex than those enjoyed by animals, but all the basic principles still apply.

---

[1] If we take a moment to think about this, it should be apparent how truly extraordinary this is.

[2] See Raph Koster's book, *A Theory of Fun for Game Design* (Paraglyph Press, Scottsdale, AZ, 2004), for similar sentiments.

Aptitude for Gameplay

All around the world, people, adults as well as children, play games in which the rules are easy and even intuitively understood. This suggests that we as a species are very good at *"speaking the language of games."* We know, for example, that we can play games with people whose linguistics aren't ours, whose culture we don't share, and whom we have never met before. It is even clear that we can play games with creatures that don't even belong to *our species*! However we choose to look at the subject, it is clear that human beings possess a certain amount of aptitude for gameplay.

Universal gameplay grammar

One could even argue that human beings use something akin to a *universal gameplay grammar* that allows us to understand and play games easily, often without regard to their origins.

Although beyond the scope of this book, it would be fascinating to study this topic further, as has been done in the field of linguistics, where much study and discussion exist around the field of *generative grammar*, for example through the work of Noam Chomsky, not least because of his work in the field of *transformational grammar*. Here are some key concepts:

> [T]ransformational-generative grammar, [a] linguistic theory associated with Noam Chomsky, particularly with his *Syntactic Structures* (1957), and with Chomsky's teacher Zellig Harris. Generative grammar attempts to define rules that can generate the infinite number of grammatical (well-formed) sentences possible in a language. It starts not from a behaviorist analysis of minimal sounds but from a rationalist assumption that a deep structure underlies a language, and that a similar deep structure underlies all languages.[3]

Exciting as a "unified theory of gameplay" sounds, I think I will leave further examination of this for another book for now.

Support from Within the Field

Many notable people within our own industry have reached the same or similar conclusions. Raph Koster, the author of *A Theory of Fun for Game Design*, has the following things to say:

---

[3] "Transformational-Generative Grammar," *The Columbia Electronic Encyclopedia*, Sixth Edition, http://www.encyclopedia.com/topic/transformational-generative_grammar. aspx, 2001–2007.

One of the subtlest releases of chemicals is at that moment of triumph when we learn something or master a task. This almost always causes us to break into a smile. After all, it is important to the survival of the species that we learn—therefore our bodies reward us for it with moments of pleasure. There are many ways we find fun in games, and I will talk about the others. But this is the most important.

Fun from games arises out of mastery. It arises out of comprehension. It is the act of solving puzzles that makes games fun.

In other words, with games, learning is the drug.[4]

Taking inspiration from *Flow Theory*,[5] which offers a scientific and well-researched approach to "happiness," Raph Koster describes processes that are very similar to our findings. Although he was talking specifically about *game design*, it is nonetheless as relevant to *level design* if one thinks of level design as *applied game design*. (See Chapter 1, "Game Design vs. Level Design.")

To find more support from the game industry community, let us also consider the following from Carolyn Handler Miller:

> The earliest games were developed not for idle amusement but for serious purposes: to prepare young men for the hunt and for warfare. By taking part in games, the youths would strengthen their bodies and develop athletic skills like running and throwing. By playing with teammates, they would also learn how to coordinate maneuvers and how to strategize. Over time, these athletic games evolved into formal competitions. Undoubtedly, the best known of the ancient sporting events are the Greek Olympic games.[6]

In these ancient games, we find another clear indication of gameplay as a teaching device for events in real life.

Many other examples illustrate that there is some support for the view that gameplay has a strong basis in teaching mechanisms.

Support from Other Fields

This notion that human beings possess a native ability to understand and engage in gameplay is not a new one. People in other disciplines who have been studying

---

[4] Raph Koster, *A Theory of Fun for Game Design*, Paraglyph Press, Scottsdale, AZ, 2005, p. 40.

[5] Explained in Chapter 8 in the section "The Zone."

[6] Carolyn Handler Miller, *Digital Storytelling: A Creator's Guide to Interactive Entertainment*, Elsevier Science, Amsterdam, 2004, p. 27.

this concept and approached it from differing angles have come up with similar conclusions. Currently, a reasonable amount of data has been collected to support these findings, and more is uncovered on a regular basis.

> Researchers suggest that social play may safely teach young the skills they will later use in aggressive social competition. However, such play may also simultaneously strengthen social bonds between group members, a process that serves to limit the amount of actual aggression between group members.
>
> If social play can mirror real aggression in appearance, what then lets animals know that their partners are only playing? Animals, it turns out, communicate playful intentions with certain stereotyped signals. The most widespread play signal is the play face, a relaxed, open-mouth expression seen in many mammal species, used virtually from birth. The human smile almost certainly evolved from this ancestral trait. If someone smiles or laughs while hitting you in the arm, you realize that his or her intentions are very different than if he or she is frowning, with a tightly closed mouth.[7]

More and more studies and articles are appearing that explore gameplay for educational purposes. Consider the following example:

> Games['] greatest potential is that they're worlds in a box. They allow you to create a world that somebody can be in and take on an identity. People learn most deeply when they take on a new identity that they really want. Let's say I really want to know what it's like to be a biologist of a certain sort. I really want to know what it's like to feel that way, to value that way, to talk that way. I can do that now. I can be in that world. That's going to be a deeper form of learning.[8]

A whole subgenre called *serious games* has appeared recently, which heavily relies on the educational aspects of gameplay and uses them specifically with the context of educational games.

Concept Summary

Our findings have taught us that from a very young age, human beings are *predisposed* towards playing games, just like many animals, *in order to learn impor-*

---

[7] Alex Hawes, "Jungle Gyms: The Evolution of Animal Play," *National Zoo| FONZ*, http://nationalzoo.si.edu/Publications/ZooGoer/1996/1/junglegyms.cfm, 1996.

[8] Joel Foreman, James Paul Gee, J. C. Herz, Randy Hinrichs, Marc Prensky, and Ben Sawyer, "Game-Based Learning: How to Delight and Instruct in the 21st Century," *EDUCAUSE Review* 39:5 (September/October 2004), pp. 50–66.

tant survival skills, in a *safe* environment. It may even be *hardwired in our brains*, and we are *rewarded* with pleasure if we engage in playful behavior. We call this pleasurable feeling *fun*. Related to this predisposition towards gameplay is our ability to easily and readily *suspend our disbelief*, when confronted with *virtual experiences*.

Games can be considered a *teaching mechanism*. One of their most important purposes is to teach vital life lessons through gameplay. This concept of educational gameplay, from a biological point of view, is far-reaching and fundamental to us as human beings. It is literally a part of our *behavioral makeup* for reasons of survival, and understanding the processes at work is vital to our understanding of level design. Many of the same underlying mechanics at work with regard to play and traditional games apply to level design. Gameplay and educational processes can form a natural match, examples of which can be found in new gameplay-based educational programs, serious games, and scientific literature.

Nonetheless, it is important to keep in mind that evolutionary play is a very controversial subject, and to this day, arguments in favor and against are still debated.

> Explanations of play that involve either proximate or ultimate cause, or both, are common in the literature. However, though evolutionary explanations—and hence ultimate explanations—of play pepper the literature, their success in answering the question, "What is play for?" has been limited.[9]

Nonetheless, play as a teaching mechanism provides a worthy area of knowledge for level designers to dip into. There is much useful data there to link to level design theory.

Theory

If we are predisposed to gameplay because it *teaches* us survival skills, it stands to reason that we examine the teaching aspects of this concept further. The idea that games can be seen as a *teaching mechanism,* born out of biological or evolutionary necessity, is certainly interesting. Based upon our finding so far, we can formulate the following statement:

---

[9] Garry Chick, "What is Play For? Sexual Selection and the Evolution of Play," keynote address presented at the annual meeting of The Association for the Study of Play, St. Petersburg, FL, February 20, 1998.

> In purely biological terms, a game is an artificial construct, designed to safely teach survival skills, and in doing so, rewarding the player with pleasure.

This statement seems fair and accurate, but how does it help us understand or apply level design? Let's see if there is conceptual overlap between this general *concept* and specific level design *theory* by rephrasing the previous statement so it fits within the parameters of video games. A translation into video game terms would look like this:

> A video game is an artificial construct that, when well made, rewards the player with fun.

If we equate the concept of *teaching survival skills* from the first statement with *well made* from the second statement, we find that they equate very well.

There is a strong correlation between the rewards we receive from play in general, and those we receive from playing video games. This is not strange, since video games are just a different form of games, and therefore are subject to many of the same underlying principles. However, we are not used to looking at video games in that way, even though it makes sense to do so.

Much traditional play is all about *teaching skills*, and *testing* the player's proficiency. It is rewarding to master a task, or to be good at something. Games teach motor skills, mental skills, skills of reasoning, and so on. Gameplay allows us to put those skills to the test in a controlled manner. A good game strikes a balance between teaching these skills and providing the player with an enjoyable testbed in which to try them out. There is no reason to think that video games are any different, and in extension, the same is true for level design.

"Good" Level Design

As we have already established in Chapter 1, "Game Design vs. Level Design," we can state that level design is the *application* of game design. We now also know that in practical terms, we can say that *"good level design teaches the player how to play and enjoy the game."*

This is one of the most important concepts in level design, and when better understood, one that good level designers will keep coming back to, time after time. It can be used in almost any aspect of level design and can relate the smallest gameplay mechanic to the largest span of levels.

Let's look at a small number of areas where this can be applied:

- the physical rules of the environment,
- the abilities of the player's in-game character,

- the behavior of enemies,
- the game's reward systems.

These are all major gameplay areas, and the game as whole would suffer if their rules were not properly taught to the player. Conversely, if the player is taught well how to deal with these areas of gameplay, this will form a solid basis for a good gameplay experience. This is part of the reason why the *game* cannot be good if the *level design* is not good. The underlying game design can be the best in the world, but if the level design does not support it by teaching the player the rules of this brilliant game, it is all for nothing. Furthermore, if the game design does not support education though level design, it will never be fully enjoyed by the player.

If we accept that this *teaching role* is absolutely fundamental to level design, it makes sense to try to define the best techniques available to us in achieving this teaching goal. This is what I mean by *teaching mechanisms*.

Good level design is not just teaching the player the rules of the game, but also allowing the player to use those rules in a way that is rewarding and fun. Much of the fun comes to the surface when the player is tested.

Teaching Mechanisms vs. Testing Mechanisms

Teaching mechanisms are meaningless unless that which is taught is tested and put into practice. There has to be a way to test the player's knowledge or proficiency within the game, or the game may lack purpose. This is another intrinsic goal of level design. If the gameplay is taught well and the player gets tested in an enjoyable manner, the level designer has done a good job. Countless lessons and techniques can be derived from this fact alone. Examples of this balance can be found in many successful video games, and throughout the book many of these will be referenced or new ones will be explored.

Testing[10] the player's skills and knowledge is an integral part of the teaching mechanisms in level design. From now on, when I refer to *teaching mechanisms*, it can be assumed that I am also talking about *testing mechanisms*.

Teaching Gameplay and Reward Systems

At the basis of much level design success lies the ability to show the player how the game's play mechanics tie in with the game's reward mechanisms. What actions and skills does the player have to master in order to get rewarded by the

---

[10] It is important to note that testing does not necessarily equal challenging. A test can constitute a challenge, but not every test has to be a challenge.

game? Where are the most enjoyable sections to be found, which weapons provide the best results, what creatures are most fun to play with, and which skills should the player train first? All these questions present a teaching dialogue between level designer and player.

Inappropriate Gameplay

When we teach the player how to play the game at its most effective or its most enjoyable, it is expected that those lessons are meaningful. Players implicitly trust the game to teach them techniques that are consistent and trustworthy throughout the game.

It is therefore important for us as level designers not to betray that trust, and to create gameplay scenarios or puzzles not only for their own sake,[11] but also in context of the gameplay appropriate to the game as a whole. To put it simply, if possible, we should not create situations where the player's skills are useless.

For example, we should avoid situations that arbitrarily or in an unannounced way deviate from the needed skill set and require something from the players that they have never been taught.

This lesson is easily (and often) forgotten. A typical example is found in *boss fights*[12] that don't use taught gameplay skills—and they are rife in game levels. Please be aware of pitfalls in this regard.

Teaching Mechanisms in General Areas of Level Design

It is impossible to try to identify all gameplay mechanics and try to find ways to teach them best to the player. Not only is this impossible due to the scope of the task; it also wouldn't cover new genres of gameplay or unexpected gameplay occurrences. Furthermore, mechanics differ wildly between genres.

A more sensible approach lies in trying to find common themes that can be applied to diverse situations. I have identified a number of areas that cover most aspects of level design and deserve a further look:

- the game's main goals and rules,
- the abilities and limitations of the game's player character,

---

[11] Although there is place for discreet isolated puzzles, or even games dependent on them.

[12] Boss fights are climactic fights between a player and an extra-powerful computer controlled opponent.

- the physics and scope of the gameplay world,
- the abilities and limitations of the non-player characters,
- success strategies available to the player.

Each of these areas covers a very wide range of gameplay issues and is worth exploring further.

The Abilities and Limitations of the Game's Player Character

A player's *in-game character* or *avatar* provides the player with much of his or her interface with the game world. To a large degree, players experiences and interacts with the world through their player character. This is of course less important to games where the main gameplay does not derive from interacting through an avatar, but the principle still stands that players need to know how they can manipulate or interact with the virtual world they are exposed to. For example, it is just as important in *Tetris* to know how to rotate, direct, or drop down shapes as it is in *Tomb Raider* to know what jump distances are viable or what surfaces can be climbed.

This need to know defines the player's abilities and limitations in context of the game's (virtual) reality. It is very important to teach this early on in the gameplay experience, because the earlier this is accepted by players, the earlier they are able to suspend their disbelief in what is after all an artificial construct.

This need is actually fairly typical in all kinds of games. In chess, for example, half of the rules are linked to knowing what the abilities and limitations of the individual chess pieces are. There is in fact no point in playing the game until you know. (This does not mean that in video games these rules can't change later on, but in most cases, these changes have to come after the player has been taught the fundamental and basic rules.)

The Physics and Scope of the Gameplay World

Just as it is important to define the abilities of the player character, it is important to teach players how they interact with the game's environment. This is important because it gives further *context* in which to perform actions. In some ways, the game world can be seen as a character in itself.

Players' actions by themselves don't have much meaning unless they are performed within a defined physical context. The game world is a large part of this.

The Abilities and Limitations of the Non-Player Characters

If a level designer works on a game that features non-player characters, which is extremely likely, the player needs to be taught how to interact with them. This does not only cover *enemy AI* (artificial intelligence) but any AI characters present in the game.

The Game's Main Goals and Rules

In most cases (there are exceptions) it is wise to assume that players need to learn what constitutes the core gameplay experience of the game they are playing. In other words, they need to know early on what the game's main objectives are and how to achieve them. This is true on a level-by-level basis as much as it is true for the game as a whole.

Success Strategies

From a player's point of view, a video game needs to be worth playing. The actions a player takes while in the game need to include gameplay that is somehow rewarding to the player, especially if linked to progression within the game. There are strategies available to the player that result in an enjoyable progression. Part of the fun of a video game is finding out what they are and perfecting them.

From the player's point of view, this is central to being taught how to enjoy the game. To players, a game is an entertainment device over which they have control. Learning how to manipulate this device in order to yield maximum fun is imperative to good level design. To learn this, a player has to determine which strategies of play yield the best results. A *success strategy* in that context is defined as a strategy that produces a fun gameplay experience.

These success strategies can be *formal* in nature, requiring predescribed solutions to gameplay questions. For example, this occurs when a player has to progress through a level by following a specific path, determined by the level designer.

Alternatively, success strategies can be informal, defined by the players themselves. Good examples of this can be found in games where players can devise their own enjoyable gameplay through nonprescribed interaction with the game's environment. Although less explicit than formal strategies, this kind of freeform play can still be encouraged through good level design.

Some Dos and Don'ts

Without trying to be exhaustive,[13] I would like to highlight some typical dos and don'ts related to this subject. They are not hard rules; use your own judgment, but they generally should be considered.

Dos

Let's start with some recommended approaches.

Teach by practical example

Always give players a chance to put the things they have been taught into practice as soon as possible. When a new gameplay mechanic is introduced to the player, it is best to let the player try it out immediately. The best way of learning for many people is by doing. And it is easier to put lessons into practice when they are still fresh in the mind of the player.

This is a good habit to get into, and once you are aware of this method, you will start to notice the principle in many other games. For example, many Nintendo games do this consistently.[14]

Positive reinforcement

If at all possible, make sure players are actively rewarded when they pass a skill-test or successfully progress through a challenging gameplay scenario.

When players are taught that there are very positive consequences for successfully navigating the game, they will become eager to engage with it.

Prepare the player fairly

Make sure that players have the right tools and knowledge available to them before they are forced to perform a skill test that they can badly fail. There is a place for lethal encounters in many games, but it is always necessary to make them *fair*. Unannounced or unavoidable instant-death traps are generally to be avoided, unless they are expected in the game's genre.[15]

When possible, teach important skills in a safe environment first. A great example of this philosophy is found in the *Half Life 2* series:

---

[13] Elements of this chapter will keep appearing in some form or another through the book, and additional tips and danger areas will be highlighted per subject.

[14] *Zelda: Twilight Princess*, to name one.

[15] This will be covered in more detail later in the book, specifically in the chapters on reward mechanisms and challenge.

Players discover that every basic skill is taught in a very unobtrusive way, especially early in the game. This includes simple challenges, like stacking the crates to get out of the windows in the Trainstation, to more complex ones, such as the Antlion Pheropod "Bugbait" training in the Coast section. The difficulty of subsequent tasks could then be increased knowing that the player had been taught the mechanics they needed to succeed.[16]

Make sure that players can comfortably learn the skills they are supposed to pick up. There is no problem with ramping up difficulty later on and providing more difficult encounters, but when first teaching the player how to play the game, the lessons should be forgiving.

Players should be introduced to new mechanics in non-frustrating ways. This can mean that a skill can be taught in such a way that players cannot fail the exercise and only need to focus on practicing the skill until they can perform the tasks relevant to the teaching exercise.

Don'ts

We also need to be careful to avoid some problems. The following examples are situations to look out for:

Don't start with failure

Sometimes level designers are tempted to start a new level with a very serious challenge. They want to begin gameplay on a tense note and immediately put the player in grave peril. This may sound good on paper, but a game is not a book or a script. If there is serious danger, there is a serious chance that the player will fail the gameplay challenge. Imagine how frustrating it is for those players who don't pass this test and end up failing badly right at the beginning of a level. Rather than being enjoyably tense, the experience is likely to be off-putting and tell the player that the game will be a frustrating affair. In fact, it discourages the layer from playing, and that is something we generally want to avoid.

Don't taunt the player

It is strange that I even feel the need to write this, but this advice is too often ignored. It is crucial that even when players are struggling to pick up a skill, that they be encouraged in a positive manner, and not scolded for not being able yet to master a mechanic or meet a gameplay challenge.

---

[16] David Hodgson, *Half Life 2: Raising the Bar*, Valve/Prima Games, Roseville, CA, 2004, p. 277.

When a gameplay section is supposed to be about teaching, play mechanics make sure the results are positive, even if the player takes a long time to master the skill. Don't shut off award paths or use taunting language or employ any similar tactics, as you will just put off those players who for some reason or another struggle a bit more than others. You will end up punishing those payers who have the most to gain from an encouraging approach. If that happens, you may well lose them completely if they get fed up with the game and put it down for good.

Theory Summary

There is a direct and useful link between level design and the educational aspects of gameplay. Level design can be seen as a vehicle to teach the player among other things, *how to play and enjoy the game.* Gameplay, and by extension level design, functions as a teaching mechanism. The techniques and strategies that can be derived from this conclusion cover almost every aspect of gameplay.

There are too many ways to employ this knowledge to focus on individually. This chapter has identified a number of important ones, and future chapters will explore even more.

Practice

Example 2.1: Teaching by Doing— Mandatory Skill Gates

Summary

Generally the most enjoyable way of learning a skill is by "doing": the player actually trying to perform the necessary actions, and adjusting and adapting until he is able to put the lesson into practice. Because levels often make heavy use of *interactivity* and *player agency*[17] to a large degree, this method is very suited to the form.

There are times when a level designer needs to be sure that the player possesses certain skills or is in possession of specific knowledge. A guaranteed way

---

[17] The ability to act in the world.

of teaching the player something like this is by making absorbance of the lesson a condition for progress.

The two aspects can be combined in a discreet level design scenario that is very useful in many circumstances.

Game Genre

The technique is suitable for any game where progress can be halted if a game mechanic is not yet mastered (either naturally, or by scripted means).

Goals to Achieve

- Showcase a natural way for the player to pick up skills through gameplay actions in level design scenarios.
- Make sure the player cannot progress unless they have been taught how to use the new skill.
- Teach new skills in a controlled setting.

Description

(Example type: Original/general)

If a level designer wants to make sure that players pick up a certain level of proficiency when introduced to a new gameplay mechanic, he or she can consider the use of a *skill gate* in a locked-off gameplay arena.

Such a setup is realized by establishing a dead-end area where the player finds or is introduced to a new gameplay mechanic. This can be a new skill or perhaps a new item that is to be used throughout the game from then on. Imagine a player needing to jump down one-way drops (too high to jump back up) all the way to the bottom of a ravine. Once at the bottom, the player is trapped there unless they can find a way to backtrack along the path they just used. If the player is then confronted with a new skill—for example, an increased athletic ability—he can now practice that skill by using the new athletic ability to travel back along his original route. This will only be possible if the player becomes proficient enough with the new athletic capabilities to be able to scale the heights that were prohibitive before.

The designer can include extra difficult areas off the main path, filled with rare collectables, to encourage the player to exercise and practice the new skills even further. By the time the player has left the ravine, she will have learned the new skill—or would not have been able to escape—and have been given the opportunity to find extra rewards through extra efforts, showcasing that the new skill is enjoyable and useful.

Further Notes

This technique is extensively used in Nintendo's "Zelda" games. Upon the introduction of a new skill, the player is typically confronted with a use for that skill close by.

There are many more ways that these skill gates can be part of a teaching mechanism. A puzzle may need to be solved before the player receives an item that unlocks the next area of the game. A creature needs to be defeated by using a specific gameplay mechanic to its full potential. A locked dungeon may have to be cleared of enemy creatures before it unlocks. Game history is full of further examples that can be adopted for new level designs.

A further advantage lies in the fact that, since the player is guaranteed to have learned the skill at the end of the gameplay scenario, the level design can now take this into account.

Example 2.2: Teaching by Example

Summary

By showing players certain actions or outcomes in the game world, you give them the opportunity to learn by observation and example. This principle is easily translated in custom-made gameplay lessons that are effective and appropriate to the level setting.

Game Genre

The technique is suitable for all games that allow the level designer to create an observable sequence of gameplay-related actions.

Goals to Achieve

- Introduce a new enemy into the level, at a safe distance from the player.
- Show conditions in which it becomes a threat.
- Demonstrate the severity and nature of the threat.
- Show to the player what tactics work against the enemy.
- Give the player a chance to practice this in a safe setting.

Description

(Example type: Original)

A classic scenario in level design is found in the introduction of a new enemy in the game. If this encounter is of sufficient importance and the level designer has time to turn the encounter into a mini set piece, it can be turned into a scripted teaching mechanism. By showing how the creature reacts or how the creature can be defeated through the actions of others, the player can learn and strategize without being directly exposed to any immediate danger.

The trick is to find a natural way for the player to be separated physically from the action but still be able to observe a scenario played out in his presence. This can be done simply by providing a distance barrier (the player can't get close enough to the action before it runs its course) or a physical barrier that still allows the player to see the action unfold. The example may play out on a balcony the player can't reach, or some similar restraint.

Let's take, for example, an adventure game where the player is part of an archaeological dig on the side of a mountain. The other members of the party are human, as is the player character. When the player reaches a certain position near some loose rocks an event is triggered. One of the party members slips on the rocks and falls down onto a precarious ledge, which houses a big bird's nest. The nest belongs to a condor pair, and the mother can be heard squawking from far away. The sound becomes louder, however, until the irate bird flies into view and starts attacking the fallen archaeologist. It does so by either flying over the NPCs head, trying to scratch him with its claws or by flapping its wings in front of him trying to push him off the edge. The NPC takes initial damage, but eventually notices that crawling protects him from the flyover attacks, while throwing rocks at the bird interrupts the flapping attack. Other NPCs get the clue and also start throwing rocks at the bird, but are not able to hit it. The player, on the other hand, is given the opportunity to do the same, and when he or she successfully strikes the bird with a rock the bird is scared off. The NPC is subsequently rescued by his colleagues.

The player has learned a number of things:

- the existence of these condors in the level;
- the fact that they become aggressive if their nest is disturbed;
- aspects of their behavior: time to arrive on the scene, different attack modes;
- the amount of damage they can do;
- several strategies for coping with them;
- how to dispatch them.

All in all, that is a decent amount of gain from one custom-made lesson. From now on, the level designer should be able to use the condor threat in several circumstances. The player may be confronted with a path that is blocked by a nest, or the player may be accosted by a pair of condors to up the challenge. Many other scenarios can be imagined, but the player will at least be familiar with key aspects of the creature.

Further Notes

It is vital when employing this technique that the player is subject to the same rules as those entities around them. To give a simple example, it would be unfair to show a non-player character who is physically the same as the player character to be more resistant to environmental damage than the player. So, for example, if an NPC of the same abilities jumps off a high roof and survives, the same outcome should apply to the player (unless there is a good explanation for a different outcome).

Example 2.3: Formal Tuition—Overt and Covert

Summary

Sometimes it is valid to teach a player something through a tutorial or training sequence. The player is aware that he or she is being taught something about the game and needs to pay close attention because of this. This example shows a way to do this that does not break the game's immersion.

Game Genre

This technique is especially suitable to games that require the player's suspension of disbelief to stay intact.

Goals to Achieve

- Teach the player game related skills.
- Do this in a formal manner; the player knows they are being taught something.
- Show overt and covert ways of doing this.

Description

(Example type: Existing game)

Many games require at one point or another that the player go through a tutorial in order to learn a new ability. This can, however, be done both in *overt* and *covert* ways. *Overt* in this context means that the tuition is not hidden within the game world. The player is literally told that they are being taught without pretending it is part of the game proper. This is what happens with tutorial sequences outside the levels of the game, a bit like an interactive manual.

Covert, on the other hand, means that the teaching occurs within the story or within the reality and logic of the game world. The game stays "in character" and does not break the fourth wall. This is a very useful technique as it has a number of valuable side effects beyond the content of the tutorial. This kind of teaching mechanism can achieve the following goals:

- teach the player a skill (or range of skills),
- maintain immersion,
- maintain suspension of disbelief,
- add to the level content.

Halo—Covert camera calibration tutorial. In Bungie's *Halo: Combat Evolved*, [18] we can see this technique utilized with great intelligence. The game is played with a first person camera; preferences with regard to camera calibration is one of the peculiarities of players: If you press the camera stick on the joy-pad up, should the in-game camera look up or down? As it turns out, Microsoft has studied this subject through extensive usability testing, and they found that there is a 50-50 split of preferences on this subject. This meant that whatever the default setting for the game camera was, it was going to be wrong and frustrating to half the players. They decided, therefore, to let the player calibrate the camera themselves in-game, in a covert camera calibration tutorial. This was a very clever and useful solution to a problem that should not be underestimated.

The resulting level design solution was to place the player character in a setting where the game could measure the player's input when asked to perform a task. In this case, the player is given a new combat suit and asked to "test" it for optimal performance. The player is literally asked to look left and right, up and down, and the resulting player choices tells the game what the player's preference is in this regard.

This solution shows that it is possible to maintain suspension of disbelief even when teaching or calibrating very technical aspects of gameplay.

Further Notes

Other classic covert tutorial or teaching scenarios occur in games that use an obstacle course for in-game training of operatives. This occurs, for example, in the first *Splinter Cell*[19] game, where the player is asked to finish an obstacle course to assess if the player has received enough training.

---

[18] Published by Microsoft Game Studios, developed by Bungie Studios, released November 15, 2001.

[19] Published by Ubi Soft Entertainment Software, developed by Ubi Soft Divertissements Inc., released November 2002.

Example 2.4: Teaching through Experiment

Summary

A very pure and natural way to discover abilities and other things is by *experimenting* with things. Playful experimentation is a cornerstone of education, not only for children but for adults as well. ("What does *this* button do?")

This method can be used to much effect as it tends to produce very enjoyable results.

Game Genre

The technique is very suitable for sandbox games. Additionally, it is a very useful technique when there are multiple uses for a game object.

Goals to Achieve

- Create a situation that allows for self-taught gameplay skills.
- Create an environment that encourages experimentation.

Description

(Example type: Original)

There is a funny cliché associated with 2D point-and-click adventures that you often need to combine the use of completely disparate objects in your inventory to find a solution to some obscure problem—the (valid) complaint being that there is no logical sense to many of these item combinations. Those games do highlight, however, that it is fun and rewarding to find uses for things through experimentation.

This principle can be expanded on in level design by making sure that there are instances where the player can freely experiment within the interactive parameters of a level to learn new skills, or find new uses for objects.

To try to encourage this kind of experimental yet educational gameplay, you may find it worthwhile to create specific areas where the player can indulge—a "safe zone" with no loss of, say, expendable items.

A good way of doing this is by creating a situation where there are multiple uses and outcomes built into the level design scenario from the outset. To do that, we take a number of desired outcomes and characteristics and use them as the building blocks for our level design scenario. Taking, say, the humble game crate[20] as a starting point for an example, we can list a number of ways in which this can work. We can say, for example, that the crates can

---

[20] Discussed in Chapter 8.

- block NPCs,
- be stood on,
- be climbed,
- be stacked on top of each other,
- be pushed over,
- be moved about.

If we take these basic abilities of the crate, add a player character's abilities to the mix, and combine those two with an environment containing aggressive NCPS, collectibles that are out of reach and additional crates that the player can't get to, we end up with a recipe for great potential experimental fun.

The player could try to do things like

- create a stack of crates that can be climbed to reach high areas (to get to collectibles),
- create a stack of crates to reach other crates to add to the mix,
- prepare traps where the crates can be shoved off ledges onto enemies,
- create towers of crates to be pushed over on top of enemies,
- create pens in which enemies can be trapped,
- create structures that are pleasing to the eye,
- stand on crates in order to review the environment form a high vantage point.

Many other uses can be found depending on the level in question.

Look at all the things the player has the potential to learn—many ways to find new objects, interact with enemies, manipulate the environment—and all without any explicit tutorials. Anything the player learns will feel like something they have earned through intelligent gameplay and as such is very rewarding to the player.

Further Notes

There exists the danger that this technique does not aid the player in finding the right solution. It is therefore best implemented in situations where the teaching mechanic is optional—i.e., one very specific solution is not required to complete the challenge.

Level Design Goals and Hierarchies

3

Just like in any other creative endeavor, it is important in level design to define a set of clearly understood goals before any major work is done. However, this is easier said than done, if there is no consensus on just what those goals may be. Can we even speak of goals specific to level design, or are such goals related to the game design as a whole? Do level designs for differing games share similar goals? Should we even try to formalize a set of specific level design goals?

The longer we look at these questions, the clearer it becomes that they are important and fundamental questions that need to be addressed early in the level design process. This chapter will address a number of level design goals that are important to keep in mind.

Success Definition

> What are you trying to achieve?

This is a question that should always have an answer. The *why* and *how* aspects of the same question are addressed separately, but those are all moot if the *what* question is not answered first. Being able to define clearly what it is you are trying to achieve means that you can clearly describe a number of goals that need to be met. That is to say that any goals that are set are subject to an overall *success definition*. This means that the goals are not arbitrary, but instead are set to achieve a desired overall result, which is a *definition of success*. A goal is just part of a strategy for achieving this successful outcome. This may seem too obvious to state, but in my experience this most basic element of level design is often forgotten.

The success definition(s) can be game-wide[1]; indeed a clear definition should exist at the top of a game's *hierarchy* of goals. It can be level-wide, or can

---

[1] Some game companies refer to such a game-wide goal summary as *The X*.

even occur on smaller gameplay scales. For example, a hypothetical level-wide success definition could state:

"Train players' combat skills throughout the level and build up the players' level of confidence and ability in order to prepare them for the introduction of a new enemy creature."

A game-wide success definition might read:

"Create an action-horror hybrid that can be described as "Dracula meets The Terminator.[2]"

In our case the success definition describes what the *level designer* needs to achieve. This is something that should remain in focus as the ultimate goal throughout the level design and level creation process. All other goals are by definition subordinate to that overall aim. Whatever the final success definition(s) incorporate, we need to be aware of what they are.

External Level Design Goals

There are all kinds of goals that may need to be taken into consideration when determining success definitions. Some are independent from direct gameplay considerations, insofar as they that they refer to goals outside of the gameplay experience. The level design may have to

- be appealing to both genders,
- stay true to the brand image,
- sell X amount of units,
- push new engine technology,
- win a BAFTA award,
- receive a meta critic[3] rating higher than 75%.

These are the overarching goals that are derived from the requirements of the game's development as a commercial or even artistic production. They describe the purpose of the level design components as much as they define the internal level design goals, which are derived from direct gameplay considerations. It is a mistake to dismiss these external factors, as they are the ultimate reason why a game is made in the first place.

Good examples of external goals like this can be found in the marketplace, so let's take a closer look at commercial considerations:

---

[2] I have seen worse pitches.

[3] See www.metacritic.com.

Commercial considerations

It is important to note that, aside from alternative funding models and independent game development, in most cases, games are supposed to make money. There are many ways one can try to achieve this goal, but it should not be forgotten that for many people it is the fundamental reason for developing a game in the first place. It is wise to note this simple fact. In the case of publisher-funded development, for example, a game that does not sell is likely to be seen as a failure by the financing publisher. *The most important reason that publishers fund game development is because they think it is likely to make them money.* I am not saying this is bad or good, but merely stating a fact that offers another point of view on the function of a game and, by extension, of its design. If the game design within this context doesn't support a commercially viable end product, it has failed to fulfill its basic function *from the publisher's perspective.* This is a possible interpretation of game design that, even if unwelcome[4] at times, nonetheless needs to be understood.

Only after a game's creation has been approved through these external goals can the production go ahead. However, these goals do not in themselves determine fun gameplay, which is the realm of internal level design goals.

Internal Level Design Goals

As stated earlier, internal level design goals *are derived from direct gameplay considerations.* Outside of the external macro goals described earlier, there will always be level design goals that are just part of the art form itself, driven by internal factors. They are the goals that contribute to the overall good gameplay. They deal with requirements such as the following:

- Empower the player.
- Teach the player how to have fun with the game.
- Don't break the player's suspension of disbelief.
- Give the player a sense of achievement.
- Reward the player for exploration.
- Provide addictive, fun gameplay.

These are requirements that stem from supporting the game or the gameplay on a very pure level. They are as important to define as external factors.

It is important to never forget that it is the job of a level designer to implement, interpret, and exploit the game design to give it its best possible applica-

---

[4] It is good to note that commercial considerations do not have to be crass or in conflict with artistic merit.

tion. A game's *level design* is not an isolated construct, just as *a game design* does not function independently. They need to complement each other, or both will suffer. (See Chapter 1, "Game Design vs. Level Design.")

Internal level design goals are the bread and butter of our profession. They give us very specific goals to aim for in order to provide a good gameplay experience. In a hierarchy of internal goals, the game's *overall gameplay experience* always comes out on top, and the level design needs to support this.

This also means we have to start putting our level design goals into some type of *hierarchical* order.

Level Design Hierarchies

We looked at level design goals before and determined that they must support and put into practice the game design. This is easier said than done, of course, since the level design components will have to fulfill a number of requirements. This is their *purpose*. Nonetheless, let's assume that we have a clearly defined set of goals, and that we have translated them into requirements.

So how do we know what value to assign to these goals and requirements? What components do we focus on first when we start working on a new level? Which elements are more important? *What if it doesn't work?*

These are all typical questions that come up during a game's development. They are all related to the component's importance and place in the project. To determine these factors, we first have to take a step back and devise a way to assign value to individual level-design components. We have to give them a place within a logical *level-design hierarchy*.

Development Hierarchy

To create a situation where we can measure the value and implementation of such things as AI encounters, item placement, puzzle design, and hundreds of other level design components, it is helpful to define some kind of hierarchy. If we can figure out where things fit in the scheme of things, we can make choices on what and how to prioritize, and where dependencies occur.

In a game-design setting, here are a number of known stages and areas of development. They tend to fit into a structure where one area supports another in a certain hierarchical order.

Generally, we have to look at the following questions:

- Why are we making the game?
- What game are we making?
- How are we making it?

Figure 3.1. Game-wide hierarchy.

When we have answered these questions and have logically placed our general development components in this framework, we can see a hierarchy emerge. For some games, this general hierarchy may look like the image in Figure 3.1.

In this pyramid shape, each segment is supported by the segments below it, and were we to try to answer our why, how, and what questions with it, the following would emerge:

- Success Definition (Why),
- External Goals (Why),
- Internal Goals (Why),
- Game Design (What) – Level Design (What/How),
- Technical Design (How) – Art Direction – Audio Plan (How).

This diagram gives us a possible insight on where level design exists within the overall context of the game's development. I won't go into too much detail when it comes to production issues, as that is not the focus of this book. However, it is at least interesting, insofar as that it shows some relationships between level design and the rest of the game's production areas.

Things become more relevant when we try to find a similar approach within the level design parameters for a game. We might ask those questions again:

- Why are we making the level?
- What levels are we making?
- How are we making them?

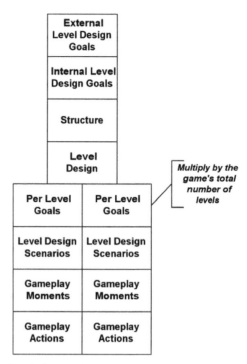

Figure 3.2. Level-wide hierarchies.

To answer those questions, a game's level design hierarchy might be made up of the elements shown in Figure 3.2.

And to repeat the exercise once more: in this pyramid shape, each segment is supported by the segments below it, and were we to try to answer our why, how, and what questions with it, the following would emerge:

- External Level Design Goals (Why),
- Internal level Design Goals (Why),
- Structure (What),
- Level Design (What),
- Per-Level Goals (How),
- Level Design Scenarios (How),
- Gameplay Moments (How),
- Gameplay Actions (How).

From this point on, we can go into real detail and start to assign things like function and resulting tasks to the broken-down elements.

Dyson, a Case Study

To illustrate some of these concepts against a real world example, I am going to use the game *Dyson*,[5] designed by Alex May and myself, as a case study. *Dyson* was created in a one-month competition for the *independent games focused* website and community *TIGSource*. The game development competition was defined by the following rules:

> The theme of the game is PROCEDURAL GENERATION, with an emphasis on generating new content every time the player starts the game. Procedural generation, or procedural content generation, is a term to describe the creation of content algorithmically "on the fly" (i.e. after the software executes, rather than before). In video games it is generally used to either generate "random" content (like graphics or levels), or to reduce file size. This competition is focused on the former, but you may choose to apply the theme however you see fit.[6]

With this background in mind, we can now examine the *why, what* and *how* questions and the level design hierarchy they imply. In the case of *Dyson*, all these elements are represented, as discussed below.

External level design goals

Dyson's levels first and foremost had to show off the concepts of *procedural generation*, as defined by the competition rules. They had to do so in such a way that they still ended up being enjoyable to play, without the procedural nature being a gimmick. In other words, the procedural elements of the game needed to be explicit in the levels and the gameplay they would hold.

All this had to be achieved within 30 days with a very limited amount of time and resources. (The team consisted of only one programmer, one designer, and one audio designer.)

Resulting strategy. To meet these goals, we decided that *Dyson* would be a game that Incorporated scientific theories that show off procedural generation in a gameplay format. Freeman Dyson's *Dyson trees* and *Astrochicken* met John Von Neumann's self propagating machines, and everything was turned into a design that allowed small seeds of data to grow into complex environments.

---

[5] This is not meant to promote the game, but simply to provide a clear example of the concepts we have just discussed. A fully featured version of the game is still being developed at the time of writing this book by Alex May and myself, with music and audio being done by Brian Grainger. Have a look at it here: http://www.dyson-game.com.

[6] "Procedural Generation Competition," *Procedural Generation Competition*, http://forums.tigsource.com/index.php?topic=1646.0, 2008.

To restate that in understandable English: *Dyson* was chosen to become a game of space conquest. Flying robot seeds conquer territory and exploit resources in an asteroid belt. Other seedling factions compete for the same resources, and almost all the game art was to be procedurally generated, rather than modeled.

Internal level design goals

To meet the external goals, we decided that the levels had to provide strategically interesting choices despite a very limited amount of resources at hand. This meant that the levels needed to work as a replayable experience, where players would get different content every time they play.

Resulting strategy. To provide enough variation within a limited number of levels, we decided that almost all factors in the game had to be affected by a select number of variables. To do this, a limited number of variables had to lead to a maximum sense of interesting complexity.

To facilitate this in level design terms, we decided that the levels had to work in two dimensions, and that all territory was governed by simple and recognizable attributes. In the game, the seeds are planted on asteroids, and they turn into trees whose genetic makeup is influenced by the asteroid's variations in natural resources. The trees produce seedlings, which are also affected in their abilities by the mother asteroid, and they can in turn be used to conquer other asteroids.

Structure

Because of the need to make the most out of very limited resources, the levels for *Dyson* had to be replayable. The level structure therefore had to support open-ended strategic choices from the beginning of play, in order for multiple playthroughs to feel very different, depending on the choices that were made by the player early on.

Resulting strategy. To achieve this, we decided to create one very large level, with interesting gameplay complexities introduced by AI agents that all vie for the same resources as the player. Because the resources and layout of the asteroids change every time the game starts, replayability is guaranteed.

Per-level goals

In this case, only one level was chosen to be in the game, but it had to have the appeal and scope to keep the player interested for as many playthroughs as possible.

Resulting strategy. For this to work, the gameplay goal of the one level we ended up with for the competition had to be one of *total conquest of a territory*. The win/lose conditions for a level had to be simple, so that players could easily understand the task at hand and try again if it didn't work out.

Gameplay scenarios

The level in question could only maintain its long-term appeal if a number of discreetly interesting gameplay scenarios would play out time after time, without losing appeal. The level had to be balanced in such a way that these kinds of gameplay loops would occur often enough and be enticing throughout.

They had to be those kinds of moments that operate at a level where the player is trying to find and perfect success strategies.

Resulting strategy. Out of the possible scenarios to evolve from the core gameplay elements, we focused our attention mainly on the following ones:

- Invest and grow: Choose to keep seedlings close by and use them to plan more Dyson trees).
- Grow and expand: Try to create an army of conquest and take over other territory.
- Choose units and attack enemy: Focus on the variations in seedling abilities and pick seedlings best suited to defeat other seedlings in the game.
- Defend: Take a defensive approach and try to hold territory while repelling attacks from enemy factions.

Gameplay moments

To have lasting appeal, gameplay scenarios need moments of excitement or must otherwise be engaging. These are the decision moments that involve players at a deep level and have them watch the game unfold with real interest.

Resulting strategy. We tried to make sure that enough of these special moments would occur to serve our other goals in the level-design hierarchy. We focused on gameplay moments that included

- choosing a strategically strong asteroid to attack,
- finding the right moment to sacrifice seedlings and plant a new tree,
- setting up forces, to swoop to a heavily fortified enemy asteroid,

and so on.

Gameplay actions

Finally, the immediate actions the player can perform had to be balanced against the overarching goals and had to fit the environment. Fundamental level-design choices had to be made with basic actions like

- planting a tree,
- sending units to a target.

Resulting strategy. To keep things interesting for players, a number of restrictions, or conversely abilities, had to be considered with regard to those gameplay actions. For example, *planting a tree* had to be balanced by an associated cost; in this case a number of seedlings had to be sacrificed. (This had the added advantage of making seedlings work as currency). On the other hand, *sending units to a target* was made to be as easy as possible; all units' seedlings orbiting an asteroid could be sent off simultaneously.

To facilitate the use of these actions, and to serve several of the other goals of the game, we also decided to include tutorial text that helps the player pick up the game rapidly.

Note that it is surprising how easy it is to fit all the disparate elements of a game and its level designs in a fairly sensible and logical hierarchy. The fit is not 100%, and some elements have been left untouched. For example, music and audio play an important role. However, the example illustrates how it is possible to construct a view of the level design process where each individual feature is shown to support many others. The interrelationship within such a hierarchy is useful and shows up important areas to focus on when designing and implementing levels.

X Factor

Another way of looking at the concept of a success definition is by dubbing it the *X-Factor*. I am highlighting this subject, as it often doesn't get the attention it deserves.

A good game is more than the sum of its parts. This can be seen very clearly in some very famous example, for instance in *Grand Theft Auto: Vice City*,[7] which was a phenomenal success, both financially and creatively. However, if studied in isolation, many of the individual game components were lacking in some way or another.

---

[7] Developed by Rockstar North.

- The aiming mechanic was cumbersome.
- The third-person character controls were frustrating.
- The camera often couldn't cope.
- The geometry and architecture were very low on detail.

There are many other examples as well, but the key point is that deficiencies or excellence in these areas do not necessarily make a bad or good gaming experience.

Many people have tried to copy *Vice City* and have even improved upon individual gameplay mechanics, yet have come away with less enjoyable games. Apparently it is not that easy to copy gameplay mechanics and end up with something of equal quality. The answer lies in the fact that there is an art *and* a science to games development, and that both have a strong impact on the final game. (I am using the term in this context as something different from the art direction). The science is the pure implementation of the required mechanics, but the art comes into play by taking those gameplay mechanics and making them work as effectively as possible within the game's success definition (including the game's level design goals).

To go back to *GTA*: what the game does very well, however, is to place all these individually lacking gameplay elements and put them in the service of the game's ultimate goals, both internal and external. Players forgive the frustrating moments, the repetitive NPC dialogue, the camera issues, and so on, because they are still successful in achieving those goals that the level designers and game designers have put at the top of the hierarchy.

Additionally, what gives *Vice City* added appeal is how all its disparate elements have been made interesting by giving them cultural relevance. The music in the game, the references to 80s pop culture, and the humor, can all be seen as *essential* contributions to the final appeal of the game. It is also interesting to see that they are all integrated in the level design of the game in a way that is deep and practical.

In practical terms, the game successfully combines the art and science of making games. And by applying all these things expertly in its level design, mission-based or sandbox, it manages to fulfill its game-wide and level-wide success definitions and hit the target of the elusive x-factor that so many games strive for.

A Modular Approach to Level Design

So now we know that is useful to try to place our level design components within the context of an *overall level design hierarchy*. A good next step is to make sure we can have level design components (modules) that are multi-purposeful and effective.

The *modular* aspect of this approach comes from the idea that once you determine what the *function* of a component is, you have more freedom in the way you try to hit the requirements that this functionality implies.

A classic problem with inexperienced level designers is that they have insufficient grasp of the overall purpose of the particular level design task they are working on. It is easy to get trapped in problems due to tunnel vision, I certainly have done so myself on many occasions early on in my career. When this happens, the micro details of a particular level design component become more important than its actual function in the grand scheme of things. Suddenly, that ambush encounter you are working on HAS TO BE about using a particular weapon or enemy, while it may be entirely possible that that encounter can fulfill all its requirements while being staged against a completely different backdrop or by using an entirely different class of enemies.

Realizing that this danger exists and always asking oneself, "What is the function of this component?" goes a long way towards avoiding that trap.

Contingency Planning

Not only does this way of thinking help in designing levels in a more effective manner; it also provides great scope for contingency planning. This is something that within the high-pressure environment of commercial game development is extremely important.

It allows us to create level design components that are scalable. For example, if we know that a certain combat situation in a level is mainly included in order to introduce a new gameplay mechanic to the player, we can of course try to make the event as spectacular as possible by introducing complex scripted events, incorporating intricate enemy behavior and pulling out all the bells and whistles. This section will probably "read" very well on paper, especially early on in the development cycle, when the level designer is assured that the creature AI would eventually be more than up to the task of supporting such an amazing encounter.

Now let's fast-forward twelve months in time. We are now two months away from having to ship the game, everybody is severely stressed and overworked, and unfortunately, the AI of this particular enemy had to be scaled down several levels due to time constraints and will no longer be usable within the original plan for the level design. *Oh dear, what now..?*

This is an example where it is extremely important to realize why the encounter exists in the first place: *to introduce a particular new gameplay mechanic.* With this overall goal in mind, we find that it really does not matter through which AI encounter this gameplay mechanic is taught and introduced to the player. It can be substituted and made to work by using existing and working game assets, and the final value to the game as a whole will be the roughly the same.

This may seem completely obvious, but it is very easy to get lost in insular goals.

Anybody in games development is constantly bombarded with the following question: *"Wouldn't it be cool if we… (Insert idea X)?"*

As it turns out, idea X may well be cool, but does it really need to be there? Can it be done in a different and more cost-effective way?

Those are the kind of questions you should ask yourself if you want to be able to apply level designs with enough flexibility that you can react to unexpected circumstances.[8]

Application of Modular Hierarchy

If we take all that we have said before into account, we should now have a practical framework for our criteria and requirements that has great value. We should be able to take any game component, find a place for it in this hierarchy, and be able to ask the right questions regarding its place and value in development. This is no minor thing and can save a difficult project from disaster if done correctly. It means that there is much less dependency on specialist or bespoke solutions, and that the developers can be much more flexible about the implementation of the designs without compromising too much on quality.

Conclusion

Hierarchies can offer a very useful tool. They give us a way to break level designs down into individual components and formulate a plan in which all of the level design components fulfill their ultimate requirements. Furthermore, it allows us to check the value and importance of individual components and refer to their place in an overall hierarchy.

Viewing the level design process through hierarchical steps may not always be a perfect fit. For one thing, one level design hierarchy may look different than another, and your mileage may vary between different projects. But it is always useful to try to find a way to define the *why, how,* and *what* questions within a logical order or hierarchy that allows you to make judgment calls on the implementation of your levels.

---

[8] You should always expect unexpected circumstances.

This gives us the practical means to assess what function any individual component or element fulfills, what it relates to, and how important it is. This has obvious uses that go beyond the need of the level designer; it also helps in establishing clear goals and criteria that are understandable to anybody involved in the development of the game.

Level Design Structure and Methodology

4

A level's structure and methodology are important early choices for a level designer, and they can have a large impact on the actual creation of the levels. We will look consecutively at structure and methodology, because the choices of the former impact the likely choices for the latter.

Structure

Once we have decided on the type of content a level requires, and where it exists within the hierarchy of the game, we need to determine which *structure* to apply to the level. In most cases this will be determined as part of the game design, since that determines structure as a whole across the game. Nonetheless, it is often the case that at least some choices are left to the level designer, at least on a smaller scale—for example, within the levels themselves. This kind of structure is one of gameplay flow, which is very much in the hands of the level designer.

Typically there are three main approaches to choose from in most game types: *linear*, *semi-linear* and *non-linear*. Sometimes the distinction is not clear-cut, and hybrids may occur. For example, a level may be divided between content that is 60% linear and 40% non-linear. Ultimately one of the most important determining factors of structure is a game's genre. A classic shoot-em-up is much more likely to follow a linear structure than a freeform RPG. But even within these genres, there is scope for differing progression models.

Let's look at the distinction between linear, semi-linear and non-linear in more detail.

Linear Levels

Linear level design, as the name implies, is level design where the gameplay events follow a strict *line* laid out for the player to follow.[1] Sometimes this is referred to by saying that the gameplay is *on rails*. Events unfold across this line in a strict order that the player cannot deviate from. Progression through the level is only possible if the player goes through the gameplay events in the order predetermined by the designer. To look at a diagram of such a level structure, we can envision something like the structure in Figure 4.1.

Although pure linearity is becoming less prevalent than it used to be, it still has a place in video games. There are a number of advantages to the technique. If they are appropriate to the gameplay needed for the game design, linear levels can work well.

Figure 4.1. Linear level structure.

Advantages

The most important advantage to linear level design is the amount of control it gives a level designer over the play experience. It is much easier to carefully design the experience of playing the level if the designer can determine the order in which gameplay events occur. Since this type of overall control allows the level designer to determine matters of pacing, consistency, story development, learning curve, and many others, it is as close as a level designer can get to *directorial* control. And in keeping with the analogy between directing a film, it can be compared to being allowed *final cut* on a movie.

Disadvantages

The main disadvantage of linear level structure lies in the danger that it can make players feel constrained in their gameplay freedom, possibly *arbitrarily* so. The designer needs to make sure that the roller coaster ride is an enjoyable one, as the player is not allowed to get off and find his or her own fun. If this is not done correctly, there is a possibility that the player will start to *resent the game*, which is of course to be avoided.

---

[1] Generally this is done in advance by the level designer.

Furthermore, if things start happening *regardless of the player's own actions*, a perception of futility may be created. And since the linear structure of a level is not the most flexible one, it is fairly common for certain gameplay events to be forced onto the player. This can be a dangerous approach. If the player's actions don't matter, than why act at all? If this is allowed to get out of hand, the experience of the entire game will be tarnished or even ruined.

Implementation Strategies

In linear level design it is vital that the designer has a good understanding of *pacing* and *play psychology*.[2] Most players will accept this kind of directed experience as long as they are directed with a sure and steady hand and the gameplay is always rewarding or interesting. If the player does not have time or inclination to *question the direction*, the level designer is successful. Unfair gameplay challenges, or dreary boring stretches, must be avoided if possible, as the player does not have a choice in engaging with these gameplay sections. Since these events are forced upon the player, they have to be worthwhile for them not to grate.

Some Typical Examples

There is no hard rule on when to choose linearity in level design, although there are times when it best supports the game's structures or general internal goals. For example, some puzzle games work best when the next puzzle will only be presented if the previous one has been solved. *Tetris* would not be very compelling if it were a free-roaming affair where the player would not feel the pressure that its linear approach enables. There are also story-driven games that rely on the progression of the story in a strictly linear fashion. These kinds of games may be becoming less fashionable, but if expected to create levels for them, we have to be prepared to rise to the challenge.

Semi-Linear Levels

As a compromise between linear and non-linear gameplay the level designer can opt for a hybrid form. Semi-linear gameplay allows players to direct their own experience in some instances, but it requires that players follow a script in other instances. This can be done by a system where players can perform a certain number of gameplay tasks or follow a number of paths of their own choosing, but eventually are led to a bottleneck. This bottleneck can be a *physical* one such

---

[2] All covered in great detail throughout the book.

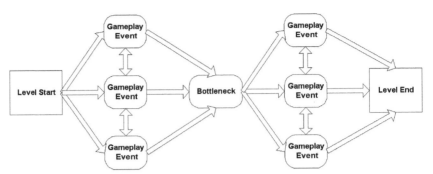

Figure 4.2. Linear level structure.

as progress to a next area via a single door, or it can be a *conditional event*. The event can be anything from reaching a certain number of experience points to hitting a time limit or having collected a certain amount of items. There are plenty of possibilities available within most game genres. (See Figure 4.2.)

Semi-linear gameplay progression is widespread in games, as it fits many game types and allows sufficient control over the experience.

Advantages

Semi-linearity, if used correctly, can offer the best of both worlds. It gives the level designer a reasonable amount of directorial control over the events the player will experience, but leaves enough freedom in the hands of players for them to feel they are authoring their own experience.

Furthermore, adroit level designers will do their best to create the *illusion* of full player freedom, to maximize players' involvement in the experience and deepen their immersion. This is an important aspect of level design and one that will be further developed in several chapters later in the book.

Disadvantages

On the other hand, semi-linearity can represent the worst of both worlds. If applied in a lazy manner, it can arbitrarily lead players by the nose when uninspired, while leaving them to their own devices at inappropriate times. When a level designer starts to give the player *some freedom*, more freedom will be expected throughout the level. If they are allowed to perform certain gameplay actions at one point in the game, it is only natural that the players expect this to be possible at other points. If the level designer does not carefully think this through, a logically inconsistent world can be the painful end result. This can completely undermine the expectations the player has of a level and can destroy trust in the fairness of a game. At least with strict linearity, players know what they can expect.

Implementation Strategies

It is important in this kind of level design to observe consistency. Players will be acutely aware of when they are treated unfairly, and because of this, the level designer should make sure that restrictions or player direction does not feel too arbitrary.

Where possible, techniques should be used that hide as much of these restrictions as possible, and that successfully create an illusion of player freedom and choice. If players have limited progression choices, but are made to believe they have many, the best of both worlds has been achieved. The level designer has in that case invisibly guided the player's experience.

Application

The semi-linear approach is probably the most popular one in level design circles. It avoids the limiting constrictions of pure linearity and steers clear of the logistical problems of freeform gameplay. Multiple play styles can be incorporated so the levels cater to a wider variety of game players, contingencies can be included for when players find it hard to progress, and the world can be made to feel more responsive to players' choices, even if in fact the choices are limited.

These are serious advantages, and they make it easy to see why so many levels follow this kind of approach.

Non-Linear Levels

In a *non-linear level,* the order of gameplay actions is mostly left to the player. This is one of the reasons why non-linearity is linked to *sandbox design* and to *emergent* gameplay.

True non-linear gameplay is very rare indeed, but some games and game types come close to it or feature moments where it does occur. Often, this type of gameplay goes hand in hand with interactivity; in a game where it is viable to create one's own gameplay, a high level of interactivity can be very helpful. A good example of this is games where a physics system allows players to manipulate their environment on their own terms, but within the restraints of the physics system, thus leading to non-linear and non-scripted gameplay events.

The clearest example of non-linear gameplay lies within the realm of some multiplayer games. Since it is the other players, and not the level designer, who provide the bulk of gameplay, multiplayer games can be highly non-linear.

Advantages

Because the players themselves exert maximum control over the gameplay experience, they are likely to take responsibility for their own failures. Since the level designer does not directly dictate the progression choices, players can experience a sense of ownership over gameplay. This is generally perceived as a positive outcome.

A game that allows players to manufacture their own gameplay experience produces an added bonus of *free* content. After all, if *automatic* generation of gameplay occurs, it does not require work from the level designer. It is gameplay content created by somebody else, which in the busy schedule of professional level design is a very good development.

Disadvantages

A non-linear gameplay world is much harder to test and is therefore harder to design in a robust way. It may be impossible to test every single permutation of player action that may occur, which is inherently dangerous. Unforeseen player actions or tactics may "break" the game in unforeseen ways, possibly by allowing some players to dominate others in an unacceptable way, or by finding loopholes in gameplay logic that allow the player too much power.

Requirements

In non-linear levels, the level designer has to make sure that players have enough tools to play with the game world. A requirement for non linear gameplay is that players must be allowed to write their own gameplay story. To do this, a certain amount of interactivity is required. There is a need for deep and engaging gameplay resulting from the player's own actions, rather than prefabricated scenarios. Where possible, the conditions for this must be provided by the level designer.[3] This can take the shape of strategic depth, for example in layout design in multiplayer games, or of purely physics-based interaction in single-player games where the player treats the world as a toy.

---

[3] Also, in this case, extra responsibility is laid on the shoulders of the *game designer* to allow for this. The level designer can only implement what he or she is given in the game design.

Methodologies

Earlier in the book I mentioned that this text is not meant to be about level *construction*; instead, it is focused on level *design*. But this does not mean that we should not look at *methodology*. When eventually faced with technical construction issues, it is good to have spent time researching a number of methodologies. This allows us to structure a level well in advance of level creation and gives us a chance to prototype on paper. Potential problems can be found early, and the level creation process can be scheduled easier.

This part of the book will not attempt to be a detailed listing of all possible level design methods, but will rather focus on a number of *general methodologies* that may provide hints on how to proceed in other unique cases. The main goal is to give examples of various approaches that a level designer can adopt, depending on the situation he or she is in. It is up to the designer to determine what to include in the level design documentation.

After having looked at structure, methodologies are a logical next area to look at. A number of useful methodology types are shown below.

Annotated Maps

Most people are familiar with the concept of *annotated maps*. This is a method widely used throughout the game industry, where the level design is described through a gameplay breakdown of all the physical spaces in a level. This is often done by creating a map on paper, providing a legend and numbers that indicate the "rooms" or other gameplay areas. This can be extremely effective, as it allows not only the level designer, but also other team members, to retrieve useful data from the level design document.

Example of Annotated Level Design: *Stolen*, Level 4

Annotated maps are commonplace in professional level design and is an approach I have had to take myself many times. To show how this may look, the following example details a section of a level heavily weighted for stealth gameplay, made for the game *Stolen*.[4] The game's player character, Anya, needs to traverse a heavily guarded area without being spotted, as shown in Figure 4.3.

---

[4] Developed by Blue52.

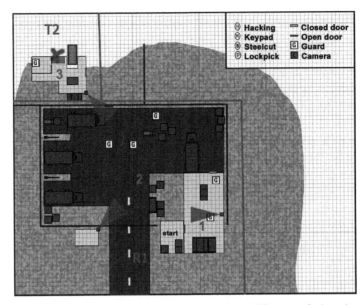

Figure 4.3. Level design detail: Satellite Array Level. (Source: *Stolen*, developed by Blue52.)

Here are some annotations for the map:

02 Lower compound (links to 3 and 1)

Anya will be in an outside area where she can clearly see the building that houses the cable car docking bay.

The player has to approach the cable car dock without being spotted, using stealth mechanics. A route is available via the roofs of several trucks and a number of poles but the final jump cannot be made.

In order to finalize the route the player needs to get near a forklift truck and raise its forks that are holding a pallet. After this the player will be able to get on the roof of the docking bay, and enter through a vent

Several guards patrol in key positions.

Anya can get to the main entrance of the docking by evading the guards and sticking to the shadows, but there will be no way in from the ground floor.

An alternative route takes her around the edge of the compound. She has to evade the guards patrolling and somehow get past a guard at the checkpoint of the area.

03 Docking bay

The player finds the cable car inside, but it is not reachable from the ground. A little tower/building gives access to it but is locked. A gantry connects with the cable car but is too high to be reached. This is the destination in this area.

A ledge route along the walls of the room leads the player to a vent system high up, and can be reached by a ledge jump. Eventually the player lands on top of gantry that triggers a real-time cutscene.

The guards holding her equipment leave the building to board the cable car. Anya quickly jumps on top of it to stay out of sight. The cable car starts to move up towards the mountain.

As you can see, the method can become quite involved. A very large amount of gameplay information is recorded in a useful manner. Other people than the level designers can also benefit. Take the following addition of information for game area 02. It is meant to provide notes on required game assets or other related information useful to other members of the development team:

Special Assets Needed/ Notes:

Code

    Interactive Objects/Other:

    Forklift truck needs to have operable forklift.

    Two different collision states are needed.

Art

    General:

    Forklift model.

    Special:

    None

Production

    Sound:

    Forklift engine.

    Forklift raising its forks.

    Story Events/Cutscences:

    Forklift raising its forks.

Concept art

Even more information can be added to the level design. For example, concept art can be very useful to provide the reader with a better visual guide of the environment and its content: see, for example, Figure 4.4.

All of this builds a picture of the final shape of the level design even before construction begins.

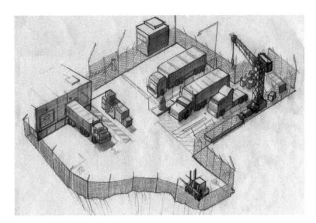

Figure 4.4. Concept art. (Source: *Stolen* Level Design, Blue52.)

Dangers

When so much information is collected into a limited amount of documents, there is a real danger that the resulting level design may become too cumbersome. A monolithic, unwieldy, and inflexible level design is problematic for all parties involved. It is hard to keep up to date and may provide too much information for some, but too little for others. If a level design document like this *is* appropriate, it still may require further explanatory documents or visual support, some of which will be shown below.

Flow Charts

To combat some of the clunkiness of annotated maps, we can express level design progression through flow charts. There are many positives attached to this method. They can be created and modified quickly, which is very important if the level design has to be flexible. They are much better able to express conditional data and, in doing so, provide a logic check for the level designers. (This can also be very important if any amount of scripting is involved.).

Here is an example of conditional level design data expressed through the flowchart in Figure 4.5:

> A player enters a room and activates a floor switch that locks the room and releases two guards. Only when the two guards have been defeated

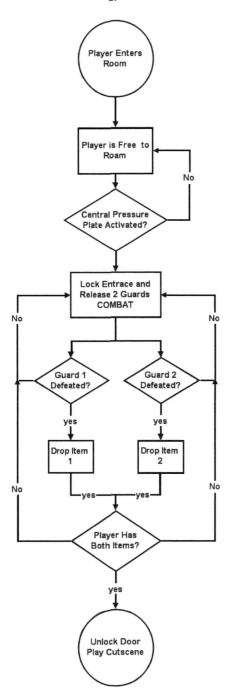

Figure 4.5. Conditional combat situation.

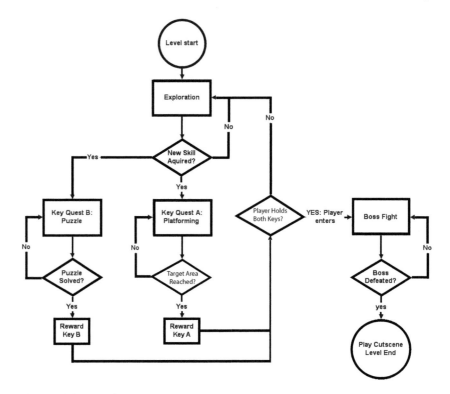

Figure 4.6. Level flowchart.

and two objects they were carrying have been collected[5] can the player leave the room. A cut scene is played to signify this.

This kind of information is hard to capture in annotated maps, no matter how complete the annotation is. Flowcharts are very good at capturing specific information and showing *how it relates to other elements*. This makes them very useful indeed to create an easy-to-read and coherent overview.

Figure 4.6 shows a flowchart applied to a whole level. Note how this kind of flowchart shows progression by providing questions and answers that signify gameplay or game states.

---

[5] I am sure you can figure out why this is so.

Dangers

The large degree of concision and logical overview comes at a price. There are several dangers and problems that may occur when using his method. Out of many, here are some typical examples:

- There is no information on the level's environment.
- Emotional impact is not represented.
- There is no temporal data (outside of chronology).
- There is no room for unexpected results.[6]

These and other dangers make it doubtful that a flowchart can express a level design fully. (But I have personally seen people attempting to do just that.) However, this is an extremely powerful method to be used in conjunction with other methods. The use of flowcharts, for example, is very complementary to annotated maps, described earlier.

Level Arc: Freytag's Pyramid

In 1863, Gustav Freytag published an important book on dramatic structure called *Die Technik des Dramas*. The book aimed to provide an overview of dramatic components as seen in classic plays, namely Greek tragedies and Shakespearian drama. Freytag argued that all these components follow a specific order, one component leading to the next one. The well-known visualization of this underlying structure is called *Freytag's Pyramid*. (See Figure 4.7.)

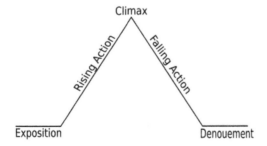

Figure 4.7. Freytag's pyramid.[7]

---

[6] This can also be an advantage.

[7] "Freytag's Pyramid," *Wikipedia*, http://en.wikipedia.org/wiki/Dramatic_structure, 2009.

Freytag's Five-Act Progression Breakdown

As Figure 4.7 shows, Freytag divides drama into a number of consecutive steps: *exposition, rising action, climax, falling action,* and *dénouement* or *catastrophe,* each represented as an act within a play.

Act 1: Exposition

In Act 1, the basic story elements are introduced for the first time. We learn enough about the setting and about some of the characters to form a framework in which the drama takes place. This exposition ends with an *inciting moment.* The inciting moment creates the catalyst necessary to allow the unfolding of an interesting drama. Without this, there would be no reason to tell the story to begin with. It often takes the form of a conflict of some kind.

Act 2: Rising action

After the story has been kick-started by a central inciting moment, further depth and drama is added during Act 2, *rising action.* This is done by introducing further layers of drama (possibly including new conflicts, hindrances, and obstacles to the protagonist's goals) and by introducing new characters and other complications.

Act 3: Climax (turning point)

The rising action leads naturally to a climactic moment. This is a turning point to the story: a key moment where a change occurs that is fundamental to the story. This change can be for better or for worse, depending on the type of play. Typically, in a comedy the change is for the better, while in a tragedy the opposite occurs.

Act 4: Falling action

The conflict between the protagonist and antagonist reaches a critical stage during the *falling action* part of the play. The drama will progress towards a resolution that serves either protagonist or antagonist. The final direction of this resolution can be kept ambiguous for a certain amount of time to create *suspense.*

Act 5: Dénouement or catastrophe

The final resolution of the play comes in the form of a positive conclusion (*dénouement*) in case of a comedy, or in the form of a negative ending in the shape of a *catastrophe.* Both conclusions show a progression in the experience of the protagonist. In a dénouement, the protagonist is better off than at the beginning of the play, while a catastrophe leads to the opposite conclusion. Either way, the drama gets resolved.

Five-Act Progressions in Level Design

Nobody suggests that the above description of a five-act classical play or drama is representative of all plays. It is merely a description or analysis of a particular kind of drama that has often been used in the past. Judging by how many plays have followed this progression, it must have been very popular with a great many writers. Perhaps this is because it creates a recognizable format in which to tell the story: a frame of reference that an audience can relate to. In truth, the five-acter is still very much alive and is used throughout the arts, not in the least in Hollywood cinema.

If we extrapolate from this, it may be possible to identify similar principles within level design. Let's take Bungie's *Halo* as a test case:

Halo as a five-act level design progression.

Halo is a good subject for this experiment, because despite a certain amount of freedom in the way the game can be played, the story progression through the game is fairly linear. In other words, many of the methods are up to the player, but the gameplay goals are predetermined.

Act 1: Exposition

In Act 1, we are introduced to the protagonist, Master Chief. Through exposition, we learn much about the background to the story and the story's environment. We learn that the protagonist is a soldier and that the current action takes place on board a space ship. The inciting moment that functions as a catalyst that escalates the story takes the form of an alien attack on the space ship.

Act 2: Rising action

Act 2 serves as a vehicle for introducing elements to the game that deepen the experience. The player has landed on alien structure *Halo* and has to learn how to combat the resident hostile alien forces. In the meantime, we learn more about the background story of the conflict.

Act 3: Climax (turning point)

In the climax of *Halo,* the player learns that a far greater danger than the alien protagonist exists. It is a viral life form known as the *Flood.* It infects and takes over other life forms in such a way that the Flood ends up corrupting and controlling its victims. The Flood have started to infect both the aliens and the humans, and their threat lies in infecting entire planets.

Act 4: Falling action

Much of Act 4 is defined by the player's epic struggle to contain the threat of the Flood.

Act 5: Dénouement and catastrophe

In the final act, we already know that Master Chief has been successful in his main goal, stopping the Flood from spreading by destroying *Halo*. The final outcome of the story centers on the personal survival of the hero.

Problems Associated with Freytag's Pyramid

Although there are many uses to the pyramid, and there are many examples of dramatic creations that fit its definition, there are a number of criticisms that can be aimed at Freytag's pyramid that are worth investigating.

Oversimplification

It can be argued that to create such a neat overview, the subject must be oversimplified beyond the point of being useful. One could argue in the case of *Halo* that the story features several turning points. Should we ignore some of them in order to point at one specific climax? If we don't, does it mean that Act2 sometimes appears after Act 3?

Restriction

Restriction is the enemy of creativity. At least, arbitrary restriction is. What if we want to start with a catastrophe and a climax, and through exposition and falling action slowly tell a compelling story? We may want to write a comedy with a fatal ending or a tragedy with a happy ending.

All of these criticisms are valid to a point. As a device for forming an interesting dramatic construction, the pyramid *is* hopelessly restrictive and oversimplified. But the pyramid's value is not one of dramatic creation; rather, it is a tool for *dramatic visualization and analysis*. After all, Freytag intended to analyze and show the dramatic structure of classical plays. Considering the ubiquity of his work to this day, he was very successful in achieving this goal. There is no need to slavishly follow this particular method, but it can inspire us to devise our own methodology to suit our own needs.

Applications for Level Design

If we extrapolate from this, we should be able to devise similar techniques that successfully aid us in level design analysis and visualization. This is something that in the hectic and often stressful reality of professional level design can be of immense benefit.[8] There are several techniques and approaches available to level designers, but the ones most commonly used are based on *event diagrams*.

Event Diagrams

An *event diagram*[9] is a graphical representation of the content of a level, potentially including representations ranging from emotional impact to duration, or combinations of several factors. There are many elements that can be included in these diagrams, but typically they will show one of the following things:

- type of event,
- duration of event,
- chronology (if applicable),
- impact (color-coded).

Take the example in Figure 4.8.

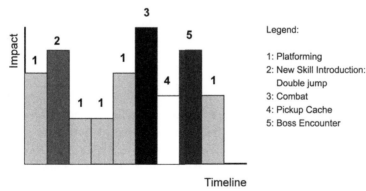

Figure 4.8. Event diagram.

---

[8] In fact, it is beneficial in all circumstances.

[9] Admittedly, an entirely made-up term.

As we can see in this example, the following elements contribute to a clear picture of the level:

- type of event (legend),
- event Duration (column width),
- chronology (column order),
- impact Value (column height).

These elements can each make a valuable contribution to the level design. Using this method, it is easy to identify and read them.

Type of event

The *type of event* can consist of any gameplay event intended by the level designer to occur at a specific moment. This can range from the very important unique moments (Set Piece X) to more generic or modular occurrences (Scripted AI Encounter Y). In the above example, other gameplay events include: *new skill introduction, boss encounter, pickup cache,* and *master key found.* Alternatively, or as a complement, less specific event descriptions can be used, like *combat, platforming* or *puzzle,* which still provide a good overview of a level's content.

Event duration

It is unlikely that this data can ever be exact, but it is still possible to convey helpful information. For example, it can be useful to show duration in relation to other events, or one can show patterns in gameplay that may be problematic, like a sequence of long, but low impact, gameplay. This may indicate a section of gameplay that the player may find boring. If precise information is known, this can be included alongside less specific descriptions, such as *short, medium* and *long.*

Chronology

As noted earlier in this chapter, chronology is partly dependent on linearity. Nonetheless, even in very open freeform games with a non-linear structure, things still often happen within a certain sequence. Skill trees may have to be developed, some areas may only unlock if a certain item has been found, defeating a specific creature may unlock a new skill, or the collection of a specific amount of items may allow the player to buy new gear.

In the above example, the *boss encounter* does not occur until after the *master key* is found. This kind of information makes it easier to maintain continuity and avoid many bugs.

Impact value

Emotional impact is a very vague term. How do we measure it? There is no satisfying answer to that, especially in instances where one player's subjective experience may be different from the next player's experience. But this does not mean that we should not try at all, especially in the type of levels where we are able to author the general experience of all players. Let's say, as in the above example, that we have included a set piece event in the level. Naturally, we assign a high value to it, most likely higher than for any other events in the level. If later playtests show that its impact on the player lies well below other events in the level, we know that we need to do something to raise the impact value of the event.

Instead of a general value like emotional impact, it can often be a better idea to represent a more specific element. In a survival horror game, this can be a *scare factor*, or in an action adventure it can be an *action quota*. Use whatever is right for the game you are working on.

How this is represented in the diagram is also open to many choices. Typical choices are *color coding* and column height, the latter being the one shown in our example. A line diagram can be used, or even a pie chart; it is up to the level designer to determine what is appropriate.

Event Diagrams Summary

Event maps provide an often-useful visual overview of important level design data. This allows the designer to quickly assess the level's overall *tone* and makes it easy to give others on the team a quick summary. However, in most cases it should not be seen as an alternative to a detailed and thorough level design document; instead, it is more effective in conjunction with one. This is especially true when it comes to highlighting specific elements within a level, as shown in previous examples.

It is of course entirely up to the level designer to decide which data to include and what type of visual representation to use.

The methodology is easiest to apply to linear level designs. Nonetheless, the methodology has applications even for completely open level designs.

Note that his methodology is not to be confused with *beat maps*. These provide a graphical overview of the player's "heart rate"[10] at specific moments in the level, but this is almost never a sufficiently useful technique.

---

[10] Typically by displaying a number that signifies heartbeats per minute.

Object-Oriented Level Design (OOLD)

As already touched upon in Chapter 3, "Level Design Goals and Hierarchies," it is helpful to think of level design components as modular objects. Another way of describing this methodology is as *object-oriented level design*. This term is based on an idea that originated in the world of computer programming, known as *object-oriented programming*. *Object-oriented programming* is:

> a modular approach to computer program (software) design. Each module, or object, combines data and procedures (sequences of instructions) that act on the data; in traditional, or procedural, programming the data are separated from the instructions. A group of objects that have properties, operations, and behaviors in common is called a class. *By reusing classes developed for previous applications, new applications can be developed faster with improved reliability and consistency of design.*[11] *(Emphasis mine.)*

One does not have to be a programmer to realize that from a design perspective, *reuse, improved reliability,* and *consistency of design* are major advantages. These are things that as level designers we always should try to achieve. If we look at *object-oriented programming (OOP)* in greater detail, we find further useful principles. There are a number of fundamental principles associated with OOP. These include these are: *encapsulation, inheritance,* and *polymorphism.* All of these should be of interest to a level designer.

These terms have been defined as follows:

> *Encapsulation* refers to the creation of *self-contained modules* that bind processing functions to the data. These user-defined data types are called "classes," and one instance of a class is an "object." For example, in a payroll system, a class could be Manager, and Pat and Jan could be two instances (two objects) of the Manager class. *Encapsulation ensures good code modularity...* [I]nheritance allows the structure and methods in one class to be passed down the hierarchy. That means less programming is required when adding functions to complex systems .... The ability to reuse existing objects is considered a major advantage of object technology....
>
> ... *Polymorphism* in the object-oriented approach refers to the ability of a programmer to treat many different types of objects in a uniform manner by invoking the same operation on each object. Because the

---

[11] "Object Oriented Programming," *The Columbia Electronic Encyclopedia*, Sixth Edition, http://www.bartleby.com/65/ob/objecto.html, 2001–2007.

objects are instances of abstract data types, they may implement the operation differently as long as they fulfill the agreement in their common contract.[12] (*Emphasis mine.*)

Practical Examples of OOLD

In Chapter 3 we discussed modular level design. OOLD is a method that takes the principle of modular level design and applies it in practice, ensuring modularity and other similar concepts. The previously described elements of *encapsulation, inheritance,* and *polymorphism* can be easily incorporated into level design. Let's go through them one by one.

Encapsulation

In ID Software's game *Quake,* the player can often traverse a level with the aid of teleporters. The player just walks into one and is teleported to a different location in the level. This can be considered a *class* in level design terms. Once the basic elements are in place (such as trigger areas, destination areas, and three-dimensional models), we can have a class called a *teleporter.* Individual teleporters, as objects, can be one-way teleporters, or might feature different 3D models and have unique destinations and starting points. But they will always be teleporters and belong to the *teleporter* class.

Let's take a less literal example next: encapsulation applied to gameplay scenarios. Let's say that a level designer has spent a significant amount of time setting up a combat situation that makes use of specific aspects of the environment. (For example, cover, line of sight, and height difference.) If this particular situation works well in the game, the level designer may decide to replicate it by keeping the essential elements in place, but then providing different-looking environmental details, such as different AI opponents. The encounter's integrity stays in place, but the original benefit of the gameplay is encapsulated in each instance. (Or the environmental detail may stay the same and the combat can change.)

Inheritance

Early in the level design process for a game, we may want to create a generic object called a *treasure chest,* scripted in such a way that when the player opens it, a random item of limited wealth is generated (once). This may require a certain amount of scripting from the level designer, but once it has been set up, this treasure chest should be useful throughout the game. Say that play-testing now

---

[12] "Object-Oriented Programming," *The Free Dictionary by Farlex,* http://encyclopedia2.thefreedictionary.com/Object-oriented+computer+programming, 2009.

shows that players highly enjoy these moments of excitement where a random award is received, and the game team decides that this type of occurrence should be more prevalent in the levels. To avoid littering the level with treasure chests, the level designer decides to create a number of new objects, such as cupboards, filing cabinets, desks, or any furniture or similar object that can be opened and closed and used as a container. Players can now find treasure all through the level by opening up these new objects, without the objects feeling out of place.

Although these physical objects are new classes (in programming terms), when programmed as the same type of *object*, they can inherit much of their function from the behavior of the original *treasure chest* object.

Polymorphism

When a level designer can incorporate polymorphism into his or her work, a huge amount of flexibility is gained. Let's go back to our earlier example of treasure chests and the creation of other classes with overlapping functionality. Say that the game is nearly finished, the designer has placed hundreds of these chests and cupboard and drawers, vases, you name it, throughout the level. The publisher however now demands that a cash register sound should play whenever the player receives treasure. If polymorphism has been factored in the designer should be able to associate this sound to any object that makes use of this behavior simultaneously. This means that *making the change* once, *to the behavior* applied to all of these objects, not to all the objects individually.

Dangers

If we go back to our earlier example of *Halo,* we can find a good example of a persistent danger of this technique: if not careful, the level designer risks creating highly repetitive gameplay sections. In *Halo* this took the form of the now infamous "library levels." The library levels were created in such a way that they reused environments and gameplay in a very thorough manner. This was done in such a manner that the player is confronted with arbitrary repetition. Even if assets and gameplay sections are re-used, they still have to feel individual and worth playing. In the library levels, the player literally has to play the same thing over and over again, which is more akin to dreary work than to rewarding gameplay.

OOLD Summary

Applications of this kind of thinking, of borrowing these programming concepts and applying them to level design processes, are widespread and far reaching.

They range from simple puzzles to extended gameplay sections and even whole areas of level geometry. The examples themselves are not important; it is more about locating moments when this kind of thinking can be applied to anywhere that benefits from it.

Dense Level Design

An example of a level design methodology that combines elements of previously discussed methods can be found in *dense level design*. We speak of dense level design when a larger-than-normal amount of gameplay is incorporated in the physical environment of the level. This type of density can be achieved in many ways but generally occurs through reuse of the environment in time. New gameplay elements can be introduced to the level when a player revisits a section.

Another aspect of dense level design is density of gameplay *space*. All aspects of the gameplay space are exploited if possible. This can mean that a level will make much deeper use of vertically layered gameplay, incorporating all architectural features. For example, many doors can be opened and rooms can be entered, even if they serve no direct gameplay purpose.

Advantages

There are many clear advantages to this approach. So much so that in most cases, I advocate the use of this technique as one of the first things to look at in many level design tasks. Let's look at some of the advantages.

Reuse of assets

In most cases, as level designers we are expected to make the best use of the assets we have. If interesting gameplay can be replicated over several iterations without changing the assets needed, the resulting gameplay comes at a lower cost to the game's development.

Reuse of gameplay

This reuse of gameplay has many advantages, but an extremely important one is that it allows the level designer to teach players how to enjoy the game more easily. This is the case because the designer can take initially simple gameplay sections and slowly upgrade their difficulty and skill level in a controlled manner, without alienating the players. In this case, repetition and familiarity are your friends.

Immersive effect

If an environment is used to its fullest, if all of its features, be they interactive, artistic, or physical, are incorporated consistently in the level's gameplay, it will create a much more immersive experience. It gives the environment a sense of reality. Even if set in a non-realistic framework like fantasy or sci-fi, the environments still have to conform to the logic of that framework.

Dangers

There are several dangers associated with this technique, and some of them are hard to avoid.

Spatial confusion

Game levels are experienced through a two-dimensional interface. In most cases, this is a computer screen or television monitor and some kind of game controller. While this method is fine in principle, it does require certain concessions that in normal life do not occur. A good example of this is the way gameplay spaces in levels are often simplified to facilitate orientation.

Lack of gameplay readability

Most level designers are weary of reusing the same environment too many times without serious modification, as it is much easier to give a level area a specific purpose that is understandable to the player. If the player revisits an area and the gameplay has changed, it may need some re-evaluation on the player's side. This is not necessarily a problem, but there needs to be a good reason for this, or the player will feel ambushed. Something can only be done so many times before it becomes annoying.

An example: MINERVA—Metastasis 2

MINERVA is a modification for *Half Life 2*, consisting of a number of episodic levels designed by Adam Foster. The *MINERVA* mod actively reinterprets the gameplay of *Half life 2* by introducing a much stronger emphasis on density of play.

> Instead of relying on horizontally-sprawling, immense maps that stress the engine's area-capabilities to its max, *MINERVA* maps are *incredibly* small. This is because of Foster's ground-breaking idea to utilize every possible area to its maximum potential, and instead of expanding horizontally, he expands vertically. Rather than leave large areas wasted with inaccessible buildings, "fake" corridors and rooms to give the impres-

sion of an immersive, realistic environment, Foster makes *every* area accessible. This doesn't mean that one can simply travel all over the maps in any manner one chooses—but instead through the use of very creatively-placed barriers Foster is able to funnel the player around the maps in a spiraled fashion.[13]

All throughout this level, it is notable that the gameplay is extremely layered. The player almost constantly revisits areas that have been traversed before, but which are updated with new gameplay features. This is especially true for combat with the game's enemy soldiers (Combine soldiers), presumably because they can use the same paths and doors as the player. So it is not illogical for them to make full use of the environment as well. The end result is that the action comes and goes, but the environment stays consistent. In most cases this is good enough, as the available tactical variation is strong enough to support this kind of repetition. Furthermore, it also contributes to the environment feeling very *real*, as if architecturally properly designed.

Where the level fails, though, partly because of the use of dense level design, is in readability. Quite often, players find themselves lost or unclear where to go now, a danger that is especially great if routes are backtracked several times. A player who has already been down a known route several time now has to wonder at every corner: "I've been here already, but has something else opened up?" Nonetheless, through the consistent use of dense level design, the final experience is very powerful. The player develops a real bond with the environment, which is very important in level design.

Further Examples

There are, of course, many other methodologies applicable to level design, some more obscure than others. Some level designers like to start their design by first working on key elements of the levels, to make sure that all the impressive features are worked out in time. Others work in a completely opposite manner, sketching out all the lighter detail first to make sure that a functioning outline of the level exists early on.

---

[13] "MINERVA: Metastasis 2," *MINERVA: Metastasis 2—Planet Half-Life*, http://planethalflife.gamespy.com/View.php?view=HLMotw.Detail&id=7, 2009.

Single-Player vs. Multiplayer Considerations

5

One of the approaches taken for this book is to make the text independent of genre and technology. Wherever I can, I try to explore concepts and theories that have as much range as possible and lend themselves to multiple applications, without being dependent on things like existing technology or game engines. If at all possible, I try to avoid too much focus on specific genres to make general points, although I do examine aspects that are unique to specific genres to make sure their pitfalls and idiosyncrasies are understood.

This book applies the same philosophy to *multiplayer* and *single-player* aspects of level design. When possible, it tries to provide material that is useful to both game modes. However, at times, chapters will deal with specific and custom-made elements on a case-by-case basis.

Before we reach those specific aspects of multiplayer and single player level design issues, I would like to make a number of general observations, which can function as a useful background against which we can place more specific issues in upcoming chapters. This chapter will highlight some of those specific elements.

Single-Player

We speak of *single-player gaming* when the gameplay occurs in isolation from other players. In basic terms: when the player can enjoy the game without input from other people. This does not mean a game cannot have both single-player and multiplayer *content*, just that it has to be able to provide an experience that allows a single player to enjoy it. This is sometimes referred to as *solo play*.

Single-Player Level Design Considerations

There are a number of very clear considerations that are relevant to single-player level design, sometimes aiding the level designer, sometimes providing obstacles. Here are some typical examples.

Control

A major advantage of designing for a single-player experience is that it gives the designer more control over what happens to the player. There are no other players involved whose input may cause unpredictable outcomes, or whose input can counter the themes and moods the designer is going for. Imagine a dark and atmospheric survival horror game filled with perverted Freudian overtones meant to disturb the player on a psycho-sexual level. Now imagine that all the time, two co-players in the background are constantly giggling at those dark sexual themes. This would simply devastate any efforts to slowly build up a carefully crafted experience.

Single player levels don't have these problems at all. Designers can do their work in providing a directed experience without fear of third parties ruining it for the player.

Balancing issues

A potential negative lies in the possibility that the designer may misjudge the mindset or experience or skill level of players and create bottlenecks that needlessly frustrate players, or that even stop them from progressing.

This is not a rare occurrence unfortunately. A level designer should be careful when it comes to implementing such harsh bottlenecks. The fact of the matter is that the level needs to provide a good experience for all kinds of people, and that this is harder than often imagined.[1] Generally, it is a bad idea to try to please everyone, but that does not mean that we shouldn't try to balance the game for those people who are deemed the target audience for the game. Later chapters go into much detail on this matter. For example, see the sections on *flow theory,* dynamic *difficulty adjustment,* and *pacing* later on in the book.

Either way, single-player levels require great empathy for the player in order to create a balanced game experience

Narrative possibilities

Although multiplayer levels provide plenty of opportunities for narrative content, it can be easier to aim narrative elements at a single person, rather than at

---

[1] Sometimes it is even impossible.

a group of players. The game can check for certain player acts or events to occur and can be certain that they have been triggered and experienced by the same person, while this cannot always be easily determined in a multiplayer context. This mostly applies to games where it is important that information be experienced linearly and absorbed in such a way that the game can rely on the player having certain knowledge. This can occur in text adventures or point-and-click adventures, for example.

Multiplayer

We speak of *multiplayer gaming* when some of the game content or experience is provided via interaction with other players. Although most video games are designed with a single-player component, multiplayer video gaming has taken a real step forward with the advent of *online* play. Some of the most successful games[2] ever created are mostly multiplayer affairs. One cannot be a fully rounded level designer without taking into account the needs of a multiplayer audience. Let's look at the most typical multiplayer modes.

Multiplayer Cooperative Play

Sometimes it is fun to help each other and tackle challenges together. It can be fun to solve a murder mystery with a friend, or go row-boating together. Video games are no different, and some of them provide this specific type of multiplayer gaming. This type of gameplay has become much more normal with the advent of *Massively Multiplayer Online games*, like *World of Warcraft*, where groups of players band together to tackle the game's obstacles cooperatively.

Multiplayer Adversarial Play

A very common type of multiplayer gaming consists of people competing against each other as adversaries or opponents. There are more subcategories of this kind of play than we need to go into, but some of the more popular ones are the following:

- Coop: This is the traditional cooperative mode where players can jointly take on the single-player game's challenges, although often with enhanced difficulty and optimized content.
- Versus play: Chess, backgammon, table tennis, beat-em-ups.

---

[2] Blizzard's *World of Warcraft* provides a good example.

- Deathmatch: Players fight each other in arenas and score points by annihilating each other.
- Capture the flag: Two teams fight each other by trying to steal the other team's flag and returning it to their own base.
- Competitive sports gaming: Just as in real sports environments, video game versions of sports games can offer human opponents.

Many other examples exist; it is a very popular way of playing games.

Multiplayer Level Design Considerations

Depending on the type of multiplayer game, there are some very interesting differences than those found in single-player level design. In one form or another, level designers working on these kinds of games are likely to have to deal with content that features the following characteristics.

Enhanced routes and challenges

In games where player characters traverse an environment, the multiplayer component allows the level designer to create routes that make use of this extra dimension. Routes and challenges can be devised that require players to cooperate in order to progress. A player may need to stand guard and fight off marauders while another player picks a door lock to open up the escape route. Two players may need to throw a switch simultaneously. It is easy to think of content in this regard. Possibilities abound, and that is very useful for level designers, as it is almost always enjoyable to solve game challenges with another player. It automatically grounds players' actions into the game world, and this really deepens the game's immersion and enjoyment.

The human element

Another bonus to multiplayer games is the opportunity to include human capability in the game's experience. What I mean by this is that the content of the game can be directly enhanced by other people in ways that programmed or animated or modeled content cannot. In a deathmatch game, for example, it is much more exciting to play against human opponents than against artificial intelligence opponents, normally known as *bots*. Not only are humans better at coming up with completely unexpected strategies; they are also able to adapt to those of others.

Additionally, other players can introduce elements of real emotion into gameplay, such as a passion to win a match, empathy for other players, or just the ability to converse with others within the game.

Where possible, this needs to be enhanced within the level designs. It is useful to give players well-defined moments of human-to-human interaction within a level. Place people in predefined face-off situations. Provide players with cooperation dilemmas: can I trust the other player or not? How to engineer those moments depends entirely on the game and genre in question, but it is always good to keep this principle in mind.

Clearly defined competitive challenges

When it comes to competitive play, nothing is simpler than creating a situation where two or more players compete with each other on the same task to see who is better at it.

To a degree, this can be emulated in single-player games. But the human face of an opponent is often the difference between a pastime and a serious competitive challenge. For example, this really comes to the fore in deathmatch- or team-based adversarial play. The level designer needs to do no more than provide an environment that is balanced for the competing teams, and then allow the teams to fight it out in whatever game modes are applicable. There is no need for fancy extra special challenges; these will be provided by the players themselves.

In *capture the flag*, for example, it is quite normal for a level to consist of two halves that are roughly mirrored in order to guarantee that both sides have the same advantages or disadvantages. In *deathmatch* levels, we often find simplified environments that act as smooth flow in arenas, with very few bells and whistles. The gameplay is largely enjoyable because the level simply gives the players a good excuse to compete against each other. The same goes for multiplayer racing games, and for too many other genres to mention.[3]

Single-Player and Multiplayer Hybrids

Although rare, there are examples of games that manage to fuse both single-player and multiplayer mechanics. This sounds like a paradox, after all; how can a game be both a multiplayer game and a single-player game? Isn't it true that the moment more than one player is involved, the game type automatically has to be seen as multiplayer? Well ... maybe not. What if a player is not aware of other players? Is it possible to design a game where players can choose to experience the gameplay as if it were solo play, while still surrounded by other players? These may well be inconsequential questions, but some of these types of games have emerged in recent years and may be worth studying.

---

[3] There is easily enough material there to fill another book.

Simulated Multiplayer

This is a relatively rare phenomenon, but it can occur when human opponents are absent, but their roles are played by AI opponents. Good examples of this can be found in multiplayer games that provide tutorials where players can practice their skills against computer AI. Additionally, we see it in games that are meant to have humans playing each other, but that provide a simulated setting for when no other people are available. As previously mentioned, bots in *First Person Shooters* (FPSs) are often used in this context to provide opponents to simulate human players.

Special mention needs to be given to *Alternative Reality Games*, which often blur the line between real players and simulated players. This will be explored in more detail in Chapter 12.

Towards a Shared Grammar for Level Design

6

*L*anguage is often used as a metaphor when describing aspects of art. We talk about how a painting speaks to us, or how a movie has much to *say* on a particular subject. We speak of an artist's *vocabulary* or comment on an artist's *voice*. There are plenty of further examples relating to almost all art forms, so it is understandable that this is such a useful metaphor. Everybody understands statements such as, "Artists want to *speak* to an audience, to get a *message* across that hopefully, the audience wants to *hear*."

There is no reason not to employ the same metaphor when discussing level design. Unfortunately, people are not yet used to looking at our field in such a way, perhaps because level design is such a young profession. Nonetheless, regardless of how many people are aware of it, the field is slowly developing its own voice, language, syntax, dialect, or whatever you want to call it. It is important that level designers understand this and try to become fluent within the language of their own field.

The next part of the book is mainly about level design *concepts, theory,* and *practice.* But hopefully, as a consequence of studying these things, level designers or other interested parties will be aided in understanding, or contributing to, *a shared grammar of level design.* Hopefully, we can work to gain a better understanding of the language of our art form to allow us to get our message across loud and clear.

Conventions and Language

When a new art form develops, it starts to recognize that there are certain techniques available to it that are more useful than others. Artists start to learn how to effectively communicate with their audience, while the audience becomes better at recognizing which techniques the artist is using. There is a dynamic at play here, where both the audience and the artist develop together on an individual level, as well as scaling up to a societal and cultural one. There is in fact a constant dialogue of sorts between artist and audience. This dialogue is only possible when artist and audience can communicate, at least to a small degree, in a mutually understood language. Before we can develop and better understand our own language for level design, we need to understand a bit more about how an art form's language develops in general. And to do this, we need to look at our understanding of conventions.

Conventions

When artists, or any entertainers, for that matter, try to make a connection with an audience, they use certain techniques they know to be effective. Some techniques come from natural reactions; a loud bang will make you jump, slow movements are non-aggressive, etc. Other reactions, however, are conditioned ones. Those techniques are based on repeated usage through time; the audience *recognizes* them from previous encounters. For example:

- The scarred man is the villain.
- The hero gets the girl.
- The villain ends up dying a terrible death.
- The comedy will have a happy ending.
- Lassie will come home.

These are events that we have come to expect from many Hollywood stories, pulp novels, and other creative genres, to the point where they have become clichés. They may not be the best thing for an original story, but they are something that the audience will easily recognize as genre staples. They are part of a *formula*. These genre staples can also be described as *conventions*.

The idea of conventions refers to nothing more than an *accepted* truth or an accepted way of looking at something, and it covers many more things than entertainment clichés. Conventions in general occur when a culture or significant group of people accept a certain set of rules that govern something they are exposed to. If this sounds needlessly vague, let me give you some examples to show the scope of this concept.

Fashion

Most people conform to accepted conventions of dress and fashion. It is extremely rare for men to wear miniskirts, wear pajamas outside the house, or wear a suit to work that features a giraffe motif. Some people flaunt these unspoken rules; but they are seen to be eccentric, or indeed *unconventional*.

Social Behavior

There is a large amount of behavior that is conditioned and based upon a mutual understanding of conventions. We don't speak with our mouth full, throw change on the ground, pinch a stranger's nose, or steal each other's property without it being frowned upon. We decided upon these conventions a long time ago for diverse reasons, but we now agree to stick by them.

Literature

In most books, it is common to gain insight in the motivation of the protagonists. Most stories feature some kind of conflict, and events occur in such a way that they make chronological sense. It is often asserted that only a certain limited amount of stories can exist, and that all stories fit within these kinds of archetypes. Books that flout these rules are seen as experimental, difficult, or indeed once again, *unconventional* (a term that is revealing in itself).

The Language of Art

As we have seen so far, there are many conventions based on natural and conditioned reactions, and it is important to be able to see the distinction between the two. What matters most, however, is our ability to translate these conventions into a coherent framework. This is important in social situations, so that we all agree on how to interact with each other. But it also governs other aspects of our lives, including how we dress or even how we experience art.

Artists are often most effective if they can translate existing conventions, or develop new ones, and integrate them in their art in a way that enriches the work. Playing with conventions directly touches the experience for the audience, as it plays with their expectations and conditioned responses. These conventions become part of a toolset for the artist, or put in a different way, they become part of the artist's vocabulary.

When a set of artistic conventions has existed long enough that it has become stable, it can develop into something deeper. The conventions start to take place within a coherent context, or they form a prism through which the medium as a whole is perceived. For example, this has happened with conventions in film. People almost universally understand the use of certain filmic conventions even when they are quite abstract in nature, like screen distortion in a flashback scene, or complicated camera moves that nonetheless are accepted by the audience. These kinds of integrated and coherent sets of conventions are part of what is often described as the *language* of the medium.

The Language of Level Design

Just like any other art form, level design is subject to the same principles of conventions and the medium's language. Game players can *read* many aspects of level design these days. Many conventions already exist and contribute to an evolving and ever-richer level-design-specific language.

- We know that a health pack lying in a sealed-off area implies that access to this area can be gained.
- It is understood that a cut scene showing a lever and a door explains a relationship between the two.
- It is accepted that in most 2D platform games, jumping on a creature's head is an acceptable action to perform.
- It is clear that searching behind a waterfall may yield the discovery of hidden loot.

At one point, not so long ago due to the youth of our profession, all these conventions were new and fresh. We need to recognize these achievements so that we can use them in our own work, or even develop our own conventions. The most important aspect to integrate in our understanding is that we are all constantly using and working on developing a coherent language of level design, complete with its own syntax and grammar.

Note that when dealing with these elements of conventions and a medium's language, it is extremely important to be consistent. Even if new conventions are established within the game the level designer is working on, it is vital that unless there is a very good reason, the convention has to apply all through the game. If this rule is not followed, the player is basically taught that the game world is arbitrary, unreadable, and ultimately unfair. This kind of betrayal of a consistent set of rules is a perfect way of alienating the player.

Level Design and Art

Over the course of this book, I will often use the terms *fun, entertainment,* and *art.* The terms will frequently be used to describe level design goals, or desirable outcomes. The terms are not interchangeable, and all three can be attained in a level simultaneously. Quite often they are connected or even interdependent. This is especially true for art and entertainment, which form a complex relationship with each other. There is no consensus on where one thing starts and the other ends. To make matters worse, the meaning can mutate and change over time as one era's entertainment can form the next era's art.

As every art student knows, it is pointless to try to create a shared definition of art. In fact, it is a sure-fire way to start a heated argument, unfortunately one that can have no resolution. Nonetheless, I often speak about level design as an art form. Although this notion of level design as art is disputed by many people, I see it as an irrefutable fact. The fact that most games are not art may be true, but this does not mean that games can't be art. This argument is true for many other creative fields, like music and film. Level design *can* create art, and therefore in my opinion it is an art form. (Nobody thinks film is not an art form because of the overrepresentation of formulaic box-office creations.)

Conclusion

What more established art forms have in common with each other is that there is a language assigned to them that allows for critical analysis and discourse. They have developed a shared grammar of the medium that applies to all their disparate elements, and this is something I feel we should also aim for. Sir William Thomson (Lord Kelvin) said: "*If* you cannot measure it, you cannot improve it." I would like to add to that the notion that "*if* you cannot discuss it, you cannot make it better."

It is important to grasp the significance of a medium's language and study it, as it teaches us how and when communication occurs in the medium. Just as with a language in a linguistic sense, it is much easier to express oneself in a language when the underlying culture is studied as well. Level design as an art form also features a shared artistic language. Some elements are related to other art forms, like film, storytelling, or photography, to name a few. But it also features elements that explicitly belong within the field, based on conventions and ideas developed specifically for level design.

It is this combination of elements, if properly studied and understood, that can turn our designs into a powerful message spoken with a clear voice.

Emotional Feedback Systems

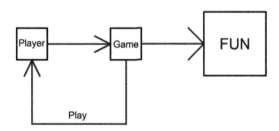

One of the ways in which the success of an art form or an artistic expression can be measured is by gauging its emotional impact. Can it *move* us emotionally? Can it cause anger or sadness, create hope or explain despair? If we look at other art forms, this question is easily answered; many examples can be quoted from films, books, photos, musical compositions, etc. All of these art forms have found a way to touch us in some way or speak to our inner self. They have learned to reach an emotional core and can become part of our inner life.

What happens if we look at level design, and its attempts to reach the inner life of a game player? Can we honestly aspire to similar achievements on an emotional level as other more established art forms?

I think we can, although we have far to go when it comes to fine tuning our proficiency in this matter. Nonetheless, it cannot be denied that level design has created its own set of *emotional feedback systems*. We have developed tried and tested methods for creating and feeding emotional responses from our audience. As level designers, we have a strong advantage over most other art forms when it comes to his kind of engagement. Our audience will actively participate and contribute to the experience. This willingness to engage with our work is a key aspect of understanding the power of level design. Because of this participatory

---

Simplified gameplay feedback loop.

aspect of the art form and the final control we have over content, we can predict many of the actions and emotions of the player. This means we can take these player contributions and enhance them, alter them, reward them, and reflect them. Such reactions provide the underlying principles of the use of emotional feedback systems in level design, based on an understanding of the player's own emotional investment and contribution.

The following chapters will look at a number of these systems that are available to us and provide clear and practical examples that show how we can best use them. Ultimately it is vital that as in other art forms, we can to engage with the player's inner life. It is important that we can create a real emotional response through our work. The good news is that we have many ways of doing so.

Reward Systems

7

The carrot or the stick?

While the answer to this age-old question depends on the situation, it is generally accepted that one is meaningless without the other. If carrots are the norm, they will not be seen as anything special, just a fact of life, no more special than other omnipresent elements. Alternatively, if the stick is the only thing available, it ceases to have any motivating power; it just offers abusive coercion and does not foster any innate motivation. Both examples are extremes that unfortunately do happen in real life and in most cases have been shown to be deficient. If you work somewhere where your boss only screams at you and never praises your achievements,[1] chances are that you will leave. If you are a runner and never lose a race, there is not much incentive to train to become even faster.

There is, however, a *third* way. If somebody who is holding all the carrots beats you with a stick, it would be very satisfying if you were to wrestle the stick away from your tormentor and make him give you all the carrots. I know which way I would prefer.

The following chapter will look at some fundamental principles of reward systems and positive or negative motivators. Some of these occur within an everyday context, while others are more specialized or unexpected. Eventually we will seek ways in which to use them in our levels in a manner that is effective and entertaining, rather than there being something as crude as being hit repeatedly with a stick over some measly carrots.

---

[1] Not unheard of in the game industry.

Concept

Reward Systems and Schools of Behaviorism

Like most mammals, human beings are fairly predictable in their reaction to rewards and punishments, insofar as that they have been studied extensively in this regard, and behavior tends to fall into a number of typical[2] responses. Without wanting to go into a detailed exploration of behaviorism and its many schools of thought, I would like to suggest that it covers a lot of ground that relates to level design. A key factor in level design is the use of rewards and punishments to enforce (or reinforce) or discourage certain behaviors. This is a massive subject, and one that is laced with controversy and difficulties. I suggest that readers find their own path through subjects such as operant conditioning, intermittent reinforcement, Pavlovian reactions, and other related subjects.[3]

For the purpose of this book, I think it is enough to look at a number of reward systems that apply directly to its subject matter. As a preamble to their uses in level design, I would like to shine a general light on the following reward systems.

Escapism and Wish Fulfillment

There are many reasons why we turn to art or entertainment: enlightenment, a need to expand boundaries, a quest for an alternative point of view, or other equally valid motivations. However, sometimes all we need is a certain amount of *wish fulfillment*, sometimes referred to as *escapism*. Generally these words are not used as terms of appreciation; indeed, they are often used as terms of ridicule. "That book is just an escapist fantasy" or "The movie has nothing to offer but flights of fancy and empty wish fulfillment." It is a big mistake to do so. Critics who employ this kind of language may well be right about the artistic merit of the work they are reviewing, but they tend to make a grave error by mistaking the effectiveness of the artist with the method employed, or even the goal of the work. In other words, the problem is not that the work is *escapist* (one can insert

---

[2] Insofar as this is possible when it comes to the often *irrational* behavior of people.

[3] "Behaviorism," *Wikipedia*, http://en.wikipedia.org/wiki/Behaviorism, 2009.

other similar concepts); the problem is that the artist has not been successful in providing *enjoyable* (or artistic) escapism.

Nobody would criticize a person for going on a long walk in the countryside or reading a travelogue (clear escapism). There are no problems with somebody listening to music from another country and in the process being transported there (obvious wish fulfillment.) Who begrudges somebody reading Tolkien's *The Hobbit* (a flight of fancy)? Tolkien himself had the following to say on the exact same subject:

> I have claimed that Escape is one of the main functions of fairy-stories, and since I do not disapprove of them, it is plain that I do not accept the tone of scorn or pity with which "Escape" is now so often used: a tone for which the uses of the word outside literary criticism give no warrant at all. In what the misusers are fond of calling Real Life, Escape is evidently as a rule very practical, and may even be heroic. In real life it is difficult to blame it, unless it fails; in criticism it would seem to be the worse the better it succeeds. Evidently we are faced by a misuse of words, and also by a confusion of thought. Why should a man be scorned if, finding himself in prison, he tries to get out and go home? Or if, when he cannot do so, he thinks and talks about other topics than jailers and prison-walls?[4]

The fact of the matter is that sometimes the here and now is not a desirable place to be and can even be *punishing*, and that we can *reward* ourselves by engaging in creative expressions that recognize this and provide an alternative. This has been the motivation, and even the subject, of some of the most enduring pieces of art in the history of mankind and should not be sneered at. To do so risks inviting cynicism, closed-mindedness, and contempt for other people. Not only can escapism provide wish-fulfillment for the subject involved, it can also constitute a form of *rebellion*: as a way of taunting the world by saying: "You can't touch me while I am in here!"

Submission and Release

There are times when we decide that it is all right for us to relinquish control over a situation or even (mostly temporarily) our lives. This occurs when we decide that somebody is able to teach us or help us in some way and we are told that this can only occur if we follow the other's lead. Although human beings are naturally social creatures, this does not mean that they are naturally submissive.

---

[4] J.R.R. Tolkien, *Tree and Leaf*, Allen & Unwin, London, 1964, p. 53.

There are of course many times when people espouse a group mentality, but that is not what we are discussing right now. I am rather talking about those times when people willingly, in exchange for some kind of reward, submit to others, or at least take somebody else's lead.

There are countless examples, both humble and significant. We can see this principle at work in something as fanciful[5] as ballroom dancing. There can only be one person in that situation who leads. It also occurs in a very formal context, for example in education. This does not only apply to children, who are naturally much more submissive, but also to adults. For example, driving instructors or music teachers must be listened to, or they can't do their work.

Consensual (Temporary) Submission

In the case of most adult examples, the submission we are talking about is purely consensual. Nobody is forcing you to submit to some arbitrary figure of authority, yet it happens frequently and willingly. There are no punishments for not submitting in this manner, unlike (for example) in the case of submission to the law, which if refused, would lead to serious punitive consequences. Instead, these are moments of subordination or submission that we actively seek out, which is an interesting fact, considering that we would never behave like this in other circumstances. If your music teacher told you to do his or her shopping, you would laugh in that person's face. This is because it is a ridiculous request that yields no discernible reward to the person asked to submit to this "authority." It is ridiculous because there is no *agreement* in place to do so.

In almost all similar cases there is an agreement, written or otherwise, that exists between the parties involved. This agreement is essential and generally quite clear in scope. We don't need to see in a detailed contract that explains all the legal parameters that state that the person blowing the whistle in a soccer match is to be listened to.

You don't run away from your guide in the jungle because he or she gets cross with you for picking up some venomous lizard. We submit to this kind of authority on a regular basis because there is an agreed-upon reward. We learn how to play an instrument, enjoy a fair and enjoyable match of soccer, or enjoy a safe and fascinating trip through the jungle. After the activity ends, temporary submission is abandoned and authority is released.

Not only does this kind of system yield its own rewards, it can also be closely tied in to other systems, and can in fact be the reason why we would even engage

---

[5] Perhaps not the best word to describe it.

in them. A good example of this will follow later in this chapter and discusses *catharsis*.

Challenge and Empowerment

It is often asserted that hard work rewards itself, not just in a sense of achievement, but also in more practical ways. If we take off our cynical hat for a moment, we will realize that this is true in many situations.

There are positive challenges. If you go running for an hour every day, you will become very fit. If you study a language diligently for ten years, you will become fluid in its use. If your work is better than that of your colleagues, you will get that promotion. (Well, you *should*, anyway.)

And there are negative challenges. Stand up to that bully and he will stop harassing you. Deal with the tragedy of a loss for a long enough time and it will hurt less and less. Resist smoking for a year and your cravings will be gone.

The main point to recognize is that life is full of challenges, both positive and negative, and that meeting them, sometimes even just attempting to meet them, gives people a sense of control over their own life. This is a massively important principle, which is often referred to as *empowerment*. The word is overused at times, and it is often coated in sugary, feel-good language. But at the basic level, it is nothing more than finding the personal power to take control of your own life. This is a huge motivator for anybody, and many belief-systems, books, self help tapes, motivational speaker's careers, and other things have been based on it. The reward of empowerment is so strong that it can even lead people into unhealthy behavior patterns. For example, addiction is often, paradoxically, about control.[6] Some people try to feel empowered by trying to control other people's lives. But in general, it is widely understood that reacting to life's challenges positively, or seeking positive challenges to master to ultimately gain a level of control over life's experiences, is a very positive endeavor.

Fairness

This principle only works however when life treats people *fairly*. To put our cynical hat back on: *life isn't always fair*. The notion of fairness is a very interesting one, as it is a strictly human concept. The wind isn't fair, nor is gravity. Fire cares nothing for fairness. Yet within our own lives, we attribute huge importance to it. There are few things as annoying as someone jumping ahead of you in line, a

---

[6] For example, gambling is often said to give addicts a sense of control by letting the ritual control other aspects of their lives.

lazy millionaire underpaying hard-working employees, or losing your pension in some financial corporate debacle through no fault of your own. Unfairness is a form of *disempowerment*, and it should never be underestimated how much of a negative impact this can have.

Investment and Payoff

Related to the expectation of fairness is a reward system, which has its roots in financial principles. When we put our money in the bank, we expect to receive interest payments as a reward for letting the bank hold it. If we invest in a company through buying shares or in some other way, we expect a return on our investment in the form of a profitable payout. There are many other examples, but these should suffice to recognize the principle. We invest our money in such a way that we expect to receive some kind of reward at the end. This is a fairly basic principle of financial systems. It extends to further principles, for example to buying property in a country with a growing housing market, or starting a business in a country which is experiencing economic growth.

These examples are of a purely financial nature. But the principle is equally recognizable in other areas. For example, we can invest *time* into something and expect something in return. Or we can invest *effort* and expect some kind of result. This can overlap with the principle of empowerment, but it doesn't have to. For example, we can invest time and effort to solve a difficult cryptic puzzle, which yields a reward in providing a satisfying answer. Large investments offer the expectation of large rewards. A scientist may dedicate his or her entire life to finding a cure to a particular disease or other scientific problem. Although it might not necessarily be unfair, it would be unfortunate if these investments went without rewards.

Sometimes the rewards are immediate, (the activity itself is so enjoyable that it is a reward in itself), or sometimes the rewards arrive over time, or it is reached after sustained effort or investment. Sometimes both can occur within the same activity.

An Example: Treasure Hunting

Almost every culture on earth understands the concept of treasure hunting. This is clear from representations in books like *Treasure Island*,[7] films like *Pirates of the Caribbean*,[8] legends like the *Lost Gold of the Templars*, and the iconic image of

---

[7] Robert Louis Stevenson, 1883.

[8] Published by the Walt Disney Company.

the classical *Pirate*. Furthermore, in the real world there are thousands of people who engage in amateur treasure hunting with a metal detector, as well as professional treasure finders who organize well-researched expeditions in heavily funded commercial projects.

Investment in the context of the treasure hunt can contain examples like these:

- Treasure hunting investments:
  - financial investment in an expedition,
  - effort of researching a subject,
  - spending time waving a metal detector around,
  - hard physical work during an expedition.
- Immediate returns on investment:
  - enjoying the company of other expedition members,
  - gaining knowledge,
  - enjoying the outdoors,
  - feelings of excitement.
- Long-term returns on investment:
  - treasure, of course!

Romantic as this all sounds, there are real world treasure hunters who are very successful. A famous example is Mel Fisher and his company Salvors Inc., whose most famous expedition led to the discovery of the long-lost Spanish galleon Nuestra Señora de Atocha,[9]" whose wreck was the home of an enormous hoard of treasure:

> Among the items found on the wrecks are a fortune in gold, silver bars, and coins destined for the coffers of Spain; a solid gold belt and necklace set with gems; a gold chalice designed to prevent its user from being poisoned; an intricately-tooled gold plate; a gold chain that weighs more than seven pounds; a horde of contraband emeralds—including an impressive 77.76 carat uncut hexagonal crystal experts have traced to the Muzo mine in Colombia; religious and secular jewelry; and silverware.[10]

This shows that treasure hunting is an excellent example of an activity with a multi-layered inbuilt reward system. Although treasure hunting is in many ways an obscure example, everybody can understand the reasoning behind it. It is an activity that can act as a nearly perfect metaphor for the principle in general.

---

[9] Our Lady of Atocha.

[10] "1622 Feet," *Mel Fisher Maritime Heritage Society and Museum in Key West*, http://www.melfisher.org/1622.htm, 2008.

Isolation and Social Reinforcement

People are social creatures. This may not always seem obvious, considering how badly people can treat each other, but nonetheless, almost nobody can enjoy extended periods of social isolation. We really do need some minimum amount of social contact to successfully experience our humanity. This principle is so strong that it is represented in fundamental instincts. Take, for example, human childbirth: it is well known that it is beneficial for child and mother to bond as soon as possible after birth. This process has been linked to the hormone oxytocine in women, which facilitates this bonding.[11] Regardless of the scientific explanation of any hormonal grounding, it is hard to argue that social reinforcement isn't one of the most important driving forces in our lives.

Social Reinforcement

The need for social systems does not stop with the child-mother bond. When we grow through life stages, we feel the need to be part of a family unit. The rewards are clear and easy to recognize. Through social bonds, we receive support or companionship and guidance. If this cannot be found in the family, people sometimes join another group to make sure they receive it nonetheless, like the army, or an ideological group of some sort. At times this need is so strong that people will join groups that are clearly abusive, like some cults. This shows how powerful the need for social reinforcement is.

In addition to these examples, we often join clubs, go to communal events, start our own families, and form complex social networks. And, most relevant to this book, we seek out enjoyable activities that are based on or reliant on social interaction. Have you ever been to a sci-fi convention? It is remarkable how sociable huge groups of people can become when they acknowledge that they have something in common. This can be seen in events where people just enjoy each other's company, when they share a common interest[12] or goal, or when they want to compete against each other in an enjoyable way, like at sporting events. It is hard to deny the existence and the plentiful awards that all of these social interactions can offer. It is therefore not surprising that they are all around us and we engage in them on a regular basis.

---

[11] Catherine West, "Level of Oxytocin in Pregnant Women Predicts Mother-Child Bond," *Aps Observer* 20:10 (2007), available at http://www.psychologicalscience.org/observer/getArticle.cfm?id=2245.

[12] Perhaps I should start a level design appreciation society?

Temporary Isolation

This reward system can also work inversely, strange as that may sound. Who hasn't heard the grim saying, "Hell is other people"? Although not a very nice thing to say, it touches upon an important truth. Many of the advantages of a strong social network can also cause serious distress. Sometimes all the social elements in our lives can become oppressive. Too many opinions vying for dominance, attempts at peer pressure, social control instead of social support, or even just the fact that sometimes we don't get along with some other people.

At such moments, we may decide that the best way to improve our situation is to engage in activities that enforce *temporary*[13] *solitude*, or at least minimize the number of people we have to interact with.

When we need "peace and quiet" we may go on a long walk in the countryside. It allows us to focus on *our own* thoughts, without the din of others disturbing them. There are many other examples, like painting or writing a book. We may seek an activity that, in solitude, lets us focus on the voice or on the ideas of others. Listening to music or watching a film, and even doing a crossword puzzle, come to mind. As prevalent as social interaction can be, we enjoy a comparable number of solitary activities that produce their own vital awards.

Adversity and Catharsis

It is an unfortunate but nonetheless potent truth that some rewards can only come from dealing with negatives. This is complicated at best and covers a wide range of topics. I have dedicated a whole chapter to the principle of using negative emotions (Chapter 9),[14] which goes into some detail about using negative emotions in a positive way to strengthen level design. A number of specific techniques will be discussed and illustrated by clear examples. Within this chapter, however, I want to spend some time on the principle of *catharsis* as a reward system.

Catharsis
- *Noun* the release of pent-up emotions, for example through drama.
  - Derivatives *cathartic* adjective & noun.
  - Origin Greek katharsis, from kathairein 'cleanse'.[15]

---

[13] Almost nobody is interested in permanent solitude. That would be throwing out the baby with the bathwater.

[14] Chapter 9, "Negative Emotions."

[15] From the *Compact Oxford English Dictionary*. Available online at http://www.askoxford.com/concise_oed/catharsis?view=uk.

Catharsis is a special case reward system because it is often one that we wouldn't seek out intentionally, because it cannot be achieved without also experiencing negatives beforehand. The concept is almost always described as having something of a *purging* nature, all the way back to Aristotle's early use of the word in his famous *Poetics*, where he describes catharsis as being one of the main characteristics of tragedy, where it serves as a purgation of pity and fear.

Furthermore, there are definitions of catharsis that are just as valid but come from psychology, religion, or medicine. Whatever the interpretation, though, a defining feature of the principle of catharsis is that its reward can only come about after one suffers a serious amount of pain or adversity and feels the purging nature of the subsequent emotional release. This is why it is an interesting reward system, since it feels counterintuitive to seek out negative experiences to receive a positive reward. Indeed, in many cases we don't do this and in fact try all we can to avoid it. But on further inspection, we find that in most societies there is actually a deep-rooted respect for doing exactly that. In the English language, this can be seen in phrases or sayings like "character building" or in the slightly more testosterone-tinted observation that some kind of adversity "makes a man out of him."

All over the world, people engage in initiation ceremonies, or in ritualized rites of passage. An almost uncomfortable number of coming-of-age ceremonies are associated with painful or difficult tasks or quests. Ultimately we find that the basic principle of coming through a painful or difficult experience to learn or experience something positive pervades society on all levels. Uncomfortable as it may seem, negative experiences can provide rich rewards. This knowledge is formalized throughout all aspects of society. Catharsis is the basis for all kinds of reward mechanisms, some of them formalized and accepted, others only recognized after the fact or even coerced. Thank goodness that the latter is more and more frowned upon, although it still exists in practices like initiation ceremonies. Other examples can be found in activities that take serious sacrifices from the participant, sometimes in ways that seem extreme to others, but that give rewards that otherwise cannot be attained. People have spoken of life-changing experiences after extreme challenges like mountain climbing or spelunking[16] expeditions, extremely long periods of meditation, or extended fasting.

Plenty of other examples exist, but they all require a real extended effort from the participant. It is this *extended* aspect of *enduring hardship* that in most cases is linked to the positive outcome, the sense of catharsis. It can only occur, however, if the participant is tested in such a way that failure to endure is a possibility. And therein lies the danger. Paradoxically, catharsis as a basis for a reward

---

[16] Cave exploration.

system can only work well if there is this element of danger of failure or at least of real challenge. Otherwise, the emotions released at a positive or negative[17] outcome will not be strong enough to trigger a real sense of catharsis.

Concept Summary

What most of the reward systems and structures described above have in common is that they demand a certain amount of work, sacrifice or investment from the subject. *Something is given and something is received.* It is not necessarily true that more effort equals a larger reward (although that is often the case). It is more a matter of making a task worthwhile and meaningful because seeing one's efforts rewarded is fulfilling and enjoyable. This sometimes means that a very small amount of effort can reap a large reward, or a grueling task may end in a small symbolic victory, *yet the feeling of fulfillment can be equally strong.* Often the joy simply comes from what amounts to solving a life puzzle or conundrum, or it revolves about learning and applying the right skills for a task.

Unfortunately, there is a flip side to all this, insofar as unfulfilled reward systems provide negative emotional feedback. At times this can be of comparable impact to the expected positive outcome. It can also demotivate people to engage in important aspects in their lives, if through thwarted reward systems they have been taught not to do so. What use is love if it is likely to end in tears? Why work a hard job if the promotions only go to people who cheat? Why play a game when any effort can be instantly wiped out by the level design?

One of the many things a level designer has to understand is the dynamics of all these reward systems, as well as being able to effectively use them in practical situations, in a fair and even-handed way, if possible. The following chapter will attempt to take these concepts of diverse reward systems and examine them in the light of level design theory.

Theory

> If somebody holding carrots beats you with a stick it would be very satisfying if you were to wrestle the stick away from your tormentor and make him give you all the carrots.

---

[17] Catharsis can still occur even if the participant fails at the attempted task. It is the final release of emotions that shapes the sense of catharsis.

The previous chapter discusses many of the possible ways in which reward systems and structures can work, and, as importantly, what expectations people have from life. In this chapter we will examine some of them again, but within the context of level design theory. We will derive or construct some game-specific principles, as well.

I would like to make an important initial point before we do this, however, What has to be clear from the outset is that as authors of a level's content, and therefore of much of the player's game experience, we are completely within our rights to manipulate the player's reward expectations in ways that are unexpected, but that are ultimately more rewarding to the player. Even though it falls squarely within our responsibilities to do so, this is often forgotten, or worse, ignored. As long as we don't violate other important principles of level design, we have the power to give the player the opportunity to finally take away the big stick from the universal tormentor and run away with all the carrots, *and feel really good about it.*

Escapism and Wish Fulfillment

Level designers are lucky that they work in a medium that has an audience that is already willing and able to submit itself to feelings of escapism and wish fulfillment. It is perfectly acceptable for a gamer to crave these things; it is even (erroneously) at times expected that a gamer will *exclusively* crave them. This makes us lucky, because it gives us an audience made up of people who are willing to travel with us and gives us a whole range of techniques that we can use to get them there.

We can do this by taking them somewhere that doesn't exist in this world and then delight them with amazing new sight and sounds. *Fantabulate!*[18]

Or, we can take them into our interpretation of an enjoyable activity based in real world concepts. *Simulate!*

Both have many areas where they overlap, as covered in many chapters elsewhere in this book. But they also have important differences that need to be examined. (There is also a third option that will be examined later.)

Fantabulate!

A level is a virtual construct. It may have its own set of rules, logic, physics system, ecology, and other internal systems, but they all take place in a *virtual* setting. The disadvantage of this virtuality is that somebody needs to design and

---

[18] If this is not a real word, it should be; and I am claiming it now.

implement all of these things. The advantage for level designers is that in this need, or put to put it differently, in this *license* to do so, lies a huge amount of freedom and power. In game levels with a non-realistic setting, the level designer has the license to fantabulate.

New rules

Within a fantastic virtual construct, we are free to create many things or situations that simply would not work in the real world, all with the approval of our audience. Not only may we invent these new rules; we are positively *encouraged* to do so. We have already concluded in Chapter 2, "Teaching Mechanisms," that part of our responsibility lies in teaching the player the rules of the available gameplay activities. In a fantastic setting this is especially important, as the rules may be unknown in real life.

For example, we may have to teach players that summoning a fire elemental is an extremely effective way of deterring packs of ice wolves from attacking[19].)

The real fun lies in the fact that players who enjoy these kinds of things, and there are many, many millions of them, also really enjoy learning about this new world they find themselves in. Within an escapist mindset, experiencing new fantastic concepts is an attraction in its own right. If we go back to our earlier example of Tolkien, we see a work of fantasy that partly excels because of its sheer scope of invention. The book creates a very deep *sense of wonder*, partly because it consistently and thoroughly showcases a new world with an extremely detailed and well-thought-out set of rules. This applies to almost anything in the world, including its history, its ecology, and its magic system. Reading about all of these things is a large reason for the success of the book.

Level designers have to do the same thing. They need to interpret the new rules of the world and teach them to players in such a way that it creates a great *sense of wonder*, as well as teaching them *how to play* the game.

New environments

Hand in hand with new world rules come new environments; and once again, a great amount of work and a great amount of freedom for the level designer. A great amount of *work* because within this virtual construct somebody has to do the constructing. This does not mean that the level designer has to create all the environments solely by himself or herself, although at times this is feasible or necessary. In most cases, this work must be done in partnership with the art department. But the level designer does need to design all the *gameplay space*, and the way it is used. This gives level designers a great amount of *freedom* because

---

[19] Yes, I picked this cliché on purpose, for illustrative clarity.

they are the authors of a new gameplay environment, and to a large degree, of a whole new gameplay world. This is one of the reasons why level design is such an enormously fulfilling profession; it literally gives a designer the power to create worlds.[20]

So far, so good. In fact, this is no different from most other forms of level design.

Where level design featuring themes of escapism and wish fulfillment in a fantastic setting differs from more reality-based design is in some of the intrinsic goals. A big reason for the existence of the levels is to present a gameplay environment, and a virtual environment that appeals enough in its own right that the player wishes to engage with it and spend time sampling its content. This means that it is reasonable to include enjoyable areas that don't feature much gameplay (but aid in escapism), or to go further and assert that exploring these areas is part of the gameplay appropriate to the goals of such a level. A big mistake that many people in game development make is to assume that all gameplay spaces must feature active challenges and encounters. It is actually important to also include gameplay space that celebrates escapism through the medium of *exploration*, or other ways that the player can just enjoy the world. These are some of the reasons that so many games feature a fantasy, sci-fi, surreal, or otherwise fantastic setting. For many reasons, these genres are especially suited for this kind of design.

Providing the player with many level design scenarios to achieve these goals is an important way to allow for deep and interesting elements of wish fulfillment and escapism. Level designers should always ask fundamental questions about the scenarios they create. In the case of a fantastic setting, these questions can include:

- Can I reach that strange but beautiful area?
- How do I study that new dangerous creature?
- What else can I use this artifact for?
- Who built this structure?
- How do I reach that floating fortress?

These are just a few random examples, but each one shows that interesting level design scenarios are just around the corner. And answering questions like these goes very far in providing the player with what he or she wishes for, and constitutes an effective use of a powerful reward mechanism.

---

[20] If you are interested in level design and that doesn't appeal at a very basic level, you may ask yourself some questions.

Simulate!

A completely different approach to escapism and wish fulfillment is found in *simulations*, and before we discuss level design theory and simulations, we should actually look at what is meant by the word.

Simulation and imitation

Normally, when we speak of simulation, we are talking about modeling a real-world system or situation in order to learn something new. This could be for scientific reasons; for example, a simulation and study of hunter predator cycles could be used to warn when a particular species becomes overhunted and may become endangered. It could also be for financial reasons; a simulation of a particular economic system may predict which factors contribute to inflation. In any of the examples we can find of simulations, it is generally the case that there is a need for accuracy in order to correctly extrapolate from the data that the simulation produces:

> [A] simulation results when the equations of the underlying dynamic model are solved. This model is designed to imitate the time-evolution of a *real system*.[21] (*Emphasis mine.*)

Most games are not like that at all. (The exceptions will be noted shortly.) Games are all about *enjoyment*. When we play games, we play them for all kinds of enjoyable reasons: to have fun, to exercise our brains, to have a meaningful artistic experience, and so forth. Simulation games are no different and exist to provide an enjoyable experience, in most cases by providing players with a chance to engage in a real-life activity they normally would not be able to enjoy. A game can offer a player a chance to be a soccer manager or a train conductor or a theme park operator.

These are great examples of games based upon wish fulfillment as a reward system. If we look closer, we find that they aren't games of simulation at all, but games of illusion and *imitation*. The game *imitates* real-world activities only to the degree that their fun aspects are replicated for the enjoyment of the player. This kind of imitation is, unlike practical simulations, not concerned with accuracy at all, but with the *appearance* of accuracy. The games would quickly become extremely tedious if they tried to accurately simulate all aspects of the activity in question.

---

[21] Stephan Hartmann, "The World as a Process: Simulations in the Natural and Social Sciences," http://philsci-archive.pitt.edu/archive/00002412/, 2005.

Accuracy only needs to be observed as long as it supports enjoyable gameplay. An actual racing game *simulator* (SIM) would be far too difficult for most gamers to enjoy. And what is the point of playing a grand prix SIM if the player cannot win? It would be accurate and realistic, but not much fun, especially because it fails at the first hurdle and doesn't provide the wish fulfillment element of the game's reward system.

Strangely, although the use of the word *simulation* is suspect, I still advise that we adhere to its usage in games. It is simply too confusing to do otherwise, because as a description of genre, it is too widespread to change. It is essential, however, that level designers know what simulation games are really about: enjoyable *imitation*.

This is not semantic nitpicking, but a fundamentally profound difference that causes much debate and conflict. Almost every level designer, on a regular basis, will have to argue this point against somebody who insists on making gameplay decisions that fail this test of enjoyable imitation, solely based on the argument that the game needs to correctly simulate a real world event. There are times when simulation and imitation go hand in hand, perhaps when a particular sport's league is implemented, or when the correct dimensions of a vehicle need to be followed. But even in those circumstances, it needs to be clear that these implementations still serve *an enjoyable imitation of a real world activity*.

This has tremendous impact for the level design of these games. Instead of being at the mercy of real-life rules and physics, the level designer now has the role of illusionist. The tracks in a realistic racing SIM now only have to *feel* like they are correct; as long as they are fun, the job is well done. The lack of accuracy in a wildlife photography game's terrain means nothing as long as it produces expected results that don't break immersion. It is all smoke and mirrors.

"Serious games"

There are only few exceptions to this rule, mainly in the area of so-called *serious* games and educational games. They are noteworthy because although they can display many of the characteristics of other video games, they are fundamentally different. There is no formal definition of what exactly constitutes "serious games", but it is fair to say that their main focus is that of teaching some real-world application or education. This can be a commercial focus, for example a driving game for a driving school, or a scientific one, for example a game that lets students identify certain plants as part of a biology lesson.[22] As already noted in Chapter 2, games are extremely suitable as a teaching tool, since we are already trained at a very young age to engage in gameplay in to learn all kinds of diverse

---

[22] Serious games are nearly always educational games.

skills. This and the ever-improving technological sophistication of commercial video games have led to a proliferation of serious and educational games that recognize this principle.

For example, see the Serious Games Initiative, which has done much work in this arena:

> The Serious Games Initiative is focused on uses for games in exploring management and leadership challenges facing the public sector. Part of its overall charter is to help forge productive links between the electronic game industry and projects involving the use of games in education, training, health, and public policy.[23]

Because the defining aspect of these games is that of real-world application, they are always expected to produce tangible results, or they will have failed in their basic function. And this result has to be realistic or accurate at all times, or its real-world application will be ruined. Because of this, the player has to be able to trust the game to produce teaching material that is trustworthy and cannot just be an imitation or an illusion. A serious game teaching somebody how to fly an airplane in real life has some serious responsibilities in real life to live up to.

Fantastic Simulation

On rare occasions, a hybrid game form appears that tries to provide fun game-play through "realistically" simulating an activity in a fantastic setting, or even a *fantastic activity* in *any* setting.[24] This is a strange beast indeed and initially is not easy to quantify, but some clear examples exist. Take for instance *Startopia*,[25] a game that expects the player to successfully run a spaceship colony, balancing the needs of all the diverse onboard species. Another example can be found in the famous *Tamagotchi* brand, where the player is expected to take care of a fantastical creature in a realistic manner.

These games still contain the key elements of a rewards system based on escapism and wish fulfillment, but it is up to the level designer to decide where to fantabulate and where to simulate. However, the question can be asked: how can a game simultaneously be both fantastic and realistic?

---

[23] "The Serious Games Initiative," *The Serious Games Initiative*, www.seriousgames.org/newswire/.

[24] Typically a fantastic setting, however.

[25] Mucky Foot Productions, 2001; published by Eidos.

Staying "in character"

The answer to this question lies in the assumption that a level should stay *in character*. Like an actor, the game cannot acknowledge the world outside of its own fiction. If this happened, it might not be strange for a player to take slow incremental lessons in hover board control to perfectly learn the nuances needed to enter the *Martian Circular Race*.[26] The level designer needs to be aware that although there is room for imitation and illusion, the levels cannot cheat the in-game rules at any time. I will leave this topic for now, before it all becomes too metaphysical, but I would like to advise any level designer working on such a game to treat the fake rules of the game as if they were real.

Some Further Notes on Wish Fulfillment

In most of the examples and cases discussed so far, wish fulfillment has been linked to giving players the freedom to engage in activities they probably can't in real life. This can be to shine in a career as a formula one racing driver or to captain a star ship. The activity itself is the wish being fulfilled. The principle goes much further, however, sometimes in unexpected ways. The player may be confronted with a fast vehicle, leading to a wish to drive it, or the player may spot a castle on the horizon, leading to a wish to reach it. Many of these kinds of scenarios are actually in the hands of the level designer. In wish fulfillment, we have an immensely powerful tool to entertain the player through our level designs. In this context, wish fulfillment means adding gameplay scenarios that create a desire and eventually give the player the means to satisfy it.

Avoiding clichés

A well-known criticism of wish fulfillment is that it panders to simplistic desires and that is "too easy," leading to cheap entertainment that doesn't challenge or engage the audience enough. This danger certainly exists, but it is no more a result of wish fulfillment than elevator music is a result of making music accessible. If used well, wish fulfillment is a powerful technique that can be used to reward gameplay, deepen immersion, and to challenge the player's conception of what a desired outcome is. It is up to the level designer to decide how to implement these principles, and what clichés to avoid. There are no hard and fast rules and what constitutes a cliché can be entirely dependent on the game's genre or expected audience.

---

[26] I made that up.

Investment and Payoff

Players of *massively multiplayer online role playing games* (MMORPGs) know all about this one. In fact, they have a rather negative term for when a game becomes too much of a chore — *"grinding."* The *grind* describes a painful and boring slog where players perform repetitive gameplay tasks[27] that very slowly increase their experience points, eventually allowing them to *level up,*[28] which gives them more and more of the power needed to make a real impact in the world.

Sounds terribly boring, doesn't it? Yet millions of people do this day after day without fail, simply because there is a payoff for all this investment. They may hate doing it, but they do it anyway if they perceive the payoff to be worthwhile. However, we can do much to reduce the tedium of this kind of gameplay with smart level design. I will focus more on avoiding the grind later. But first, let's look at the principle of investment and payoff in level design.

The Agreement between Designer and Player

Throughout this chapter, and indeed throughout this book, I have made it a recurring theme that artist and audience strike a deal. *The player of a video game is happy to face the challenges the game offers — if there are rewards for doing so.* It is tempting to leave it at that; but because it is such an important principle, let me try to illustrate the concept in a little more depth. As in most other level design techniques, it is important to get the balance right. In the dynamics of investment and payoff, the two sides of his bargain need to be balanced. If the reward is not high enough in relation to the investment, the player will feel cheated. If the reward is too high, the player will become spoiled and will expect too much throughout the game afterwards. If the challenges are too hard, the player will become frustrated; if they are too easy; the player will become bored. So, a few principles need to be respected:

Proportional rewards

Rewards need to be proportionate to the effort expended in obtaining them. Or at least, the player needs to know that the *potential* awards can be proportionate to the effort needed to obtain them. There are exceptions, but they *are* exceptions to the rule. If we ask players to abide by certain rules, they need to be able to trust the contract and the fact that they will receive a reasonable reward for

---

[27] Like vanquishing small furry creatures or picking berries for days of in-game time on end.

[28] Attain higher levels for their character.

their efforts. Even when there is an element of chance in play, this principle stays intact, as the potential award needs to be high enough to compensate for those instances when the player receives a lesser reward, or none. But in that case, the player needs to know that chance is a factor.

Avoid boredom if possible

Try to avoid situations where the player ends up repeating the same boring task over and over for small incremental awards. I have already mentioned "the *grind* earlier in the chapter, but it can occur in other ways as well. A good example can be found in enemy placement. For example, in a first person shooter, if the same enemy guards every pickup, the task of dispatching that enemy to gain the pickup becomes very boring, very quickly. Constantly repeating the same task for the same gain is a sure-fire recipe for boring the player witless. Instead variation needs to added, by diversifying the challenge, even if the basic components stay *the same*. The challenge can be repeated but possibly with variations in

- enemy numbers,
- enemy arms,
- strategic positioning,
- player arms,
- pickup location,
- time limit.

And so it goes. There are uncounted ways of adding variation of this kind. Doing so allows the level designer to scale content and difficulty level to a large degree. This can go quite far and can allow the player to be taught different ways of approaching the same problem. (How to get the award.) This makes it possible to stave off player boredom with a repetitive task, while at the same time teaching new gameplay mechanics.

Avoid frustration

Don't promise the player a fat juicy carrot and then just end up repeatedly bashing that player with a stick. This is another instance where rewards need to be balanced against the effort needed to obtain them. It is frustrating if it is too hard to get a gameplay award. And there is a point where any reward is too little for the enormous effort needed to obtain it. It is worth noting that many level designers, especially those just beginning, err badly in this department. Challenge levels don't scale indefinitely; in fact, quite early on, difficulty starts to become a turn-off, unless skill keeps pace with it. If your level design is based upon a concept of elite Yoda-master level skills, you have effectively turned off the majority of your players. These are players who will probably *never play your game again*, and they will tell others not to buy it. It is simply not in the contract between level designer and audience that the audience can only enjoy the game after unbelievable skill levels have been reached. Or at least this is the case in most games. There are exceptions, like certain types of shoot-em-ups where this difficulty is part of the core gameplay. And even in these games, there is still an acceptable[29] level of difficulty and an unacceptable one. Generally, it is better to think of *interesting* challenges, rather than of difficult ones. Difficulty is just one of many ways to keep a challenge interesting.

Submission and Release in Level Design

Earlier in this chapter, we saw that at times people are happy to submit to an authority they normally would not recognize.

Application

So far so good, but does this have anything to do with level design? Well, surprisingly, it does. This agreement between parties to temporarily allow a reward system of submission and release is clearly recognizable in the contract between artist and audience. Don't we submit to the whim of the writer or the wishes of the movie director? Even in the non-passive context of a video game, we still submit to the same principle, because there is the promise of a reward on the other end. Sometimes we can be held or a long time, without complaining, in a state in which we normally would not find ourselves, because the artist is assured and strong in his or her craft. I will return to this principle of an agreement, or contract between artist and audience, several times in this book, as it can lead to useful applications in creative expression, and particularly in level design.

Trust in the Machine

The most important aspect of this dynamic is the fact that players are happy to be led by the level designer if they trust the design not to betray them. This can be *overt* — players know and acknowledge that they are submitting. Or it can be *covert* — players are not aware that a direct effort in this regard is being made.[30]

---

[29] Chapter 8, "Immersion," will explore in greater detail the required balance between difficulty and skill levels through an examination of "Flow Theory."

[30] Other than the fact that they are aware that they are playing a game.

Overt submission

In the case of *overt submission*, trust is lost if the situation does not result in some tangible bonus or reward. (The mission needs to end in some form of success, or at the least in an honest chance to succeed. A tutorial needs to teach, rather than punish; and collecting all 100 gems of infinity needs to really pay off.[31] In many ways this is the same principle as discussed earlier in the area of *investment and payoff*, but it is still a useful alternative way of looking at reward systems. In this particular case, the player is aware that the game offers specific awards for specific behavior, and related gameplay tasks are actually represented as such. It would be a huge mistake to allow a situation where the player thinks that a certain outcome is guaranteed, only to find out that this no longer holds true. From this point on, trust is lost, and the player will not be able to make informed gameplay decisions.

Covert submission

Covert submission to authority is more widespread than most players realize. A lot of it is planned out early in the level design stage, since it is intended for certain things to occur, *no matter what the player decides*.[32] If players do not realize this, or if they agree not to acknowledge the fact that they are forcibly led to certain conclusions, chances are they won't resent it.

For example, a level designer may wish to teach the player how to use a certain play mechanic and therefore have devised a number of artificial encounters that act as a tutorial. Players may think they are following the request of a villager in need, while in actual terms they are gaining enough experience points to be able to wield the sword they will receive at the end of the mission. In order to present formal gameplay challenges like this in such an informal way, the challenges have to be presented through the voice of the game itself, without acknowledging the formal real-world goal of gaining X experience points or something similar. It is generally a good idea if the game "stays in character" and does not tell the player what the real reason for the task is.

Covert submission is less direct than overt submission, and therefore it is less easy to define what a betrayal of trust means. There are some definite danger areas, however. It is often a bad idea to present the player with any of the following situations:

---

[31] Perhaps by providing a nice porcelain dog? (I am kidding.)

[32] This is why, although it sounds paradoxical, it makes sense to classify this as submission. Chapter 10, which covers topics like immersion and suspension of disbelief, goes into great detail on how this works.

- Don't repeat the same covert task too many times. The player is sure to catch on sooner rather than later.
- Don't arbitrarily use this technique. It is much easier to pull off when there is a good in-game reason for doing so.
- On completion of the task, don't inform the player that it was all just a ruse. The player will feel manipulated and resent it.

These are just some general examples. There are many others, all of which depend on genre and conventions.

Empowering the Player

Unlike real life, games provide us with an opportunity to face challenges without penalties that go beyond the limits of the game itself. This is a real advantage, since it allows the player of a game to experiment with different strategies for overcoming challenges, or repeating attempts at solving the same problem. It is entirely possible for a player to face initial impossible odds, yet through repetition or experimentation, manage to finally overcome them. As level designers we are uniquely placed to provide the player with interesting challenges, as well as the tools and means to successfully overcome them. In other words, we can design levels that are geared towards player *empowerment*.

As a reward mechanism in real life, this is hard to beat, and it is no different within the virtual setting of a game. The difference in a game setting is that as level designers we can shape the actual world and the contained gameplay scenarios. We can lend a helping hand by rigging the game in favor of the player, eliminate much of the fairness inherent to real life, and provide players with multiple chances to overcome the same challenge. And we can determine much of the final reward offered to the player, sometimes including the type of empowerment that the experience rewards. To be able to wield these godlike powers wisely, we should examine these advantages a bit farther.

Shaping the World

One of the most fundamental acts that a level designer undertakes is that of *creating the environment*. It is literally a matter of *world building* and is therefore an area that has far-reaching consequences for gameplay. Crucial to this act of creation is the design of the player's *role* in the world. How does the player *interact* with the world's dynamic systems? How much control is given to the player to affect the environment? How *effective* are the powers that the player wields? The answers to these questions paint a unique gameplay experience for every individual game, from *Tetris* to *Half Life*, and what they all have in common is that they can empower or disempower the player in a variety of ways.

Rigging the game

Life's challenges tend to be fairly random. They just pop up, and we have to cope with them, regardless of our ability to do so. As level designers, however, we can tailor the players' challenges, and we can have much to say over their ability to deal with them. In most cases, we can and should make sure that the fix is in, and that the game is slightly rigged in favor of the player. The player finds just the right keys to open just the right doors. The player has just enough training to be able to just win the tennis tournament. The ambush area features just enough cover for the player to make a fighting escape. Often, we can engineer these moments in such a way that the player makes the key decisions, or is tricked into thinking so,[33] thus deepening the sense of empowerment.

Keeping it fair

Most people are painfully aware of the fact that life is not inherently fair. We want it to be, and sometimes the outcomes of our life's challenges are pleasingly positive, but just as often they simply aren't. This is why we often seek out challenges that can guarantee a fair outcome. Video game challenges fall in that category. As designers, we can facilitate players in this wish by making sure that we keep the challenges they face firmly in the realm of fairness. We have the power to create a world where taking action *does* mean taking control of one's destiny.

Allowing the player to cheat

Although we can add a sense of fairness to gameplay, on the other hand, there is nothing wrong with us *allowing the player to cheat*. I don't mean cheating in the sense of breaking existing rules, and we can't let the player rewrite code. But we can present situations, such that the player can approach them in ways that the real world doesn't allow. For example, say we create a jumping puzzle where failure means that players will fall a long way down, normally to their death. However, nothing prevents us from placing a trampoline at the bottom of the drop, which bounces the player back to the start of the jumping sequence. We might engineer a fight sequence to take place in a location where the player is less vulnerable and can approach the fight from a position of strength that is normally absent, perhaps by giving the player access to a shielded vehicle. We can even engineer situations where the player can attempt to do something like stealing

---

[33] I will return to this theme of *benign deceit* several times throughout the book.

an item from a museum and make the price of failure much lower than in reality. In this case, tripping an alarm can be temporary, and the museum security would reset after five minutes, no matter how many times the player trips the alarm.

The final reward

The sense of empowerment after overcoming an interesting challenge is rewarding in and of itself. This alone is sufficient grounding to make it a useful reward mechanism. Additionally however, we can reward the player with enhanced means to *exercise* power, or with an environment that itself is easier to control, as a form of *literal empowerment*. These kinds of awards can be quite literal. The player may receive an upgraded weapon or gain access to a level's security systems. Subtler methods may be employed as well. For example, the player's relationship with non-player characters (NPCs) can change for the better, or some player skill can be enhanced from now on, making it easier to deal with future challenges. Whatever the reward may be, in this particular reward system, it is important that the player ends up feeling empowered in some way that matters.

Social Dynamics in Level Design

In the earlier section on isolation and social reinforcement, we have seen that these social principles can both reward and punish, depending on the context in which they are used. As in real life, in level design this is something that is not always clear to the player. Sometimes these principles can be quit subtle, but that does not necessarily take away from their impact. In other circumstances this principle can be the central one of the design and may be clear to anybody involved. Either way, social dynamics can be of the utmost importance to level designers and can be used as strong and important reward systems.

Multiplayer Aspects

In multiplayer games, the social dynamics we have discussed cannot help but come to the fore. By their very nature, multiplayer games need to be conducive to social reward systems. Therefore, the level design has to incorporate this where it can, to support the game's design. This can be done in diverse ways and on many levels of sophistication. The question, as always, has to be "what are my level design *goals*?" In this case, some of the answers may lie in areas dealing with issues as diverse as *spatial considerations, fostering group interactions*, or conversely, by enforcing *social bottlenecks*. (The latter case shows that even in multiplayer games, temporary isolation can be a positive factor.) All of these examples are elements that can occur in real life and are easily adopted or translated into level design theory. Let's take a closer look.

Spatial considerations

Have you ever seen a group of school children enter one of those mazes made of hedges, which are often built in the garden of some castle or ancient mansion? It is hardly a coordinated and cohesive affair. In fact, if the children are too young, it may lead to some rather distraught scenes. What only moments ago was a nice group affair is now a disjointed and confused scene, filled with individual accounts of fear and dismay.[34] The maze, while conducive to individual exploration, or at least to use by small numbers of people, ceases to be enjoyable if the group becomes too large and is expected to stay together. Imagine what would happen if the group consisted of hundreds of people!

If we translate this scenario into a typical gameplay one, we get a similar need for spatial consideration. Depending on the size of the game, it is likely that the gameplay space itself needs to take special steps to support the game' social dynamics. For example, a game that requires large groups of people to explore old ruins can be made much more enjoyable if the ruins themselves allow for this by providing wide and high corridors and large rooms. This means groups can travel together and intermittently take stock of the situation by being able to gather en masse in a single room, without anybody being left behind or outside.

Fostering group interaction

A classic way of strengthening communities is by involving them in some kind of group task that benefits the whole. This is especially true if the group can perform a task much more effectively than a collection of individuals. Take for instance a support group for parents with children who suffer from diabetes. All the individual parents may have much knowledge of some of the issues and have developed coping mechanisms that are helpful to them some of the time. Task them to improve things collectively, and it becomes clear that the support group however allows them to pool the information and knowledge and make it available to all other parents. They can set up a network that can cover for parents with specific needs, set up an information network, lobby the government as a pressure group, and so forth. Not only is this group much more effective than a collection of individuals; it can also forge real bonds of social reinforcement because others in the group understand the individual needs and problems and can react to them.

---

[34] Ok, perhaps it is not quite *that* bad, but it could have been!

If social reinforcement is a desired result of the level design, it makes sense to foster similar types of situations, where the whole can be more effective than the individual parts. Since we can author specific challenges and scenarios within the level design, it is within our power to create challenges that require group solutions or at least are more effectively handled by people working together. Furthermore, this can be done in such a way that it strengthens an online community.[35] This can happen in multiplayer games ranging from team-based first person shooters like *Counter Strike*,[36] which is best played on levels where a well-trained clan can cover big parts of the map strategically by communicating well and assigning supporting duties, or in games like *Gears of War*,[37] where the level design is geared towards a separation of tasks that are vital in order to achieve a common goal. In both cases the level design is crucial in fostering positive social reinforcement by providing gameplay scenarios that require or encourage this.

Social bottlenecks

Sometimes in a busy multiplayer environment, the constant human interaction, or worse, constant attacks or abuse, can become too much. Sometimes it is fun to be a loner, to save the girl as a unique hero, or to just collect one's thoughts. Or sometimes it *is* better to serve the group through individual actions. This makes the act of breaking away from the group or the masses a positive and can be seen as a reward in its own right.

This does not mean that it cannot be done while in the service of the greater communal good. The level designer can use *social bottlenecks*, for lack of a better term, that provide gameplay opportunities for individuals. A sniper may be able to find a lone perch on top of a building and hold off an advancing group of enemies while his friends make an escape. The sniper is sure to enjoy a great deal of social reward when he or she rejoins the group later on when they are safe. A scout can forge ahead unseen by the enemy and report on the best route forward. Plenty of other examples exist, but the main point is that it helps to think about these principles early on, as they can be just as rewarding as group interactions.

Single-Player Aspects

It may seem a bit odd to talk about social dynamics and single-player games. Aren't these games played in solitude, i.e. the opposite from a social dynamic?

---

[35] However, this tends to happen as a consequence anyway.

[36] Developed by Valve Software.

[37] Developed by Epic Games.

This is true to a degree; the player is not with any other *people* while playing the game. Nonetheless, this does not mean that social dynamics and social reward systems cannot have an impact in *the absence* of people. Two important topics present themselves: the player can still be exposed to non-player characters (NPCs) and the player can still be rewarded by, or subjected to, rewarding situations *derived from solitude.*[38]

NPCs

Just because the other people in the game are digital doesn't mean that they cannot have an impact, or more to the point, that they cannot be subject to the systems we described in multiplayer games. This means that spatial considerations, fostering group interaction, and social bottlenecks are still techniques and areas that can be explored. NPCs may not be as intelligent or many-layered as real people, but that is in many ways beside the point. What matters is that they still need space to maneuver, can work more effectively as a group, and can be subject to social bottlenecks.

Where NPCs differ from human characters is that the level designer can control them. While in a multiplayer situation the level designer needs to create an environment that is conducive to the people themselves creating socially rewarding interactions, in a single-player game, the game the designer is able to determine or predict many of the actions of the NPCs. The designer therefore can design specific gameplay scenarios that are socially rewarding. This is an important advantage to have as a designer, as it means the design is not dependent on the fickle nature of real people.

The player can even form relationships with NPCs. It is possible for a level designer to foster player bonding with non-player characters, in the absence of real people to bond with. NPCs can at times provide a similar function to real players, sometimes with surprisingly strong results. One of the best ways to do so is by letting the player invest emotionally in the non-player character, as well as giving the NPC a direct gameplay function. Giving the player the proverbial puppy to care for can provide direct gameplay gains when the puppy grows up to be a fiercely loyal guard dog.

Solitude and isolation in single-player games

Sometimes the absence of a thing makes it more powerful in the mind of a person. Think of becoming homesick or missing a loved one while at work. Or in a slightly more ominous scenario, imagine being locked up and awaiting an inter-

---

[38] Often presented as a contrast to social interaction.

rogator. Imagine traveling through the ruins of an ancient culture, or through a city mysteriously devoid of any occupants, even though there are signs of recent habitation everywhere. These are all examples of social dynamics being in play in situations of complete solitude, a paradoxical but real situation.

Even in single-player games that are normally filled with NPCs, there are very direct advantages to providing opportunities for solo gameplay. Solitude can provide breathing space that allows the player to form new social strategies. Eventually it can even engineer a situation where the player misses the company of others, thus creating a mechanism that reinforces bonding the next time the player meets an NPC.

Catharsis and Level Design

We have discussed earlier when people come out of extended periods of enduring some kind of hardship, or engaging in an extreme challenge, this can lead to a very strong release or purging of emotions. Together with the resulting positive feelings, for example a sense of renewed purpose, empowerment, and revitalization is often referred to as *catharsis*. This cathartic effect is a recognized outcome in many situations and can even form the basis of formal reward systems. This makes it an interesting subject for level designers, since we may be able to use some of these principles to create emotional feedback mechanisms for our levels.

Before we continue examining how this can work, I would like to show an example of how the principle has been successfully used in filmmaking and see if the use in another art form can give us knowledge applicable to our own craft. The best example I can think of is found in the film language developed by Alfred Hitchcock throughout his career. Hitchcock is famous for many reasons, but chief among them is his particular use of *suspense*.

Alfred Hitchcock and Suspense

Hitchcock was a past master at manipulating an audience's experience, and his influence also reaches other chapters in this book, including Chapter 13[39] with regard to set pieces. But in this chapter, we are going to look at the rather nuanced fashion in which he used tension and release in a way that was revolutionary in its time.

A key aspect to the success and effectiveness of a Hitchcock movie is the use of *suspense* to captivate the audience. Suspense in filmic terms is the technique whereby the director creates a large amount of tension in the audience, but then

---

[39] In the section on "Making Your World Memorable."

waits a certain amount of time before allowing the tension to be resolved. This state in which the audience is waiting for a resolution is what we call suspense. While in this state of suspense, the audience will be highly focused and receptive to onscreen actions.

Compare these two scenes:

Scene 1:

A train is racing across the tracks. We can see that it is filled with passengers. The camera *zooms* in on a family scene, two parents and a child sitting around a table in a carriage. The parents are talking while the child is playing with a toy train, making it crash and providing the appropriate sound effects himself. The couple now seem content to look at their son playing with the toy, they smile at each other. Clearly, they are happy. Suddenly, the carriage lurches, people scream loudly, and mayhem ensues. All of a sudden there is quiet, the camera zooms out, and we see that the train has stopped on a bridge that seems partially collapsed. It is hanging over the edge of the broken bridge, precariously balanced!

This scene may be effective[40] as it stands and cause fright out of a sense of surprise. I even included a small amount of foreshadowing through the child's play with the toy train. Let's see what happens if we introduce the element of suspense:

Scene 1 v.2:

A grim-faced man is connecting wires to a small box and sweating profusely. It slowly becomes clear that he is setting up a timer, one that is linked to a large amount of explosives. *Cut to:* a family scene, two parents and a child sitting around a table. The parents are talking while the child is playing with a toy train, making it crash and providing the appropriate sound effects himself. *Cut back to:* the man with the bomb. We can see more of the environment around the man. He is attaching the timer and the charge to a large pillar. We can now see that there are many other charges connected to the same timer, attached to other pillars. *Cut to:* the family we have seen earlier. The boy is still playing his train crash game. The camera reveals that the family is seated within a train carriage. *Cut back to:* the man with the explosives. We see he is ready with his work. He checks his watch and looks at the timer.

The camera zooms out to show that the explosive charges and timer have been attached to a very high and large train bridge. Furthermore,

---

[40] Although perhaps not a masterful piece of script writing.

we can see the plume of a train appearing further down the tracks. A train is approaching. *Cut to:* the family in the train. It is now clear that the family is heading for disaster, together with everybody else on the train! *Cut back to:* the man with the explosives, who is now hiding behind some rocks with the timer, watching the approaching train. A figure approaches slowly from behind (a policeman) and suddenly lunges for the timer, trying to wrestle it from the bomber. A struggle ensues. *Crosscut several times between the fighting men and the approaching train.* The policeman is losing the struggle and the bomber is nearly able to retrieve the timer. *Cut to:* a large explosion; debris flies through the air. *Cut to:* the approaching train.

Suddenly, the carriage lurches, people scream loudly, and mayhem ensues. All of a sudden there is quiet. The camera zooms out, showing that the train has stopped on a bridge that seems partially collapsed. It is hanging over the edge of the broken bridge, precariously balanced! The bomb exploded early and the train was able to stop just before plummeting down the now-broken bridge. *Cut to:* the family in the carriage, clearly shaken but unhurt. The boy is still clutching his toy train.

Despite the laughably clichéd content of the second scene, it illustrates clearly how much extra tension, depth, and meaning can be added through the use of suspense. For a long period, the film is able to heighten the tension in the audience, drawing its complete focus onto the onscreen action. This audience is finally rewarded for enduring the suspense by a strong and enjoyable resolution to the tension. This is a clear example of a practical reward system employed to achieve greater artistic impact.

Including the audience

This was by no means a new technique, even when Hitchcock was making his films. But what made much of Hitchcock's work special was that he added an extra dimension to the use of suspense by giving the audience more information than the protagonist onscreen, and extending the duration of suspense. Since the audience cannot alter the events onscreen, this allowed for a large amount of tension to be created, leading to a subsequent powerful resolution.[41]

Hitchcock was very aware of the power of this technique and made it a vital part of his filmmaking. He was notably successful in incorporating audience

---

[41] This resolution does not have to be a positive one. If it is rewarding for the audience, it may well be a disturbing or frightening one, or whatever the artist finds appropriate.

knowledge into a scene, meaning that the audience knows more about the on-screen situation than the protagonist, which creates even more tension and suspense. A typical Hitchcock classic where this occurs is *Rear Window*,[42] where at a key moment the viewer is allowed to see things unfold while the protagonist is asleep.

This principle has become so well known that scenes or entire films are now is referred to as being *Hitchcockian*, and many famous directors have taken the old master's lessons and incorporated them into their own style. Brian de Palma is a director who comes to mind who has often used Hitchcockian suspense in his own movies.[43]

What this kind of suspense shows us is that it is possible to use the principle of catharsis, the release of emotions after enduring a lengthy and serious challenge, to create sophisticated artistic techniques. If it can be done in film, it may well be possible in level design.

Suspense, Catharsis and Level Design

Suspense works as a technique of a cathartic reward system by using a key aspect of it, namely the endurance of a challenge over time. It actively sets out an exceptionally challenging[44] situation and artificially extends its duration, *suspending* the outcome until the director feels that maximum emotional impact can be reached in the moment of release. The other main components are *challenge* and *release*. Let's examine these three in level-design terms.

Exceptional challenge

Catharsis works differently from other reward mechanisms in level design because of the nature of the challenge necessary to produce the desired emotional release at the end. The challenge has to be one that goes beyond the expected and actually tests the player's ability, and his or her will to cope with something on a deeper level than regular game mechanics. This is an extremely difficult thing to pull off well and one of the more dangerous techniques in level design. The problem is that is easy to create something that is extremely challenging, but not so easy to make that challenge one that players are willing to finish. Get the balance wrong, and the player will just stop playing in disgust and never come back to the game. Why would players have to put up with fighting some unbe-

---

[42] Paramount, 1956.

[43] His film *Body Double* comes to mind, and in fact it can be seen as an ode to Hitchcock.

[44] To the audience.

lievably strong opponent that just kills them when even one small mistake is made? Whatever the level designer's plan is for challenge, a number of considerations have to be taken into account. It helps if the player *is motivated* to take on the challenge, the challenge itself *makes sense*, and it looks at the beginning of the challenge like there is a *chance of success*.

Motivation. Why cross a desert if it is known that it will be a gruesomely hard experience? Why single-handedly take on a whole gang of dangerous criminals? Why decide to go into the awful dungeons that are clearly haunted? If all of these challenges deliver on the seriousness of the challenge that they imply, a good answer to these questions is needed. The level designer can answer them by providing a good *motivation* for the player to adopt. The stronger the motivation, the more willing the player becomes to accept an exceptional challenge. A player may not want to put up with a long and extremely dangerous trek through a miserable wasteland, but will become totally committed to doing so if it is to stealthily follow a group of thugs who have kidnapped the player's favorite in-game companion.

Nonarbitrary and focused gameplay. Once a degree of focus is attained through providing the right motivation, the player still needs to be confronted with actual challenging gameplay. To keep that focus in place, it helps if the gameplay is immediately linked to the motivation of the challenge itself. It helps if the actions required are somehow logically linked to the main task at hand and not blatant arbitrary hoops to jump through, put in place by the designer.

Viable strategies. Although moments of despair and futility can be allowed to creep into the challenge, it is vital that at the start of the challenge the player is not overcome with a sense of hopelessness. The aim of the exercise is to lead players to catharsis, not to immediately put them off. This means that it is important to make sure that the player thinks it is worth proceeding. To do that, the level designer has to provide the player with viable strategies for progress. This doesn't have to be a strategy for success; in fact, it can be as humble as allowing the player to follow an overwhelmingly strong foe and ponder what can be done.

Suspended resolution

Now that an exceptional challenge has been created and the player is committed to taking it on, the level designer needs to make sure that the challenge plays out over a sufficient amount of time. It is of no use creating a difficult situation that can be resolved in ten seconds, as this does not provide enough of a test. The player will either feel lucky or simply not challenged after all. Instead, just as in Hitchcockian suspense, the challenge grows in meaning and impact if extended through time. Feelings of panic and doubt can come into play during this ordeal, but they can be taken away again by a sense of progress, the addition of new viable strategies, and small successes. This resulting extended gameplay works as a pressure cooker where the player's need for a resolution starts building up and provides the energy for a sufficient emotional response at the time of release.

Release (Catharsis)

Finally, now that the player has been guided to a moment where a release of tension can occur, it is very easy to forget that it has to be a *rewarding* release of tension. This can be done in several ways, but it is vital that it is done, or the whole exercise would end up feeling futile and depressing to the player.[45] Rather than risking this, the level designer needs to make sure that the rewards and the accompanying feelings of catharsis are strong enough. This can be done by making the method of release really satisfying, for example by providing a particularly enjoyable gameplay scenario that allows the player to overcome the challenge. It can also be helped by providing an extremely positive outcome, for example by giving the player a long-coveted item, or restoring an emotional bond with a previously lost companion. There are countless ways of rewarding the player, but each level designer must make sure that this indeed happens. If chosen correctly, the resulting emotional release will create a game moment that the player will cherish for a long time to come.

Associated Dangers

Catharsis is a dangerous technique to use in level design, yet it is a tempting one because the potential reward is so high. What the level designer needs to understand is that the technique easily breaks one of the level design fundamentals, namely making sure that the skill level and challenge are in balance. Frustrate players long enough with difficult gameplay and they will leave the game for good. And the nature of the extended challenges we are discussing here is by definition frustrating, as the resolution desired by the player is purposefully suspended by the level designer. Tread carefully!

Furthermore, as in all art forms, the artist has a certain amount of responsibility to the audience. In this case the responsibility is not trivial, as we are talking about highly manipulative techniques used to elicit an emotionally strong response. This does not invalidate the technique, but it should at least prompt

---

[45] Another chance to lose a player forever.

the artist to check to make sure that no ethical lines are crossed. It is not up to me to suggest where these lines lie, but I do think that the question should be asked by level designers who find themselves in this situation

Practice

Example 7.1: Investment and Payoff— Awarding Exploration

Summary

A basic reward mechanism that all levels should feature is one of investment and payoff. The player should not only be rewarded for their efforts, but the rewards should be proportional to the amount of effort required to do something. This applies to many aspects of gameplay, including exploration.

Game Genre

Most games where the player can explore an environment.

Goals to Achieve

- Encourage explorative gameplay.
- Provide subtle direction.
- Provide proportionate rewards.

Description

(Example type: Original)

Abandoned house. When choosing a setting that rewards exploration gameplay, it is worth taking a moment to think of something that really speaks to the imagination of the player. This is a nice general goal to maintain, but it is essential in the case of exploration gameplay, as we have to create an environment in which the player's imagination leads them to explore.

An example of such an environment can be a grand abandoned old house. The concept immediately puts certain images and desires in the mind of the player: images that can be incorporated into the level design, based on exploration gameplay principles.

House areas. We can list areas in the level that are subsequently more and more off the beaten track, but can yield bigger rewards, both in terms of in-game items that can be found and of new interesting areas that the player can discover (the latter can function as a reward in its own right):

- corridors,
- main rooms,
- secondary rooms,
- locked rooms,
- hidden cupboard,
- out of reach attic (pull down ladder),
- locked basement,
- secret passageway,
- secret garden.

These are all easily incorporated into subtle and imaginative level design scenarios. Faint footsteps on a dusty floor can lead to a hidden cupboard. Locked rooms are a clear invitation to explore and find a master key. A locked basement demands to be accessed one way or another. A secret garden in the middle of a folly maze can yield real revelations.

Each of these examples can reward the player in one way or another, but they are all subject to explorative gameplay. If the player is willing to put in the effort, then he or she can uncover deeper and more exciting secrets and be rewarded in the process.

Further Notes

It is always useful when thinking of a setting for this kind of gameplay to take this into account. Is it easy to provide deeper and deeper layers of exploration? If the answer is yes than the level design process should be significantly easier.

Example 7.2: Escapism—Safe Haven

Summary

Providing escapism can operate as a strong reward system in its own right, and can appeal to people at a very pure level. Few things are as human as the occasional wish to get away from things, to escape from the troubles of our lives. Although games are often wrongly derided for this, we should celebrate the fact that game levels can be a fantastic vehicle for achieving this escape.

Game Genre

The technique is suitable for use within specific levels or a dedicated level that functions as a hub for all other levels.

Goals to Achieve

- Provide a reward mechanism that uses escapist desires to be effective.
- Incorporate this directly into the level design.
- Tie this into other uses, like providing a practice space for the player.
- Incorporating exploratory or other rewards into the general setup.

Description

(Example type: General)

The extendable safe haven. If a level can feature a safe house or an otherwise safe area (for example, one that can function as a hub), the level designer has a good opportunity to create an area that fulfills the desire for escapism. This is done by creating an area the player returns to regularly, at will or otherwise, in which no harm can befall the player. Instead, it is a safe place in which the player can indulge in exploration, strategize, practice skills, store loot, and enjoy a rewarding environment. Other uses can be added as well.

The safe haven—let's take a fenced off forgotten industrial area as an example—can be made into an *extendable* safe haven by treating it as a playground and a home base that features rewards that get slowly unlocked. In this example, the player can start in a single building at ground level where they can store loot and decide what to do next. Subsequently, throughout progressing through the level (or through a hub for all levels), the player will acquire additional skills, abilities and equipment, which can be used to extend the safe haven. New athletic abilities can make the player reach high places that were previously out of reach, including a new building with new secrets to discover. New equipment, like a blow torch or a fence cutter, can open up previously locked areas. The more the player progresses, the more environmental rewards they may achieve, like great panoramic views, finding new creatures to interact with and other rewards. As long as the whole area provides an entirely safe playground for these principles, the chances are that it will feel like an escapist retreat or playground.

Further Notes

This is a setup that has been used in a number of games, but is especially well implemented in the *Tomb Raider*[46] games, where the safe house is actually Lara Croft's in-game house.

---

[46] Published by Eidos Interactive.

Example 7.3: Giving the Player What Whey Want—Wish-Fulfillment

Summary

Similar to escapism, wish-fulfillment identifies a desire in the player and fulfils it. This desire can be created, however, which makes it a viable technique to use in level design.

Game Genre

This technique is suitable for most games.

Goals to Achieve

- Create a desire in the player.
- Build the desire up to a degree that it can become a real reward if fulfilled.

Description

(Example type: Existing game)

The most effective way of providing wish-fulfillment in a level is by creating and then building up a desire or by strengthening an existing one. In this example we do this by confronting the player with something desirable all the way through a level, and making sure that that desire is granted only when this has the greatest impact.

"Wouldn't It be cool if?" Every gamer has moments when they wish they could do something, or experience something in a level, that they can't for one reason or another. This technique is based on the idea that the player is *led* to think this, only to be extremely pleasantly surprised when they can do it after all.

So, the object of this technique is to create a desire that may seem out of reach but can be fulfilled after all. The exact subject of the desire is completely fluid and depends on the game and the specific level.

Some great examples are found in a few very famous games (no coincidence, in my opinion). In *Half Life 2: Episode 2*[47] the player is confronted with an extremely powerful AI companion, a robotic sidekick named Dog. Dog is shown early on in the game to be extremely strong. (This goes back to a previous installment of the game.) The creature helps the player out on a few occasions, show-

---

[47] Published by Buka Entertainment, developed by Valve Corporation, released October 10, 2007.

ing prodigious strength and ability. The player slowly starts to wish for DOG to be able to do more than provide sporadic help, and a subtle wish enters the player's mind that it would be really cool if DOG were pitched against one of the game's super powered opponents. This never happens, however, and it stays a wish in the player's head every time they see DOG. Until suddenly, this *does* happen when the AI creature suddenly reappears when the player really needs him and gets into a fight with an enormous robotic tripod creature, known as a Strider. The resulting fight is pure wish fulfillment.[48]

Further Notes

Including moments like this can be combined with the need for set pieces and memorable moments in a game. Get a few of these right, and players will fondly remember the game.

Example 7.4: Social Reinforcement through Codependency

Summary

Cooperative multiplayer games rely on groups of players enjoying a game together. Some of this can occur naturally, but there is much we can do to make our levels foster social interactions. A strong example of this comes out of engineering a level environment where codependency leads to positive social reinforcement.

Game Genre

This technique is suitable for cooperative multiplayer games.

Goals to Achieve

- Reward cooperative play.
- Provide a level design set piece based on cooperative principles.
- Teach the player the value of communication.

---

[48] This moment was so successful that it has been turned into a poster available from Valve's online store: http://store.valvesoftware.com/productpages/prints/product_ HL2DogvStriderPoster.html.

Description

(Example type: Original)

A cooperative multiplayer game's core game design should be such that social interaction is rewarded, and in most cases this goal is met in basic gameplay decisions. Players may share resources, commands can be given to a whole group, or group attacks can be subject to damage multipliers.

This is all valid and on its own can do much to reach the game's desired goals, but the level design needs to provide a context for the cooperative actions and enhance them or instigate them when possible. This can be done by providing the players with challenges that are only solvable, or are better solvable, by players working together in concert. The idea is to create a sense of codependency where players need to be aware of each other and fulfill roles that support the group as a whole.

Codependent group defense. In this scenario the players need to defend a specific area—let's say a base—against an attack or invasion of sorts that is coming in waves from all directions. Codependency is guaranteed if the base cannot physically be defended by a collection of isolated individuals, but requires a group working together, in constant communication with each other.

Imagine that the players can defend their base through the use of turrets, which are mounted with the only weapons strong enough to stop the invaders. There is, however, only a limited number of turrets available, too few to cover the entire base, and they are very slow to be redeployed. The only way that the defending players can position the turrets in time to repel the waves of attack is by receiving advance notification of the directions from which the attacks are coming. To do so, a number of players will have to leave the base, scout out advancing enemies, and report their locations back to the base.

To create an even deeper sense of codependency, we can make the scouting job too dangerous for one player, and instead require a guard to go along and protect the player while he do his scouting work.

When all the waves of attack have been stopped, all players involved will have individual stories on how they helped the group as a whole, which in turn will yield a large sense of accomplishment both on an individual level and on a group level.

Further Notes

This is a specific set piece that requires the level designer to plan and orchestrate the gameplay to a certain degree and make sure that players understand what their roles are. Easier implementations can be construed that employ the same principles but are less dependent on polish and extra level design work: for example, a t-junction where two players need to cover each other's backs, or a bottleneck where players need to perform various diverse tasks simultaneously in order to progress.

Immersion

8

The concept of immersion constitutes an interesting metaphor. It brings to mind the sensation of being immersed in water or some other fluid. When immersed we are completely enveloped, and in many ways it speaks of an all-encompassing experience. We speak of being immersed in a story or being immersed in work. When this occurs, we temporarily exchange our wide view of the world around us for one that employs a very narrow gaze or focus. There are many ways this state can be reached, but the one that is of most interest to us within the context of this book is the state of immersion reached through artistic constructs, although I will touch on other forms of immersion as well.

We cannot speak of this kind of immersion and immersion techniques without looking at the concept of *suspension of disbelief*, which lies at the core of these matters.

Concept

Suspension of Disbelief

George Orwell famously coined the term *double think* in his seminal dystopian novel *1984*. The concept of double think is fascinating, if initially difficult to comprehend (by definition). This is the description offered in the book[1]:

> the power of holding two contradictory beliefs in one's mind simultaneously, and accepting both of them.... To tell deliberate lies while genuinely believing in them, to forget any fact that has become inconvenient, and then, when it becomes necessary again, to draw it back from oblivi-

---

[1] George Orwell, *1984*, Penguin Books, New York, 1968, p. 171.

137

on for just so long as it is needed, to deny the existence of objective reality and all the while to take account of the reality which one denies—all this is indispensably necessary. Even in using the word doublethink it is necessary to exercise doublethink. For by using the word one admits that one is tampering with reality; by a fresh act of doublethink one erases this knowledge; and so on indefinitely, with the lie always one leap ahead of the truth.

Perhaps with the exception of politicians or the mentally ill, it is hard to understand how human beings can have this capability of holding two contradictory beliefs simultaneously. Yet without realizing it, we engage in this behavior pretty much every day of our lives. We do it when we go to the cinema, watch a play in the theater, read a book, engage in a role-playing session, or play a game. During all of these activities we readily, actively and often wholeheartedly *believe in something we know to be untrue*. We know that the people on the silver screen are actors, or that the book describes a fictitious world, yet we let ourselves be convinced of this fantasy in order to experience things we otherwise would not. We *suspend our disbelief*.

Suspension of disbelief is no less an extraordinary concept than Orwell's notion of *double think*. Both concepts rely on a human being's capacity for *make believe*, to believe in an artificial reality of our own construction, while knowing it to be false.

Cognitive Dissonance

At times this ability can be so strong that it takes us to too far, into areas where it isn't appropriate. An example of this is when it occurs within the realm of a person's worldview. In other words, it can occur outside the realm of make believe, fantasy or other accepted forms of artificiality, which is of course very dangerous. How can we make correct judgments of the world around us if we submit to contrary beliefs? The simultaneous belief in contrary facts, when exposed to evidence that threatens this belief, can lead to strange results. It can cause mental friction and conflict, which need to be resolved. When this happens we speak of *cognitive dissonance*, which has been defined as

> anxiety that results from simultaneously holding contradictory or otherwise incompatible attitudes, beliefs, or the like, as when one likes a person but disapproves strongly of one of his or her habits.[2]

---

[2] American Psychological Association (APA): cognitive dissonance (n.d.), Dictionary. com Unabridged (v 1.1). Retrieved June 02, 2009, from Dictionary.com website: http://dictionary.classic.reference.com/browse/cognitive dissonance.

What is essential to understand about cognitive dissonance is that people can force themselves to maintain the contrary beliefs by going to extraordinary lengths to reconcile their worldview with their expectation of it, which may not be factual at all. This need to fix the facts of the world around a belief system is a need that can be manipulated, and history shows us that this is often done for exploitative reasons.

The Need for Self Deception

What all this points at is that human beings have a strange capacity, and sometimes a strong need, for self-deception. (Sometimes this reaches the point of detrimental self-delusion, as cognitive dissonance shows.) Some of the origins for this phenomenon have already been discussed in Chapter 2, where it is concluded that this ability is needed to allow us to construct artificial mental arenas in which we can learn lessons, or experience environments in a safer context than reality allows us. In other words; *sometimes self-deception can be a survival skill.* This need, however, can be appealed to in ways that constitute mental manipulation.

Throughout history, but increasingly in the last century to the present, people have understood this phenomenon and used the knowledge to manipulate other human beings, sometimes with catastrophic and even genocidal results. Here is a passage of an interview with Hermann Goering:

> We got around to the subject of war again and I said that, contrary to his attitude, I did not think that the common people are very thankful for leaders who bring them war and destruction.
>
> "Why, of course, the people don't want war," Goering shrugged. "Why would some poor slob on a farm want to risk his life in a war when the best that he can get out of it is to come back to his farm in one piece? Naturally, the common people don't want war; neither in Russia nor in England nor in America, nor for that matter in Germany. That is understood. But, after all, it is the leaders of the country who determine the policy and it is always a simple matter to drag the people along, whether it is a democracy or a fascist dictatorship or a Parliament or a Communist dictatorship."
>
> "There is one difference," I pointed out. "In a democracy the people have some say in the matter through their elected representatives, and in the United States only Congress can declare wars."
>
> "Oh, that is all well and good, but, voice or no voice, the people can always be brought to the bidding of the leaders. That is easy. All you have

to do is tell them they are being attacked and denounce the pacifists for lack of patriotism and exposing the country to danger. It works the same way in any country."[3]

In this case the manipulation occurs by appealing to the human need to feel protected, through the use of propaganda. Other examples can be given where manipulation occurs by appealing to a need to protect, nurture, mate, or one of many other natural human urges.

Positive Uses

It is important to understand that the mechanisms described so far, although open to malicious manipulation, are not negative *in themselves*. There are of course many legitimate ways to use this knowledge. Techniques to enhance immersion and encourage suspension of disbelief have been practiced and honed for millennia by storytellers and other artists across many disciplines.

There is nothing sinister about a skillful storyteller enthralling an audience around a campfire. We don't resent a filmmaker for using meaningful camera angles to add strength to a scene. Cognitive dissonance, for example, can be used to create tension in a story or to engineer an audience's need to resolve within a fictional setting. Artists and entertainers rely on manipulating the audience in order to be effective, and the audience is willing to subject itself to this kind of positive manipulation. Crucial to these positive examples is that the manipulation occurs *with the consent of the manipulated*. (As opposed to, for example, political propaganda.) We could describe this process as one of *benign deceit*.

Pianist Hal Galper describes this implied understanding between artist (or entertainer) and audience as follows:

> A mutual social contract is unconsciously agreed upon between artist and audience. The conditions of this contract must be fulfilled by both performer and listener and entail emotional risk for both parties. Contrary to popular belief, most people are afraid of freedom, of "letting go." Suspension of the sense of self is a rare, pleasurable experience that is not an everyday occurrence in most people's lives. Audiences gravitate toward live performance situations because they offer a safe way to let go. However, letting go can suggest the possibility of emotional

---

[3] Gustav Gilbert, interviewing Hermann Goerring during the Nuremberg Trials in April 1946. Later published in the book *Nuremberg Diary* (G. M. Gilbert, 1961). Available at http://www.snopes.com/quotes/goering.asp.

risk because the listener's defenses are let down. Listeners, by showing up paying and paying an attendance fee, have willingly entered into an agreement with the performers. They feel comfortable with the fact that, along with other members of the audience, they've agreed to open themselves up to any influence the performers may exert upon them. As suspending one's sense of self creates a unique sense of freedom, the listener can then derive pleasure from this experience allowing themselves to be swept up by a musical performance without emotional risk. The audience has, for that moment, put the state of their emotional well-being into the hands of the performer, a responsibility the performer must accept with care.[4]

There is an underlying understanding between artist and audience that this manipulation is legitimate *as long as it is not abusive*. There are of course many instances where the boundary between abuse and legitimate artistic expression is blurred, but the principle stays intact. The disagreement between artist and audience in that case is one born of execution, not of principle.

Other Forms of Immersion

There are also non-manipulative factors at play when we study immersion. Hormones can play a great role in focusing the mind, not to speak of other chemicals like endorphins, testosterone, or adrenaline. There are many psychotropic or mind-opening drugs that can immerse a person in all kinds of immersive experiences. Crucially, these kinds of mechanisms take control away from the subject.

Then there are many other activities that can all contribute to an immersed mind. On a regular basis most of us are

- immersed in work,
- immersed in a moral conundrum,
- immersed in sport,
- immersed in beauty.

There are many more, so many that it is pointless to try to name all genres or areas where immersion can occur. More so, it is beside the point. What matters is that it is completely clear that this capacity to be immersed is deeply ingrained in the human psyche and that *it will often occur*, especially in situations where this is beneficial to us.

---

[4] Hal Galper, "The Social Contract: Presentation And Creativity," *Down Beat Magazine*, http://www.halgalper.com/13_arti/social_contract.html, December 1994.

Concept Summary

A human being's capacity for immersion and suspension of disbelief is all-pervasive and deeply ingrained in all aspects of our lives. In many cases this is a benign, even necessary phenomenon. It occurs on a daily basis on a natural and often subconscious level.

One should be aware, however, that it can also be manipulated, especially by those who understand what underlying mechanisms are at play. This can be done in amoral and illegitimate ways (without explicit approval), or this can be done with the consent of the user to create a positive experience (as in the arts). If it is done well, the various elements that allow an audience to suspend its disbelief contribute to a general sense of immersion. In effect, the artist creates a coherent virtual environment or experience in which the audience can believe. We can find this immersion in artificial environments through suspension of disbelief all throughout culture. Examples are rife and include books, films, music, and video games.

Further factors that can contribute to immersion but are independent of suspension of disbelief are also at play. These are too wide-ranging in scope to cover in one book, and they often occur outside the context of art and entertainment. Nonetheless, it is important to study them to create a deeper understanding of immersion and immersive factors, since this knowledge can help by improving or discovering new immersive techniques. What all these concepts tell us is that human beings are subject to, and have *inbuilt mechanisms* that allow them to enjoy, deeply immersive experiences.

A solid understanding of a broad scope of immersive techniques lies at the core of most aspects of level design. As level designers we have the capacity to fulfill our end of the unwritten contract between artist and audience by making sure we employ all the knowledge we have of mood manipulation without betraying the trust of our audience.

Theory

Immersion and Level Design

It is legitimate within the arts to engage in *a benign deceit* to create a positive experience for the audience. The audience knows it is being deceived but chooses to suspend its disbelief willingly, as it is part of the process of enjoying art. Or at least this is what happens if the artist is skilful enough in the necessary manipulation techniques. This is extremely relevant and applicable to level design because video games often operate as artificial worlds. We want players to believe in those worlds so that they accept as a consequence the game's formal rules.

If level design acts as a *teaching mechanism*, it helps if the pupil is willing to believe the teacher.

It is not enough for the level designer to just focus on gameplay mechanics in an isolated way. We need to be able to bind the player to the gameplay world in a manner that is not objectionable or overly coercive. We need to be able to charm players, engross them in a new universe, and make sure they *want* to spend time in it. This can be done in a positive way, by providing a beautiful or engaging environment; or just as valid, in a negative way by realizing a nightmarish dreamscape. Key to this is that we make sure that the player is willing to suspend disbelief in what clearly is an artificial reality. (In most cases, immersive gameplay will trump other elements of immersion.)

There are hundreds of ways to achieve the goal of immersion, and throughout this book we will cover a large number of basic techniques that can be adapted by any level designer. This chapter will look at a number of general principles and allow for ways of extrapolating to practical theory and application.

More on Suspension of Disbelief

I have so far spent a considerable amount of time on the topic of *suspension of disbelief*, although with regards to immersion it is not the only factor of importance. This partly comes from the knowledge that to play a game *is* to suspend one's disbelief. If this voluntary self-deceit doesn't occur, either the game isn't being played or the player is delusional and doesn't understand that the activity is in fact *a game*. This is the original conceit that is necessary to even begin talking about games, just the same as a reader knows the difference between fiction and fact, and a moviegoer or theatergoer knows the difference between drama and reality. This is more important than it may seem on the surface, where it appears as just common sense. It *is* important to explicitly contemplate this concept since, as shown in the previous chapter, it brings to the fore a number of important underlying psychological processes, all of which have direct bearing on level design.

However, there is another layer of immersion in play, which has to do with the actual content of the game. The in-game actions, events, environment, etc., are all subject to their own processes of immersion, including (but not limited to) suspension of disbelief. This type of suspension of disbelief is covered throughout this chapter, especially in the section on *game logic*, and will be extrapolated upon when appropriate. This topic is too wide ranging to be covered in its own section; instead, I will raise it as it occurs in relation to other elements, whenever they occur.

The Zone

Many classic eighties movies feature a scene where somebody, often the hero, is completely engrossed in a video game, typically played on a machine at an arcade. Take for example that seminal piece of eighties filmmaking, *The Last Star Fighter*,[5] in which the main character is so good at an arcade game that he is identified as "The Last Starfighter," an elite starship pilot destined to save the universe.

Or consider the opening scene in the film *War Games*, where Matthew Broderick displays an unmatched mastery of arcade games, foreshadowing his later conflict with, and understanding of, a pentagon computer on the verge of unleashing thermonuclear war.

I am not including these examples of eighties cinema just out of some sense of nostalgia (although I was one of those kids chained to the local arcade's game cabinets, in the town where I grew up). The reason I mention them is twofold;

1. Video game developers started to become really good at tying players to their games,[6] and gamers started to experience a state where, for prolonged periods of time, they were completely immersed in the game they were playing, often at the height of their ability.

2. Society in the eighties showed a genuine interest in this phenomenon of video-game-induced deep focus, and this fascination was reflected in countless eighties movies that have built scenes around this concept. The two previous examples are typical in that they showcase the players of games as people with extraordinary powers, echoed in their mastery of video games. These players were able to stay "in the zone" for extended periods of time.

This jargon of being "in the zone" became widespread[7] and accepted, and was subject to serious study and research. *The zone* is a concept where players are kept in a completely immersed and entertained state of mind by the game they are playing. The interaction between game and player is completely harmonious, the game is working well, and the player is playing well. Often this leads to play-

---

[5] Directed by Nick Castle, distributed by Universal/Lorimar, a joint-venture (original release), released on July 13, 1984.

[6] To make sure they kept pumping quarters into the game.

[7] Previously limited mostly to the field of sports.

ers performing at the peak of their abilities, which is often referred to as being "in the zone." The concept goes further than degrees of proficiency, however. It may be more accurate to describe the zone as a place where the player is utterly *engaged* with the game, or in other words, a place where the player is *completely immersed* in the game. A place where as level designers we would like to lead players, and keep them for as long as possible.

An Introduction to Flow Theory

Much that is known about the concept of being in "the zone" actually comes from "flow theory," a concept pioneered by Mihaly Csiksczentmihalyi, which has many implications for level designers.

Optimal experiences

Flow theory was originally linked to the study of happiness. Through years of academic research and interviews with thousands of people around the world, Professor Csiksczentmihalyi has been trying to determine how people experience happiness and what causes this state of being. One of the terms he uses in his books is *optimal experience*. He describes the happiness inherent in optimal experiences as follows:

> Getting control of life is never easy, and sometimes it can definitely be painful. But in the long run optimal experiences add up to a sense of mastery—or better, a sense of participation in determining the content of life—that comes as close to what is usually meant by happiness as anything we can conceivably imagine.[8]

These optimal experiences describe *life experiences,* and the professor does not differentiate between activities that can cause this happiness to occur. The source can be any experience, ranging from work to childrearing to survival sports. What is more important is finding out what makes these (optimal) experiences enjoyable.

Elements of enjoyment

Throughout many interviews, and from further research, the professor found that all respondents, regardless of culture, location, financial status, etc., shared a number of "elements of enjoyment" that are fundamental[9] to being happy. He has formulated eight principle *elements of enjoyment*:

---

[8] Mihaly Csiksczentmihalyi, *Flow: the Psychology of Optimal Experience,* Harper Perennial, New York, 1991, p. 4.

[9] Although not all of them need to be experienced simultaneously.

1. The activity is challenging and requires skill.
2. It requires full concentration (action and awareness merge).
3. It must provide clear goals.
4. The task undertaken must provide immediate feedback.
5. The person involved stays concentrated on the task at hand (it removes worries of everyday life).
6. It provides a sense of control over our actions.
7. The activity involves loss of self consciousness (we lose the sense of being separate from the world).
8. The activity involves the transformation of time (hours can pass in minutes, and vice versa).

These principles of enjoyment are fundamental to happiness as optimal (life) experiences, but in practice they can easily be applied to level design, if interpreted as optimal *game experiences*. It is remarkable just how closely they can correlate with gameplay. These principles would not look out of place as a quality checklist for most levels.

When enough of these factors are in effect, the professor describes the resulting happiness as that of a person who is in a state of flow.

Csiksczentmihalyi has described being in a state of flow as follows:

> ... being completely involved in an activity for its own sake. The ego falls away. Time flies. Every action, movement, and thought follows inevitably from the previous one, like playing jazz. Your whole being is involved, and you're using your skills to the utmost.[10]

And more specifically, there is

> ... a sense that one's skills are adequate to cope with the challenges at hand, in a goal directed, rule-bound action system that provides clear clues as to how well one is performing. Concentration is so intense that there is no attention left over to think about anything irrelevant, or to worry about problems. Self-consciousness disappears, and the sense of time becomes distorted. An activity that produces such experiences is so gratifying that people are willing to do it for its own sake, with little concern for what they will get out of it, even when it is difficult, or dangerous.[11]

I would be hard pressed to find a better description of what I would consider an optimal immersive game experience, and therefore what we should aim for in

---

[10] From an interview with Wired magazine, "Go with the Flow," *Wired*, http://www.wired.com/wired/archive/4.09/czik_pr.html, September, 1996.

[11] Mihály Csíkszentmihályi, *Flow: The Psychology of Optimal Experience*, Harper Perennial, New York, 1991, p. 71.

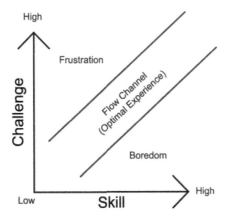

Figure 8.1. Flow channel diagram.

our level designs. This becomes even more exciting if we look at the basic mechanics at play when we look at the circumstances under which flow occurs.

Flow channel

According to professor Csiksczentmihalyi, being in a state of flow can occur when a person is participating in an activity that is balanced between the person's *ability* and the activity's *challenge level*. This is clearly illustrated in the diagram in Figure 8.1.

When the challenge is in balance with the person's skill level, that person is in the (*flow*) *zone*. But if the activity is too challenging, the subject will feel anxiety. Conversely, if the person's skill level is too high, boredom will ensue.

Flow Theory and Immersive Level Design

Just like the developers of those arcade games in the eighties, we should do our best to keep our players *in the zone* (in a state of flow), not so much to keep them pumping in quarters, but to keep them deeply *immersed* in the game. It is important to remember that

A player who is in the zone is a player who is deeply immersed.

An immersed player is a happy player, and a happy player is much more receptive to what the game has to offer. It should be clear that this makes immersion a central goal to good level design. It is not a separate aspect of level production, but a key aspect that permeates all other related areas. Flow theory can provide us with valuable insights on how to keep the player immersed in our levels and on keeping the levels as enjoyable as possible.

The Player Wants to Play

In most cases, we know that the player of the game *wants to play*. This is not as flippant as it sounds; we encounter many games in life that we are unwilling to play and that cause resentment if we are forced to do so. Examples include playing mind games at work, avoiding the bully at school, and facing one-upmanship in a socially competitive setting. With video games, however, we know that players want to play our levels, because they bought the game, borrowed it, or in one way or another took a conscious step to try out the game. This willingness to play needs to be awarded by the level designer and provides us with an excellent opportunity to bind the player to the game.

What Players Want

It sometimes pays off to give players what they want in the first level they play. There are of course many ways to do so, and there is no set way that always works.[12]

To "give them what they want" early on does not necessarily mean pampering the player, being overly nice, providing an inordinate amount of challenge, or that we can focus exclusively on any one thing. What it means is that we must respect players' choice in picking up our game, and understand why they have done so. What is it they expect or hope to gain? A certain amount of psychology is at play here; after all, we are trying to understand what is in another person's mind (not an exact science).

However, there are genre conventions that often help us determine certain desires. It is likely that in the case of a first person shooter, the player is looking forward to shooting things. A 3D adventurer may find joy in exploration, and a platform game may have to provide good jumping action. These examples are so generic that they are almost useless, but they nonetheless provide a basis of understanding to work from.

This understanding of basic player desires can lead to much subtler uses, for example in the case of a first person shooter, we may decide to withhold weapons to shoot with, but to provide a large number of targets anyway. (This is an

---

[12] Beware of designers who claim otherwise; they have developed tunnel vision, a dangerous affliction for level designers.

inversion of the principle, "do NOT give players what they want.") Later in the level, when the desire to shoot things has been amplified by this preponderance of targets, the level design can deliver in a dramatically impactful way, providing shooting action in spades. This is a dangerous method, since it can put off the player if taken to extremes. But if used correctly, it can be an incredibly powerful way of focusing the player on in-game events. As this example shows, from identifying player desire (the player wants to shoot things) a clear level design tactic has evolved that is relatively nuanced and ultimately rewarding to the player.

Other player desires will yield other techniques, but we must first understand what it is that the player wants to get out of the game. This can result in charming the player by rewarding this desire immediately, or it may not. Some games are best served by surprising the player, and others by giving players exactly what they want. But an intelligent choice can only be made by level designers if they know what the player's needs are in the first place. Either way, this is knowledge that through good application in level design is much more likely to keep the player immersed.

Temporal and Historic Grounding

It is sometimes disconcerting to enter a newly built residential area, especially if the architecture is uninspiring. This wrongness can be felt strongly in hastily erected touristy areas, or cheaply built reconstruction areas. The experience can feel slightly surreal or unsettling in its *artificiality,* and it is not always easy to explain why. In my experience, much can be explained by a noting a lack of *historical grounding.*

Normally our environment is strongly rooted in historic significance. There are either strong memories associated from our own lives, or there is evidence everywhere of past events. These include public art, architectural styles, wear and tear, and all kinds of evidence of human habitation for prolonged periods. If our environment is natural rather than man-made, there will be still more links to the past, which ground the area, such as vegetation, animal life, erosion, etc. We expect these things on both a conscious and unconscious level. When none of these elements are present, we experience a *disconnect.* The environment doesn't feel grounded in time, which causes use to feel uneasy, or at least to notice that something is lacking.

In level design, a great way to anchor players solidly into the experience is by providing them with this temporal grounding, to make sure that the game world feels *real.* After all, if the world shows evidence that it exists beyond our own actions within it, it must be real, right? Well, maybe not, but it provides a good argument for our subconscious mind that it is okay to suspend our disbelief. Any good storyteller knows that adding key details, even if not directly related to the story, makes a story come alive. A game's level, for better or for worse, has the capacity to convey a huge amount of historic information:

- Are the buildings old and abandoned, or shiny and new?
- Is the NPC aware of the player's history?
- Has there been a previous battle is this location?
- Are there boat wrecks at the bottom of the sea?
- Has anybody been up this trail?
- Whose skeleton is that?

The list is endless.

The downside of is that the level designer needs to be aware of all this information, but the upside is that it allows a large amount of control over what information is conveyed to the player. Because of this, it gives the level designer many golden opportunities to really deepen the immersion that a player feels in the level, something that should be embraced and used whenever possible. We can take a sterile and uninspiring piece of suburbia and age it artificially by making sure that the textures show age, and that the buildings have been adapted by their owners and imbued with their personality. We can have NPCs reference important past events, plant evidence of submerged subplots, add secret areas, and many other things besides. If this is done correctly we should be able to sketch out enough of an outline for the player's unconscious mind to accept the place as real. If this happens, we have achieved an important level design goal.

Non-Games Examples

This principle of historic grounding is known throughout art and entertainment and there are many established methods and philosophies related to achieving this goal. George Lucas, to take a famous example, has referred to it in the past as wanting to create a "used future."[13] He talks about giving the future a past by using props that are deliberately smudged or have been used in real life. Instead of a shiny technocratic future, this creates a more believable one, where objects look like they have always been there. This can be seen, for example, in his film *THX 1138*, which features an industrial setting where workers operate machinery that may be futuristic, but not implausibly so. The machines look like they are made to be used (and have been used) instead of being incorporated in the movie because they look sleek and stylish.

---

[13] *THX 1138: The George Lucas Director's Cut*, Special Edition, Warner Bros., 2004 (originally released by American Zoetrope in 1971).

Photography is another field that provides a unique insight to the subject. Ironically, in photography it is sometimes preferable to try to *remove* as much historical grounding as possible, to create an image that is *timeless* and doesn't *date* badly. Although this is an inversion of the principle, it showcases how powerful this concept can be. In these cases the photographer simply doesn't trust the viewer of the image to be able to interpret it without being affected by information that places the image in a temporal context!

Another good example can be found in the field of *Computer Graphic Imaging* (*CGI*), where it is important for the images to be able to blend in with real photography. CGI work tends to stand out like a sore thumb unless it is made to look used instead of shiny and new. With this example it is crucial that the imagery be grounded in time somehow, or the audience will know that the imagery isn't real, *even if they know it can never be real anyway.*

Game Logic

An important aspect of suspension of disbelief is indeed *believability.* Sometimes it is forgotten that suspension of disbelief does not mean that a level can incorporate any idea or arbitrary restriction that the level designer wants to use. This isn't because those ideas are too wild or too fantastical, but because they need to conform to the game's internal logic, or *game logic.*[14]

There are certain conceits that an audience is willing to put up with, even if they are not realistic in the real world, as long as they link into the game's reality in a logical and consistent manner. For example, take Tolkien's *Lord of the Rings*, famed for its detailed immersive world. People are perfectly happy to suspend their disbelief in magic, orcs, dwarves, and a plethora of other things that would be utterly ridiculous in the context of our real world. This is the case because these elements are part of a complete and logical set of *internal rules.* Imagine, though, that at Helm's deep, Gandalf suddenly would pull out a handgun and start shooting orcs in the kneecap while spouting sarcastic one-liners? Both the act and the behavior would be so inconsistent with the established internal rules that readers would immediately lose their suspension of disbelief and most likely abandon the book. (This behavior is perfectly acceptable, however in most Arnold Schwarzenegger action movies.)

The same principle applies to level design. Just because it is possible in a game to set up fantastical or science-fiction themed scenarios does not mean that they aren't subject to sustained and serious scrutiny by the player.

---

[14] The concept of game logic is partly determined by game and genre *conventions*, a topic discussed in detail in Chapter 7, "Towards a Shared Grammar for Level Design."

Please note that this also means that the level designer needs to be diligent in laying out the groundwork and must teach the player what the game's internal rules are, or in other words, must establish and maintain game logic.

The Game Crate

As an example, take archetypical *game crate*, used in hundreds of game levels. Let's assume that the level designer sets up a scenario where a number of crates can be pushed together to create an artificial set of stairs to reach a previously restricted area. The designer could end up with an engaging spatial puzzle. So far, so good. What needs to be remembered, though, is that this also creates an additional bit of game logic: *crates can be pushed around to create new routes within the level*. This game logic needs to be maintained, or the designer risks destroying immersion because the game world does not follow its own internal rules.

In our world of empirical evidence and scientific reason, it is reasonable to expect that our laws of physics are consistent. In a game the same needs to be true, or the player's acquired skills are unpredictable and thus useless. A logically consistent game world suggests a *"real"* game world, or at least one "real" enough to suspend players' disbelief and make them accept the presented fantasy as a coherent whole.

Some Typical Mistakes

There are many mistakes to be made, and shockingly, some of the easiest ones to avoid keep reappearing in game levels over and over again: to name a few,

- invisible barrier,
- cheating AI,
- impossible constructions,
- *deus ex machina* events.[15]

I am sure you can add many more yourself. Once the principle is recognized, it becomes clear how widespread the problem really is. It must be clear, however, that the problem does not lie with *realism*, but with those rules that apply to the specific game or genre. That is why jumping on enemy heads is perfectly viable

---

[15] "God from the machine." In classical Greek plays, gods would sometimes resolve a tricky situation through divine intervention. An actor playing a god (*deus*) would be literally lowered onto the stage by a mechanical crane (*machina*). The term now refers to an improbable intervention by the author to solve some problem, for example, the appearance of a will in a murder mystery.

in a cartoony platform game, but would make no sense whatsoever in a serious World War II shooter. The most important thing to remember is that everything must be *contextual to the type of game being made*.

Breaking the fourth wall

In theater and film, a well-known convention consists of not *breaking the fourth wall*. This means that the filmmaker or stage director does not allow the production to acknowledge the audience directly. No references can be made that allude to the fact that the world portrayed is an artificial one. The film or play thus *stays in character*. Imagine a serious film about ancient Rome where the extras can be heard discussing the superiority of sneakers over sandals, or a detective in a murder mystery discussing the fact that the audience also doesn't know who dies next. I can't think of many other ways that are better at destroying suspension of disbelief than actively making the audience aware that they are experiencing something artificial. This needs to be avoided where possible.

It is surprising, then, to find out that there is a rich tradition of people breaking this golden rule. We can go as far back as Groucho Marx winking into the camera, back hundreds of years in the past to find stage writers who employ the use of *asides*, a technique that allows for a commentator to expand on the actions onstage for the benefit of the audience.

Games themselves employ completely acceptable exceptions like tutorial text, or opening credits. Nonetheless, most of these instances consist of established game-specific conventions that we know we can ignore. However, there are examples of more blatant disregard of this rule. In the game *Metal Gear Solid*, the player is suddenly told by a psychic that he/she "saves a lot" and that elsewhere in the game the solution of a specific puzzle is to be found by finding a clue within the box art of the game! Although admittedly some players have made clear that they enjoyed these unexpected moments, many have declared their dissatisfaction at being pulled out of the game world in such a rude manner. In most cases it is best to err on the side of caution, and in my experience this is especially true in games where suspension of disbelief is important to the overall experience, which is a very large category indeed.

Ambience and Atmospherics

The proper use of ambience and atmospherics can completely transform a game's levels from feeling boring and uninspired to being completely engrossing and immersive play environments. With that in mind, one would expect much time and resources to be allocated to this, but that is unfortunately not the case in most games' development processes. The reason is that in the very finite schedule of commercial level design, the focus is on something that is *good enough*, not on something that is *very good*. This often means that due to time considerations, resources are focused on other matters, often as simple as getting levels to a shippable state. A shippable state is often a far cry from a very good level, however. It is essential for level designers to work to a sensible budget and specifications and be able to create good immersive levels from that starting point. If appropriate to the game, immersiveness needs to be part of its early spec and be incorporated into the level design.

Often it will be argued that immersiveness is always trumped by direct gameplay implementation, but that is too simplistic an approach. Can you imagine a game like *Silent Hill*[16] working well without a serious amount of time assigned to the level designers to implement levels with a good use of atmospherics and ambience? *Silent Hill 2* starts with an extended walk through the woods, without actual gameplay, yet the scene is riveting and completely immersive. It is an excellent start to the game and sets up the whole experience of irrational fear and dread very well.

Level designers should expect many arguments about an approach like this, but they must be able to fight their corner. For this to be possible, they must have a good grasp of what constitutes ambience and atmospherics. Vague as these terms may be, there is much known about them, even if it is subjective to a degree. Within the context of level design, I make a distinction between the two, where ambience is to do with *location aspects*, while atmospherics have more to do with general *mood enhancement*.

Ambience

Brian Eno, the inventor of ambient music, has the following to say on ambience:

> An ambience is defined as an atmosphere, or a surrounding influence: a tint. My intention is to produce original pieces ostensibly (but not exclusively) for particular times and situations with a view to building up a small but versatile catalogue of environmental music suited to a wide variety of moods and atmospheres.[17]

Note that he talks about music that is *part of the environment*, an important distinction that sets the music apart from a normal soundtrack. (Although a soundtrack can be made up of ambient music, in which case the two can coincide.)

---

[16] Famous survival horror game series, known especially for its disturbing atmosphere.
[17] Liner notes from the initial American release of Brian Eno's "Music for Airports / Ambient 1," PVC 7908 (AMB 001), 1978.

This direct link to the environmental spaces is crucial, and one that is greatly helpful to level designers, since they are the designers of the game's spaces, together with the art department. With that in mind, a number of immediate examples jump to the fore:

- ambient sounds,
- ambient lighting,
- particle effects[18] (steam, rain, etc.),
- props,
- fauna and flora.

These are just a number of straightforward examples that are easily identifiable but nonetheless need to be part of the overall spec.

Ambient sounds

We all know of a number of aural game clichés; on top of a mountain we hear wind, in caves we hear drips, etc. However, these kinds of straightforward implementations are not just representations of sounds that need to be picked from a list to complete a level's outstanding tasks. Recorded sounds not only have documentary qualities, they also have psycho-acoustic qualities, which means they have the ability to have an effect on the psychological interpretation of sound. Machine hum can be made to sound calming, *a purring engine*, or it can be made to sound unnerving, *an infernal machine*. This is a subtle but very powerful concept. Choosing ambient sounds smartly gives the level designer a way to manipulate player experience in a profound manner without things appearing overly directed.

(Much more on this in Chapter 11.)

Ambient lighting

Normally when we speak of ambient lighting we are talking about using the lighting naturally present in the environment, which can be natural (sunlight) or mechanical (room lights). In film and photography this is often not enough and additional lighting is added to the scene by the photographer or camera person. This artificial lighting is often recognizable as such, but there are tricks to make it appear natural or ambient. This is very relevant to level design, since all lighting in levels is artificial. The ultimate goal of lighting, beyond illuminating a scene, is to support it. Sometimes that means making sure the gameplay works well, but there is also a large part reserved for enhancing a level's ambience. This is mostly done by making sure that where possible, lighting is emitted by believable light

---

[18] A computer "particle" rendering effect that can simulate diverse phenomena like fire, rain, steam, smoke, sparks and others.

sources, from the sun to room lighting, glowing panels or monitors, or whatever else can be used for this goal. It is surprising how effective it is to exaggerate weak light sources in a room to create a natural feeling. Even if the light sources would never produce this much light, the brain gets tricked into believing it.

Particle effects

An easy way to add to the natural ambience of an environment is by logical and consistent use of *particle effects*. This can encompass anything from believable rain, smoke and fire, or the old favorite; steam coming from pipes and vents. The best use of this goes beyond the merely decorative. It can suggest much about things that aren't there (a working electricity net) or strengthen the impact of things that are present; an animated model of a train will look much better in the environment if it emits steam and smoke while sparks fly off its connection with the energy grid.

Props

Levels need to be populated as well. Look round the environment you are in right now, chances are that there are all kinds of objects scattered around. Newspapers, junk, furniture, crockery, you name it. Levels that don't include this are sterile and lacking in ambience. Even if the player doesn't know *what exactly* the problem is they will still notice that something is lacking.

It is even better if we can incorporate props into gameplay. We have seen the use of things like crates so often now that it is almost humoristic, but surely we can use other objects to achieve similar results. Props can be used for cover, missiles, barriers, rams, artificial steps and many other things. Just a single useful object can add to ambience, strategy, interactivity or symbolism... not bad for a humble prop!

Fauna and flora

It almost goes without saying that a lived in world makes for a more believable, and generally a more enthralling one. Curiously there is often more time allocated to inanimate objects, or the consequences of habitation that actual habitation itself. Incorporating elements of fauna (animal Life) and flora (plant life) can help suggest a whole eco system, and a living breathing eco system suggests a fully functioning world in which players can lose themselves.

As often in this book I want to note that there is no point trying to create an actual ecosystem, or anything even approaching that kind of scope. There is no need to do so as the player's mind can be tricked into accepting small manifestations of one as sufficient evidence that the world is "real". Showcasing elements of life that are *independent of player action*, suggest that the world only takes partial notice of the player, which suggests that the world is bigger than the player's imagination. This often subconscious realization in the player's mind is often enough to generate a strong desire to suspend disbelief, as enough evidence is presented that the game world is complex, coherent, and exists in its own right. If approached in such a manner the level designer can consciously manipulate a subconscious process that betters the player's gaming experience. A number of examples will be given in the *practice* section dealing with this topic, following the current chapter

Atmospherics

While ambience is defined as part of the environment, atmospherics are enhancements or additions to the environment or to the experience in general. Sometimes they overlap; an environment can be made to be atmospheric, often however they are very different, at least in their approach. They share the same goal however, immersing the player deeply into the gameplay experience and thus aiding a suspension of disbelief. Atmospherics can be roughly divided into *atmospheric additions, and atmospheric enhancements.*

Atmospheric additions

We speak of atmospheric additions when we add elements to the game world that are not normally native to it, in order to add to the desired atmosphere for the level. No definitive list of examples can be created for this as so many unique additions can be envisioned depending on genre, platform, level, or game type. I can however provide some typical examples.

Music

A very effective example of adding something that is not native to the game world, yet which still deepens immersion, is the use of music. One only has to look at film to see the potential impact music can have to a scene. This subject will be covered in great detail in Chapter 11.

Voiceover

The use of voiceovers in games is not without precedent and can be very effective. A good example of this can be found in ID Software's *Quake 3 Arena*, where the gameplay has been turned into a tournament sport, complete with voiceovers provided by a commentator who remarks on several in-game events.

Voiceover can be used in other game types, as well. A mystery game grounded in classic hard-boiled detective fiction may benefit from a film-noir-inspired voiceover incorporated in the levels, or a historic strategy game may include a sage-like voiceover, providing extra weight or mystery to the level's events.

Cutscenes and scripted events

One of the most often-used atmospheric additions is the *cutscene*. In video games cutscenes are sequences, often cinematic, where the player has no control over the onscreen events. In many ways, it is hard to imagine anything more intrusive than being forced to go through a cutscene, although these day semi-interactive cutscenes are being used more and more, which greatly improves things. It is especially in the latter where this can be used to deepen immersion in level design. Together with scripted events, an in-game cutscene (as opposed to one that takes control away from the player) can be extremely helpful, since it allows the level designer full control over a level event. If this is done with some forethought, the level designer can even use gameplay-related level cutscenes or scripted events and incorporate elements into them that help deepen immersion.

Note that you should always try to avoid cutscenes where major decisions are taken away from the player; this is often judged by the player as too much of an intrusion.

Atmospheric Enhancements

We speak of *atmospheric enhancements* when we take already existing elements, native to the game world, and enhance them to provide a more atmospheric experience. This kind of enhancement is related to ambience, but a subtle difference occurs, insofar as that ambience wants to *emphasize*, or *become part of*, the environment, while atmospherics want to enhance what is already there to strengthen its impact. Sometimes these things overlap, and sometimes one follows the other. As with atmospheric additions, atmospheric enhancements are too numerous to cover in exhaustive detail, but we can look at typical examples:

Lighting

Level design lighting performs two functions:

1. It determines what the player can see.
2. It *colors the perception* of what players see.

The first function has many practical secondary effects, including matters of direction or misdirection. This will be covered in other chapters, notably in Chapter 10, "Visual Experiences."

On the other hand, the second function has application in the area of immersion. As is clear from the fields of film and photography, lighting can completely change the impact of a scene. Imagine a normally lit room containing a character, a living area, and a bed in a typical apartment complex. This scene is functional but nothing special. Now imagine the same room like this:

> The bedroom is covered with dancing shadows cast by a slowly swinging flickering light bulb above an unmade bed, while the living area is only slightly illuminated by cold moonlight falling in through the only open window, showing the backlit silhouette of an emaciated person. A soft droning sound can be heard in the background.

Suddenly we have atmosphere in abundance, at very little cost to the level designer. The use of lighting deserves its own chapter, but for now it suffices to say that level design can really shine[19] if it is applied well.

Consider this eloquent description of the power of lighting and the need to reach a state where the audience suspends its disbelief:

> Stage lighting was once the supreme manifestation of manipulative ambience: it paints the scene; it changes to adjust the mood for the audience while they just sit there. And that of course is its ultimate limitation: in the darkened auditorium the audience remains detached and unimmersed, never—in the famous phrase about yielding to staged reality—fully "suspending disbelief" about those onstage golden verandas, spangled dancing levels, bluish dramatic storms, and rosy dawns.[20]

Lighting can have a huge role in establishing the right environment for the player to truly enjoy the game.

Game camera

Many games, but by no means all, allow a certain amount of control over the game camera. This can include camera placement, lens type, field of vision (FOV), direction (yaw, pitch, roll), camera transitions, and other aspects. It cannot be emphasized enough how greatly bad camerawork can hurt a game, or inversely, how greatly good camerawork can enhance a game, including in the area of immersion. Take survival horror as an example, including games like *Resident Evil* or *Silent Hill*, and imagine them with simple unimaginative camerawork. Do you think these series would still be as big as they are now? Furthermore, even if this is not apparent, for example in the case of first person shooters, there may

---

[19] No pun intended.

[20] Nathan Silver, "The Suspension of Disbelief," *Metropolis Magazine*, http://www.metro polismag.com/html/content_0501/chn/index.html, May 2001.

still be possible uses. For example, what if the level designer can place triggers in a level, such that when the player sets them off, this subtly changes the depth of field of the player camera?

Note that I strongly urge any level designer working on a game where this kind of control is theoretically possible to make a strong case *from the beginning* that this control is indeed made available. In an ideal world this includes at least one *dedicated* programmer and a good toolset to implement and try out camera work.

If a complex camera is needed for the game, but it is not worked on and respected from early on in the project, you are in real trouble.

Dramatic scale

Much atmospheric mileage can be derived from good use of dramatic scale. This goes beyond matters of just art direction, but much can be gained by building a strong relationship with the art department in general and concept artists in particular, since it is their job to enhance the game through visual techniques. Don't be afraid to submit a request for concept work for the levels you are working on, with specific requirements about atmosphere and immersion. For example, it is perfectly fine to sit down with a concept artist and talk through the general gameplay progression of any particular level. You could then add a request at the end, which might look something like this:

> All the way through the level, I want the player to be confronted with a continual sense of unease and dread, even if this is subtle and in the background.

Now that the artist knows the level progression and has a specific atmospheric goal to aim for, he or she may come back to you with all kinds of ideas that you would never have thought of. This coordination between level design and art is especially important when it comes to matters of dramatic scale.

A good example of this is found in Sony Computer Entertainment Japan's *Ico*, in which players are constantly reminded of their own vulnerability and the size of the task at hand by the massive and overbearing architecture. This gives the game an oppressing weight and transforms the environment from what is basically an excuse for platforming actions to something that almost amounts to a character in its own right. It is hugely satisfying to be able to manipulate such a characterful and impressive environment.

Theory Summary

In this book, I often argue that a level designer must be able to work to a spec with limited resources at hand. The reality of commercial level design tends to make this the norm rather than exception. It may seem strange, then, to focus this much attention on something that most game producers will not recognize as a key area of interest. To some degree this is to be expected; the basic-level framework needs to be guaranteed first. Often the question asked of the level designer when he or she presents ideas intended to deepen immersion and broaden the suspension of disbelief is something like: "Can the game ship without it?" The answer to this tends to be "I suppose so." But is that really the right question to ask? What happens if we change the question into a more general one: "What if our levels aren't immersive enough?" If somebody doesn't see the danger in a situation where there isn't sufficient player immersion, then that person is likely ignoring a very important question: "Who wants to play a game that does not engage enough to be immersed in?"

From both a commercial point of view and an artistic one, it would be a disaster for the game if it lacked this crucial element.

There are uncounted ways of making sure that a level provides an experience that is deep and immersive. An invaluable tool is provided by Mihaly Csik-sczentmihalyi's *flow theory*, especially when it is translated to optimal game experiences. Equally so, we can learn from theatrical or filmic principles. Look at intrinsic game logic and consider ambience and atmospherics. What stands out, however, is that immersion is not separate from gameplay, it is part of it. An immersed player is a happy player, and a happy player is much more receptive to what the game has to offer. It is of the utmost importance that level designers recognize this, incorporate immersive principles into the level's design and implementation, and fight for the level's integrity in this regard when people start to chip away at it.

The next section will describe a number of practical and useful examples that level designers can adapt or adopt, but the whole of this book should provide inspiration, as well as other examples. This particular topic is intertwined with so many other level design goals and areas of discussion that it is worth keeping in mind all the way through the level design and implementation process.

Practice

Example 8.1: Immersion—Historic Grounding

Summary

Environments that are very believable in the way they have been realized and detailed can be especially immersive to a player. The more convincing a gameplay environment is in its specifics, the easier it is for the player to accept the environment as a whole, including in other areas. One of the areas that can help foster a general sense of immersion is providing an environment with a *past*.

Game Genre

The technique is suitable for most games that use non-abstract environments.

Goals to Achieve

- Deepen immersion.
- Provide historic grounding.
- Assist a sense of agency in the game world.

Description

(Example type: Original)

The passage of time touches everything and everybody. In the real world this happens automatically: things suffer wear and tear, people grow older, the weight of historic events can be felt in the politics of the current day, and so on. In a virtual setting like a game level, temporal impact has to be *created*. This means we can have an influence over the perception of history and thereby influence the immersive qualities of a level.

A place with a sense of history feels more real than one without. After all, how can there be a history to something that isn't real? If we suggest that past events have had an impact on the environment, we suggest that current events can also impact on the game world. This in turn aids the sense of agency a player feels towards the environment.

This example will take a hypothetical environment and suggest some ways in which past events can be suggested. The chosen level environment is a small American town.

Mixing old and new. One of the more straightforward ways to suggest past events is to make sure that there is a visible temporal layering of content in the environment. What I mean by that is that we can include content that dates back to different time periods in order to show the passage of time. In this case for example we can use architecture to date the town. We can include modern buildings alongside older ones, a modern bank next to a classic 50s diner. A church can display the date it was built, as can the town hall, on a foundation stone.

Historic props. We can go further by including things like a derelict building that, on investigation, awards the player with newspapers stemming from the time the building was last occupied. A diary of a previous owner can be found giving an account of events over a specific timeline.

There are less work intensive ways of creating a past as well. Street signage may be used to date the town to a specific event or time period by consistently incorporating references that the player knows to be from a specific period of time.

Ripple effect. We can greatly improve a sense of history by showing the impact of a past event throughout many aspects of current life in the town. This can be seen as a ripple effect through the fabric of time and how it has changed the town. Our town may have experienced a large meteor impact in the 1950s, affecting almost every aspect of life from then on. The impact site itself may offer great gameplay opportunities, for example by having been transformed into a somewhat amateurish and spooky tourist attraction. Subtler little details can be adopted as well. The diner for example may carry a meteor themed menu or be named after the meteor.

Further Notes

There is not much that limits level designers when it comes to this kind of temporal grounding other than time and budget. It makes sense, therefore, to incorporate these kinds of things into actual gameplay related scenarios, and not only use the history of the place for atmospheric qualities.

Example 8.2: Game Camera and Immersion

Summary

One of the ways in which we judge our environment is by our visual perception of it. We form a mental image and make certain assumptions based on the evidence presented to us by our eyes. In level design we potentially have control over the game camera, which means we can influence the players' perception of their environment. This can be done in strong immersive ways.

Game Genre

The technique is suitable for games that employ a camera system that can be influenced by the level designer.

Goals to Achieve

- Aid immersion through inventive game camera use.

Description

(Example type: Original/real)

Safe distance establishing shot. Sometimes it really pays off to give the player a grand view of the level before they get to explore it. It can set a powerful mood and allows the player to build a mental map of the environment right from the beginning. Unfortunately, this is often made impossible due to technical and practical limitations. The scene may contain too much visual data to render and cause performance issues, or early access may ruin level design scenarios scheduled later. Whatever the reason, this can still be made to work by presenting the player with a particular *view* of the environment, not necessarily the actual environment itself. As long as the player can see the environment, it will have the desired effect. This can be done, for example, through a window or a fence or any other believable barrier between the player and the view.

For extra effect we can include vantage points that overlook each other, so when a player eventually reaches a view they had witnessed before, he or she can be made to appreciate this more if it is possible to see the original vantage point from the new location. It can be great to have a panoramic view of a massive tower, and then hours later be able to look back on where you came from standing on top of the tower in question. Excellent examples of this can be found throughout the game *Ico*.[21]

Special angles. At times it is possible to create a deep sense of immersion by employing special camera angles. The game camera can be tilted to indicate the player's deteriorating mental state in a horror game, the camera can zoom out to suddenly show an approaching danger, or the camera can move into a top down position to reveal something about the environment, for example the aftermath of a grueling conflict between the player and a group of enemies.

Many other possibilities exist.

Camera shake. Relatively easy but no less effective is the inclusion of camera-shake at key moments. Imagine a level set in a series of underground tunnels during a long bombing raid. A sporadic camera-shake accompanied by a low, far-away rumble, and possibly some falling dust created with the game's particle system, can be incredibly effective in creating a deep level of immersion.

Further Notes

If at all possible, examine the use of camera lenses to provide further effects. It is remarkable how much lens types, depth of field, color filter, field of vision (fov)

---

[21] Published by Sony Entertainment Europe, developed by "Team Ico" in Japan, released March 23, 2002.

and other aspects can contribute to a level's immersive qualities. Yet, very few level designers have been able or are allowed to make use of those possibilities.

Example 8.3: Ambient Factors—Fauna and Flora

Summary

If we can create levels that feel like they are stand alone, autonomous, living and breathing environments, we provide the player with a much more immersive experience. This process can be helped by providing an ecosystem that the player can observe and potentially interact with.

Game Genre

This is a useful technique for games that allow wildlife to be scripted.

Goals to Achieve

- Make the level environment more immersive.
- Encourage immersive deepening gameplay.
- Provide spontaneous or emergent gameplay in levels.

Description

(Example type: Original)

Catch the creature. If the game you are working on contains wildlife, or has the scope to contain wildlife, it is a good idea to include a creature that the player can have some fun with. Take, for example, a creature that needs to graze and will wander over to specific patches of vegetation in order to do so. It may move from patch to patch and otherwise mind its own business. Chances are the player will eventually try to approach the creature. Make sure the creature has some rudimentary AI that will make it run away when the player comes too close, running too fast for the player to catch up. I can guarantee that a large group of players from then on will try to find ways in which they can catch the creature. They may try to ambush it or herd it into a pen or find some completely unexpected way of catching it.

This kind of spontaneous fun directly linked to the level environment really adds to the immersion of the level. Ideally, this is rewarded by allowing skilled players to indeed capture the creature, in which case the player needs to be rewarded—for example, with a tuft of fur that can be used elsewhere in the level, or any other award that fits the game's specific circumstances.

Further Notes

This kind of mechanic can work on several levels. Flytraps can contain useful substances but the player needs to figure out how to approach the plant without it closing its petals and denying access. Birds can circle above areas of interest. Glow-worms can provide unexpected illumination at night, unveiling secret areas, and so on.

Negative Emotions

9

There are times when conventional wisdom doesn't apply. Normally we don't set out to frustrate an audience, or make them feel bad. We don't want them to feel negative emotions. In most cases this is true, we try to enlighten or entertain. What happens, however, when we try to do that through the use of negative emotions? When we use emotions like frustration or anger as a tool to achieve a higher goal? That is the subject that this chapter will explore in more detail.

Concept

People like being scared.

On the surface, this is a slightly strange statement. Why on earth would anybody enjoy feeling scared? Most people lead their life in a way that reduces risk and fear as much as they can. But on the other hand, many people enjoy such things as ghost stories, thrillers, and scary movies, so there must be something about feeling scared that appeals to people.

Let's therefore rephrase the previous statement slightly and say: *People like dealing with their fears in a safe environment.*

This sounds a bit more acceptable. If there is no real risk involved, there is nothing to worry about. This leads to a conundrum: if people like being scared in situations without real risk, what logical reason do they have to actually be scared in that context[1]?

Unreal Risk

The key to answering that question lies in the observation that there can be such a thing as *unreal risk*, which on the surface seems a contradiction in terms. How-

---

[1] There is after all *no risk*.

ever, this concept is sensible if one considers the human capacity for *suspension of disbelief*, which as we know from the previous chapter is a massively important ability that human beings possess. We have the ability to suspend our disbelief and indulge in artificial scenarios that are completely fictitious. This allows us to deal safely with concepts that, if they were physical and real, would be harmful to us. In other words: in this case, suspension of disbelief allows us to experience and deal with unreal risks. We can see now that this constitutes a clear example of a *positive* use of a *negative emotion*.

Enjoying the Negative

We already know that sometimes human beings artificially create and experience scenarios that involve *negative emotions*, for example by listening to ghost stories or by seeing a scary movie. We even talk about some of these experiences in positive terms, like the "thrill" of being scared or the "lure" of the dangerous wild. Some of this harks back to basic principles of *play*, insofar as some aspects of play have to do with learning about and preparing for dangerous situations. It seems fair to say that:

> People have the capacity and the need to deal with negative emotions and experiences, and they can do this through applying suspension of disbelief to artificial situations where such emotions can occur in a controlled and safe manner.

This principle occurs throughout human society, time after time. We have already encountered it in the discussion of reward systems in Chapter 7 where we found it at work in the principle of *catharsis*. Throughout this current chapter, we will examine a number of areas and examples that pertain to the subject matter of this book.

The Example of Fear and Other Negative Emotions

Fear is an emotion that has been studied by humankind for thousands of years, so we actually know a little bit about the subject. Throughout history, it has demonstrated a capacity to both paralyze and motivate people. At a basic level we can argue that scary films and books are about facing fears. There are certainly many stories about some kind of phobia or other deep-rooted fear, so we know that at least sometimes this applies. Fear is just one example, however. There are many other negatives in our lives that demand their own coping mechanisms. Other examples that can be included are emotions dealing with *panic, doubt, anger,* or *frustration,* to name just a few. Do they all have a place in this concept where we absorb negative emotions into an artificial scenario of our own making and turn them into a positive experience?

Let's go back to the example of *fear.* Countless books have been written on the subject, millions of songs are inspired by it, many classic films are based on it, and countless paintings have been created because of it. It cannot be denied that fear is a powerful emotion that has stood at the basis of all kinds of creative expression. But it is certainly not the only one.

Art or Entertainment as a Coping Mechanism

Works of art and entertainment often deal with negative subject matter. It is undeniable that a great diversity of artworks through the ages have been created that would not have had their impact on society without delving into this admittedly negative, but rich, vein. Can we imagine a happy, carefree version of Munch's *The Scream*? Or of *Dante's Inferno*?

I will not try to create any definition of what art is or what it should deal with,[2] but it is fair to say that at times creative expression incorporates negative emotions and provides a relatively safe way for the audience to deal with them or learn to understand its own personal instances of those negative feelings. Seen in such a way, the use of negative emotions becomes a powerful tool in the hand of the artist, a tool that allows the artist to create a profound emotional response in the audience. Sometimes it even assists the audience in devising coping mechanisms for dealing with such negatives.

This can be a powerful incentive for people to be exposed to negative content, things they would normally want to avoid. Artists have become quite adept through the ages at devising methods to deliver these positives through negative means. Let's look at a number of known techniques to see how they are implemented in practice.

A Deal with the Devil (Committing the Audience)

There are multiple ways to keep an audience interested, generally through entertainment and engagement, in the traditional positive sense. But something

---

[2] I am not that foolish.

strange happens when it becomes clear that the audience is exposed to an experience more akin to an *ordeal*. If this is done with skill, the artist will not lose the audience, but instead will *enter into an agreement* with it. This can partly be explained by the natural fascination people have with certain dark areas of life. Sometimes this is a healthy curiosity in areas that are genuinely interesting, for example, a will to understand something about a painful subject. At other times this is a more basic desire to be entertained by things like shock and revulsion. Often it is not clear where one ends and the other begins. But what *is* clear is that the audience is willing to go quite far with the artist because of the implicit promise of a worthwhile experience. If the audience is ultimately rewarded well, it will not resent the difficult route in getting there.

This is true in acceptable arenas like film, where a narrative about violent, reprehensible men can garner great critical and popular acclaim (*Goodfellas*[3]) or gruesome horror can be elevated to a celebrated film art (*Alien*.[4]) It is just as true in more obscure or specialist arenas like performance art, where people like Marina Abramovic have been doing recognized work for a long time, sometimes in ways that go beyond what is normally accepted by an audience:

> In *Rhythm 10*, she plunged a knife between the spread fingers of one hand, stopping only after she had cut herself 20 times. Having made an audio recording of the action, she then played back the sound while repeating the movements—this time trying to coordinate the new gashes with the old. Using her dialogue with an audience as a source of energy, Abramoviç created ritualistic performance pieces that were cathartic and liberating.[5]

All of these examples show successful challenges to the audience where the artist manages to make the audience commit to dealing with extraordinarily negative subject matter.

Drugging the Audience (Adrenaline Rush)

I personally am incapable of enjoying a roller coaster ride. Even while I was typing that sentence, I was getting an uncomfortable feeling in my stomach just imagining the possibility.[6] Having said that, I do understand the attrac-

---

[3] Directed by Martin Scorsese, 1990.

[4] Directed by Ridley Scott, 1979.

[5] "Marina Abramovic: Rhythm 5. 1974," *Guggenheim Collection Online,* http://www.guggenheimcollection.org, 1994.

[6] I suffer badly from vertigo.

tion in general. It is the same attraction that causes people to go wild water rafting, bungee jumping, carting, paint-balling or participate in any of a multitude of genuinely exciting activities. All of these acts are guaranteed to flood the participant's system with an intoxicating mix of endorphins and adrenaline. People often literally describe this feeling as an *adrenaline rush*, or even just as a *rush*. This rush can be so potent that people get addicted to it, and they literally turn into *adrenaline junkies*. On closer examination, it is very interesting to note that all of these activities carry some kind of potential *danger* or *penalty*, which is the reason why they so easily cause a release of adrenaline in the blood. Nothing like a bit of danger and fear to get the juices flowing, right?

It is not a huge jump to take the kind of chemical award linked to these dangerous activities and recognize the value this can have in creative expression. Is it possible to challenge the audience with comparable negatives in such a way that it causes the release of natural drugs like adrenaline? It is hardly surprising to find that it's not only *possible*; the use of this principle is in fact ubiquitous. This can be seen clearly even in the language used to market these works of negative entertainment. We have all seen movie posters and ads that scream things like: "A truly shocking story! A terrifying film!" and so forth.

I had a teacher many years ago who explained to me why he disliked *tension* in novels. It was mainly to do with the fact that readers can get so drawn in that they race through the book, ignoring the nuances of style and language. This taught me a valuable lesson, completely counter to my teacher's original intention, about the role of prose versus the desired overall goal of the book,[7] and one that I suspect is shared by authors of the exciting books he so disliked.

Learning through Shock (Forced Focus)

Most artists want to make a point with their work. They want to teach the audience a certain lesson, or let it focus on a particular theme, or perhaps make it think about a certain contradiction in society. Whatever the exact motivation, they want to get something across in an impactful way. This can be done through seduction with beautiful imagery, compelling music, beautiful prose, and many other positive means that are known to work. It can also be done by *shocking* the audience in such a way that people automatically give all their focus to the creative work, and as a result of this sudden focus and the accompanying physiological processes, the audience will be much more receptive to absorbing the

---

[7] It is legitimate to make prose subordinate to story and impact.

presented content. It is well known that shocking or stressful events can lead to enhanced memory function[8].

Realizing that this side effect of shock can cause such a singular focus and promote knowledge retention makes it easy to understand that there can be many uses for it in artistic expression. If the artist wants to focus attention on a new character, an effective way of doing so is to introduce him or her by showing the villain committing a truly shocking act. This immediately will lead to a number of questions and doubts in the mind of the audience, which may be beneficial to the work as a whole. *Who* is this person? What motivates this person to act in such a way? Will this shocking behavior continue? Is this person redeemable, or truly evil? If any of these questions are answered early on, just after the initial shock, chances are that the audience will remember this for the rest of the work. This principle applies to all information that the artist may wish to assign extra significance to.

Dramatic Impact

In Chapter 7, "Reward Systems," we have already gone into some detail on how catharsis can be used as a formal reward system. I won't repeat that content too much, but I would like to reiterate that some of the earliest interpretations of the concept come from Aristotle's *Poetics*, where catharsis is mentioned as one of the key elements of drama. I would like to note, however, that there are many more ways to use darker subject matter to create dramatic interest. If we look even further back in the book, a typical example presents itself in Freytag's pyramid, which was explained in Chapter 4. As noted there, in the climactic turning point of a *tragedy,* a change occurs that is negative to the protagonist. This has all kinds of potential dramatically beneficial consequences. The audience may feel pity for the plight of the protagonist, and the change may give the protagonist emotionally sound motivation and provide context for his or her future actions. Many other advantages can be gained from one well executed shocking or disturbing moment or development. It is easy to see why this is attractive to artists in almost any creative discipline.

Concept Conclusion

Not only do we see that the use of negative emotions is viable as a creative technique, we find that it flourishes throughout diverse disciplines and can incorpo-

---

[8] Much work on this topic has been done by James McGaugh. See http://darwin.bio.uci.edu/neurobio/Faculty/McGaugh/mcgaugh.htm.

rate almost *any type* of negative emotion. What seems to be clear, though, is that there is always a process of give and take involved, where audience members are willing to be presented with these negatives, but only if they can get something out of it themselves. Viewed in such a light, we can say that this technique of creating negatives to produce positive emotions as a final result acts no differently than many of the other reward systems discussed earlier in the book. But this does not mean that there are no reservations when it comes to adopting the use of these kinds of things in creative expression. There are a number of dangers associated with it, as we will see.

Inherent Dangers

As we all know, there is no such thing as a free lunch, and this definitely applies to the above techniques. There are a number of real dangers involved in applying these kinds of methods of playing with negative emotional impact. I will list a number of the major ones.

Audience rejection

The first one is quite simple. The audience may not wish to be exposed to this kind of manipulation, or to the particular incarnation of it that the artist chose to use. As turnoffs go, this is an extremely strong one. It can do real damage to the artist-audience relationship, even to the point of being irreparable. This is of course something that must be avoided, unless you want to press the self-destruct button.

Overshooting

Another danger comes from the possibility of overdoing it to such a degree that the main purpose is not met. In this case, the audience will focus so much on the particular technique employed that it is to the detriment of the desired result. There is no point to shocking an audience if people are left numb, or completely engrossed in the shocking event *itself*. This quite often happens to people who mistake the technique for the goal and forget that there has to be something in it or the audience as well.

Some ethical considerations

A further danger that presents itself is *ethical miscalculations*. Does the artist actually have the right to use this kind of negative emotional manipulation? There are of course many very successful examples of celebrated artists who use these techniques in their work. On the other hand, most people will find it hard to have anything positive to say about the countless exploitative or even criminal examples of art or entertainment that also exist in our environment. This includes films that revel in pointless depictions of extreme violence or build on tired racial stereotypes, and art that shocks without rationale and has nothing further to offer. I am sure you can think of your own examples to illustrate the point. This is the flip side of the power of negative art and entertainment.

How does an artist know if he or she has gone too far, or lacks the skill to pull things off without causing real harm to the audience? Does the audience have an inherent right not to be subjected to certain types of manipulation?

These are real questions that are still asked daily and can create massive, even international, controversy.[9] Although I personally take a strong libertarian stance in many of these matters, I still have to define my own perimeters on what I personally see as acceptable use. I am not going to explore the topic of ethics or freedom of speech in this context, but I do think it is important to highlight that there is a certain amount of personal responsibility involved when dealing with these issues. This is something that artists have been struggling with since classic times, and it is important to try to be aware where one's own line in the sand is drawn. I highly recommend that you do the same, even if it forces you to re-examine personal notions of artistic freedom of expression.

Theory

In the previous section I made the following observation:

> People have the capacity and the need to deal with negative emotions and experiences, and they can do this through applying suspension of disbelief to artificial situations where such emotions can occur in a controlled and safe manner.

If we try to view these concepts through the lens of video game development, we once again find that these concepts apply, and that video games are perfectly capable of dealing with serious issues and emotions. It isn't too hard to find clear examples: we fill games with scenarios that in real life would be undesirable but somehow seem appropriate to the game. Often a player is confronted with levels that feature dangerous action, war, disasters, fearsome creatures, and so on. The list is very long indeed, and as diverse as the subject matter of other art forms. It

---

[9] See the negative reaction to Salman Rushdie's *Satanic Verses*, published in 1988.

is clear that we already force the player to deal with *negative experiences*. A video game is by definition an *artificial environment*. Players have to *suspend their disbelief* in order to immerse themselves in the game world and accept its rules. Because we allow the player a certain *sense of control* over the situation, and the player deep down knows there is *no real risk* involved, the experience is ultimately a *safe and controlled* one.

So we find that the earlier observation contains many concepts that video games, and consequently level designers, already incorporate. In fact, there is so much overlap that it becomes clear that it is almost *too* snug a fit.

So how does all this help us? We know that on a conceptual level, negative emotions can be and are used in video games just as much as they are in other art forms. But, what kinds of techniques are used? Are there other more suitable ones unique to games? How do we get the best use out of them, and are there game-specific dangers we need to be aware of? These are the kind of questions we will be trying to find answers for in this chapter.

Genre-Specific Examples

In many ways, video games are especially suited to the use of these techniques. This isn't just because through level design we have authorial control over the content of a level. It is also because to a large degree, video games give *control* to players, often in order to test their skills against the challenges inherent in many games. Players have a certain expectation that they will be tested in a video game, and within certain genres they expect to be pushed very far indeed. Although the techniques in question are applicable to most games, there are a number of game genres that lend themselves especially well to them because they are part of the *core gameplay experience*. Let's look at some clear examples.

Survival Horror

Within the survival horror genre, it is part of the expected framework that the player is underpowered and up against dark and disturbing forces. This means that the player will not resent it if confronted with unspeakable horrors or gameplay moments where it *feels* as if the player is at a huge disadvantage. Everything in the game world can be used to scare or disorient the player. This includes camera work, audio, architecture, props, cutscenes, and of course enemy encounters. In other words, this game genre is more geared towards using negative emotions than any other.

Shootemups (SHMUPS)

Classic *shootemups* allow things that almost no other genre can get away with. They allow for a fundamentally different approach to difficulty and the learning curve. Although not true for all shootemups, there is nonetheless a large group of players who want to be severely tested and are happy to be *frustrated* and presented with what at first seem like *unfair* circumstances. This is accepted because much of the attraction of this genre comes from mastering nearly inhuman skills and reflexes and using them against a merciless onslaught of wave after wave of enemies. It is interesting to watch skilled shootemup players. They somehow manage to navigate a screen that is literally filled with bullets and enemies, except for a tiny moving area that the player always seems to inhabit.

Retro Games

Retro games are a special category, insofar as that they are not necessarily played for normal gameplay reasons. As the name says, they are played more to provide a gamer with retrospective and can be quite a nostalgic affair. Remakes of classic retro games are faced with the paradoxical situation that were they to improve too much on the original's gameplay, they could be criticized for not being authentic enough!

Unfortunately, some classic games feature incredibly frustrating and difficult gameplay. Many rose-tinted glasses have been shattered by the realization of how bad or unfair many classic games really were. This type of harsh and negative gameplay was often employed to make sure that the player couldn't survive too long on the coin used to start playing the game in the arcade. To this day, there are still players who relish this unfair challenge. If one wants to court them, it is inappropriate to stray too far from these harsh concepts. This type of game has become a genre of its own, where negative emotions as a level design theme are completely acceptable.

General Level Design Application

As the famous Dutch soccer player Johan Cruyff once said: "Every disadvantage has an advantage." In the case of the techniques we are discussing, it makes sense to adopt the same philosophy and see how negatives can be changed into positives in level design.

Since to a large degree we are the authors of the player's experience, it is almost inevitable that at some point we will be tempted to frustrate the player or confront the player with some kind of negative experience that goes beyond the regular gameplay challenges *in order to achieve a specific result that cannot otherwise be obtained*. Other than the inherent goals derived from the typical gameplay associated with some genres like survival horror or some retro games, as discussed earlier, there are also many techniques based on general principles. We know from the earlier conceptual examination of this topic that the right use of negative emotions can greatly enhance a creative work. What happens if we try to translate these general principles to level design principles and methods? Let's have a look at the previous general observations and see if they fit into a level design framework.

A Deal with the Devil (Committing the Audience)

Previously I stated that:

> ... the audience is willing to go quite far with the artist because of the implicit promise of a worthwhile experience. If the audience is ultimately rewarded well, it will not resent the difficult route in getting there.

In some ways, this seems unnecessary in video games. Hasn't the audience already bought the game? In other ways, this seems entirely sensible. Gamers know that they will be tested throughout the game and that reward systems are at play. Where this really matters in level design is dependent on the goal and the skill of the level designer. If the level designer wants to create *motivation* in the player to endure an extended period of hard gameplay, this can be done by providing an enemy that is so horrific that the player feels compelled to go through great lengths to defeat the enemy. If players are helpless to avoid a situation that causes great distress and suffering, they be extra *motivated* to avoid this a second time.

These are level design decisions. The level designer can create scenarios where a negative occurrence creates the commitment and framework to engage strongly with the presented gameplay. As before, this is especially viable if the reward offered to the player is worthwhile. Unlike in real life, the level designer has much to say about the play awards. So it is fair to say that this technique translates extremely well to level design.

Drugging the Audience (Adrenaline Rush)

In the virtual environments of a game, especially if they aren't abstract, there is a great opportunity to explore the psyche of game players. This may sound a bit pompous, but if we look at what happens in video game levels, it is quite easy to reach this conclusion. Aren't we putting real people in something like a virtual experience chamber? We poke them here and there, change the maze around them, bombard them with surreal experiences, and manipulate their emotions and expectations.

Within our palette as level designers, we have a huge amount of color to play with in shaping a play experience that is ultimately beneficial to the player. One of these colors comes from playing with feelings of fear and danger and turning this into a measured release of adrenaline. This can come from exploration of phobias like vertigo or arachnophobia, or from more scare tactics and unexpected shocks. In fact, there are countless ways to achieve this result and find new and original ways of doing so. Within level design, we can control gameplay, sound, camera, AI behavior, and so forth. This is all the control we need to create the circumstances to reach the desired goals.

Learning through Shock (Forced Focus)

In a good game with good level design the player is often kept within a state of heightened awareness. In some ways this is a side effect of the *optimal experience* of being in the *flow channel*[10], (being in the zone in other words) as created by the level design. The player is fully immersed and open to the game world. Furthermore, whether explicitly or not, the player is by definition, through playing a game, in a system designed to educate.[11] These factors combined suggest that there isn't much need for shock-induced focus, especially if it is designed to aid the retention of information. To a degree this is true; since the player is already actively engaged in the creative work, games have an advantage over other art forms.

On the other hand, this doesn't mean that there is no place for this technique at all; far from it. Some lessons are hard to accept, some artistic points are hard to make, and some rewards only come at a price. Add to that the fact that the player is often in partial control of the outcome of the gameplay scenarios, and one can be forgiven for sometimes seeing a need to force the issue. If viewed in this way, level design is actually not so different from other creative art forms. It is up to the individual level designer to see if there is a need, and if so, to choose how far to take the application of this technique.

Dramatic Impact

On this topic I can be short. One of the areas in which we can make great strides forward in our level designs is by making sure that the player's actions are re-

---

[10] See Chapter 8.
[11] See Chapter 2 on level design as a teaching mechanic.

warded by dramatic impact. This is of course already done throughout games, but unfortunately, the application is frequently blunt and ham-fisted. This is in some ways very strange, as drama has been studied for thousands of years and all this knowledge is available to us. We have already gone back as far as Aristotle to describe the use of fear and pity as key components to create drama, which literally is a textbook example of using negative emotions to create a positive experience. But there are key differences between stagecraft and video games, especially when it comes to building and expressing narrative. A level designer doesn't always have the luxury of linearity or a passive audience that politely sits through the whole performance. Due to the interactivity of the art form, we have to deal with some unique challenges that are at times hard to solve.

It is good to remember, however, that if level design is the stage on which gameplay occurs, we aren't just the scriptwriters, but also the sound engineers, lighting people, acting coaches, set designers, and so on. If we create a moment of dramatic tension, perhaps the loss of life of the player character's main rival, we can raise the camera to look down on the scene, have an NPC utter a suitable line of dialogue, play the right music, create a gust of wind, and more. Then on top of that we can create gameplay scenarios that feed off or link to the dramatic context just created. And that last aspect, where the drama is linked to the actual gameplay, where the player acts out dramatically interesting scenarios, is where our work can shine in unexpected ways.

Other Themes

Many of examples of these principles have been applied successfully in well-known games. It is a much richer and universal concept than generally expected.

Panic and stress

In *Tetris*,[12] the blocks stack higher and higher, and they will never cease or slow down. Nobody "finishes" *Tetris*; it cannot be beaten and it has no happy ending. This is on the surface a terribly harsh premise for a game. Yet who can deny that *Tetris* is one of the biggest success stories in game development?

Betrayal

One may wonder how this can ever be a good basis for gameplay. But this is instantly understood when one witnesses a bout of multiplayer *Chu Chu Rocket*.[13] The mayhem and backstabbing that occur in this game, in which players can

---

[12] Developed by Alexey Pajitnov, released June 1985.
[13] SEGA Enterprises Ltd., 1999.

actively interfere and sabotage each other's chances of success, is truly epic. It is very funny to see how easily even lovely people turn to the most backhanded techniques without any guilt.

These are all viable examples, and many others exist. Some of these will be described in more practical detail in the following *practice* section.

Dangers and Disadvantages

The idea that negative emotions like fear or panic can be a rich resource to be tapped for the purpose of art and entertainment is a very powerful one. Its use, though, is often dangerous and subversive to other, sometimes more important level design goals.

The biggest danger in all of the techniques described is that by attempting to deepen players' experience through the use of negative emotions, they may end up feeling negative *about the game itself*. The *gameplay* becomes a negative, is an outcome that needs to be avoided at all costs. It is essential that players maintain a sense of *fairness* and be allowed to *trust* the game. The simplest way to sum it up is that we need to make sure that we don't put players off by treating them harshly in an arbitrary and pointless manner. Instead, we need to make sure that players can *experience negative emotions* that help them *enjoy or appreciate the game*[14] (as opposed to making the gameplay itself negative). This sounds paradoxical, but techniques that work towards this outcome are used all the time in other art forms as well as in other game forms. It is a viable and valuable technique *as long as the principles of trust and fairness are not violated*.

However, the problem is that most gameplay does not really lend itself to this approach. As we have discussed earlier, level design is much concerned with teaching the player's skills and testing those skills through gameplay challenges. Fun is therefore often associated with success, and if that experience of success is frustrated too much, players will end up resenting the game itself. This occurs either because it is unfair, or because players feel they cannot master the game to a sufficient enough degree to enjoy it. This is an important conundrum that is becoming more and more understood now that so many games involve mature and emotionally challenging themes and gameplay psychology is better understood. Some of these concepts are now sporadically appearing in design literature, as the following example shows:

> Under the hood of every game is the same simple mechanism: we give
> the player a set of skills to master, and then run them through the paces,
> demanding effective performance of that skill-set. To know that they

---

[14] Or at least make it a worthwhile experience.

did well, the player requires feedback. If the player thinks they screwed
up, but the game doesn't send a clear message to that effect, they will un-
derstandably be frustrated and put off. Not to mention that the drama
will not be read as drama. This means that player's actions – and their
results – are not good contexts for setbacks or reversals.[15]

This neatly sums up a key problem facing us if we want to use negative emotions as
a reward mechanism in gameplay. It is something we have to be very careful about.

Purpose and Gameplay

There are certain dangers that are easily avoided, because we have seen them
annoy players in games of the past and can therefore avoid them in the future.
A classic misinterpretation of the technique, for example, is seen when a game
hobbles the player's abilities without good reason. This used to be rampant
among others in survival horror games that employ so called *tank controls,* which
make it very awkward to control the player character. It is often argued that this
aids the game by inducing a feeling of panic, which is appropriate to the genre.
This introduced level of difficulty is so arbitrary, however, that it is tantamount
to cheating on the designer's part.

It is not that the decision to make the player-character physically less capable
that is suspect, as this indeed can add to the tension in an appropriate manner. It
is that it is done in a way that is *unfair* and arbitrary. Why not give the player in-
tuitive controls, but impose a *logical* restriction on movement, in which case the
player won't feel cheated. This is where level design can step in. If the complexity of controls is minimal, and the challenge lies in negotiating the environment,
then much frustration will be forgiven, since it is now a question of *player* skills
and weaknesses, as opposed to player *character* weaknesses. We should always remember that there is no dramatic impact to be derived from pointless irritation. If
the gameplay challenges make sense through the level design, if there is a purpose
to the difficulties experienced by the player, then there is at least some respect for
the player's plight. Nobody wants to feel at the mercy of arbitrary circumstances.

Theory Summary

We have seen that in addition to traditional level design challenges, general principles of negative gameplay for positive results are also applicable to level design
theory. If we want to tackle mature and emotionally deep themes, we need to be

---

[15] Ben Schneider, "Losing For the Win: Defeat and Failure in Gaming," *Gamasutra,*
http://www.gamasutra.com/features/20070215/schneider_01.shtml, 2007.

able to use any techniques available to us in a responsible manner. There are both ethical and practical dangers and obstacles to overcome, but we have seen that there are many ways in which unwanted side effects can be mitigated or avoided. If we do so successfully and appropriately, we have the means to make our levels much more meaningful and rewarding, which is something that is definitely worth pursuing.

Some of the discussed concepts may feel at times counterintuitive or even paradoxical, but the following section, with its practical examples, should clearly illustrate their use.

Practice

Example 9.1: Dramatic Impact through Emotional Loss

Summary

Sometimes the player can be extra motivated or involved in the game by being exposed to something that has great dramatic impact on the gameplay narrative of the level. In the context of this chapter, we are going to look at using a negative emotional event in order to create a positive play experience, specifically through subjecting the player to an emotional loss.

Game Genre

This is especially useful in games with important AI companions.

Goals to Achieve

- Foster an emotional bond with an NPC.
- Create motivation through negative emotions.
- Frustrate the player in exchange for increased commitment.

Description

(Example type: Existing game)

Ico: A case study. In their game *Ico*,[16] Sony Japan has done a remarkable job in creating an AI companion for the player, who generates real emotional at-

---

[16] SCEE, developed by Team Ico, released March 22, 2002.

tachment. In *Ico* the player controls a young boy who needs a girl named Yorda to progress through the levels. She alone can perform certain tasks that make progress possible, but she relies on the boy for protection. This creates real codependency in gameplay terms, and through the skilled use of character enhancing speech and animations, the player comes to really care for Yorda. Time after time throughout the levels, the player relies on her powers to unlock doors and is called on many times to save her life and protect her from creatures that are trying to take her. Most players of the game eventually develop a very strong attachment to the girl.

It is interesting, therefore, to see that Team Ico decided that the way to make this emotional attachment really shine through was by making the player experience the flipside of that emotion, namely emotional loss. Without much warning, the game forcibly cuts the connection between the player and the AI character, after carefully building it up through many hours of gameplay investment. Yorda and the player are suddenly physically separated from each other, and a strong sense of loss overcomes the player.

This is a remarkably brave level design choice, one that could have backfired easily if not handled well. After making sure that the player has the capacity to feel strong emotions towards the AI character, the player is then confronted with a situation that makes the player examine how deep this attachment goes.

From that point on, the player is very motivated to progress through the game and reunite with Yorda. This enhanced motivation and the final payoff when they do reunite provide a powerful gameplay experience that could not have been achieved without the initial use of negative emotions.

Further Notes

This technique is also employed in the game *Shadow of the Colossus*,[17] which takes place in the same game universe as *Ico*. In this game the player forms a bond with their companionable steed named Agro. In fact, the game goes even further than *Ico* into mining negative emotions by expecting the player character to slay wondrous and titanic creatures that have done it no harm.

Example 9.2: Temporary Removal of Control

Summary

Players can become very motivated and involved in a level design scenario if they are faced with a situation that is fundamentally upsetting. One such scenario can

---

[17] Also made by Team ICO, published by SCEA, released October 18, 2005.

be the removal of a certain amount of control from the player, which creates a real sense of urgency and discomfort. If used well this can fuel an eventual positive resolution.

Game Genre

This technique is suitable for any single-player or cooperative game in any genre that allows the level designer to temporarily, physically trap the player inside an area.

Goals to Achieve

- Instill tension by creating feelings of *panic* and *trepidation*.
- Eventually reward the player by allowing them to remove those feeling.
- Let the player be the agent of this removal of frustration.

Description

(Example type: Existing game)

This example's inspiration comes from a level called "The Dismal Oubliette" in Id Software's *Quake*.[18] It shows a very simple way to effectively use negative emotions to engineer a positive gameplay experience. The principle applies to many diverse types of games. In this example, we will show how by temporarily restricting the player's movement, we can simply and very effectively create a tense gameplay moment. A minimum amount of scripting is necessary in order to make the example possible.

In the level "The Dismal Oubliette," the player enters a round room with a central pillar. After the player has entered the room the door behind the player locks, trapping the player in the room. The floor starts to descent and it becomes clear that the room is a giant, slow-moving lift. A sense of panic and trepidation comes into effect as the player is trapped and has no choice over where the elevator takes him or her.

While the elevator is descending, monsters start teleporting in and the player has no choice but to dispatch them one by one. It is an unavoidable combat situation over which the player has limited control for the duration of the lift's descent, and fear sets in as the player takes damage, and expends resources, without knowing the full duration or the final destination of the elevator trip.

The environment and the available resources are such, however, that most players should be in less danger than they think, and should be able to dispatch of all the enemy creatures without perishing themselves.

---

[18] Published by id Software, Inc., developed by id Software, Inc., released 1996.

When the elevator finally reaches the ground floor the player will feel rewarded in a number of ways:

- relief because the creatures have stopped attacking,
- pride at their accomplishment,
- relief because they are free to move again.

To some degree, this kind of setup has become a bit of a cliché, but if implemented in a novel or interesting way, it still provides a very effective setup.

Further Notes

The technique can easily be applied to almost any kind of game environment as long as it allows the player to be limited in some way or another.

Example 9.3: Sound-Induced Shock and Subsequent Tension

Summary

Extreme sound can completely overwhelm a person's thinking. If loud and abrasive enough, it will disrupt normal cognitive processes and force the attention of the player since it can't be ignored. This kind of negative reaction to sound can be used in positive ways in level design.

Game Genre

This technique is suitable for most games that are looking to scare or disturb the player through ambient sound.

Goals to Achieve

- Create an unforgettable moment in a level.
- Engineer a lasting feeling of dread.
- Strengthen the sense of immersion.

Description

(Example type: Existing game)

Dead Space[19] is a survival horror game that makes heavy use of sound to deepen the dark and horrific atmosphere of the game. The game's sound design is an in-

---

[19] Published by Electronic Arts, Inc., developed by Electronic Arts Redwood Shores Studio, released October 24, 2008.

tegral part of the level design and is used in a multifaceted and very effective way throughout each level. There is a standout moment, however, when the player starts playing one of the earlier chapters. Right at the beginning an incredibly abrasive, deeply unsettling and disturbing sound engulfs the player. It seems to be part of the environment, although there is no clear source for it.

This is what the game's Audio Director, Don Veca, has to say about it:

> I have lived in the San Francisco Bay Area most of my life, and was in high-school around the time that the "Bay Area Rapid Transit" (BART) system was built, which in one section literally tunnels underneath the San Francisco Bay. I'm not sure why, but for some reason the tracks really scream down there… but in a very "scary" way—lots of high, screechy over-tones, big bottom end, and very dynamic. In later years as a sound designer at EA, I started thinking that this sound would be perfect for a game, but I didn't know what game or where. Fast-forward to *Dead Space*—the perfect place for it. The sound we actually used in the game was recorded in the tunnel while standing between two cars (where it says "Do Not Stand Between Cars"). I didn't really know where in the game to put it, but in our early demo there was a very inconspicuous room right after the first "zero gravity/zero air" moment that seemed to have no pur- pose. Since the Horror genre is also known for its heavy use of contrast, audio-wise, it seemed to be the perfect place to use this sound. When you open the air-vac door from the virtually silent "zero G moment" into this next room that has air (and therefore sound), you immediately get this deafening, screechy, scraping, pseudo-mechanical ambient roar. The art team jumped on this, and turned that room into a dark but strobing visual environment to match the audio. It was pretty cool.[20]

When this sound eventually stops, the player is left completely rattled and un- balanced, wondering what happened and feeling a real unease about an environ- ment that can expose them to such an assault. The sound is never repeated but its effect stays with the player for a very long time. It is a perfect introduction to a new level for a horror game like *Dead Space*.

Further Notes

Although this may seem too "cheap"[21] a way of producing results, it is actually quite hard to do this well. Get the sound itself wrong and the player may mis-

---

[20] Jayson Napolitano interviewing Don Veca, the audio director for *Dead Space*, on the Original Sound Version blog, http://www.originalsoundversion.com/?p=693, October 7, 2008.

[21] As in "lacking in class" or "exploitative."

interpret its occurrence. Misjudge the intensity and the player may get irritated. Mess up the timing and it may occur at an inappropriate time.

If done correctly however the level quality as a whole will go up substantially.

Game Environments

R eality is that which, when you stop believing in it, doesn't go away.

—Philip K. Dick

"We experience the world through our senses." To most people this is hardly a controversial concept. We define our reality through sight, sound, smell, taste,

"Labyrinth 1" from the Nordisk familjebok, *Wikipedia*, http://commons.wikimedia. org/wiki/File:Labyrinth_1_(from_Nordisk_familjebok).svg, 2009.

and touch. When it comes to video games, however, several of our senses are taken out of the equation. There is no smell associated with a game environment.[2] Likewise, we cannot taste our game environments, which is something that may well be for the best. We do have a very limited sense of touch, depending on the platform and its input/output mechanism, rumble, force feedback steering wheel, analogue pressure-sensitive buttons, motion sensing, etc. Diverse as these are, they still provide a fairly basic and limited experience in comparison to the final two: sight and sound.[3]

This section of the book is about how people experience game environments, and how we can design levels that make full use of the sensory possibilities this experience can offer. *Touch* is still too underdeveloped a dimension in game development, or at least level in design, which after further discounting *smell* and *taste* leaves us with only two chapters based on *visuals* and *sound*. What rich and important subjects they are, however! Some of the most enjoyable contributions to level design language are made within the context of these topics, at least insofar as they are important in helping to realize game environments, which is the main focus of this section of the book anyway.

---

[2] At least not until games are developed using *smellovision*.

[3] Or sound and vision, to quote David Bowie.

Visual Experiences 10

Most established art forms have had a profound impact upon each other. A healthy cross-pollination occurs, and the result is that art does not exist in a vacuum, but keeps evolving through exposure to the rest of the world.

Since making video games is such a young art form, there is still much to be learned from other art forms. This is true, for example, of some elements of storytelling or sound design (areas that are covered elsewhere in this book), but it is especially true for visual design and visual direction. Although not exclusively so, most level design is highly reliant on conveying visual information. Yet surprisingly, not much is known in level design circles about the underlying processes at work. There are a number of basic areas that need to be examined to help us use visual techniques to their fullest potential. This is true for any creative medium that is reliant on visual communication with the audience.

Concept

The Physiology of Sight

I have to admit that before I wrote this book I only had some vague notions on how eyesight works. I already knew that it was important somehow to processes that one would not immediately associate with eyesight, but how and why was a mystery to me. I am happy to say that in my limited research I did indeed find out some very interesting facts about how eyesight works, and crucially that it has great bearing on the subject matter of this book. Let me share some of the findings with you.

The Human Eye

One of the easiest ways to explain sight is to think of the human eye as a biological camera. Light falls through the *cornea* and a hole called the *pupil* (diaphragm), is focused by a *lens*, and is projected onto an area at the back of the eye called the *retina* (film). The retina then takes the information it collects and sends it to the *optic nerve,* which develops the image into electric signals sent to the brain. The brain then constructs a mental image from those electric signals.

The Act of Seeing

Seeing is of course so much more than just *sending electric signals to the brain.* There are some very important processes at work that have massive bearing on how we experience the world visually. It is the interpretation of data that produces some special characteristics. For example, human eyesight (and that of many other species) seems to be particularly good at processing visual data as *patterns* and *motion:*

Pattern recognition (and recognizing pattern breaks)

Our brains have evolved in such a way that they have become very adept at processing data in ways that are important in our daily lives. Of these skills, *pattern recognition* stands out particularly well, since we use it so much. How else do we differentiate between all the differing visual inputs we receive via our eyes? Pattern recognition allows us to process visual data at a much-enhanced speed because it lets us carve up the visual input into useful chunks to which we ascribe further meaning and behavior. This process is actually called *chunking*[1] and is key to our intelligent understanding of our environment. Chunking occurs when we encounter large amounts of visual data and summarize it into abstract patterns or visual models we can deal with much quicker. For example, a master chess player can mentally recreate the location of all the pieces on a chessboard by recognizing the underlying strategic patterns involved.[2] When we lose something in the grass, we don't have to process each blade of grass visually in order to find the lost object. Instead, we have a pattern (the grass) and we look to see where the lost object breaks it.

Although we don't often think about this aspect of our cognition and intelligence, it is actually a key part of our ability to process information in the world.

---

[1] I kid you not!

[2] Tellingly, this skill falls away if the pieces are placed randomly.

Interestingly within the area of robotics and other related fields like artificial intelligence, it has become clear that it is incredibly difficult to artificially recreate this ability. Some even see it as a necessary hurdle that has to be jumped on the path to full artificial intelligence. An enormous amount of research is done in this field as a consequence; so much that it has spawned dedicated journals[3] and academic gatherings.[4] It is clearly a fascinating and important field and it leaves no doubt that pattern recognition is fundamental to our ability to create abstract recreations of the world around us. And that is something that marks us even further as strangely evolved creatures.

Motion tracking

On a similar note, we have the ability to pick out, track, and process the movement of countless objects in our vision. We know about the amazing skill of a hawk to pick out the movement of a tiny mouse on the ground, or a cat focusing on the movement of a wriggling insect. But in our own lives we can recognize similar feats of motion perception just as easily. Take a moment to think of the real complexity of a person crossing a busy street in a major city. That person has to successfully track and judge the motion of dozens of moving bodies and make individual assessments on how to react to them in many cases. It is not rare for such a mundane act to require the person to process data dealing with several other pedestrians, many cars moving at different speeds, the person's own motion, sudden changes due to traffic light fluctuation, and so forth.

Op-art

One of the best-known art forms that deals with visual techniques is op art. Op art deals with optical illusions elevated to the level of art. Often, through the use of patterns, scale, or color, op art can create tension in impossible images. (See, for example, Figure 10.1.) It examines the psychological reaction to physically impossible or confusing images or other art works. Although not the most self evident of techniques, when studied, it actually shows a wealth of understanding of how human beings deal with visual input, and how easy it is to subvert these reactions.

---

[3] *Pattern Recognition: The Journal of the Pattern Recognition Society*, http://www.elsevier.com/wps/find/journaldescription.cws_home/328/description#description.

[4] International Conference on Artificial Intelligence and Pattern Recognition, http://www.promoteresearch.org/2007/aipr/.

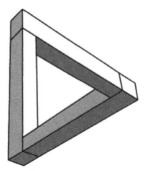

Figure 10.1. Penrose triangle.[5]

The Psychology of Sight

Beyond the physical, there is a further, even more interesting dimension. What is it we actually do with all this visual information on a psychological and mental level? How does sight affect how we *feel*?

Emotional Associations

Aside from the way human beings react to visuals on a mechanical level, there are factors at play that are more nebulous.[6] Certain visuals evoke an emotional reaction within us, sometimes completely independent from physiological causes. We are scared of the dark, clutter makes us nervous, towering architecture may make us feel insignificant, and so forth. Why is it that we may label one visual experience as beautiful and another as ugly or depressing? There isn't one all-encompassing answer to all these questions. There are many factors at play, and some of them cannot easily be explained. Let's look at a few of them.

Aesthetic sensibilities

Aesthetics is a rather large and complex discipline, sometime even a contradictory one. It studies the senses' reactions to things like art, but I won't spend time trying to explain the full scope, or even attempt to give my own understanding of what it means. It suffices to say that most people when asked about aesthetics

---

[5] The original drawing of this object appeared in Lionel Penrose and Roger Penrose, "Impossible Objects: A Special Type of Visual Illusion," *British Journal of Psychology*, 49:1 (1958), 31–33.

[6] But important nonetheless.

think of the study of that which makes things beautiful or enjoyable to the senses (or ugly and repugnant).

We can learn many things from aesthetic principles in regard to making a visual scene pleasing to look at, but the deeper lesson lies in the fact that aesthetics gives us a measure of control, a tool, for influencing the audience's mindset. Instead of using aesthetic principles to create a pleasing scene, the knowledge can be used to create a disturbing scene, for example by sabotaging an earlier carefully established sense of aesthetic balance.

Primal reactions

Some emotional responses to visual scenes or stimuli seem to be hard-coded in our brains (or taught at such a young age that they are involuntary). Who doesn't feel a slight tremor in their legs when standing on the edge of a precipice? A large percentage of the population freaks out when confronted with insects crawling on them, *even if they are known to be harmless*. We react well to smiles, not so well to a stranger or strange animal running straight at us.

"Taught" reactions

At other times we are confronted to what amounts to long established visual *conventions*. In nature an animal is taught by experience which colors to avoid when gathering food. In human culture we have many conventions as well. In a movie, a shaky point-of-view handheld camera may indicate a stalker. Red is often the color of *danger*. Different creative fields have different sets of conventions, but many visual ones are shared across disciplines. This is ripe picking for anyone who wants to enlarge his or her vocabulary of visual techniques. Many books have been written on the subject, so there is no excuse for ignorance in that regard. Even a trip to the museum can do wonders.

Visual Direction

When we take all of these examples and the associated knowledge we gleam from them, we suddenly find that we have at our disposal a huge toolbox for artistic expression. The techniques available to us are often surprisingly effective and versatile, and it should come as no surprise that they have many well known and practical applications. When these principles are being applied to aid artistic or creative expression[7] we speak of *visual direction*.

---

[7] They have other applications as well, but I don't want to stray away too far from the core of this book.

Few fields are as knowledgeable about the psychology (and physiology) of visual direction as filmmaking. The field has been discovering and refining techniques of visual direction for over a hundred years. There are thousands of fantastic examples of directors of photography (DPs) or cameramen who have been adding their own twist to the subject. A beautiful example can be found in a scene in the movie *Lawrence of Arabia* that showcases one of the most famous sequences in cinema history. It describes the first meeting between Sherif Ali, played by Omar Sharif, and Lawrence of Arabia, played by Peter O'Toole).

Lawrence and his guide Tafa have just quenched their thirst from a well in the middle of the desert. The camera shows Lawrence lazing about and the guide getting more water from the well. The whole horizon can be seen for many seconds. Finally it becomes clear that somebody is appearing on the horizon (Omar Sharif's character) and approaching. It becomes clear that it is somebody riding towards them on a camel. Suddenly Lawrence's guide runs off to get a pistol, grabs it, and takes aim. He is shot by the approaching rider. The following dialogue takes place:

Lawrence
Who is he? Tafas!

Ali
He's dead.

Lawrence
Yes. Why?

Ali
This is my well.

Lawrence
I have drunk from it.

Ali
You are welcome.

It is a well-written scene with dialogue that is original and interesting. Had it not been preceded by the approach on the horizon by the rider who appears as in a mirage, it would not have been as famous as it is now. On location filmmaker David Lean and the director of photography (DP) Freddie Young, realized they had a particular problem with the focal point of the viewer. Omar Sharif was supposed to ride into the scene appearing far away on the horizon, slowly becoming visible to the audience. Unfortunately, with such a clear and wide horizon and the otherwise empty desert, the viewer's eye started to wander. Since the viewer wasn't directed where to focus he or she would start scanning the screen, missing the point where Sherif Ali was to slowly materialize on the horizon. This meant that Omar

Sharif's character would not get the introduction that the scene demanded and the whole sequence would fall completely short of the impact that was required.

Freddie Young's solution was ingenious. He painted the desert. He literally had his crew paint a line of desert sand reaching all the way to the spot on the horizon where the Sherif Ali character was to appear. The line was slightly lighter than the normal desert sand, just enough so the eye and brain would pick up on this and follow it to the beginning, the intended focal point. It worked perfectly; the viewer's eye is now naturally drawn towards the trail in the sand, and is focused in the right area of the screen even before Sherif rides into view. Without realizing it, the audience now is looking *exactly* where the DP wants it to look. It makes the scene perfect, and has become a classic example of visual direction in cinema. Most people who watch never realize that their eyes are being directed.

Visual Direction and Film Language

This description of the famous scene from *Lawrence of Arabia* is highly significant, as it shows a practical and applicable example of visual direction in a creative art form and can teach us many things. It shows that it is possible to direct the emotional impact of a scene, without being too overt, *with simple visual direction*. This is extremely important if we want the player or movie viewer to be immersed and willing to suspend disbelief. It is just one example, but it hints at a whole toolset or language of visual direction that may be of use to level designers as well. In filmmaking terms, this kind of visual direction is part of a larger body of expressive and artistic means often referred to as *film language* or *film art*.

Film language constitutes an ever-evolving and vital body of knowledge[8] that level designers would do well to study and incorporate in their own level design language.

Related Disciplines

If we take a high concept approach to the topics we are discussing in this chapter we start to see that there is much overlap with other fields of interest, some of which are associated with a huge body of work.

Architecture

Architecture is often named as a logical subject of study for level designers, and to a degree this makes sense. Architecture has much to do with designing spaces

---

[8] Bordwell and Thompson's work is a good starting point: http://www.davidbordwell.net/blog/.

for human beings, and since architecture has been around for a few thousand years, this gives us a wealth of information[9] that could apply to level design. We can look at aesthetics, construction and technology, visual direction, social manipulation (in a benign way) and so on.

Planology and urban planning

Some of these matters are also related to choices made on a societal level. How do we design and plan public spaces to be effectively used by millions of people? How do we reach a consensus that will appeal to the people forced to make use of those spaces in the future? Answers to these questions can have much bearing on multiplayer level design issues, especially in the areas of MMOGs and other virtual worlds. Again, much important research has already been done and can be of great help to us.

Environmental psychology

There is no shortage of interesting areas to study across the whole spectrum of applied visual theories. In fact, the way we act in and interact with our environment within this context touches on too many disciplines to name. There is, however, an area of study that tries to unify many of these loosely related topics into a general area—*Environmental Psychology*. It is a field that is not clearly delineated but has much to offer to level design, and in my personal opinion, level design actually has much to offer to this field in its own right.

Concept Summary

All of the above examples, be they physiological or psychological in nature, provide us with creative opportunities. The knowledge we have of how human beings process visual information and how they react to visual stimuli on an emotional level allows us to create situations where premeditated reactions can occur.[10] In other words, we can influence the reactions of people around us (only with their consent of course) by manipulating what they are exposed to visually. Creative expression is filled with examples of artists doing this successfully. Sometimes it has even been elevated to an art genre in its own right, as we can see in the op art movement.

We can even go as far as saying that visual direction is a key part of the *language* of many art forms, film being a notable example. Whatever the terminol-

---

[9] A good starting point for study is Francis Ching's book *Architecture: Form, Space and Order,* Third Edition, Wiley, New York, 2007.

[10] That sounds much more sinister than intended.

ogy used, however, these forms are only relevant if we take lessons from them that we can use in actual level design theory and practice. This is something we will explore in more detail in the next part of this chapter.

Theory

The previous part of this chapter goes into some detail explaining the core principles of visual processes. It covers underlying physiology, general comments on sight and psychological impact, and to a degree, artistic viability. The first and the latter are mostly straightforward examinations, but the middle one dealing with psychological principles deserves extra scrutiny within the context of level design theory. In what cases can we use principles of visual direction established in other disciplines? When do we need to make alterations to them? When do we need to define our own principles and techniques? In other words: we need to establish visual direction techniques and principles as part of level design theory. We will look at this and other aspects of visual direction in the next section.

Camera

We cannot talk about as visual a medium as video games without spending some time on the subject of the camera. The camera system of a game is the medium through which we view the game directly. It provides our eyes with the visual data that the game wants to player to receive. For that reason it is of the utmost importance that the subject of game camera be taken seriously. There is a good chance that on any given project the level designer will have some control over the game camera. This makes it extremely important that the designer have at least some knowledge of the capabilities of the game camera.

The introduction to Sidney Lumet's chapter on cameras in his book *Making Movies* reads as follows:

> The Camera
> Your best friend
>
> First of all, the camera can't talk back. It can't ask stupid questions. It can't ask penetrating questions that make you realize you have been wrong all along. Hey, it's a camera!
>
> But:
>
> - It can make up for a deficient performance.
> - It can make a good performance better.

- It can create mood.
- It can create ugliness.
- It can create beauty.
- It can provide excitement.
- It can capture the essence of the moment.
- It can stop time.
- It can change space.
- It can define a character.
- It can provide exposition.
- It can make a joke.
- It can make a miracle.
- It can tell a story.

If my movie has two stars in it, I always know it really has three. The third star is the camera.[11]

This is about as ringing an endorsement of the value of good camera work as can be found.

Without disagreeing with Mr. Lumet, it is nonetheless important to note the difference between game camera and film camera. Although many principles overlap, the two aren't the same. A major difference between film and video games lies in the fact that while a film audience has no influence whatsoever on what is displayed onscreen, games allow for a huge range of freedom in this regard. Not only in respect to what scenes are shown, but also in what order they occur, and in some cases games can even allow the user to change the actual *environment*. This means that in most cases the traditional controlled version of visual direction goes out the window. Other techniques have to be employed.

Let's first look at some typical game camera situations so we can judge potential limitations. These are of some importance because the choice of game cameras determines how the player sees the game.

First Person

We speak of *first person* camera when the camera view is shown from the perspective of the player. Imagine the scene shown as if seen through the player's eyes. There are many variations possible, but the following are the most prevalent. (They are not mutually exclusive.)

On rails

In this variation the camera moves on a predetermined path and the player has little or no control over the direction it looks at. (Although the player may have

---

[11] Sidney Lumet, *Making Movies*, Random House, Inc., New York, 1996, pp. 75–76.

control over the direction it moves in. A good example can be found in *Myst*,[12] a puzzle-based adventure game, or in a similar vein. *The Seventh Guest* [13]"is a game with similar play mechanics.

By today's standards, this type of camera control would seem overly limited and even old fashioned. From a purely level-design-centric view, however, the advantages are massive. The designer rather than the player controls the camera, which gives him or her much more license to direct the gameplay.

A further advantage lies in the fact that designers and artists can build environments based on predetermined camera positions, only having to build those parts that the player can actually see. This is just as on a film set, where a street only needs to consist of the fronts of buildings, since nobody will ever see the inside or the back.

Player controlled

This is by far the most prevalent form of first person camera in games. Imagine a camera glued between the eyes of the player, and you'll get a pretty accurate picture. Camera direction and movement are controlled by the player, which means that the designer will have to use all kinds of techniques of visual direction in order for the player to follow his or her lead, receive specific in-game information, get the right emotional messages, and so on.

The disadvantage of not having as much control over the player's experience can be seen as a major advantage, as well. Through the use of subtle visual direction, the designer can shape a play experience without leading the player by the nose. This helps make the player responsible for his or her own actions, greatly reducing resentment for being presented with lack of choice.

Much more detailed environments have to be built to accommodate all the player choices, but on the other hand, this delivers increased chances for exploration.

Third Person

An easy way to imagine third person camera views is to picture a floating camera, disassociated from the player's in-game presence. In most cases it follows the player character, but this can be done in quite diverse other ways as well. The most typical ones are discussed below.

---

[12] Published by Brøderbund Software, Inc., developed by Cyan Worlds, Inc., released September 24, 1993.

[13] Published by Virgin Interactive Entertainment, Inc., developed by Trilobyte, Inc., released 1993.

Side-on

Classic two-dimensional platform games feature a camera that tracks the player but is stuck in a side-on, 2D plane. Some minor control by the player may be possible, for instance by "pushing" the camera slightly off center to reveal more of the playing field, but most of the time the camera will be stuck in one position relative to the player character and will not leave the 2D plane of movement.

These limitations produce their own unique problems and opportunities. It is difficult to apply any traditional dramatic touches or to create a sense of foreboding due to camera placement or something equally filmic. On the other hand, it is an excellent camera system for showing the player things explicitly and safely, away from player influence. A room with a monster might move into view, forewarning the player of a situation that is yet to occur. Whole scripted sequences can take place just outside of the player's reach.

Third person free-cam and follow-cam

One of the most prevalent camera systems in modern video game is used in third person games with a controllable player character. These include *Tomb Raider*,[14] where the camera can move about in 3D space, but follows the player. This can be further divided in games that allow player positioning of cameras (*free cam*), and games that don't.

Third person free-cam. This allows the player to rotate the camera, and sometimes to adjust pitch and yaw. Since the player has almost full control over where the camera is at any time and may have much control over where the player character can go, much will be asked of the game environment. It needs to be much more realized and must stand up to the scrutiny of being explored and looked at from many angles and directions.

Third person follow-cam. This employs a camera that follows the player around, as in the 2D side-on game example, but it is not limited to one plane of movement. Instead, it is generally the level designer who determines where the camera can go and how it gets there. (However, they may still have some control over pitch and yaw.)

This allows for a much more controlled style of level design, where visual direction can be planned with more accuracy or knowledge of what the player will be able to see at any time. This has fairly obvious advantages, which are further enhanced by the fact that the designer is also able to employ techniques dealing

---

[14] Published by Eidos Interactive, Inc., developed by Core Design Ltd., released 1996.

with camera height and framing in general. In many ways, this camera system presents the best compromise between player needs and directorial control. Games like *Zelda: Twilight Princess* have employed this with much success.

Placed (static)

In some cases the camera can be placed in 3D space, but it doesn't move around relative to the player position. (However, it may well keep the player centered onscreen, within the limits of the camera's pivot distance.)

This is generally done to add drama and tension to an environment, as in survival horror games, or to aid specific environment-specific gameplay, like jumping sequences that may be hard to judge with a moving camera.

Whatever the reason for this system, whether temporary or used throughout the game, it features some unique problems and opportunities.

Other Types

These examples all spring from game types that feature an in-game presentation of the player. There are of course many game types where this is not the case; chess, for example, is generally depicted through a camera that just shows the whole playing field. In those cases many of the third-person circumstances still apply; the camera is just not associated with a specific player character.

Camera as a Level Design Tool

Depending on the project and the people involved, chances are that the issue of camera use will not be taken seriously enough. People may argue that they are making a game and not a movie. They are missing the point. What *matters* is that, just as in filmmaking, the camera has an enormous influence over the final quality of the game. Ideally, if appropriate, this means that the level designer is given as much control over the camera as possible. Therefore, it is almost always of the utmost importance that camera is given serious thought early on in the project, and that there be sufficient code support and cooperation. I cannot stress the point enough. Although this is a crucial component of level design and game quality, it is rarely understood by other team members. The designer nonetheless should argue this point as strongly as possible. The level design can be strengthened immeasurably by giving the designer a set of tools that allow for camera movement, lens changes, field of view changes, shot transitions, camera types, etc.—whatever is deemed appropriate for the game.

This responsibility must also be recognized by designers themselves, who must study and build a repertoire of video game camera techniques and limitations. Books like this one can hopefully be of great use, but it is also extremely useful to be up to date on real world camera techniques, especially motion picture camera principles. This includes subjects like framing a shot, set design, camera moves, and lenses. A good book on the subject is *The Camera Assistant. A Complete Professional Handbook*, by Douglas C. Hart, which is one of the key reference works within the discipline.

Carrying Information

A fundamental aspect of camera work, and a key part of level design, lies in the realization that every scene or shot contains *information*. This is pretty much always true, even if the information isn't always very interesting. Once we get beyond the almost banal simplicity of this statement, we are nonetheless presented with a very important question: *what information do we want to convey to the player?*

This is actually a very interesting question, with a limitless number of potential answers. *Every single visual decision* made in the course of the design will make an impact, and that includes "simple" decisions like item placement. It is an old level-design cliché, for example that a room full of powerups signals an imminent boss fight.

This principle can be extended to include other areas as well. Scripted sequences can carry information useful to the player. The original *Half Life*,[15] for example, would signal danger to the player by letting Very Bad Things happen to NPCs in view of the player, often in scenarios that would also give the player information on how to avoid a similar fate. In a game with a day/night cycle, dusk may tell the player that it is time to find shelter from night crawlers. The way somebody is dressed in MMORPGs may indicate rank and experience. The list is endless. We need to be as aware as possible of the impact of the things that the player can observe, and try to incorporate this knowledge in the visual direction and the visual design of the levels.

Visual Design

There is no doubt that at times, as level designers, we need to be knowledgeable of the visual arts, so we can create real impact on a visual level as well as on a gameplay level. Furthermore, quite often the two should not be seen as separate disciplines at all.

---

[15] Developed by Valve Software.

Darkness and Light

Photography is often described as *painting with darkness and light*. Although color can clearly be a part of the equation, the description still holds true in general if we accept that color still comes from the consequence of lighting a scene. In most cases it is the use of darkness and light that bring out all the distinctive or interesting aspects within an image. This principle can be applied to games as well, so we should at least look at some basic aspects of the use of darkness and light in a scene, and at the interplay between the two.

Use of darkness

Traditionally, darkness is used in games to create fear and unease. Although easily turned into cliché, this is not a bad application per se. However, we must to be careful not to create a lazy *darkness = scary* attitude. At least not without understanding why it can be scary. The key aspect of darkness is that it takes away sight. This is an obvious observation, but it becomes more interesting if we look at what that can mean in practical terms. For example, if the point of darkness in a level is to create fear, taking away sight can work, because the player loses a sense of control. If we can't see dangers anymore, but they are still around, we rightly become rather nervous. Dangers can also be hinted at. An imagined creature accompanied by sounds, for example, is scarier than a visible one.

However, darkness can be used in all kinds of other ways. If the gameplay is about staying undetected, darkness can be a real friend. Darkness can provide cover for exploration, or provide the play mechanic for a puzzle.

Use of light

In contrast, light is often used to create a sense of safety, a positive to counter the negative of darkness. Again, this is not necessarily a bad application, but there are many other ways that light can be used to create interesting gameplay and therefore perform more functions than just lighting the scene. Good lighting is as much the provenance of a good level designer as that of a game artist. A level designer may decide to use the lighting in a level to create gameplay sequences that simply cannot be done in another way. Take for example typical stealth gameplay where the player needs to remain undetected, and therefore out of the light. There is great fun to be had by giving the player the chance to control lighting that affects the game AI, by being able to switch lights on or off, or perhaps by allowing the player to blind AI opponents with a searchlight.

There are plenty of possibilities where lighting can be used in an original way that enhances gameplay. Some more will be highlighted in the practice section of this subject.

Patterns and Motion Tracking

Since video gaming is such a visual medium, it is a good thing that so much of level design is about teaching mechanics, as we have seen in some of the earlier chapters. It is a good thing because many powerful techniques make use of patterns and pattern recognition. It is thankfully very easy to create level design scenarios where these innate skills are used to their fullest and tested through gameplay. Take for example classic platforming gameplay, for instance the ubiquitous section where the player has to navigate underneath a set of pistons smashing down on the player's route. This is almost always only possible to do by observing the pattern in which the pistons smash down and basing a timed run on that pattern.

Pattern recognition isn't only applicable to movement patterns. Sometimes it is just as clear in a static visual setting. In a shop with hundreds of multicolored vases, one row of ten blue vases would stand out very clearly. Or in actual game terms, the player can easily recognize the difference between environmental props and (for instance) powerups. That makes them very suitable to help direct the player visually or to suggest possible accessibility to areas in the level that the player hadn't considered. If there is a powerup, the player can surely reach it— right?

Level design is absolutely full of potential uses for our innate ability to recognize patterns and motion, and we should make full use of this principle.

Scale

Scale can have a huge impact on the ultimate feel of a level's design, and many scale-related decisions have very specific results. Some situations are easily understood and can be implemented without too much fuss. A player may feel a sense of elation after having conquered a long and difficult climb up a huge tower. The scale of the tower when the player first looked up at its base, and the reversed situation when the player has reached the peak and is now looking down at the tiny objects back at the ground, is bound to have an impact. This can be further enhanced by giving the player some useful visual information related to being at such a high vantage point, or awarding the player with some rare object for reaching this area.

Negative feelings can be stirred as well. Imagine the horror of seeing the scale of a growing mushroom cloud after a nuclear explosion. Populating a level with big looming buildings that tower over the player can generate feelings of oppression. A further sense of claustrophobia can occur by making the player navigate small, cramped corridors. Whichever way you look, matters of scale become relevant to level design issues in diverse ways. If the designer decides to make a set piece out of scaling a very high mountain, space must be reserved in the level to accommodate the scale of the mountain. Furthermore, is it actually fun to traverse the real distance this would entail? Perhaps some shortcuts are in order, possibly an action-filled cable car ride, and a further hitch on a lift built *in* the mountain.

Clearly, seemingly small[16] decisions on scale can have a huge impact on the content and feel of a level.

Visual Style

Some of the art decisions that need to be made for the game are about choosing an appropriate *style*. This is a decision that influences many things beyond the actual look of the game. Real gameplay issues come into the picture and must therefore be looked at before any art style is chosen.

We can initially make a rough decision between a style that is based on realistic imagery (realistic in depiction, though not necessarily in content) and a direction that is much more stylized, like the use of toon-shading or super-deformed proportions.

Realism

The advantage of a realistic style is that we can use the real world as an inspiration and a resource. It is very handy that if we want to use a car in a realistic game, we can just go outside and take the dimensions of a real car, or get some blueprints from the manufacturer. Consistency and believability can be guaranteed by sticking with real world parameters, an advantage that shouldn't be underestimated.

Trying to achieve realism has its own problems, however. There are a number of dangers, some of them unexpected. First, there is the problem of *detail*. In a realistic setting there is just more work to be done to ensure that realistic representations are supported by sufficient levels of detail. There will be certain expectations that must be met in order for the environment to be convincing. A door on hinges will have to swing, a car will have to behave in a recognizable way, and so on. To further complicate matters, the game's AI needs to be realistic enough, especially the AI of human characters. It is very easy to underestimate the damage that can be done by not preparing for this problem. Level designers can easily find themselves in a place known as *the uncanny valley*.

The theory of the uncanny valley was made popular by the Japanese roboticist Masahiro Mori. In his work dealing with the creation of realistic

---

[16] No pun intended.

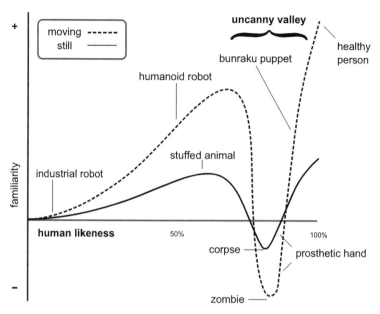

Figure 10.2. "The uncanny valley."[17]

human-looking robots and people's emotional responses to them, Mori has formed an interesting theory. He postulates that people react well to robots that greatly resemble humans, but only to a certain point. When the robot's look gets very close to lifelike, the small differences between real humans and robots start to take on an eerie quality. Imagine for instance a robot that looks lifelike except for eyes that are too wide apart and blink too often, and that moves around in a shambling gait.[18] It doesn't take much imagination to picture some very disturbing, but close to human, behavior. Figure 10.2 shows the principle clearly.

It is very rare that level designers need to design the look of human AI characters in the game, but what we do often need to do is to design the way they need to *behave*. And this is where some real problems can occur. Scripting AI behavior in a realistic game offers some well-known dangers. Lines of speech

---

[17] "Uncanny Valley," *Wikipedia*, http://en.wikipedia.org/wiki/Uncanny_valley, 2009.

[18] I am creeping myself out here!

can be inappropriate, the AI can be too oblivious to its surroundings, its path through the environment can be strange, idle animations can play at the wrong times, and so forth. Many of these can be very detrimental to immersion, or even worse, open to exploits. In other words: tread carefully!

Another problem within a realistic style is the lack of creative license if we opt for realism based on our natural world. That is to say that the game is naturalistic by only including elements that can exist now or that could have existed in the past in the real world. Having to be realistic in this manner quite often means that for an element to be believable, its use must be explained. In a cartoon, sci-fi, or fantasy setting it is quite easy to create an impenetrable barrier that the player can see through, but that will not allow anything else to pass. A magic fence or a nice force field would do the trick, with few questions asked. Internal game logic still needs to be established and followed, but more creative license can be used to achieve these things.

Stylized expression

The extra creative license just described is not the only advantage in a stylized setting. In some non-realistic styles, less detail is needed to create a clear image. Cartoons can create very clear images by using very few brush strokes, and similarly, a game that uses toon shading needs much less detail to paint a clear picture for the player. To the level designer this can be a huge advantage. It makes it much faster to create basic functioning game environments, and much easier to change them around when needed. This in turn has a subsequent effect on flexibility and iterative prototyping. These are all massive bonuses.

As always, though, there are downsides. The style may be so alien that no real-world reference can be used. Alien technology and road signs may make it hard to direct the player or to make sure the player cannot get lost. There may be the need to portray fairly complex and detailed mechanisms within a style that is too bulky to easily facilitate this. As always, we have to be very careful not to fall into any of these traps. Luckily, there are many techniques available to us that can help us navigate these issues.

Power of Suggestion

To make sense of the world, our brains are able to take limited information and extrapolate a more detailed picture from it. They literally fill in the blanks. We don't need to see every individual brick in a wall to know that the whole wall is there. If something comes running towards us, we can judge pretty quickly if it is on a collision course with us, and roughly how long before it is time to get out of the way.

We can do these things for a number of reasons. Most of them are neurological in nature, reinforced by previous experiences. When taken together, these factors give us a very decent predictive mental view of the world. However, we may still be fooled, at times in surprisingly easy ways.

Let the Player Fill in the Blanks

I have already given the example of a movie set with streets, where only the fronts of buildings need to be seen. As long as the camera doesn't enter a building, there is no need to show, and therefore build, an interior. This principle applies just as strongly to level design. The example given is a very direct and literal example. A gaming example would be a house with a locked door that the player cannot enter. Put some curtains on the window and we can forget about the interior. We can do better than this however; more interesting and versatile examples can be found.

The principle of visual suggestion doesn't just apply to things that we can observe. As we already touched upon in the chapter on immersion, sometimes the presence or absence of something in the environment suggests deeper levels of information.

- Train tracks suggest a train.
- Smoke suggests fire.
- Hot tea suggests a recently present person.
- Political graffiti suggests factions.
- A radar post suggests planes.

These are just a few.

Much better or more appropriate examples are easily found when we examine individual projects. What we wish to suggest depends completely on the game and on the situation. It can be the presence of a certain kind of creature, or perhaps shelter from environmental hazards. It doesn't really matter. What does matter is that we have a cheap and convincing method at our disposal that can convey information about the game environment in many useful ways, often indirectly. A good understanding of this principle is a major addition to the arsenal of visual direction. Sometimes this can take the form of *misdirection* as well.

"Filling in the blanks" like this is sometimes referred to as *closure*. This has much wider application potential than is suggested here, but to keep matters organized, I want to revisit these concepts in more detail later in the book.

Misdirection

Have you ever seen a magician at work? One of the main techniques of any magician is the use of *misdirection*. The famous magician Jean Hugard once said the following about misdirection:

> The principle of misdirection plays such an important role in magic that one might say that Magic is misdirection and misdirection is Magic.

This is a quote that level designers need to take to heart. After all, we deal exclusively in virtual, and therefore in many respects illusory, worlds. This is not unlike how a magician deals with illusions to create magic. The principle behind misdirection is simple enough: focus the audience's mind and expectations in one direction, while performing an act of some sort (undetected) that suggests that something magical has happened. (For example, while a street magician is focusing our attention on a complex maneuver with his right hand, he has already reshuffled the deck with his left.[19]) Of course it is unlikely that we will use card tricks or anything like that within level design, but sometimes we do want some actions in the game world to distract the player from others. Sometimes this is done to hide immersion-breaking activities, or sometimes to set up a specific gameplay surprise or scripted sequence. You will be surprised at how effective this technique can be when used well.

Theme

What is it all about? I don't mean what happens (that is plot), but why is it all happening? What is the underlying reason or the intention? Generally, these kinds of things can be attributed to *theme*. Theme is a subject that pops up a few times in this book, and although it sounds imposing and serious, it isn't something we should be scared of. In Stephen King's book *On Writing* we find the following thoughts[20]:

> Writing and literature classes can be annoyingly preoccupied by (and pretentious about) theme, approaching it as the most sacred of sacred cows, but (don't be shocked) it's really no big deal. If you write a novel, spend weeks and then months catching it word by word, you owe it both to the book and then to yourself to lean back (or take a long walk) when you've finished and ask yourself why you bothered–why you

---

[19] I don't know if that at ever happens, but the principle is clear.

[20] Stepheb King, *On Writing: A Memoir of the Craft*, Pocket Books, New York, 2002, pp. 200–201.

spent all that time, why it seemed so important. In other words, what's it all about, Alfie?

He also notes that:

> . . . Not every book has to be loaded with symbolism, irony or musical language (they call it prose for a reason y'know), but it seems to me that every book—at least every one worth reading—is about *something*.

This applies as much to writing as it does to level design. And one way to really express this well in level design is by defining a well thought-through visual theme, or more likely a *set* of themes. A good partnership with the game artists is of great importance in this case. (More on that later.)

Once a clear idea emerges on theme(s), it is easy to start to apply it in several aspects of the visual design. It is actually important to make sure that theme is reflected throughout several areas of the level, or it won't have the impact it should have. If a sense of death needs to permeate a ghost town, it is perfectly valid to sprinkle the environment with graves.

Beyond these kinds of direct visual implementations, there are subtler ways to incorporate theme in the level design. Much can be achieved via the use of *symbolism* and *metaphor*, even without the player being aware of this.

Whose Job Is It Anyway?

Some people will argue that many of these aspects of visual design fall exclusively within the domain of the art department of the project team. They are partly right, yet at the same time *completely wrong*. They are partly right because much of the relevant expertise will lie in the art department. A good artist will be able to offer far more, and sometimes better, input on how to achieve these goals of visual direction than many level designers. On many projects I would even go as far as to say that the level designer has no chance whatsoever to do a great job unless the art department is fully involved and on board.

Where they are wrong, however, is when they claim that visual design is the *exclusive* domain of the art department. Nothing could be further from the truth. Level design is applied game design, and the art of the game should support this first and foremost. Function comes before form. Anyone who suggests that this sabotages artistic expression is working in the wrong field. Imagine Martin Scorsese having to direct a gritty scene that calls for harsh lighting but being unable to do so because the cameraman or DP insists on shooting a tranquil tableau in soft focus, independent of the dramatic needs of the shot. If this were to happen, that cameraman or DP would be out of a job faster than you can say "Print!"

The same danger exists in an inverted manner if level designers think they can do the visual direction by themselves. In most cases this would be a laughable conceit.

Theory Summary

The visual direction used in a level touches every other aspect of that level's design. It simply cannot be left till last; it is the designer's responsibility that the consequences of related choices be well understood and implemented. This means that the designer must act as a liaison to the art department in order to coordinate and cooperate, and with programmers in order to receive the right tools for the job. It also means that the designer must study the craft from all angles. This includes studying many aspects of film and photography, including the areas of cinematography and set design. When all these things are done, the designer has in visual design a tool that can completely transform the experience of a level. What at the beginning was a set of planned gameplay sequences can now be full of meaning, beauty, drama, backup for gameplay, and more. Therefore it deserves to be treated with a certain amount of seriousness.

Practice

Example 10.1: Use of Light—Visual Direction and Mood Manipulation

Summary

Light can be used to focus attention as well as change the mood of an area. Combining these two concepts can be very effective.

Game Genre

The technique is suitable for most games that require the player to navigate non-abstract environments.

Goals to Achieve

- Guide the player towards a goal through visual direction.
- Equate light with a positive outcome.

- Alter the general mood of the environment.
- Build towards a rewarding scene.

Description

(Example type: Original)

"Climbing towards the light." This example is going to take a hypothetical scenario that can be adapted to fit with all kinds of setting and games. The basic premise is that the player is to slowly work their way from an oppressive dark area towards safety, represented by light.

The example is set against the background of a partly collapsed skyscraper. The player is somewhere at the bottom level and can only go upwards. Electricity is mostly compromised and the starting area is nearly completely dark. A number of discreet stages or elements can be incorporated.

- **Starting off in near dark** gives the level a very oppressive and claustrophobic feel. The game spaces should be very tight to emphasize this, while also making sure that the player can't get too lost in the dark.
- **Use busy lights** in areas that need to unsettle as well as attract. A slow pulsating light or a stroboscopic flickering give the player a goal to aim for, and can provide local illumination. This kind of lighting unsettles by nature, so it is a good way to frame dangers. These can be environmental—electrical sparks, fire, lasers, and so on—or they can be AI based—an enemy guard using a helmet with a flashlight, or weapons fire.
- **Highlight exits clearly** to indicate to the player where to navigate toward. This also has the subconscious effect of teaching the player that well-lit areas are signposts towards safety. The exits can be diverse: they can include actual doorways lit by an exit light, or a hole in the ceiling leading to the next area lit by a nearby strip light.
- **Start adding windows and additional light sources.** As the player progresses through the level and advances from area to area, it is useful to slowly increase the intensity and the number of lit areas to give the player a clear sense of progression towards an escape point. By adding windows or other lookout points, the player can start to gain a better mental map of the level, as well.
- **Make the gameplay areas bigger** as the player progresses towards the level exit. To ease up on the sense of oppression and claustrophobia, the environment should slowly become more spacious and bright. The player is to be encouraged to keep following the path that leads up to brighter and less negative environments.
- **Have encounters start from farther away** so the player can use the light to their advantage. Enemy encounters or environmental dangers

should become recognizable from farther away as this will give the player a psychological boost that they are starting to be in control of their progress. Note that the gameplay does not need to get easier at all, just less panicky and unsettling. The encounters should become an obstacle between the player and his or her progress, rather than a consequence of the darkness.

- **Reward the player with a final exit** that is both bright and expansive. When he or she finally reaches the exit point of the level, the player should receive a real reward for achieving the escape from the darkness—a fitting finale for the journey they have been on. A good way to do this is to reward the player with a grand and expansive view over a bright and warmly lit vista. In this case it may be the roof of the building providing a sudden unrestricted view over the whole city.

Further Notes

The example environment and setting above can easily be exchanged for one that is more suitable to the game you are working on, like an underground mining complex or a gothic wizard's tower, for example. It should be easy to come up with an original concept that allows the use of these techniques.

Example 10.2: Direction and Misdirection—Camera Reveal

Summary

Every visual scene carries information. This is true in film, theater or level design. The way this information is delivered to the player can be manipulated to add impact and drama, especially if we use the game camera to underline the effect we want to go for.

Game Genre

This technique is suitable for all games that have a camera system that can be manipulated by the level designer. (This example uses a third-person game camera.)

Goals to Achieve

- Frame important information in a level to grab the interest of the player.
- Reward the player for exploration.
- Deliver a revealing scene that adds drama and quality to the level.

Description

(Example type: Original)

We can use the principles of direction and misdirection to create a sequence of events that add great value to a level. If we control what the player sees, through our control of the game camera, then we can in effect create a little narrative sequence—*narrative* because the images tell their own story, played out onscreen and accompanied by the player's unfolding understanding of what it is he or she sees.

The gradual camera reveal. The gradual camera reveal is a technique that is based on showing the viewer bits of scenery that, unbeknownst to the viewer, actually comprises a much larger whole. As more and more of this whole is revealed, a new understanding of the actual scene forms in the mind of the viewer, until eventually a dramatic realization takes place when the final picture falls into place. Difficult as it sounds this technique is relatively easy to implement on a technical level.

Imagine the following sequence:

- **Camera position 1:** The (third person) game camera is positioned diagonally above the player character.
  Scene: We can see the player character and some of his or her surroundings. The player seems to be on a dusty road, going through a desert.
- **Camera position 2:** The camera is positioned farther away, and tilted more towards the horizon.
  Scene: We can see the player character, and more of the road. The road appears to be quite wide and long.
- **Camera position 3:** The camera is positioned even higher and farther away. A further tilt at the horizon is established.
  Scene: We can see the player character and a near panoramic view. The road is littered by burned-out wreckage and rusted debris. The road is going towards an enormous structure on the horizon; we cannot yet make out what it is.
- **Camera position 4:** The camera is lowered behind the player and finally the full horizon can be seen.
  Scene (final reveal): The horizon now shows the famous Cape Canaveral space shuttle launching pad. The entire structure including the space shuttle is a smoking wreck. Pieces of debris are seen across the landscape, along the road as well as elsewhere. Some enormous disaster has befallen the installation.

All that is needed to frame such a scene is camera trigger boxes that tell the camera what position to take, based on the player's location. The result is a very dramatic and interesting setup. The player could subsequently find transportation to the sight, on which the next level may take place.

Further Notes

The principle can be simplified if necessary. A top down camera view can be zoomed out revealing that the player is surrounded by enemies, or a player can reach the top of a hill revealing a new landscape that completely changes the player's perception of his or her environment.

Example 10.3: Visual Impact Techniques— Scale

Summary

Use the dramatic scale of a thin bridge over a large and deep chasm for a strong visual impact on the level.

Game Genre

This example is especially suitable for games that use a third or first person camera mode and allow for action-adventure style gameplay.

Goals to Achieve

- Use dramatic scale in order to enhance visual impact.
- Successfully use the physical implication of scale and environment in a level design scenario with multiple outcomes.
- Incorporate the physicality in a dramatically interesting sequence.
- Provide a strong set piece.

Description

(Example type: Original)

This practice example has the player engage in a set piece that has an outcome that is crucial to gameplay and narrative progress. Whatever the outcome, it will create a literal chasm between the player and the past. This can be done in a binary fashion where success gives the player a sense of resolution, while failure creates a *temporary* setback that can later turn into a delayed and therefore more rewarding victory.

Setting and background. The player chases the game's main villain to a rope bridge spanning a chasm. The villain dispatches a group of henchmen to intercept the player. The player has to engage the henchmen and defeat them in time before the villain crosses the bridge and starts cutting the ropes.

Victorious outcome. The player defeats the henchmen in time to reach the villain and capture him before he cuts the rope bridge. Now on the far side of the chasm, players can cut the bridge ropes themselves, which will stop more enemy creatures from following. (This act can be shown in a cutscene including the arrival of hordes of furious but thwarted enemies on the other side of the chasm.)

Negative outcome. The player is delayed too long to reach the villain in time before he or she can cut the bridge's ropes. The bridge is cut while the player is on it and the player falls down onto a ledge on the wrong side of the chasm. The villain got away and the player is now forced to find a path down to the bottom of the chasm, in the hope that a crossing can be found. There is now literally a chasm between the player and the villain. Potentially a horde of further enemies in pursuit can once again be seen to arrive, this time taking on the role of trying to stop the player from finding a path across the chasm.

Further Notes

There is a level in *Half Life 2* that successfully uses a bridge as a visually strong backdrop to the action, as well as providing a vertiginous quality to the gameplay that enhances mood and atmosphere to a large degree.

Audio Design

11

As important as the visual dimension discussed in the previous chapter is, there is a further important aspect to game environments. Although often overlooked in creating our *inner vision* of the game world, the aural definition of the gameplay space and our reactions to music and sound is vitally important. This is heady stuff indeed, and something we should only attempt after taking a look at the basic fundamentals of the way human beings experience audio.

Concept

The Physiology of Sound

The visual experiences chapter has shown us that studying the basic physiological properties of sensory perception can teach us a great many things that are applicable to artistic expression. To build the same kind of foundation, we should do the same thing when it comes to examining audio.

How Does the Human Ear Work?

Just as was the case in the chapters on visual direction, it is useful to get a general idea of the physical principles involved in the subject we are exploring. By what mechanisms are we able to hear? I am no expert on the matter, but in basic terms that even I can understand, the following processes are important.

The cups on our head that we normally call *ears* are, as you know, just part of the whole apparatus. They are called the *pinna*, and their main function is to capture sound waves in the air and direct them towards the *ear canal*. Incidentally, the way that sound bounces around lets us judge it positional origin. The ear canal ends at the *eardrum*, a thin membrane that can be caused to vibrate by even the slightest pressure changes. When the eardrum vibrates, that signal is amplified in the *inner ear,* whose function is to transform the air pressure differences picked up by the eardrum and turn them into fluid pressure fluctuations. This is done by the *cochlea.* The fluid waves are picked up in the *organ of corti,* a part of the ear lined by thousands of tiny hair cells, which translate the fluid waves into electrical signals. These electrical impulses are taken by the *cochlear nerve* and sent to the *cerebral cortex,* where they are finally interpreted.

Audio information

Audio waves carry information that can be vital to our well-being. As one of our major senses, hearing is constantly used to dissect the world around us and give us information and context in all kinds of circumstances. Our hearing range and the stereo setup of our ears allow us to judge aural distances, and as importantly, to judge the direction of that which produces the sound. (Is that tiger close? Is it getting closer?)

If we think of the aural picture we have of our surroundings as a list of audio information, we can construct a list of contributing factors that is surprisingly long. Our environment provides us with echoes, the Doppler effect, muffled sounds, clear sounds, soothing sounds, mechanical sounds, natural sounds, and so on. All this information needs to be digested and interpreted.

Sound Interpretation

What we need to understand when dealing with the subject of sound is that even though the physical aspects of hearing are quite well understood, human interpretation of sound isn't an exact business.

The previous dry description helps us understand the process to a degree, but let's look at another way of describing it:

> Imagine that you stretch a pillowcase tightly across the opening of a bucket, and different people throw ping pong balls at it from different distances. They can each throw as many balls as they like, and as often as they like. Your job is to figure out, just by looking at how the pillowcase moves up and down, how many people there are, who they are, and whether they are walking towards you, away from you, or are standing still. This is essentially the problem your auditory system has to contend with when it uses the eardrum as the gateway to hearing.[1]

If seen in those terms, it is a miracle that we can hear at all. Indeed, we often do get things wrong, sometimes in strange ways.

---

[1] Daniel Levitin, "It's Just an Illusion," *New Scientist*, February 22, 2008, pp. 34–37.

A limit to sound perception

Human capability means that even being able to make this much sense out of sound input is very impressive indeed, especially if we take into account the complexities involved. It is nonetheless not limitless, and is subject to some strange pitfalls. We may not always be aware of these things, but sometimes in a studio environment they come to the fore with real clarity. The famous sound engineer Walter Murch, who made films with people like George Lucas and Francis Ford Coppola, talks about an interesting practical example that he encountered while working on *THX 1138*. During the mixing phase of the film, he had trouble making the footsteps of robots sound good. He discovered what the problem was and offered this realization:

> Somehow, it seems that our minds can keep track of one person's footsteps, or even the footsteps of two people, but with three or more people our minds just give up—there are too many steps happening too quickly. As a result, each footstep is no longer evaluated individually, but rather the group of footsteps is evaluated as a single entity, like a musical chord. If the pace of the steps is roughly correct, and it seems as if they are on the right surface, this is apparently enough. In effect, the mind says "Yes, I see a group of people walking down a corridor and what I hear sounds like a group of people walking down a corridor.

> Sometime during the mid-19th century, one of Edouard Manet's students was painting a bunch of grapes, diligently outlining every single one, and Manet suddenly knocked the brush out of her hand and shouted: "Not like that! I don't give a damn about Every Single Grape! I want you to get the feel of the grapes, how they taste, their color, how the dust shapes them and softens them at the same time. "

> Similarly, if you have gotten Every Single Footstep in sync but failed to capture the energy of the group, the space through which they are moving, the surface on which they are walking, and so on, you have made the same kind of mistake that Manet's student was making. You have paid too much attention to something that the mind is incapable of assimilating anyway, even if it wanted to.[2]

This indicates that as important as the ability to make sense of audio information is, it is also subject to mistakes and confusion. How we *process* audio information is an important aspect of the complete picture.

---

[2] Walter Murch, "DENSE CLARITY – CLEAR DENSITY," *Volume Bed of Sound*, http://www.ps1.org/cut/volume/murch.html, no date.

As stated before, it is no easy task for the brain to get things right all the time, and indeed it has to rely on extrapolation and inference. This leaves the door wide open for manipulation of our audio perception, something that has been raised to the level of high art in the field of music recording. Therein we find that just as important as the *physiology* of sound is the notion of a *psychology* of sound.

The Psychology of Sound

Beyond the physical there is another, even more interesting dimension. What is it we actually do with all this audio information on a psychological level? What feelings do we experience that are triggered by sound? Are there rules or general principles we can look at? There are many questions like these that can be asked about the way we experience sound mentally, so let's look at some of the basic areas of interest.

Describing sound

The mechanical explanation of sound is very useful, but it still doesn't give us enough of a vocabulary to *describe* sounds. For some people this language exists in *music theory*, a comprehensive language that even has a written from in all kinds of music notation. Although the world would undoubtedly be a more entertaining place if everybody were taught this language from infancy, it still does not provide a common vocabulary for our general experience of sound. Indeed, it is interesting to see that most of us really struggle to discuss sound without the aid of terms that are comparative with other senses. Sounds are described as *warm*, or having a certain *color*, or being *sad* or *melancholic*.

Describing sound in this way shows that there is a deeper psychological dimension to our aural life.

Emotional Associations

Sound is a strongly associative medium. Almost everyone knows examples of how sound is associated with specific emotions or events pertinent to their life. Consider the pop hits of the time you were a teenager, or the TV shows you used to watch as a child. Take any emotive memory, and chances are that a specific inner soundtrack accompanies many of them.

This basic principle of sounds and emotions being associated with each other is not limited to personal experience. Indeed, there are many emotional associations that we can share with other people, often at a universal level. This is where we can find a multitude of uses for level design. Find the general shared associations that can work in a creative scenario, and you have found a remarkably powerful tool to help deepen the experience for the audience.

Aesthetic Sensibilities

The combination of cultural background and the properties of sound itself makes us judge sound on an aesthetic level. This is especially true for music. There are not many clear rules on what makes a sound pleasing or jarring; indeed, people often completely disagree on this topic. Jazz can be irritating noise to one set of ears and the ultimate musical expression to others. One person's soothing wind chimes are another's insomniac nightmare. There are some historically and culturally determined guidelines to be found in music theory; principles of harmony and dissonance come to mind, although these are often open to interpretation. Nonetheless, we know that ultimately a judgment is made in many cases, and often this judgment is predictable to a large degree.

This means that the aesthetic qualities of sound and music can be used in a creative context. If one can predict that a sound will be pretty or calming, it can be used as a contrast to something ugly or distressing, or it can be used to strengthen the effect even more. The aesthetic sensibility of the audience is open to all kinds of creative techniques; those involving sound and music are particularly clear examples of this.

Primal Reactions

Some qualities of sound cause a reaction on a purely primal level and cause emotional responses that cannot be ignored. This can be a matter of volume; nobody can help but be startled by an unexpected loud sound, or this can be a matter of pitch. The low rumble of an earthquake is bound to cause some serious unease to the listener. Other qualities of sound may cause equally strong reactions—human laughter or growling predators, to name a few. A mother's reaction to her crying baby is hard to describe as anything but primal.

Taught Reactions

On the opposite side of the equation, we find emotional reactions to sound based on a cultural basis. That is to say, emotional reactions to sound that society or our parents teach us. To a degree, these reactions can be seen as *conventions* of sound. That is why rude workmen whistle after women or why we give a wide berth to a truck that makes a repetitive beeping sound as it backs up. We know what a disapproving *tut tut* means and can easily comprehend an overly sarcastic comment due to the sarcastic *tone* with which the comment was made. Our daily lives are filled with moments where we react to sounds that have meaning due to conventions that we have learned to recognize.

Types of Sound

Within creative disciplines like film, television, theater, and so forth, there are distinctions to be made between certain types of sound. There is a need to differentiate and categorize for practical purposes, although there is no complete consensus on how to do so.

Diegetic and Non-Diegetic Sound

One distinction that is often used is between *diegetic* and *non-diegetic* sound. They are useful terms but require some explanation:

Diegetic

Sound is *diegetic* when it emanates from the actions visible onscreen, or when the sound is explained by the implied sources coming from the film environment. This can include dialogue, objects in the set, the weather, and so on—anything that has a natural source in the story world of the film.

Non-Diegetic

In direct opposition is *non-diegetic* sound. This is sound that comes from outside the story world of the film or other medium and has no natural source linked to the onscreen action. For example, mood music and voiceovers are in this category.

This distinction between diegetic and non-diegetic can be very useful, but it may also at times be a bit limiting, or too specific to film. I personally tend to make a distinction between music and non-music first.

Music

When people speak of the music of a particular film or similar creative product, they tend to refer to a number of diverse types of musical content. Some of these types feature some unique properties that are worth looking at. For the sake of brevity, the following examples are from the medium of film, but they often apply to other media as well.

Mood music

Mood music is music created to specifically create or enhance certain moments within a film. This is generally not a complete song, but emotive music with minimal structure, if any. It is not meant to stand alone as a musical piece, so it is free from principles of song construction. The use of mood music is incredibly ubiquitous in film, precisely because it is such a free and powerful emotional tool. Some people dislike it for that exact reason; they see the emotional manipulation inherent in the use of mood music as inappropriate. The authors of the rules of the DOGMA 95 school of film making even stated it as one of the key techniques to avoid:

> The sound must never be produced apart from the images or vice versa. (Music must not be used unless it occurs where the scene is being shot).[3]

I am not advocating for or against mood music, but it is always interesting to see how naked the content of a film can be if mood music is taken away. There is no denying the impact of its presence *or* its absence.

Original score

The *original score* is just what the word suggests: the music originally and specifically written or recorded for the work. The music has typically been scored in partnership with the film director and is frequently thematically consistent. Just as a movie can feature some strong themes and recurring motifs, the same often occurs in the original score. This is of course no coincidence, since the score is meant to bring out the best of the work it accompanies. Some of the best musical scores are highly rated because they are a particularly strong companion to the underlying work, sometimes even on an equal footing.[4]

Soundtrack

Soundtrack and *score* are words that are often wrongly used as if they were interchangeable. This is understandable, as there can be much overlap between the two. But generally, the soundtrack is a product of music research and not of composition. That is, the soundtrack generally consists of songs *used in* the film, but not necessarily *written for* the film.

---

[3] "The Vow of Chastity," *Dogma 95,* http://www.martweiss.com/film/dogma95-thevow.shtml, 1995.

[4] The *Kooyanisqatsi* score by Phillip Glass is a good example.

Non-Music

Non-Music, sometimes called *noise,* is a term used in the film industry. Within that discipline it doesn't have the negative connotations that the term normally has. In fact, it means no more than all the sound that *doesn't consist of music.* That is a very large group of sounds, so it is useful to identify some more specific categories. Many of these categories are not as clear-cut as they appear to be, and definitions vary from filmmaker to filmmaker. My personal understanding[5] yields the groupings of sound categories discussed below. They are not strict definitions, but are intended more as a rough guideline.

Sound effects and Foley

We speak of *sound effects* in cases where the sound is supposed to underscore specific physical things or actions onscreen. Sound effects tend to be short but can last a little while in some circumstances. In most cases they can be attributed directly to things we can see onscreen. Good examples of this include *footsteps* made by the onscreen characters, a *gun* fired by an onscreen character, a *door* closing, and so on.

Another term for these kinds of effects is *Foley.* The best way to think of Foley is when specific sound effects are created to imitate actual actions. In the case of footsteps, rather that recording the actual footsteps of an actor, a sound effect is created that does the job in a more convincing manner. Strangely, in film it is quite often more practical to create *artificial* sounds to represent *actual sounds.* What the film ends up with is a sort of hyper-reality where sounds imply the reality of the scene in a much stronger way than the actual sounds could achieve. This also allows for more control over audio and enables the sound engineer to try out all kinds of tricks and techniques to benefit the film.

Incidental sound

Incidental sound forms a different kind of sound effect, different enough to warrant its own category. Like mood music, incidental sounds are designed to give power to certain psychological states of the viewer. For example, we all know (and dread) the moment in a horror movie when something in the film produces a sudden and unexpected scare. In almost all cases, this moment is accompanied by some kind of loud sound effect that adds impact to the "incident." It is not a *natural* sound; it is created purely for the incidental purpose. These

---

[5] I have studied some film at the university level and have and dabbled a bit as an amateur filmmaker.

moments can also occur when the protagonist suddenly realizes something, or when a dramatic moment is about to occur.

Ambient sounds

Ambient sounds, as already discussed in Chapter 9 on immersion, are linked to the environment itself, as opposed to specific incidents or actions. They exist to help give a general definition of a space or the environment that the audience is experiencing. This creates a deeper sense of immersion, but it also conveys a great amount of information. An ambient sound like machine-room hum tells us that the machine room is active and purring along nicely. Hubbub in a meeting tells us that everybody is talking among themselves, while fading out this ambient sound can signify that the group is focusing on a single speaker. Every environment features ambient sound; it is almost impossible *not* to hear something. Even when it is quiet, we tend to hear our own breathing or sounds like footsteps or the rustling of clothes.

All of these sounds matter a great deal to the mood portrayed, and to the information divulged to the listener. This can be enhanced even further by manipulating the sound itself. Earlier we spoke of the extra information we get from our environment by naturally occurring sound alterations like the Doppler effect and echoes. We can add many others to that: reverb, cutting out frequencies to create a muffled sound, resonance, and so on. It is not that hard to manipulate sound in a studio, but the results can be incredibly powerful.

Concept Summary

We perceive audio through a diverse set of circumstances and experiences. There are important physiological rules and restraints that allow us to hear in the first place. These in turn are processed in our brains in very interesting ways, which are not always correct. What is striking is how applicable many of these ideas and principles are to creative expression. This is not just in a predictable manner as musical accompaniment or performance, but along a whole range of uses of audio, often in the subtlest of ways.

Luckily, there are numerous artistic conventions and techniques available to us for study. What we should take from this is a spirit of open-minded interpretation of audio principles and ideas and try to find applications within our own craft.

As we will see in the next section of the book, there are many ways in which we can do so.

Theory

The previous section shows how universal many auditory principles are. It also shows how relevant knowledge of audio can be to creative application. Level design offers a huge amount of scope and context in which we can place audio design theory catered to our specific needs.

Level Music

Most game levels use music of some sort, sometimes to underscore in-game events, sometimes to provide pleasant background music. This music isn't always seen as something of great importance, and indeed in some games the music used is inconsequential. But that is not the point. What we should do is look at the role music *can* play, and when we adopt that view, we find that there are many good reasons to incorporate meaningful music choices in our levels. As in film, we can make a rough distinction between the *score* of the game and other types of music, most prominently *dynamic music*.

Dynamic Music

We speak of *dynamic music* in video games in those cases when the music played is dependent on dynamic in-game events. The use of dynamic music can greatly enhance the emotional impact of a gameplay scenario. If used correctly, the music can be triggered or cued to underscore moments that enhance the player's enjoyment of a game, for example by rewarding a victory over a tough enemy or setting the mood at the start of a new level. The latter is an example where games differ from films and require different choices. In a film the mood music can be painstakingly composed or researched to fit every scene and situation at exactly the right time. In video games on the other hand, there is very little predictable linearity; most in-game actions are dependent on player choice and therefore can occur at mostly non-specific times. This means that the use of mood music has to be flexible to some degree and must fit numerous situations.

Dynamic music can also be used to give the player information related to specific gameplay or in-game events. Just as background noise of a scene can provide information that is vital to the experience, so can the music in a game tell the player additional things that pertain to the onscreen action but may be hard to convey in a different manner. If a player is close to losing control of a situation, the right mood music can indicate this and enhance the tension inherent in the situation. When a player needs to know that an environment is safe to explore, specific music can indicate this. Whatever game you are working on will have its own set of requirements, and it is generally up to the level designer to formulate them.

This use of music to convey gameplay information has the added advantage of giving *direction* to the player's actions or understanding of game events. And as level designers we should always be interested in tools that give us possibilities to direct the gameplay experience.

Score and Soundtrack

Video games are much more dynamic than films and therefore offer less room for the effective use of a musical score or soundtrack. That isn't to say there is no place for it. Indeed, some game types are perfectly comfortable with a set of looping musical themes or songs, often in addition to moments where dynamic music takes over. Specifically, classic arcade games and early console or computer games often feature a traditional score accompanying the main gameplay. Who can deny the genius of scores for games like *Turican*,[6] Ghosts *and Goblins*,[7] or *Outrun*[8]? The music research[9] done for those games is of such quality that many years later, these games are still associated with and remembered by those scores.

Finding or composing the right score for a game is not a trivial process. Try to imagine films like *Pulp Fiction* or *The Godfather* without their soundtrack or score. Choosing the amount and implementation of this kind of music is completely dependent on the individual game's requirements. In all cases, some thought needs to be given to a few specific questions.

Noise

As already discussed, *noise* is what we call all audio that isn't music. As a descriptive category, that doesn't give us enough information however. We need to divide it into further subcategories. Or at least, into the ones that are typically used in level design.

---

[6] Developed by Lorriciels.

[7] Developed by Capcom.

[8] Developed by Sega.

[9] The process by which the right music is found for the product in question.

Ambient Sound

In the chapter on immersion, I said the following about ambient sound:

> We all know of a number of aural game clichés; on top of a mountain we hear wind, in caves we hear drips, etc. However, these kinds of straightforward implementations are not just representations of sounds that need to be picked from a list to complete a level's outstanding tasks. Recorded sounds not only have documentary qualities, they also have psycho-acoustic qualities, which means they have the ability to have an effect on the psychological interpretation of sound.

It is worth examining these types of sounds a bit closer. It seems that a further distinction can be made between ambient sounds and their *documentary qualities* and their *psychological qualities*.

Documentary

The *documentary qualities* of sounds are those that make it possible for them to help define a game's space, and to even help describe what happens within that space. This may seem straightforward, but in reality is far from it. Here's a simple test: look around you and identify every single thing[10] that can create sound, no matter how loud or frequent. Chances are you won't finish this exercise because the list is too long. This shows that we cannot go into a level design process thinking that for documentary ambient sounds we can just assign a sample to every potential sound-producing item. Not only will this completely destroy our budget (both of money and memory); it will also create an aural mess that muddles the definition of space, as opposed to helping define it. Remember that we are experiencing these sounds through speakers or headphones; it is not like we are actually there.

To create a clearer sound plan to describe the environment for most levels, it makes sense to identify the key audio components and implement them wisely. In essence, this is an impressionist approach: we pick those sounds that let us paint a picture that is so descriptive that the player's mind fills in the rest. Generally, this means we need to find those sounds that the player will associate with a complete set of environmental expectations. A reverberating dripping sound can be enough to define an environment consisting of watery caves.

Additionally, some sounds may have to support certain aspects of gameplay[11] and therefore are even more important than others. Let's go through some typical examples:

---

[10] Or creature.

[11] More on this in a bit.

- Gameplay related:
    - footsteps (allow the player to judge others' locations),
    - AI states (allow the player to react to behavior of creatures/NPCs),
    - engine frequency (allows the player to judge speed).
- General documentary audio:
    - crickets (define the desert at night),
    - hubbub (defines crowds of people),
    - rain (speaks for itself).

Psychological

Just as important as the purely descriptive nature of the sounds types discussed so far are the psychological aspects involved: the psycho-acoustic qualities of sound. Just as color theory gives us insight into a person's reactions to certain colors, and as scale can affect people's emotional state in profound ways, sound can have an emotional impact or cause a very specific reaction. Is there anybody who doesn't associate a countdown timer with haste or stress? Or to take a subtler example: the sound of seagulls can exert a calming or even relaxing influence on the player due to its association with the coast.

Documentary aspects in sounds help describe a *physical space*, while psychological association helps describe a *mental space or state*. This is a very helpful phenomenon for level designers, as quite often we try to exert influence over the player's state of mind.

Seagulls or countdowns are just two examples. In practice, each level and each game will have a unique sound signature, and it really pays off to spend some time thinking about which sounds best serve the overall experience.

Sound Cues

Many aspects of a level's ambient sounds have to do with the fact that they are information carriers. They tell their own story by way of the information they carry within themselves. Sometimes this information is relevant to gameplay decisions. When it is, we can classify them as *sound cues*, or, even more likely, we can include sounds that were designed to *be* sound cues. We have encountered some of these already when we were discussing documentary aspects of ambient sounds, and those examples still stand. However, we can add to this by realizing that sound cues don't have to be a side effect of environmental noise. They can (and often should be) specifically designed to aid gameplay.

In other words, designing the speech of enemy AI in a level shouldn't just be a function of documentary sound design. It should be exploited in such a way that it also fulfills specific gameplay goals. For example, if the AI has three distinct behavioral states (such as passive, alert, and aggressive), it makes sense to gear its speech to express those states in a clear way. That way, the player can correctly read their behavior and the level designer can exploit this to create appropriate gameplay scenarios.

This doesn't just apply to character or creature sound cues. Anytime there is a gameplay consequence or dimension to sound, it can be incorporated into the level design. Electrical hum can be turned on or off in order to say whether electricity is live. A dry click can indicate it is time to reload a gun, and so forth. At times these decisions will be made within the context of the game's overall design. But just as often they are within the responsibility of the level designer, or at least are fueled by level-design needs.

Sound Effects

At other times the level needs to communicate information through sounds that don't fit within the natural environment of the game. In those cases we generally speak of *sound effects*. In *Zelda* games these may be sounds that are played when the player solves a puzzle. In *Unreal Tournament*[12] they can represent the respawning of an item. There are thousands of examples for each individual game. The nature of these kinds of sounds is almost always decided at a *game design* level. However, in some cases, the use of these sounds is up to the level designer, perhaps within the context of a scripted sequence or if the game's development tools provide extra leeway in these matters.

A surprising amount of knowledge is needed to design effective sound effects, and likewise, the level-design implementation of sound effects also requires great care. If you are in a position where the level design is required to deal with this matter, make sure that you don't underestimate this task. Some questions to ask include:

- Do the sound effects jell with the soundtrack or score?
- Can they obscure important sound cues?
- Do they clash with the general tone of the level?
- Can they be repeated often without causing irritation?

Questions like these at least need to be considered to make sure that no problems occur in the implementation of sound effects.

---

[12] Developed by Epic Games.

Soundscapes and Level Design

In some games the use of sound is so fundamental to the experience that it requires extra attention during the level design process.

For example, the independent game developer Nifflas[13] has always made clear that in his games, the music is as important as the gameplay. The way he makes this musical aspect count is by providing environments that are strongly underscored by the ambient music that he creates to accompany it. The two cannot be separated; the joy of exploration that is central to his games is partly caused by the music that fills the new environments or game areas that the player encounters. Quite often these discoveries of new areas and music form the de facto reward of the gameplay. In that important sense, we have to conclude that the music becomes an integral part of the level design itself.

Music Games

A special case in this chapter has to be made for *music-based games*. In these cases, the music often IS the level design, so I want to spend at least a few words on the subject.

Rhythm Action Games

The classic form of music game is the *rhythm action game*. This is a form of game not unlike an elaborate game of "Simon says," where the player is asked to perform specific actions to the rhythm of the game's music. There are many examples, but a typical one can be found in *Parapa the Rapper*,[14]" where following the onscreen prompts to press joypad buttons in time causes the game's protagonist (a rapping dog, no less!) to win musical duels against a diverse set of opponents.

Games like this, and there are many, mostly test the player's rhythmic skills. The design of the difficulty levels often focuses on the speed of the task and the ability of the player to pick out the right instrumentation in the music tracks and the subordinate rhythms they perform. Examples include a string section in a classical piece or a horn section in a funk piece.

The recent success of the *Guitar Hero*[15] franchise shows how much mileage this genre has. Watching a skilled *Guitar Hero* player shows somebody completely immersed in the flow channel of an optimal game experience.

---

[13] Real name: Nicklas Nygren. See http://nifflas.ni2.se/.

[14] NaNaOn-Sha.

[15] Developed by Harmonix.

Music Creation/Emulation

There are games that take a less strict approach and allow a focus on actual music *creation*. This is an area of gaming that is much less defined, so consequently the level design can take many shapes. An interesting example of this is the musical toy *Audio Plankton*, which asks the player to create compositions by manipulating the behavior of musical plankton.

A giant in the genre is Sony Europe's smash hit *Singstar*, a game that requires players to actually sing the part of various well known songs and be judged on how well they keep to the correct pitch.

With games like this it is hard to talk about actual level design, although to a degree there is significant overlap. For example, the difficulty level of the songs and the songs themselves, or the expression possibilities of the electro plankton all feature aspects of applied game design.

Music as Level Design

In some cases the level design is actually generated by the music itself,[16] and a few games have found a measure of success following this principle. *Vib Ribbon* is a classic and clear example of this kind of gameplay. The game follows a simple platform game formula, with the added twist that after the game has loaded, the player can use any music CD in the console's drive to generate a new platforming landscape. Other games exist in this genre, but much more can be made of his principle than has been attempted so far.

Theory Summary

Game audio is a vital component of the potential enjoyment of a game. Its implementation covers many diverse areas, including player psychology and mood, gameplay information, and at times specific gameplay design. In other words, we cannot create a level design without at least spending some time on the impact of these decisions.

Audio Plan

For that reason, it makes sense to create an *audio design* or *audio plan* for each level you work on. The shape this takes depends on the type of game and on the type of audio assets required, but just going through a process that takes into ac-

---

[16] A worrying idea for those of us who are paid to do level design.

count the impact of the aural dimension on the level design can be invaluable to the final quality of the level.

Practice

Example 11.1: Psychological Impact— Tension and Sound

Summary

We have established previously that sound can impact on the mood of the player. It can have properties that can have a major impact on how the player feels about a situation on an emotional level. This impact is easily recognized when we see efforts aimed at adding tension through sound.

Game Genre

This technique is suitable to most games.

Goals to Achieve

- Disturb and unsettle the player though sound.
- Enhance the impact and mood of the level.

Description

(Example type: Existing)

The sound design of Alien. Two good examples of this technique are found in the film *Alien*,[17] by Ridley Scott. They are based on the same principle, but each adopts a different approach.

Heartbeat sound. A subtle but effective trick throughout the film is the use of a heartbeat sample in the film's audio track. Throughout the film, as the tension increases, the heartbeat sound increases in tempo. Most people are not even aware of this, but the increasingly rapid heartbeat is disconcerting and creates a

---

[17] Directed by Ridley Scott, distributed by 20th Century Fox, released May 25, 1979. The film follows the ordeal of the crew of the space ship "Nostromo" as they are stalked by a murderous alien.

palpable tension in the viewer. We can't help being affected by it as we associate a rapid heartbeat with danger or fear if experienced in the right context.

A similar effect can be achieved with breathing, turning calm and slow breathing to rapid and panicked breathing.

Proximity sensor. While the heartbeat example is covert and subtle, we can also find a more explicit example in the film when the endangered crew builds a device that acts like a proximity sensor. It emits a low beep at regular intervals, but when it picks up movement the intensity and the pitch increases if the movement is getting closer to the emitter. The crew uses it to try to find or track the alien that has been terrorizing them. It is a very simple conceit but one of the most effective tension devices in the film. The audience (and the crew) cannot see what the sensor picks up, and when the emitter starts to emit ever more frequent and higher beeps, the tension mounts to very high levels indeed.

Example 11.2: Sound as Information Carrier—Environmental Dangers

Summary

Sounds tell us a great deal about a space, and they can tell a great deal about the gameplay or purpose of a space in level design. Sounds carry information to us whether we are aware of it or not. Level designers can use this fact to greatly enhance the level design, by providing crucial gameplay information through the use of sound.

Game Genre

This technique is suited to nearly all games.

Goals to Achieve

- Create a level environment where sound conveys gameplay information.
- Translate this information into something perceivable to the player.
- Tie it into a gameplay scenario.

Description

(Example type: Original)

Once we start seeing sound as a potential information carrier, it becomes relatively easy to tie sound directly into gameplay. All we have to do is provide a situation where the sound carries information that is necessary for the player to successfully deal with a level design scenario. This example shows how a number of sounds can work together, in concert,[18] to provide a comprehensive amount of aural information of great use to the player.

Dangerous factory. The player finds him or herself in a fantastical factory environment and has to navigate a route through dangerous machines. The player can get hurt by *stomping pistons*, *jets of flames*, *manufacturing robots* armed with *automated nail guns*, and so on.

The machines cycle between dangerous and unsafe states, but these cycles are not predictable through visual observation. They are not regularly spaced out across a timeline. However, the machines all employ their own characteristic sounds that precipitate a state change. In other words, the player gets an audible warning when a machine is about to become dangerous or safe.

Careful listening and timing can then do the rest.

Further Notes

We have to be careful with these kinds of audio-dependent gameplay scenarios, as they can completely ruin a game for the deaf and the hard of hearing. Alternative routes may be an appropriate way of dealing with this, or perhaps optional visual indicators can do the trick.

Example 11.3: Sound as Information Carrier—Multiplayer Sound Cues

Summary

As the previous example established, sound can carry information that is vital to gameplay. This is true in single player games, but takes on an extra dimension in multiplayer games, specifically in the area of sound cues.

Game Genre

This example is suited to multiplayer games where sound carries over distance.

Goals to Achieve

- Incorporate sound cues in a multiplayer context.
- Make it multifunctional.
- Tie it into interesting gameplay choices.

---

[18] Half a pun, my apologies.

Description

(Example type: Original)

In multiplayer games it can be a matter of great importance to know where one's opponents are and what they are up to. Based on this information, players make choices on what their next actions are and formulate strategies accordingly. This is especially true in games where the same levels are played over and over again, as this repetition means that the player can have a repertoire of strategies that are derived from their knowledge of that specific level environment.

This should be acknowledged and utilized in the level design for such games. There are, of course, all kinds of ways this can be done: the geometry of a level can provide strategic viewpoints to facilitate this, the level can be made of mirrored sections, balanced for all teams, so players can predict routes and distances, and so on.

Less prevalent is the use of sound to give gameplay critical information. There is much to be gained by employing this technique, however. In Figure 11.1 we can see a number of corridors that lead to an important pickup, let's say heavy armor (A). Several rival players (P1–P3) can potentially get to the armor. This is not an atypical scenario, and there is nothing wrong with it per se.

We can make much more of this scenario, however, by introducing sound cues to the mix. If we surround the pickup by puddles of water, and make sure the audibility of running through the water encompasses all the potential player positions (grey circle) then we suddenly have an entirely more interesting setup. (See Figure 11.2.)

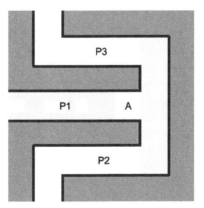

Figure 11.1. Multiplayer corridors with pickup and players.

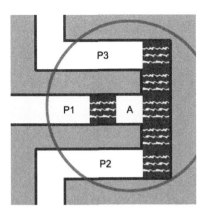

Figure 11.2. Multiplayer corridors with pickup and players, and added sound cues.

Player 1 can see the armor, and he or she could hear if somebody (Player 2 or 3) runs through the water and approaches the armor from the other side. If Player 1 decides to run to the armor, Players 2 and 3 can tell by the sound from which corridor Player 1 comes, as there is less water there than in the other corridors. (Players 2 and 3 can make that same distinction for each other, as well, if one of them approaches the armor.) They can also hear in which direction Player 1 goes after picking up the armor.

All this adds much depth and strategy to what previously was no more than a few corridors and a pickup. Yet, it terms of assets or work, the technique is very cheap to implement, and therefore a good addition to the level designer's toolbox.

Further Notes

It isn't hard to add further sound cues to this scenario, but it is dangerous to add too many. Beyond a certain number of sounds, the players will just get overwhelmed and cannot easily react to all the aural input coming their way.

Game Stories

E arlier in the book we discussed the alleged disagreements between ludologists and narrativists and concluded that play and narrative aren't mutually
exclusive. Play is covered to a degree in almost every chapter in this book, because it is natural to do so. However, concepts of narrative and story haven't been

"Medieval Writing Desk," *Wikipedia*, http://commons.wikimedia.org/wiki/File:Medie
val_writing_desk.jpg, 2009.

discussed much yet. This is partly because I made the decision that most of the narrative-related topics are better handled in a separate and focused area, rather than constantly addressing them in each subcategory. The result is the following chapter, which explores general concepts and tries to apply them to level design theory and practice.

Story and Narrative

12

Almost all the arts and entertainment forms we are exposed to deal in some way with narrative elements, storytelling, and creation of dramatic content and meaning. This is obviously true in most films that we see, books that we read, and plays that we watch. We find it in comics and graphic novels, and to some degree it often applies to less straightforward examples like painting, music sculpture—you name it.

These expressions occur for many reasons, sometimes artistic, sometimes informative or intended to make people laugh. There is a wealth of narrative content that dates back thousands of years to cave paintings and probably even farther. So, what lessons can we learn when we look at all of these types of narrative in different disciplines? Are there unified concepts that transcend notions of *genre* or *art form,* and if so, can we take this commonality and distill general concepts from it?

To try to achieve something of that nature, this chapter will not try to write a treatise on "the elements of style" or to find the ultimate definition of storytelling. Instead, our approach will take us much further down the line and will simply assume that we all agree that elements of narrative and story play an important part in most art forms. We will also put forward that it follows that to be effective in those instances where this is applicable, artists and entertainers through the years have developed useful tools and techniques that help them bring *dramatic value* to their work. This chapter is mostly interested in that specific aspect of the craft and takes a look at a number of commonly used dramatic tools.

Concept

Dramatic Tools

There is a thing that most forms of art and entertainment have in common with each other. They all want the audience to *experience* something, as intended by the artist. They all want to get their ideas across in such a way that it makes some kind of impact in the mind of the audience. In the cases of static art forms like photography or sculpture, this impact comes from the audience contemplating what it is observing. However, when it comes to non-static forms of art or entertainment (and by *non-static* I mean work that progresses along a timeline), the author has time to assert some control over the experience. Artists try to influence the audience as much as possible, so that it will perceive the work to have dramatic (or artistic) value or impact. Almost every field has developed a large array of dramatic tools that are employed to manipulate the audience in such a way that the work is most powerful. Let's look at a number of general examples.

Theme and Mood

Let's assume that in most cases artists have something to *say*. It is fair to assume that they generally want their art to have some *meaning* or at least be *about* something. There will be ideas that the artist is more eager to get across than some other specific points. What we are talking about in this case are the major themes of a work, and to a degree, the mood that the work tries to capture.

Themes can be major epic affairs that comment on society as a whole, Tolstoy's *War and Peace* or Dostoevsky's *Crime and Punishment* come to mind. Equally valid are works that deal with specific emotions or subjects that are less sweeping, like the innocence of childhood in coming-of-age stories or the moods evoked by the seasons.

One work can cover several themes and moods, such as a long-running TV series. Others may focus specifically on one aspect, as is often seen in poetry.

The easiest way to think of theme is to ask the question: "What is this work about?" More often than not, the answer will list the themes of the work.

Something that is related but slightly different is the *mood* of the piece, which generally is found by asking how the work makes one *feel*.

Theme and mood rarely operate in isolation; generally, they touch on many other aspects of the work. Other choices about the content are often made to strengthen the impact of the main themes and overall mood. Good examples of this are choices of *setting, form* and *style*.

Form and Style

Form and *style* define *how a story is told*.

Once it is known what themes and moods are to be explored in the work, a choice has to be made on how to effectively shape it. It needs to have a *form* in which it can be defined, and a *style* in which it can be approached.

Form

The *form* (or *format*) is no less than the *chosen form of expression*. This is something that is governed both by personal choice and by the theme and mood of the work. "A lyrical expression of love" can be shaped as a poem or a western pop-song, among other possibilities. Each choice will bring with it numerous defining attributes that will have a huge impact on the final work.

Style

Style is the way in which the final content is approached. So to go back to our earlier lyrical expression of love, if we chose poetry, we can make a further stylistic choice. Are we going for a traditional Japanese haiku or an experimental tone poem?

If we chose the western pop-song format, we can also choose from many styles, such as 80s new romantic, indie guitar music, reggae, and so forth.[1]

Any of these choices can prove to be effective, but they all heavily impact how the work will be experienced.

Setting

Setting tells us where things happen.

In order for the major themes and mood to really resonate, a choice of setting (if applicable) can have a huge impact on the dramatic effect of a work. *Blade Runner* would be less respected as a work of noir science fiction if it had been set in some bright future kindergarten.

The best settings let the artist underscore the chosen themes and mood in a clear and effective way. This can be done through a direct connection between setting and story. When commenting on what war does to humanity, it is effective to tell the story against the backdrop of a major war.

It can also be done through the juxtaposition of contrasting elements. What I mean by that is that sometimes certain themes have more impact if contrasted with a setting where they stand out. An explosion will have more impact in a silent library than in a carnival setting.

Dramatic Progression: Plot and Pacing

Many creative works feature some kind of progression over a timeline. If there is a discernable plot or narrative, it tends to follow a path through time, allowing the narrative to unfold. In those instances, choices have to be made dealing with

---

[1] Please don't snort and just insert examples of current pop music, okay?

the right order, speed, and way in which to progress the story in such a way that it has the desired dramatic impact.

We have already discussed this to a degree in Chapter 4, where we looked at the traditional theatrical five-acter, as demonstrated through Freytag's pyramid. But other, non-literary, examples can also be found as well. Musical composition, for example, also tends to follow a time line, and in some cases this has led to dramatic progression through chord progressions or similar musical forms. Ask any professional musician about the importance of the 12 bar blues and you will see what I mean.

Whatever the field in which dramatic progression occurs, there are choices to be made dealing with the order in which to tell the story and its individual components (*plot*) and the timing and speed applied to the use of these components (*pacing*).

Plot

Plot is often confused with *story*. Quite often, when people try to explain the story of a movie, they resort to telling you about what happens in the movie in chronological order. But this does nothing to explain the story's overall themes, moods, and intentions. It merely tells us in what order "stuff happens."

A well-plotted narrative employs plot choices with a great regard for the overall purpose of the work. It can include delayed revelations to heighten a sense of suspense, or early background information to strengthen character motivation.

Absence of plot

Just as important as including events in a plot is excluding them from the whole. A plot can skip many years in a character's life so the audience can feel a sense of mystery about how that character has progressed from an earlier encounter. It can set a character on a specific path of dramatic progression and examine what this has done to the character's life twenty years later. In the process this can strengthen the themes of the story as a whole.

The ultimate point of plotting in any of its incarnations is that it gives artists and entertainers a tool that enables them to exert control over the way their work is experienced. It allows them to direct the experience over a specific timeline, determining which emotions are felt at what time.

Pacing

Pacing, on the other hand deals with the speed and rhythm in which plot is exposed to the audience, generally in such a way that they are continually engaged by it. This matters greatly, as the audience experience is subject to fatigue or boredom or other distractions throughout.

Editing

To go back to the film example, imagine a film-editing suite where the editor and director are looking at hundreds of reels of films with many takes of unedited footage. When they start to splice it all together,[2] they will constantly be faced with very specific choices on how long to let scenes and shots run in the final edit. The movie footage will be put in order (plotted) and then made subject to durations; or in more practical terms, the film will be paced in a certain way.

These are not minor decisions. A deep, wistful ghost story may not be best told at breakneck speed with furiously fast scenes racing the audience through it. Time is needed for reflection and for a sense of foreboding and fear to gather.

Concept Summary

A helpful way of thinking about these choices regarding dramatic tools and elements is by placing them in a hierarchy. We have done this earlier in the book by trying to formally place level design (and game design) elements in a specific development hierarchy to determine an approach that lets us assign goal driven values to the design process. We can do a similar thing on a smaller scale with narrative elements. In this case the hierarchy looks as follows:

- **Theme/mood:**
  - form,
  - style,
  - setting.
- **Dramatic progression:**
  - plot,
  - pacing.

Theme/mood. Theme and mood tell us what the work is about and how it makes us feel.

Form, style, and setting. After choosing the theme and mood, we can enhance them by choosing an effective setting, the right form, and an appropriate style. These choices now tell us where our story occurs and how it is told.

Dramatic progression: Plot and pacing. Finally, the story or narrative itself is constructed and placed in some kind of progression over time. The story unfolds

---

[2] Well, the contemporary digital equivalent of slicing film.

from a beginning to an end of sorts and is made up of individual (plot) elements. Plot gives the story a cohesive narrative.

Then there are choices to be made on how much time to give individual plot elements, which determines the pacing of the whole.

These dramatic elements don't always apply. For example, I don't know the "plot" of Rodin's *The Thinker,* but we do now have an overview of sorts of a number of useful dramatic tools from which we can choose when we need to. Let's see how they relate to level design and *its* dramatic elements.

Theory

In the previous section we discussed a number of ways in which creators and artists use specific techniques to create or strengthen dramatic impact. They construct their narratives in many diverse ways and all kinds of creative expressions, but there are specific things they do that seem to overlap between disciplines.

What I want to do in this chapter is re-examine these kinds of tools and techniques through the lens of video games and level design, see where they apply, and find our own ways of implementing them. Additionally, I want to examine where games are different, and where they require entirely new or different ways of dealing with narrative and story aspects.

To do this effectively, we should look at those types of games where story matters most, as games like that will have had to deal with these questions in the past. Let's look at a number of story-reliant game genres, including non-video games, and then see how they can be approached with the previously discussed techniques, as well as with potential new ones.

Story-Dependent Gaming

Before we try to define our own methods of in-game storytelling, we should find out if others have already dealt with this subject matter before. I have highlighted three types of gaming where storytelling takes centre stage, yet interactivity and gameplay are still massively important, or even defining to the experience. They are *point-and-click adventures, artificial reality gaming,* or *ARGs,* and traditional *pen-and-paper role playing games,* or *RPGs.*

All of these genres have in common that the story or narrative elements are crucial to the experience as a whole and therefore provide good examples for study. They each have their own level design conundrums to deal with.

Adventure Games

Games like *point-and-click adventures* and *text adventures* belong to a genre of games where the player takes on the role of a character, and performs tasks and solves puzzles in a story-led adventure. These games can be purely text based, or they can take place in a 2D side-scrolling environment, as seen in classical point-and-click adventures. There are many famous examples, including the likes of *King's Quest*, *Hitchhiker's Guide to the Galaxy*, and *The Secret of Monkey Island*. There are even 3D examples of the genre, with *Grim Fandango* deserving a special mention.

In pretty much all examples of the genre, the story matters and cannot be removed from the gameplay. Slowly uncovering the story threads and seeing the adventure unfold through the eye of the character(s) in the game is a core element and a major attraction. Most of the actual gameplay will consist of puzzles that have to be solved. At times they are fiendishly hard or infuriatingly illogical, but the central experience is undeniably story led.

Adventure game level design implications

Because so much of the medium is based on taking the player through a predefined storyline, these games tend to end up as fairly linear affairs. There are ways to branch off story events and reconnect them later to the main story line, but the end result is in most cases fairly rigid. This limitation is not necessarily a weakness of the genre, though, as long as the story is compelling, and the puzzle solving is rewarding. Interestingly, the player actions and story development often overlap. Dialogue is presented interactively by player choice, generally through conversation with NPCs. This is often absent from more interactive games, where story exposition frequently takes place in non-interactive cutscenes. This may well be because the story is so important to the experience of the game that it is only natural to include the player's actions in the overall narrative when possible.

Alternate Reality Gaming

A relative newcomer to the (video)game family is *the Alternate Reality Game*, normally abbreviated to *ARG*. ARGs are communal games that allow players to take on the roles of participants in a story unfolding in an alternate reality (created by the game makers[3]) and told via various real world media. The online component is very important to these games, but other real world media are

---

[3] Known as *Puppet Masters*.

used as well. A player may find clues to a puzzle on a website, have to ring a real number, and then find an item in a real world location. Yet despite the overlap between the real and the virtual, a key aspect of these kinds of games is that they tell a specific story, and the players are characters within this story.

It is a fascinating genre, which at times is able to attract large numbers of players, yet its successes are fairly unknown to most people. Famous examples include *The Beast,* a seminal ARG created as a marketing tool for the Spielberg move *AI,* and *Perplex City,* a game that included the additional uses of collectable cards and a cash award of 100,000 pounds on finding a real world object called "the Receda Cube."[4]

A particular quirk of ARGs lies in the fact that gameplay and story span several forms of media, and as such, the genre comes with interesting and unique challenges, and therefore with unique solutions. One such quirk is that it is a general rule in ARG etiquette that the game and its players stay in character, no matter how unlikely or fantastic the content. Although the puppet masters formally (and secretly) design the gameplay and the story, they never allude to this in any way or form. All communication and actions within an ARG universe are *in character* and treat it as if it is not a game. This principle is often referred to quite literally as *TINAG,* which stands for *This Is Not A Game.* The point is that the interest of the game comes from people communally "living" and influencing the game narrative. The puppet masters may largely control the immediate story events and the puzzles, but the *memorable actions* come from the choices of the players.

ARG level design implications

ARG level design issues are complex and interesting. How does one tell a story that is to be enjoyed by many thousands of players at the same time, but whose progress is partly dictated by the pace of the players? How can somebody jump into an ongoing storyline like this when most of the players have already experienced it months ago? This is not a small problem, as the core gameplay is really about participating in the story, which makes it hard to be engaged when many of the story events are already handled by players who have come before you. It is a balancing act, where events are created that need sufficient players to crack the puzzles and obstacles, but the game as whole cannot always rely on having large groups of people all the time.

Because human nature is unpredictable, many ARGs can revel in the fact that their story lines unfold in a way that is partly dependent on player action. In that sense, ARGs are very democratic games. Level designers (puppet masters)

---

[4] Don't go looking for it; it has been found, and the prize money is gone. GONE!

are very much facilitators, people who create rough outlines to be explored, experienced, *and influenced*, by the players. This is an exciting prospect, key to the success of many ARGs.

RPGs (Role-Playing Games)

RPGs are *role-playing games*, which might sometimes be described as "playing a dark-elf-smiting-warrior in pen-and-paper role-playing games," as in *Dungeons and Dragons*.[5] For more information, see the section on "Level Design in a Historic Context" in Chapter 1, but it may be worthwhile to recap somewhat here.

So-called *pen and paper role-playing games* have been around for awhile, but the most famous example of the genre is the fantasy role-playing game system *Dungeons and Dragons*, developed in the early 1970s by David Arneson and Gary Gygx. The genre typically consists of a Game Master who leads the gaming session, presiding over the rule system and the adventure that is presented to the players, who act out the actions of the characters they portray. The Game Master interprets those player actions and makes sure they relate and interact properly to the game's official rules.

In addition, the Game Master narrates the consequences of players' actions and the independent events occurring in the prepared adventure. In many ways the Game Master acts as the player's eyes and ears in the virtual world and provides the simulation data that follows the game's rule set. The players inform the Game Master of the actions they wish to take and communicate in character with the other players. The resulting game is one where players partake in virtual adventure stories in a fantastic, interactive simulated gameplay session, bound by a set of formal rules that provide the necessary level of simulation and logic to bind the whole thing together.

This all may sound a bit complex or even contrived, but once a group is used to the system, it is remarkably immersive and effective. RPGs can cover many themes and moods and form a fairly diverse genre. Others include FASA's Shadow Run, which mixes cyberpunk with fantasy, *Middle Earth Role Playing*, based on the Tolkien books, or *Call of Chthulu*, which has a Lovecraftian setting.

RPG level design implications

To understand the concept of pen-and-paper role playing well, it is important to acknowledge that the ROLE PLAYING elements are as much part of the genre

---

[5] Nor does RPG stand for *Rocket Propelled Grenades*, or horrible simulations at the workplace about *dealing with a difficult client*.

as the GAME elements. In strict terms, one could argue that the game elements and the world simulation elements are no more than a backdrop for the chance to play the role of a character and interact with the virtual world though its acted-out actions. This leads to interesting results; if the role playing is interesting enough, the player can have a rewarding experience trying to light a fire for hours in some featureless tundra.

Once again, the level designer, this time called the Game Master, is an enabler of dramatic and interesting player actions. As before, the player's actions form the central story. Drama comes from the player's responses to the environment and its interactive contents, as presented by the Game Master. Even though the Game Master will have prepared a detailed "module,[6]" the player's actions in reaction to its content are what defines the gameplay session.

Just as in ARGs, immersion is key, and role-playing games require players to stay in character in order to make it all work. The Game Master performs the role of level designer and is responsible for framing the story in such a way that it becomes an enabler of dramatically interesting player choices and subsequent actions.

Similarities between Story-Reliant Game Genres

The above examples show that even in those game genres that rely heavily on story there still is plenty of scope for interactivity.

The main problem that arises from these discussions is one of definition. "Story in games" can mean many things, from traditional linear cutscenes to the actual gameplay experience itself. Video games are so diverse that story or narrative can have an entirely different emphasis, depending on what it is used for.

An important strength of video games lies in their interactive nature, and because interactivity and traditional narrative structures are hard to combine, many people seem to think that this hampers the possibility that any real story could be encompassed in a game. Many people even argue that story should be eliminated from video games completely.

This is wrong because it is based on a misunderstanding of what story can mean *within the context* of a game. Some people look at story in games through a prism of linearity and other structures derived from film or literature, areas that are suited to linear and passive kinds of story, instead of trying to understand the meaning and purpose of "game-story." But it does not have to be this way.

---

[6] The RPG equivalent of a level.

Personally, I feel that the act of playing a game actively writes a story in the mind of the player. For example, *Elite* has hardly has any story to speak of, except for some background information. Through playing the game, though, a story always emerges, based on the player's actions, immersion, and choices made while playing the game. That said, something like *Super Monkey Ball* relies much less on this, but the principle still stands. In other genres, "classic" story implementation is much more central to the act of playing the game. *The Secret of Monkey Island* is a great example of this.

Throughout this book I have been arguing that we need to develop our own voice, through the acceptance of a level design language. A major component within this goal is to come to our own understanding of how to tell stories within our medium, and level design is by far the most effective way of expressing this knowledge.

We write the script, author the play, and set the stage of our game's experience.

Interactivity and Storytelling

Through our exploration of ARGs and pen-and-paper role-playing games, we have found that they have many things in common, and that those similarities might exist within video games and their narrative aspects in general. If this is the case, we are coming close to defining a number of techniques that can work within our field. Although video games occupy a unique position within the overall family of games, they are not the only *interactive* game types.

And since we have already found out that the whole principle of interactivity—of gameplay—seems to many people to form the defining *obstacle* to in-game storytelling ,it may prove useful to look at interactivity and storytelling in more detail.

David Freeman gives the following summary of the conundrum as most people experience it:

> At first it seems obvious that the player should be in charge of what occurs in a game, or at least the agent of much of what takes place. But in games that involve stories, or sequential missions, creating the feeling that the player is in charge can become a challenge. For isn't the player following a pat laid down by the game designers?[7]

This is a prime example of the term "story" being used as a static and preordained concept, as in books and in films. However, story in games is not necessarily much about written story/literary connotations.

---

[7] David Freeman, *Creating Emotions in Games*, New Riders, Berkeley, CA, 2003, p. 328.

In a game the story's *plot* is the sum total of the player's actions throughout the game. Many of the *themes* and the *subtext*[8] are the emotions experienced by the player, and how they are dealt with through the filter of play.

Where many people go wrong is by trying to force these things into a linearly controlled and developer-constructed "story." This misses the point about how games work. Instead, we should craft levels in such a way that gameplay moments form *dramatic markers* and *narrative focal points* that can be interacted with by the player in all kinds of different ways (gameplay). If this is done well, the actions of the player throughout the game then write their own story—one that is incredibly compelling and worthwhile. Game tropes like challenge and interactivity do not impede this kind of story at all, games make use of them by making them dramatically interesting to the unfolding story of the player's interaction with the game.

Nonetheless, traditional snippets of story can still be used. We can have moments of exposition or talking heads in cutscenes, and so on (when appropriate). However, these are only a small part of the narrative as a whole.

Agency and Story

David Freeman acknowledges the role of the player in the story and offers the following:

> By feeling your actions have consequences, you have an impact on the game. To the degree that impact is either real or feels real, it creates the sense that you are playing, to some degree, a *self created story*.[9]

What David is talking about is often referred to as giving the player *agency* in games.

Agency

Agency is an important aspect for level designers, since it ties in directly with what they are trying to do. We speak of it when describing the ability of an "agent" to act in (and make an impact on) the world. This agent can be human, which opens up the discussion to matters of choice, as well as to matters of morality and ethics. (With choice comes responsibility.) When we look at this concept in the context of this chapter, we can describe agency as something given to the game player in the game. The player has the ability to act in the game world, and

---

[8] The underlying thoughts and motivations of the character, not explicitly expressed.

[9] David Freeman, *Creating Emotions in Games*, New Riders, Berkeley, CA, 2003, p. 328.

ideally his or her actions have an impact on that world and on the progression of the game. This kind of agency is much more likely to happen to players of video games than, for example, to readers of a book or to a cinema audience.

So what this all seems to boil down to is the notion that the player is a participant in the unfolding game story, and that it is often desirable to give the player the opportunity to take an active part in the content of the narrative. People call this kind of narrative or story different things; we have seen David Freeman refer to it as *self-created story*. That is a good term, but to me it avoids the fact that level designers still have some influence over what stories can be created by the player. I often refer to the process of telling and experiencing a game story as the *Gameplay Narrative*.

"Gameplay Narrative"

It is becoming clear that in video games there are two types of narrative. There is the type of narrative we normally associate with books, plays, and scripts, and the type that is built as the sum of the player's actions. This latter one is in many ways the most important one for us to grasp, as it applies to pretty much all games. Let's call it *Gameplay Narrative* for the purpose of this book. In a gameplay narrative it is the gamer who tells the story, through his or her own actions.

Seen in this light, the narrative occurs in most cases during or after the gameplay event. It is a natural *result* of gameplay. Because players have the ability to *act* within the game world,[10] they write their own narrative.

For all practical purposes at any moment, it is the player who experiences the emotions and the emotional commitment of the character. The levels themselves can push and pull and steer and provide an outline and a setting for the player to experience the game in, but in most cases it is the player to whom it all happens, not a pre-written character in a static story arc. In fact, it can clash terribly if the game tries to make the player the same as the *character*, insofar as it *tells* the player how to feel. This is the opposite of using techniques to solicit appropriate emotions.

The goal has to be to provide a chance for the player to create experiences that form an interesting narrative.

Agency and interactivity

If the most important narrative actions come from agency, that is to say, from the player's actions .This gives us an excellent opportunity to create specific

---

[10] Yep, "agency" again.

story points to occur throughout the game's levels. If we provide moments of interactivity that are geared towards letting the player experience a compelling action-narrative, we contribute greatly towards the gameplay story of the game as a whole.

In this case, story and narrative are not necessarily classic, literary story points. We don't have to have interactive sequences that are only about story exposition or similar literary devices. We are talking about meaningful actions within the gameplay narrative.

Example: many old FPS games feature a dramatic moment when the player finds a powerful new weapon. This is a specific and meaningful narrative moment within the sequence of actions that form a game's narrative experience.

It is important to allow the player to make the decisions, or in other words, to exercise player agency, in those circumstances where the resulting actions have dramatic impact.

Temporal aspects of gameplay narrative

In all this it is crucial to realize that a game's narrative plays out alongside the actions of the player. It does not exist until the player makes the choices that define the plot and story that the player experiences. This is different from linear stories like books or films, where the audience is confronted with an accomplished story.

In game levels, the player needs to be an active participant within the story, or at least must have an influence over the telling[11] of the story. In practice this means that story events (gameplay scenarios) can occur on a *fluid timeline*. If we accept this as a fact and embrace the possibilities this gives us, we are ahead of the pack. Rather than lamenting the loss of control for designers, we can celebrate the increased dialogue and interaction with our audience.

Level design outline

To do this, the level designer is best off to create an outline of a dramatic progression, and not a strict linear plot line. Think about the kinds of experiences the player is likely to encounter on a per-level basis, and use this to create tools for players to paint their own picture.

If these dramatic focal points can be encountered in a non linear fashion, it will add even more to the immersion of the player in the game world. His or her sense of place and impact on the world will be much strengthened if encounters happen on the player's schedule, rather than on the designer's.

In the player, we have an active and complicit partner in the story. This participation is subconscious when the player reacts to what we put in his or her

---

[11] As often occurs in classical text adventures.

path. It is more explicit when the player knows that certain actions are expected or that a suspension of disbelief is required to enjoy the experience.

Emergent Stories

To a degree this makes gameplay narrative somewhat *emergent*. The level designer only provides seeds that grow in ways that are not entirely predictable. Even better, some of these emerging stories can interact with other gameplay-provided experiences. Things that have happened to the player previously can directly fuel a player's current experience[12] in the game. For example, a tense survival subplot may open up because the player has been wasteful with resources in an earlier part of the game. As level designers we can make sure there is space for this kind of fluidity to the way the game is experienced, which gives us a more natural approach to story in games. Rather than having a formal storyteller approach, we are better off using an approach where we sketch the boundaries of the world, add some dramatic focal points, and give players the tools to deal with them as they see fit. This gives the added advantage of having levels that allow for a whole spectrum of experiences and are never exactly the same between different players.

Dramatic Tools for Level Design

Now that we have examined the types of story and story elements that games deal with, and the way these manifest themselves within the medium, we should look at how we can use them as level designers.

We can take the findings from our examination of story-reliant game genres and the nature of gameplay narrative and see how they relate to the basic dramatic elements explored in the previous section. Here they are again, as a quick reminder:

- **Theme/mood:**
  - form,
  - style,
  - setting.
- **Dramatic progression:**
  - plot,
  - pacing.

Each of these applies directly to level design, if in particular ways that may differ in execution from most other forms of entertainment and art. Nonetheless,

---

[12] Gameplay narrative.

many of the goals are still fairly similar: we want to create levels that have some kind of emotional impact, whether that is pure gameplay enjoyment as found in a game like *Tetris*, or orchestrating a sense of deep fear in a survival horror game like *Silent Hill*.

We address these topics one at a time, but I want to stress one point. All these elements are in a codependent relationship with each other, where one choice heavily impacts the next choice.

Theme and Mood

When we ask questions about the themes and moods of the levels we are making, we are really asking about purpose. This is where our earlier examination of a hierarchical approach to level design becomes really helpful. What are the level's external goals? What are its internal and intrinsic goals? Where does it fit in the overall picture of the full game?

If we have followed up on the advice in earlier chapters,[13] we should be able to answer all those questions and determine what that means with regard to setting, form and style, and how we can make those elements work for us to create a dramatically interesting experience to emerge for players of the game.

Form and Style

Now that we know the *"what"* of the levels, we should look at the *"how."* In most cases, game levels are fairly complex. They are multidisciplinary affairs that combine all kinds of media elements into a coherent whole. Nonetheless, there are still identifiable *elements* of form and style that we can look at, and in some cases there are even well-defined formats to choose from.

Form

Form elements are often determined by the genre conventions of the game in question, as well as by the game design. Strategic team-play games may suggest "capture the flag" levels, while racing games will be best served by certain types of looping racing circuits. The choices of these kinds of forms are as important as any others in level design and should be considered carefully.

Style

Within the forms there are certain types of gameplay that keep surfacing in levels to the extent that they can be described as *styles*. This is reflected in some typical

---

[13] See Chapter 3, "Level Design Goals and Hierarchies."

style elements that can be used in a level. There are obviously too many to consider here; the use of styles entirely depends on the kind of game you are making levels for. But we can name a few: timed sequences, stealth sections, and run and gun can all be incorporated in levels, either as the sole basis for gameplay or as one of many other gameplay styles.

We can have levels that deal with mirrored player bases (to maintain balance between the teams), capture and hold scenarios, and time limited scenarios where a team has to fulfill a task within a certain timeframe. In a survival horror game we can have levels based on *fleeing* (escape an area before it is too late), or *defend to survive* (being barricaded into a room while an enemy tries to get in).

There are many advantages to using well-known gameplay styles. The level designer will have lots of information on how to implement them, the player will have a very recognizable gameplay environment to enjoy, and the programming teams will know what to look out for. The downside, of course, is the lack of originality that can come with these kinds of pre-made styles. Having said that, innovative play environments can be considered a style in their own right.

Setting

Finally, we need to address the *where*. The setting of a level can be one of the defining features that determine much of the content the level will carry. It is potentially one of the most important decisions that can be made, as it will lead to certain restrictions and boundaries to the gameplay action, which in effect makes it a practical *framework* for the level content. If this framework is chosen well, the level can be very appropriate to the gameplay that the level designer wants to implement. If it is chosen poorly, it can become a huge obstacle to the desired gameplay. So let's look at some of the things to consider in choosing a setting.

When choosing a setting, we should check against a number of things that should be on our wish list for levels:

Depth and versatility—Can the setting sustain the level design goals it needs to support for a long enough period without becoming boring or too samey? Does it allow for flexible and varying application of gameplay mechanics?

Take for example a level of a real-time strategy game, one where terrain influences the troop movements a lot. It may be more interesting to place the action in an old European city built on two flanking hills than on a large homogenous and perfectly gridded city, as seen in many American states.

AI—Does the setting allow for the AI to shine? Does it offer the right environment for path planning, showing off their best decision making skills, allow for good interaction with the player, and whatever else can be thought of to make them as effective as possible.

Player Character Abilities—Similarly, does the environment jell with the player character's ability to navigate and interact with it? Is it a fiddly environment with many obstacles? Is it easy for the player to get lost or get stuck looking for exits? Is it easy to signpost in the environment?

Appropriateness—Does the setting fit the desired mood and themes you want to establish? Does it jell with the plot and the background story? Will it show off the rendering capability of the engine and the art style the game is supposed to convey?

There are hundreds of additional factors that we can add to this; it is all about finding the right setting for the level design elements you have in mind. For example, many levels take place in underground bases for very understandable reasons: they easily support corridor/room/corridor settings, are suitable to having lock-and-door gameplay, can be very easily provided with navigation direction in the environment, and so on. The trick is of course to tick off many positives in settings that feel fresh and original.

Dramatic Progression

If we do our work well, levels should provide some form of dramatic progression. We can affect this by a number of methods, including the use of plotting and pacing and their level design equivalents.

Plot

In level design the plot is the sum total of the player's actions. This means that we don't know the entire plot when we design a new level, since the player's actions have not yet occurred. An immediate natural reaction of many level designers is to start orchestrating the content of a level in such a way that we have total control over the player's actions and therefore know exactly what the plot of the game will be like. *This is a grave mistake.* While throughout the book I advocate ways of exerting authorial control over the levels and the experiences therein, I do not advocate spelling out the exact steps to be taken by the player in order to have the "right experience."

Agency and gameplay narrative

To make sure that players feel involved in the plot of the gameplay they are experiencing, we should avoid explicitly dictating all the experiences the player has to undergo. Instead, we design our levels in such a way that we give players real *agency* in the game, and we let their own choices become the focus for most of the plot progression. What we want to do is give players the feeling that *they* are the ones that matter in the world, that *their* actions determine the outcome of the narrative.

A player's self-determination is to be encouraged though creating environments that react favorably to the player's actions. It is to be encouraged to let players try out different abilities, award them when they try different things, and not punish them for exercising those skills that they have been taught.

Dramatic markers and set pieces

Even within such a free level design environment, we can still shape the outlines of important scenes and story elements. We will want to orchestrate memorable moments and at times influence the pacing of the gameplay narrative. To achieve these things without giving up on the sense of player agency or limiting the expression possibilities of the player we can make use of *dramatic markers* and *set pieces*.

An important thing to remember is that we can create these kinds of focused and important gameplay narratives without necessarily prescribing the exact time or method in which the player experiences them. If, for example, we wish the player to be exposed to a very important encounter with an NPC, we could make this encounter occur based on other conditional level elements. That is to say that the NPC encounter can be triggered by a number of different conditions, especially those that are subject to the player's actions. This guarantees that the player cannot predict when the event occurs, which makes for a dramatically more interesting world.

Pacing

As we have seen in the preceding chapter, pacing is an *authorial tool* of great power in most non-static art forms and creative endeavors. As level designers we find ourselves in exactly the same position as composers or film editors, inasmuch as we want to exert control over the timing and intensity of the gameplay experience we are creating. We may use a different vocabulary, but the overall aim is the same. However, there are elements to pacing that are specific to level design and need to be further examined.

Pacing and flow theory

One of the most important elements of pacing in level design is that of keeping players in the *zone*, that perfect state where immersion and enjoyment and other positive experiences keep players in a state of gaming bliss. As discussed in

Chapter 8, "Immersion"), keeping players in the zone has wide-ranging effects, not the least of which is that it has an impact on pacing.

This is also borne out if we look at our flow diagram again. We can see that Csíksczentmihalyi's diagram[14] progresses along a *timeline*, which brings us into the realm of deliberate pacing. As levels progress, the designer needs to make sure the right balance between challenge and ability is maintained along a learning curve that develops over time. Since we want levels that don't shut out or bore players, we have to take great care. It is easy to see why this is important to level designers, since they are the ones who control the pacing of levels.

Learning curve

It is then fair to say that closely related to a level designer's task of keeping a player in the zone is the need to maintain a sensible *learning curve*. As the flow diagram shows, it is vital not to over- or under-challenge the player. Under-challenging is bad because players may become bored, but at least in that situation players may still try to entertain themselves. Over-challenging the player is even worse, as this will make the player so frustrated that he or she may stop playing altogether.

So it is vital that the game's learning curve[15] be a function of a progression that keeps the player within the *flow channel*, or in the *zone* of an *optimal game experience*. But how do we do that? Players' individual skill sets can be wildly divergent, making it very hard to cater to individual abilities.

One way of achieving this goal is by allowing aspects of the game to behave dynamically in concert with the player's actions.

Dynamic progression

Keeping a balance between challenge and skill is easier said than done. Since we are dealing with human beings, we are also dealing with wildly different abilities and skill levels. One of the biggest dangers in level design is to create an experience that is suitable to one player, but that creates an insurmountable obstacle to another. If the latter occurs, it is not unlikely that the player will get so annoyed with the game that he or she will stop playing it *forever*. Even worse, that person tells friends not to buy it. This is pretty much the worst thing that can happen and needs to be avoided if at all possible.

---

[14] See "An Introduction to Flow Theory" in Chapter 8.

[15] *Learning curve* is actually a misnomer, since the learning aspect needs to stay at an enjoyable constant. A better term would be something like *challenge curve* or *progression curve*.

To counter these massive dangers, designers and game developers can create levels and games that employ *dynamic difficulty adjustment*. The game experience is tailored to the varying skill levels and play styles of its players. This is a technique that has been known for a few years, but that wasn't studied in detail until Jenova Chen did the game development community a great favor by writing his thesis on the subject.[16] Chapter 16, "Challenge," goes into great detail on this matter.

Typical Pacing Methods

Because pacing has such a strong impact on how games are perceived, I want to spend some extra time on it. Looking at the pacing elements of past video games, we will discover a massive amount of data available to us about pacing *methods*. We can easily distill a number of typical techniques and concepts that have become part of the level design toolbox:

Connectivity and Layout

The most obvious way of influencing pace is simply by creating gameplay spaces with navigational limitations and opportunities. This allows the level designer tight control over the progression of the player, and over how and when specific gameplay situations are experienced. This makes it an often-used tool by level designers in all kinds of situations. Let's look at some useful examples.

Bounce

We speak of *bounce* when the player encounters an impediment to progression that forces him or her to backtrack and perform an action that removes the obstacle when revisited. In the early days of level design, and indeed to this day, this was often realized by the locked-door scenario. The player would literally find a locked door and would have to go back and hunt or a key.

These days, we often find more elegant approaches to the bounce scenario, at times implemented so well that players don't even recognize it as such.

Linear progression

Sometimes a straight path from A to B is all we need from a level. Linearity has some clear advantages, and if not overused can be a very effective method of controlling the pacing in a level. It gives the player a great sense of clarity as prog-

---

[16] Jenova Chen, *Flow in Games*, http://www.jenovachen.com/flowingames/index.html, 2008.

ress is along the one path. This kind of direct challenge can be very enjoyable, especially if it is clear to players that in order to succeed or progress they must finish an "obstacle course" of gameplay scenarios. Pacing is controlled by the gameplay along the way. It is very easy for the designer to create and test such a formal environment, which makes it an attractive proposition from a production point of view.

Loops

A *loop* is a very similar method of controlling pacing, with the difference being that players end up at the starting point. All the other linear advantages apply, but we have the additional bonus of being able to show players their goal from the get-go. This can greatly enhance the sense of context in which players perform actions.

Sandbox

A *sandbox* approach allows players to come up with their own gameplay solutions, or at least must create the illusion that they can. The central point to sandbox games is that players must feel that the world doesn't feel too prescribed. Instead, players must be able to bend it to their own will. The sandbox provides players the raw building material (like sand) to create their own mark on the world. It isn't always easy to influence pacing in such an environment, although much can be done by placing certain conditional events in the world, and by creating natural-looking bottlenecks. Perhaps a player character needs to be of certain strength to pass a particular area, or a specific type of enemy creature is only released into the environment after the player obtains a particular weapon

Stickiness

A good way of subtly influencing pacing is to slow the player down by creating areas that are *sticky*. This stickiness is achieved by providing positive reasons for staying in an area, for example by providing a safe area in which the player can indulge in some fun activity or by creating a tempting discreet challenge that may yield a great reward. If these instances of stickiness are optional, players will never feel resentful about this kind of manipulation, since they are engaging with it by choice.

Many good examples of sticky areas can be found in *Half Life 2*, where all throughout the game completely optional areas can be found, filled with opportunities for almost carefree play. Some of these are almost banal in implementation. I have once stopped my progression on the main path after spotting a large number of crates and decided it worth my time to try to stack them as high as possible in order to gain an enjoyable view of the world. (The game allows a playful approach to physics.) From a level-design point of view, all that was needed to give the player this experience was a deep understanding of the fun of the game's physics engine and the placement of some crates in an eye-catching area.

Push and Pull

Push and pull mechanics are born from elements in the environment that seek to influence the player's progression, either forcibly or by necessity. Take for example the scenario where in order for players to progress, they need to go down a lift, but after they have reached the desired location, the lift breaks down and makes backtracking impossible. This is a clear example of a *push*. Now imagine an alternative scenario where the player is nearly out of health and being chased by a strong enemy creature. Somewhere in front of the player, a health-pack can be spotted. Chances are the player is drawn to the health-pack. This is a clear example of *pull*.

If we take these principles further, we realize that a game level is full of opportunities for pacing adjustments by pushing here and pulling there. If we do this with skill, it can come across as perfectly natural. The level can become a gameplay engine, and items placed among many other things can be used as fuel.

Alternative Methods and Ideas

There are many other ways in which to influence the pacing in a level. Some are yet to be invented, and others are fairly obvious or well known. It is pointless to try to capture them all in this chapter, but it may be useful to at least make some notes on possible areas of interest:

- fear (scare players into adjusting their pace of progression),
- hurry (create a necessity to rush),
- time (affect the progression of time to create pacing changes),
- physics (make the properties of the environment determine progress),
- AI (Let the player depend on the progression of a NPC).

Many others can be added, and in fact it may be wise to create a list of useful ones for the game you are working on. It is always nice to have a large repertoire of techniques. Please check the upcoming practical examples for a whole raft of them.

Puzzles

A special mention needs to be reserved for the use of puzzles as pacing devises. Puzzles are among the best and most versatile tools that level designers have at their proposal. Among their many uses is their ability to influence the pacing in a level.

Because puzzles can be designed to fit a certain solution, they are extremely useful in exerting control over a gameplay/puzzle situation.[17] If we can determine the likely duration of a puzzle sequence, we are in effect given control over the pacing of a level, or at least we have it to a significant degree.

Space

> Davis understood that the space between the notes was sometimes just as important as the notes themselves. But he also understood that too much space between the notes, and people would think that the concert was over and go home....[18]

In level design, pacing is as much determined by what you *leave out* of a level as by what you put in. Almost every professional level designer will at one point have a serious disagreement with somebody about level areas being "too empty." In almost every case when I have had this argument in my own professional life, I was right to fight my corner. The spaces between the gameplay events are incredibly important, and in fact, are part of the gameplay experience as a whole. Mark Hollis has been reported[19] to have said that:

> Before you play two notes, learn how to play one note—and don't play one note unless you've got a reason to play it.

Not only are these wise words, they can be expanded on to fit video game development even further. *Sometimes leaving empty spaces is a level design event in its own right.*

There is *need* in level design for spaces where nothing happens. Don't listen to producers or other meddling colleagues or bosses who want to have something happen every two seconds without rhyme or reason. They don't necessarily understand that the full picture has to incorporate room for the player to breathe. Allow for reflection and space within the player's head to do things like think, observe, contemplate, and strategize.

---

[17] For all kinds of additional ways to include puzzles in level design, please look at Chapter 14 on Puzzles.

[18] From the *Genius Guide to Jazz*, July 2001, cited at http://www.allaboutjazz.com/php/jazzquotes.php.

[19] Quotation from the unofficial Mark Hollis and Talk Talk website: http://users.cybercity.dk/~bcc11425/.

These things are as vital to the action in the level as the action-packed moments are. And last but not least: they provide a powerful tool to affect pacing.

Theory Summary: Tying It All Together

This chapter shows that there are several ways to think about story and narrative processes in level design.

Despite what many people claim, there is much storytelling involved in level (game) design, but it is focused on providing the player with the right setting and tools to experience the game in a *dramatically interesting* way. The level designer's job is to create a level in such a way that it forms a compelling narrative of the player's interactions within it. It is a self-created story or a *gameplay narrative*.

This type of story is different from stories in books and from other written stories, which are different from film stories, which are different from other stories yet again. Gameplay narratives are the sum of the player's actions and experiences and are subject to their own rules and techniques with regard to dramatic progression.

It is also a misconception that typical game elements like interactivity or challenge are unique to video games. Other game genres like *ARGs (Artificial Reality Games)* and role-playing games have to deal with the same obstacles and are well worth studying in that respect.

With that focus in mind, we still have similar goals and tools to other media that employ story. We deal with overarching *themes* and use tools to enable *dramatic progression*. It is the translation of those goals into level-design-specific tools and methods that can make the difference between levels that provide a compelling gameplay story and levels that are hampered by traditional or non-applicable notions of what "story" is supposed to be. The next chapter will show a number of practical examples that showcase how this can be done.

Practice

Example 12.1: Themes and Moods— Practical Application

Summary

To enhance the game's themes and moods, we create levels that support thematic gameplay. This can be done through the use of symbols: content that represents more than its *literal* interpretation. What does this mean in a practical sense, however? This practice example shows straightforward ways to tie themes, moods and symbolism into everyday level design situations.

Game Genre

The technique is suitable for most games.

Goals to Achieve

- Identify main themes and moods.
- Assign thematic and symbolic value to gameplay scenarios.
- Use this to underline the themes and moods the level needs to convey.

Description

(Example type: Original)

We generally try to make our levels *about* something, even if that something is solely the gameplay mood that pervades a level. In most cases it makes sense to emphasize certain themes and moods that the level needs to convey, and use this as a framework for the gameplay that occurs within the level.

We can do this by taking *general* gameplay that would occur regardless of thematic goals, and making it specific so that it ties into the required themes or moods we want to portray.

If we take a hypothetical set of themes and moods, we can show how this could work.

Powering the town. Our hypothetical game is a third person action adventure, where the player can traverse and explore the environment and perform simple context-sensitive actions: throw switches, push objects, and so on.

In this example the main themes we want to put forward are based on the universal struggle for freedom, and the mood we want to portray in the level is one of hope and positivity.

We can achieve our goal by providing an environment that is restrictive in a number of ways at the outset, including the player's ability to act within that environment, and slowly transforming it through the actions of the player to become one of wide-ranging freedom and promise.

Take, for example, an abandoned town filled with ancient machinery, doors, lights, vehicles, and so on. All of these used to be powered by electricity derived from wind and solar energy. The original inhabitants of the town have abandoned it after an earthquake damaged all the sources of power, like the windmills and the solar panels. They now live a hand-to-mouth existence in the local countryside.

To fit with the theme and mood of the level, we will allow the player to perform a number of context-sensitive actions that slowly transform the town, enable things in it, increase the player's ability to move around and interact with it, and lure back the original inhabitants.

- To begin with, the player can *rotate a windmill back into the path of the wind*. This will allow a system of aqueducts and pipes to start to power the town's running water system.
- This then enables the player to go around town and *clean the dirty solar panels* with the water pipes now running again.
- The new electricity from the solar panels allows the player to *repair the broken generators* with electric tools that can now run again.
- With the generators running, the player can *charge the battery of an aircraft*, which is able to reach previously unavailable solar mirrors.
- The player then *repositions the solar mirrors* to make them shine light on the town's massive central solar panels.
- This finally allows the player to *kick-start the whole electricity net*, enabling the town's streetcars, residential equipment, and so on.

All the way through this process, a number of things occur that are in keeping with the level's thematic goals:

- The player can navigate more and more of the town.
- The town becomes bright with all the new sunlight and electrical illumination.
- Life starts to return to the town: villagers start to occupy the houses again.
- Music is heard throughout the town.

Further Notes

An approach like this one allows the level designer to create interesting and appropriate gameplay sequences all through a level. It is more a matter of choosing the action that supports the general moods and themes than of having to painstakingly come up with a large number of individually interesting but incoherent gameplay actions.

Example 12.2: Non-Linear Narrative— Dramatic Components

Summary

There are times in which we like to avoid linearity in level design and still make use of a progressing narrative. This example shows a way of approaching the problem that allows for this to happen.

Game Genre

This technique can be used in any game where a dramatic progression does not have to follow a set order.

Goals to Achieve

- Allow for a non-linear but still progressive narrative in a level.
- Let the gameplay narrative be assembled by the player.

Description

(Example type: Original)

The dramatic components technique assumes that the player is able to form a narrative out of individual components that are presented in an arbitrary order, or in an order determined by player choice. If enough components have been assembled, the narrative structure is complete.

One way to do this is by treating the narrative as a meal that is made up of specific ingredients. The level designer provides the meal's ingredients, and the player is the cook who is putting it all together through gameplay actions and choices. It is key to accept that the player takes individual narrative ingredients and slowly constructs a whole in their mind regardless of the order in which the ingredients are discovered.

Another way of looking at this is by imaging a criminal case that can be solved if enough evidence is found. The level designer spreads the evidence throughout the level, and it really doesn't matter in which order the player uncovers it. The final picture of the narrative is the same regardless.

Whatever analogy we employ, the idea is to break up the narrative—be it factual content, dramatic sequences, set pieces, or any other components—and break it down into discreet individual instances that can be placed throughout a level.

We can envision dramatic components like the following *arsonist scenario:*

- The player rescues a child from a burning building.
- The player discovers that several buildings have burned down in the past.
- A letter reaches the player, telling him to deliver $100,000 or another child will die.
- The Player finds a diary of a psychiatrist, mentioning the case of a deluded arsonist.

Each of these components can be experienced by the player in any order, without harming the narrative at all. So, what we end up with is a coherent narrative whole, but it is presented in a way that respects the non-linear interactivity that can be so valuable in our levels. It is the player who pieces the individual parts together, and it is the player who will feel as if he or she plays a vital part in this narrative.

Further Notes

If necessary the level designer could tie it all up by allowing the next sequence in the level design to unfold only after these four events have happened. This would turn it into a semi-linear progression, based on conditional events. In that scenario, some control is applied, while still allowing for the dramatic component technique to be used.

Example 12.3: Pacing Techniques—Bounce

Summary

As defined earlier in the book, we speak of *bounce* when the player encounters an impediment to progression that forces him or her to backtrack and perform an action that removes the obstacle when revisited.

Game Genre

This technique is suitable for most games that feature physical progression through a level.

Goals to Achieve

- Control pacing by introducing a bounce scenario.
- Make this stand out from the preceding action.
- Present this in a way that is appropriate to the setting.

Description

(Example type: Original)

In this example, the player is traveling by car along a path through the level. The player is progressing along this main path when the tire blows, and he or she is subsequently forced to stop. This is the event that triggers the bounce situation (E in Figure 12.1).

The remainder of the main path is of such a nature that progression on foot is not viable, so the player has to find a solution to the problem. The only path accessible on foot is the *bounce path* that takes the player past a number of chal-

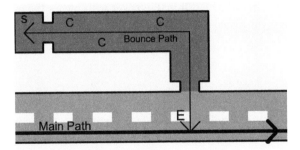

Figure 12.1. Bounce scenario.

lenges (C). These challenges are up to the level designer, but should be of a nature that significantly changes the pacing of the gameplay.

Eventually the player reaches the solution (S), which in this case is a spare tire found in a room off of the bounce path. The player now bounces back to the position where the vehicle was abandoned, and is confronted with more challenges along the way.

Finally the player returns to the car and is able to progress along the main path.

Further Notes

In practice this is no more that a lock-and-key situation: the lock is the broken car, the key is the spare tire. The situation can be embellished without difficulties, however: the path can be more complex, the bounce event can consist of a number of sub-events, and so on.

Designing Gameplay

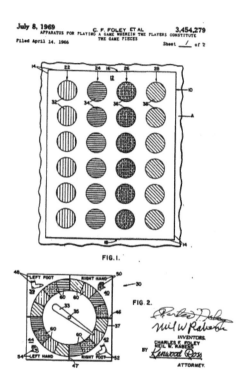

July 8, 1969   C. F. FOLEY ET AL   3,454,279
                  APPARATUS FOR PLAYING A GAME WHEREIN THE PLAYERS CONSTITUTE
Filed April 14, 1966   THE GAME PIECES
                                                    Sheet __/__ of 2

FIG. I.

FIG. 2.

I n a book covering a field as encompassing as level design, it is very hard to organize data in a way that is not too contrived or constraining. There is no ideal

---

Charles F. Foley and Nell W. Rabens, "Apparatus for Playing a Game wherein the Player
Constitute the Game Pieces," US Patent 3,454,279, issued July 8, 1969. Available at "The
Twister History," http://www.mathematik.uni-bielefeld.de/~sillke/Twister/history/,
2000.

way of doing it, and this book is no exception. I have done my best to organize chapters in a sensible manner, but some explanation is needed.

The following set of chapters is organized under the heading of *Designing Gameplay*. This is because the chapters cover areas that are most directly connected to gameplay mechanics and their implementation. They are the bread and butter of level design and often work as part of larger gameplay systems. Ultimately, this will be true to a certain degree of most topics covered in this book, but it is most true for the chapters explored in this section.

World Building

13

An interesting aspect of what we do in level design is that we create imaginary worlds for players to enjoy. This is an aspect that isn't unique to video games of course; the same thing occurs in books and theater and in all kinds of creative disciplines. However, we do have a heightened emphasis in our imaginary worlds on player input and participation, perhaps more so than in other artistic endeavors.

Either way, no matter which way you look at it, the act of level design is partly an act of *world building*. We create a headspace for players to spend a lot of time in. Since these worlds are *virtual* rather than *of this world*, normal rules don't apply. We need to take a good look at how to approach world building through that filter.

Concept

Terminology

I want to spend a small moment discussing terminology, just to make sure I don't create the wrong expectation for these chapters. In a subject as wide ranging as this one, it is very easy to lose focus and get tangled up in definition problems, so I want to avoid that trap completely. The term *world building* can be used in many more ways than I am going to discuss in this book, and although they may all be interesting to look at, I am limiting myself to those aspects that I find relevant to the subject matter we are dealing with directly.

The way *world building* is used in this book is generally not a metaphorical one. I think it is completely valid in other instances, like the worlds that can be conjured through the notes played in an evocative piece of music or other such examples, but it is not really what we deal with in level design. I am mostly focusing on the actual creation or recreation or simulation of actual or possible worlds. Sometimes this is as complete and grand scale an effort as can be seen as in *Lord of the Rings*. At other times, it is a small aspect of a world, as in a theatrical play that takes place in one set. These smaller-scale examples may themselves act as metaphors for other things, but they still employ the art of world building in a direct and recognizable manner.

Some Examples of World Building

It often pays to look at a subject like this through the various filters provided by the approaches taken by other disciplines. Various points of view are likely to yield more diverse insights, which is very helpful, while overlap between diverse art forms suggests commonalities that can be forged into general techniques.

So let's look at some typical examples of the art of world building.

Science Fiction and Fantasy Literature

It is hard to think of a clearer example of world building than the many efforts found in science fiction and fantasy literature, and in related genres. This includes utopian or dystopian books like *Brave New World*[1] or any other book set in a world that isn't our own. Many of these books are meant to invoke a *sense of wonder* in the audience. This term specifically describes a feeling of wondrous realization that is carefully built up through world building techniques.

Good science fiction or fantasy does not engage in world building simply to create a background setting. The point of the exercise is to create a world that supports the main themes of the work in an integral way. That is to say that the world-building aspects are not incidental or separate from the core of the work.

We can say without a doubt that the detail in the world described in George Orwell's *1984* matters greatly to the impact of the whole. The posters stating "Big Brother is watching you" are so apt and appropriate to the themes of the book that they have touched a real nerve in people who have read the book. So much so that the iconic image of Big Brother has been adopted across the cultural landscape. Concepts like these can closely mirror the realities of our own society, but by presenting them through the lens of science fiction or fantasy, they can be viewed in a way that gives us a new perspective.

---

[1] Aldous Huxley.

Equally interesting are the efforts to evoke an imaginary world that stands up to scrutiny and has the power to immerse and delight, simply by being conceptualized in the text. Or to put it in less flowery terms: it is really nice to read stories set in imaginary or fantastical places, if these places are realized with real skill and thought. Many readers have lost themselves in the nooks and crannies of Mervyn Peake's *Gormenghast* or the haunting places of Ray Bradbury's *Martian Chronicles*.

It is very educational to see what kinds of choices are made in this field when it comes to describing what these worlds actually *contain*. What is put into the text that makes it so successful?

Detail and symbols

The examples given above (the iconic concept of *1984*'s Big Brother or the fine descriptive detail in *Gormenghast*) show two sides of the same coin.

Regarding detailed meticulous descriptions, we have this:

> Over their irregular roofs would fall throughout the seasons, the shadows of time-eaten buttresses, of broken and lofty turrets, and, most enormous of all, the shadow of the Tower of Flints. This tower, patched unevenly with black ivy, arose like a mutilated finger from among the fists of knuckled masonry and pointed blasphemously at heaven. At night the owls made of it an echoing throat; by day it stood voiceless and cast its long shadow.[2]

And regarding the creation of iconic symbols, we have something like Figure 13.1.

Things like these two examples all function to achieve a similar end: using world building to express the work's themes and ideas.

This high level of detail is often needed because the reader is dealing with unfamiliar territory. Sci-fi and fantasy deal with unknown places, and the required sense of wonder is hard to achieve without creating a very precise picture in the mind of the reader.

The use of symbols and icons, though not specific to sci-fi and fantasy, is especially useful in these genres, since it becomes a shorthand for some concepts and ideas described earlier. The author cannot keep expressing every bit of detail in this constructed world. Some of the world's content needs to be able to function on the iconic or symbolic level.

---

[2] Description of *The Tower of Flints* from *Titus Groan*, available at http://www.goodreads.com/author/quotes/22018.Mervyn_Peake.

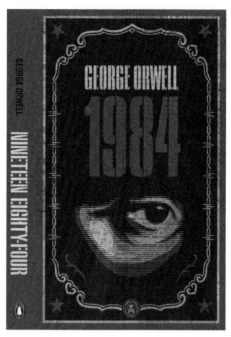

Figure 13.1. Book cover for *1984.*[3]

Simulations

While the previous example of world building deals with creating new and imaginary worlds, we also have world-building examples that deal with recreating worlds or environments as *simulations*. In this case there is no direct artistic goal, but an educational or scientific one. In simulated environments, certain characteristics and processes are examined within the context of a specific formal system. This can be an ecosystem or a weather prediction model or a geological process simulation. The principle of these kinds of simulations can scale up all the way to simulations of the universe itself, and can therefore be seen as a subclass of world building.

Again, because it is impossible to incorporate all aspects of the world into a created simulation, the makers of these simulations have to make choices on what to include and what to leave out.

---

[3] Newly commissioned book cover for Penguin Books by artist, Shepard Fairey. George Orwell, *1984*, Penguin Books, London, 2008.

In simulations, what matters most are those factors that determine the accuracy and predictability of the data they produce. So for example, when studying cloud formation above oceans through a simulation, we do not have to include data on the mating rituals of the fish beneath the waves. The difficulty lies in deciding what data is pertinent and what data is superfluous, which isn't always clear.[4]. Difficult or not, however, in this kind of world building *relevance* is a key concept.

Cinematography

In cinematography we deal with an art form that has experimented extensively with ways of suggesting and showing a vast array of possible worlds. Few art forms have become so adept at mixing techniques and methods to portray imagined worlds, showing detail when needed, yet bamboozling the audience and suggesting all kinds of implied (but nonexistent) content with smoke and mirrors.

Midgets and magic

One of my favorite examples of this is the final shot in the classic movie *Casablanca*. If I were to tell you that the famous final scene is filled with midgets, you wouldn't believe me, right?

Here is what Snopes[5] has to say on the subject:

> That final scene, in which Rick Blaine (Humphrey Bogart) and Ilsa Lund (Ingrid Bergman) say their final goodbyes as the plane to Lisbon (the one which will carry Ilsa out of Rick's life forever) warms up in the background is one of the most famous scenes in cinematic history, and this is the scene Disney recreated in their Great Movie Ride, for which they needed a real Lockheed Electra 12A.

> However, when Warner Bros. filmed the scene, they found their soundstage was too small to accommodate a real airplane, so the studio's prop men constructed half- and quarter-size models of a Lockheed Electra 12A out of plywood and balsa. *Midgets garbed in jumpsuits* were hired to move in and around the replica planes to camouflage their smaller-than-life scale, and the whole scene was swathed in machine-generated fog to further conceal the artificiality of the setting. (Fog certainly wasn't add-

---

[4] Especially when dealing with chaotic systems in which small factors can have large consequences. But let's not go into chaos theory right now.

[5] Snopes: the famous myth-busting website. See www.snopes.com.

ed for any touch of realism, as foggy nights are a rarity in Casablanca.)[6]
(*Emphasis mine.*)

This is a clever use of *forced perspective*, which is also used to great effect in the *Lord of the Rings* movies[7] to show the hobbits as being smaller than humans. In some ways this can be described as a special effect, and to a degree that is all it is. But on another level, it is way more than that, especially because the audience doesn't interact with the scene on that level. Viewers experience the available information, onscreen visuals and audio, and construct the world in their minds, following the blueprint of the director and cinematographer. When it comes to world building in film, this kind of direction occurs all the time. It happens in the audio cues given to the audience, the cutting of consecutive shots, the framing of the scene, the content of the dialogue, and so forth.

Theater

Theater is an interesting art form when it comes to world building, since it is so limited in its available space and time. All action takes place on one stage (in most cases), and since performances are by definition live, there is only limited scope for set changes. This is very different from film, for example, where many locations can be used and meticulously prepared for the best possible shots.

In most theater productions it is necessary to work with broad brushstrokes. Is the setting a temple in ancient Greece? One or two foam Greek pillars will suffice. Does the action occur underwater? A blue theater light with some waving cloth will do the trick. French front in World War II? Use an evocative soundtrack of battle noises and French and German soldiers shouting at each other. What is key is that theater set designers are able to evoke a whole world with very limited means, not only because there is only so much that fits on stage or because set changes need to be quick and simple, but also because it is just more efficient. Why build a whole temple if the one pillar will do?

Theater set-designers are very good at finding iconic visuals and sound to transport the audience to where they need to be. The dialogue and acting are of course of the utmost importance, but intelligent use of props, sounds, and lighting really places everything in a fully realized world. They serve as *symbols* that represent far bigger concepts and ideas, places, and emotions in a way that is

---

[6] "The Plane Truth," *Snopes.com: Casablanca Plane in Great Movie Ride*, http://www.snopes.com/disney/parks/casablanca.asp, 2007.

[7] New Line Cinema.

elegant and powerful. The ability to quickly sketch out the core of what matters is a valuable technique that benefits all kinds of artistic projects.

Comics and Sequential Art

Finally, and often mistakenly seen as least, there is world building as it occurs in *sequential art*. Sequential art is a term that almost nobody knows and even fewer people use, but it is in fact a very useful collective term for things like comics, strips, graphic novels, and so on.

Scott McCloud's book, *Making Comics*, features a chapter on world building that opens with the following words:

> The world is a BIG PLACE.
> Capturing all of its sights and challenges in little rectangles can be a daunting CHALLENGE.
> But with knowledge –
> Effort –
> And a willingness to go beyond the merely "adequate" –
> – your worlds can seem as POWERFUL and VIVID as any others, real or imagined.
>
> Sweating such details can make the difference between drawing a page in SIX hours and drawing it in TWENTY—
> – but for your readers it can make the difference –
> – between KNOWING where your story takes place –
> – and BEING THERE.[8]

Even without seeing the images that he accompanies these words with, these words very effectively describe many of the feelings I have towards level design.

The almost unthinking dismissal of sequential art as a non-serious art form, or even less than an art form, is tragic and wrong. Tragic because it denies people an incredibly rich and dynamic source of worthwhile experiences, and wrong because the form is capable of so much that it does not deserve to be seen in this negative light.[9]

One example of the artistry and power of sequential art comes from its approach to world building, and especially its expert use of a technique or concept known as *closure*.

---

[8] Scott McCloud, *Making Comics*, Harper Perennial, New York, 2006, pp. 158–159.
[9] Just like video games, really.

Filling in the Blanks or "Closure"

In Scott McCloud's seminal book *Understanding Comics: The Invisible Art*, we can find the following passage:

> Here in the limbo of the gutter, human imagination takes two separate images and transforms them into a single idea. "Nothing is seen between the two panels, but experience tells you something must be there." Comics panels fracture both time and space, offering a jagged, staccato rhythm of unconnected moments. But closure allows us to connect these moments and mentally construct a continuous, unified reality. "If visual iconography is the vocabulary of comics, closure is the grammar. And since our definition of comics hinges on the arrangement of elements—then, in a very real sense, comics is closure. (*Emphasis removed.*)[10]

This should really be read in context with the images and preceding chapters of the book, but I wanted to highlight it nonetheless, as it points at an important concept that we use throughout this book in one way or another.

What McCloud is talking about is what happens *in between* the panels of a comic book. Something almost never thought about, but almost magical in nature. The human brain has an enormous capacity to see patterns, recognize relationships between concepts, and extrapolate detail from those relationships.

Imagine three image descriptions presented as the panels of a comic strip[11]:

Image 1:
A rude young man throws a banana peel on the sidewalk. A finger-wagging old man looks on disapprovingly.

Image 2:
The youth is walking elsewhere now.

Image 3:
A loud sound startles him and he runs off.

Image 4:
In his rush, he fails to see a banana peel, slips on it and falls on his behind. He is laughed at by the old man we saw earlier, now holding a horn and a peeled banana.

This is a very banal example of a sequence of events that could occur in a newspaper comic strip. Yet if we examine it a bit closer, something extraordinary has

---

[10] Scott McCloud, *Understanding Comics*, Harper Perennial, New York, 1994, pp. 66–67.

[11] Be warned, it is a terribly bad one I just made up.

occurred. Somehow the reader has constructed a coherent world view in which four drawings placed side by side tell a story and give detailed information on the world in which it occurs.

For example, we know that a little humorous revenge story has unfolded. We know that the old man got his revenge by scaring the youth with the horn and placing a banana peel in his path to enact some poetic justice.

All these realizations and connections occur in *between the panels*, which is why McCloud has dubbed comics the "invisible art." Our brain takes information from the world (in this case the panels from a comic strip) and reconciles them by creating cross-connections between the sequential images, thereby adding meaning and relationships to the events depicted.

The process of resolving these images into a narrative or conceptual structure that we feel we can understand is called *closure*. It is one of the most important processes that an artist needs to understand. If employed well, closure allows us to do much more with much less, and we can let all the hard work of building a world in the mind of an audience be done by *the audience itself*.

Connecting the Dots

The mind needs VERY little to construct a view of the world that it can understand. We discussed this process previously, in the discussion of the physiology of sight in Chapter 10, but it is important to return to the concept for a moment. Let's recap what I said earlier:

> Our brains have evolved in such a way that they have become very adept at processing data in ways that are important in our daily lives. Of these skills, *pattern recognition* stands out particularly well, since we use it so much. How else do we differentiate between all the differing visual input we receive via our eyes? *Pattern recognition* allows us to process visual data at a much-enhanced speed because it lets us carve up the visual input into useful chunks to which we ascribe further meaning and behavior. This process is actually called *chunking*[12] and is *key to our intelligent understanding of our environment. (Emphasis added.)*

Previously I was speaking of pattern recognition and the ability to differentiate between all the data presented to us specifically, but this also applies to the concept of closure. Because we cannot help trying to make sense of the data we are presented with, we more often than not try to organize what we see into a world view. This can be done with *very little data* indeed, and it provides us with enormous artistic firepower. Our brains are always engaged in this process, whether

---

[12] I kid you not!

we want them to be not; this means that we can tap into this process at any time we need to.

Commonalities and Lessons Learned

There are a number of parallels and commonalities in the previous examples, as well as some genre-specific insights. They offer an insight into the kind of general techniques one can exploit, or specific solutions found in various world building exercises.

We have seen that very specific use of fine detail can be made when needed, especially in fields like Sci-fi and fantasy, where the artist has to paint a picture of many unknown things. But there is also a general need for iconic and symbolic content to convey important themes and content efficiently. At times there is an emphasis on relevance, as demanded in simulations, and we can use the concept of closure to our advantage in almost all world building scenarios.

Theory

To a certain degree much of what we do as level designers constitutes world building. What we build is a virtual world, a gameplay world, which players hopefully will spend much of their time in. The least we can do is do our best to make their stay a worthwhile one. But what does "worthwhile" mean to the player? And how do we make best use of the things that are or aren't available to us in the virtual world we are creating? How do we combine all the gameplay and story necessities of a game and incorporate them into coherent and rewarding game levels?

These are all important questions. This chapter will try to answer at least some of them.

The Detail of the World

To answer questions about world building, we have to look at what our resources and building blocks are. We need to be able to understand what the details of the world that we are trying to build are. To recap McCloud's comments on world building:

> Sweating such details can make the difference between drawing a page in SIX hours and drawing it in TWENTY—

— but for your readers it can make the difference —
— between KNOWING where your story takes place —
— and BEING THERE."

Now the type of detail that we need to focus on is different for each art form, and level design is no exception in that regard. So let's take a look at some areas that are typical to making game levels.

To help categorize things, I have made a distinction between two kinds of detail: things that define *how the world works* (in other words, the rules of the world), and things that exist within the world, or differently put, *the content of the world*.

The Rules of the World

Games and game levels are artificial constructs that come from the minds of human beings. Due to their artificial (and virtual) nature, they require a lot of design in order to function, let alone to function to a high degree of artistic merit. To make them do so, we have to create rules on the basis of which the world and its content can exist. Those rules are derived, or apply to, a number of areas, including the following

The game design

Unlike in the real world, in game levels we have the *game design* as the definition of what can and can't happen.[13] The game design formulates the rules of the world, which are expressed chiefly though gameplay mechanics in the context of the game's physics and overarching rules of play. In some ways this is the most fundamental set of rules, since all subsequent ones are based on these. Level design being the application of game design makes this the fundamental starting point to find the rules of the world that fit into the levels as world building vehicles.

Gameplay mechanics

In this case, when I speak of gameplay mechanics, I mean *all aspects* of gameplay mechanics, including character controls, environmental rules, and the physics against which mechanics are used. Ultimately these are the rules that govern the player's ability to act, and are therefore particularly interesting from a world building standpoint.

---

[13] And a technical design that describes how to engineer the game's creation and performance.

The technical framework

The technical and physical framework used to run and experience the game is also very important. It encompasses things like *platform* (portable device, console, personal computer, mobile phone), *display device* (television, computer screen) and input device (mouse, keyboard, joystick, peripheral, motion controller).

All these elements provide an interface between our actual senses and the virtual world in which we wish to spend some time. Their effect is therefore not to be underestimated. It has real impact on the effectiveness of world building in level design. Imagine the difference between creating a level for a portable mobile device that will likely only be used for 10-to-30-minute bouts of gameplay on a tiny screen with only a small keypad for input, and a modern PC with a good monitor, keyboard, and mouse.

The Content of the World

The content of the world is best understood by imagining those things that *exist* within the game's rule set. When we create levels, we fill this world up with all kinds of items, creatures, and environments that together form the content of the world.

Item Placement

So other than applying the rules of the world and designing gameplay scenarios or circumstances, what do we *place* in the levels? What are our building blocks for level design, and how do they contribute to world building? Since I cannot describe all the possible content of all the possible levels in all possible games, I think it makes more sense to point at the consequences of incorporating some of the more typical types of level content.

Pickups and powerups

Classic level design content is to be found in *pickups* and *powerups*. From health packs in *Doom* to stars in *Mario 64* and countless other games and items in between, pickups and powerups are as *integral to the history of video games as props are to film and theater*. Strangely, many of these items appear as if they are not of the game world, which one would expect in some way takes something away from the kind of illusion we are trying to foster. In a typical *Quake 3* level, for example we have fairly realistic[14] and cohesive environments filled with bright glowing and levitating (bobbing up and down, no less) pickups. Such incongru-

---

[14] Well, kind of. In a dark gothic sci-fi/fantasy way.

ous pickups incidentally show that immersion can be quite robust. These items perform a very important role in a *Quake* level; they fuel gameplay and help define the flow through the levels in ways that the player can clearly see. They are important demarcations of gameplay choices, and their bright and noticeable, even idiosyncratic, appearance actually helps the play mechanics in a level. Players don't tend to mind this too much, probably because they are an accepted part of the illusion and the players will happily suspend their disbelief in order to enjoy their benefits.

In other circumstances, pickups can be completely integrated in the environment, and can even contribute some functionality of their own. Keys can open doors; notes can give gameplay hints or background information. Whatever piece of the puzzle is required to progress in a level, chances are it can be done through pickups.

Rewards and collectibles

Similar rules apply to abstract rewards and collectibles, like the stars in a *Mario* game or the statues in *Vice City* or rings in a *Sonic the Hedgehog* game. The player tends to accept these items as part of the deal when playing a game, and level designers can use them to great effect. They are very powerful in directing the player along the paths the level designer has in mind, or they can make players stop in their tracks just to investigate or collect an item.

Props

Props have their own indirect ways of assisting world building. Generally, a prop is considered no more and no less than a game object constructed to sit in an environment. This is generally just for immersive purposes.

However, cleverly used props can do more than window-dress an environment. They can be made to evoke surprisingly strong emotions and reactions in a player. *Silent Hill 3* and *Silent Hill 4*[15] employ a giant pink rabbit that does nothing in and of itself. Yet its placement and appearance are so disconcerting that it massively underscores the themes of dread and horror that the game is so dependent on.

Props can be made to resemble other objects that carry a certain meaning in the game, in order to attract the attention of the player, or they can tie in to story events that only take on meaning after the player has learned about certain events. These may be items left behind by a hastily fleeing group of NPCs, or items affected by some event in the past or the passage of time, like a corroded metal toy or an overgrown children's playground.

---

[15] Konami.

If used well, props can have a very powerful impact on the player's perception of the world.

Scripted Sequences

Scripted sequences can be seen as the *deus ex machina*[16] of level design. They are the way in which we can directly influence events in ways that are not possible by the regular means with which we design our levels. They are therefore very powerful, but it needs to be understood that they constitute a double-edged sword.

Because scripted sequences essentially meddle in the affairs of the player the level designer has to make sure that they are implemented with great care. If they are used too blatantly and without care, they can be recognized for what they are: essentially, a forced experience. This is not always bad, but there are times when this is inappropriate, or when it takes away from the suspension of disbelief fostered by the level designer. If a rock is scripted to fall down the mountain every time the player goes past a trigger area, and the player has to avoid being crushed by it, a problem occurs when the player is killed by that rock. The next time the same thing will occur, and chances are there will be a sigh and an acceptance that the world is just smoke and mirrors.

On the other hand, scripted sequences can be extremely helpful in adding spice to what is basically an automated experience. A level and its players will run their course according to the basic design that has been implemented. Smart scripting can bring everything to life by providing detail and character in quirky or original moments that would otherwise not occur. Scripted sequences can be devised that are flexible in appearance and occurrence and always feel like fresh events, rather than seeming premeditated and predictable.

AI and "Actor" Placement

AI placement is another key area of interest. Populating the world with characters and *actors*, by which I mean any creatures in the game, is fundamental to level design. AI placement can be seen as adding detail to the world, like the use of props, and it can be seen as something that directly adds to or influences gameplay.

---

[16] "God from the machine." In classical Greek plays, gods would sometimes resolve a tricky situation through divine intervention. An actor playing a god (*deus*) would be literally lowered onto the stage by a mechanical crane (*machina*). The term now refers to an improbable intervention by the author to solve some problem, for example the appearance of a will in a murder mystery.

Level Design Symbols and Icons

Symbols and Icons are objects that represent more than themselves and their own existence. They also stand for larger concepts and ideas and can be used to great effect in level design and its world-building aspects. This is useful in a metaphorical sense, but just as true in a purely practical manner.

Well-Known Symbols and Icons

Symbols and icons come in many shapes and sizes, some more obscure than others. I have highlighted some instances of their usage they may be useful.

Hyper reality

Sometimes we can use symbols and icons, or other representational depictions, to enhance the player's perception of the game's reality to such a degree that we speak of *hyperrealism*. Under these circumstances, whether they are symbolic or representational, they are made to be "more real than real." Not only do they resemble real subjects; they also enhance them in subtle ways to make them representative of the core meaning of the subject (falsely or not). This may seem like a strange concept on the surface, but it is in widespread use in art and in advertising, to name a few examples.

Time to crate

Behold the crate: that most humble servant of level designers. Is there anybody who plays video games who doesn't try to interact with a crate on finding one?

Crate usage in level design has become so recognizable that it has been immortalized in satire. The creators of the *Something Awful* website have decided that a game's value can be measured by how long it takes a player to reach the first crate. This has been turned into a unit of measurement known as *Time To Crate (T.T.C.)* The lower a game's T.T.C., the better it must be.

No book on level design can be considered complete without the inclusion of this important measuring tool.

Internal Logic

We already know from our chapter on immersion that at times it can be essential to use a game's internal logic or *game* logic to maintain a suspension of disbelief. Even if something would not be believable in the real world, such as omnipresent magic crates filled with powerups, if explained well and used consistently and appropriately, they can become part of the game's identity in a way that isn't questioned by the player. The advantage of effective world building in this sense is that it allows the designer to create a much stronger internal logic than would otherwise be possible. This in turn allows for creating a sort of shorthand with which the level designer can convey messages to players about the world they are in or about actions they are supposed to perform.

Making Your World Memorable

World building heavily relies on the ability to create something that is very *vivid* in the mind of the audience. The newly created world must feel real and worth spending time in. For that reason, it helps if we make aspects of it stand out.

There are a number of useful techniques with which this can be achieved, some of which will be explored next.

Set Pieces

Remember that shower scene in *Psycho*? If you have seen the movie, you will. Or the scene in *Jaws* where the big fin first appears in the water? Or how about the beach-landing scene in *Saving Private Ryan*?

Of course you do. These scenes are amongst the most memorable ones ever created for the cinema.

Almost all great movies feature one or more scenes that are more memorable than those in lesser movies. Alfred Hitchcock went so far as to suggest that this was fundamental to the way he made films. He was known to say that most of what he did amounts to creating one unforgettable scene, and constructing a movie *around* it. Of course there was much more to the great man's art, but it is true that nearly all his masterpieces feature one or two pivotal scenes that are indeed unforgettable.

In earlier chapters we have looked in depth at level design goals. We have found that it is almost always wise to define a set of requirements before starting work on a particular level design component. In the case of designing a set piece, we can often assume that one of the requirements will include the criterion that Hitchcock has described. It has to be memorable. The way this requirement is met depends entirely on the game and its mechanics, but nonetheless it would be nice if the game featured moments that the player will always remember, hopefully fondly.

Some of these moments will occur without being explicitly defined beforehand. They can come out of emergent gameplay sequences or stem from the player's own imagination. Sometimes, however, we have to set up and design a memorable set piece ourselves. There are innumerable ways of doing this, and it is beyond the scope of this chapter to give an exhaustive list. A number of examples can be mentioned, however. Scenarios like the following are not uncommon:

- against all odds (seemingly insurmountable challenges made possible),
- boss encounters (classic video game convention),
- ambush (sudden intrusion on the player by hostile forces),
- dramatic markers (encounters that carry great meaning in the gameplay narrative that the player has embarked on).

The level designer needs to read the possibilities of the game to accurately determine what kinds of gameplay scenarios are most effective as set pieces. This will be different for each game, and will need to fulfill completely different requirements from set piece to set piece.

Relevance

A word of advice on set pieces. Just because you have a chance to go to town on a specific gameplay scenario and can design everything in it doesn't mean that you should make the player's skills and abilities irrelevant to the action.

Set pieces and suspension of disbelief

We have already covered this subject in great detail in Chapter 9, but I wanted to make sure this is not forgotten. If at all possible, make sure that the player's suspension of disbelief is guarded even in non-typical scenarios, as these often occur in set piece design.

Adding Character

Sometimes it pays to add content to the levels that doesn't necessarily fulfill an immediate or direct requirement. It is worth considering the inclusion of content, gameplay or otherwise, that helps support the general effort put into the level design as a world building exercise. These are not just inclusions that heighten a suspension of disbelief, but elements that add life and vitality to the world.

For example, take an *exploration platformer*. In this genre it is essential that the player find it rewarding to go off the beaten track and enjoy exploring the game world. We can assume that this is already covered in a formal way, through designed gameplay scenarios that make up the gist of the level designs for the game. However, we can also underline this theme by providing other kinds of rewards and content that add another dimension to the game by enhancing its character and identity.

For example, a level could feature a number of complex abandoned structures that contain texts and items that explain a certain amount of backstory to the player. This can be accompanied by formal awards to be given to the player as payment for the exploration effort. But it also contains content that greatly enhances the sense of history and the mood of the environment. It grounds the game world in a past and tells the player that there are things to learn by exploring the environment. One could even include mysteries that may or may not be solved,[17] but that effectively breathe more life into the game's character.

Efforts like these are not a luxury or a waste of resources. They are instead an integral part of making level designs that stand out and are full of character and identity.

Interactivity and World Building

We can't talk about breathing life into the game world without spending some serious moments investigating the concept of *interactivity*.

The word interactivity has the ring of something new in our current computerized environment. People speak of interactive movies, interactive online communities, interacting online with other people's avatars, interactive storytelling, and so on. It is clearly a wide-ranging concept that applies to our daily lives in all kinds of ways. Interactivity in some form or another matters profoundly to people. It has done so at a fundamental level long before we could articulate these intellectual questions.

There are many definitions of *interactive:* some apply to computer science, while others are of a more general nature. But they boil down to reacting or responding to actions or input. This has deep underlying philosophical importance.[18]

I Interact Therefore I Am

One of the things philosophy looks at is the question of self-definition:

- What am I?
- Where am I?
- Is this place real?
- Are those around me as real as me?
- Does a tree that falls in the wood....?

---

[17] Be careful not to frustrate the player's expectation, though.

[18] Please bear with me. It may sound like I am going on a self-indulgent tangent, but trust me, it will reach a point that applies to level design.

These can provide endless fun if one is inclined to ponder these matters. One of the answers to these questions lies in interactivity. We know many things about the world because we directly or indirectly interact with it on a daily basis. *Our interaction with the world is part of how we define our own existence.* Our (inter) actions show that we do not exist in a vacuum. In other words, there are consequences to our actions:

- Touching fire hurts.
- We can have an impact on other people.
- Planting a seed can lead to a new tree.

We can verify all these things through our interaction with the world. We can withdraw our hand from the fire, convince a friend that life is worth living, and eat the apples from the tree we planted a number of years earlier. Importantly, this means that to some extent we have control over some of our actions, and over their predictable consequences. This control gives our actions *meaning* and *context*.

Meaningful Interactions

Ultimately, our existence and its impact in the world are determined by our sense of interactivity. In many ways, our existence is a huge feedback system. But this would still not add meaning to our actions if we did not perceive them to have the power to change things around us, even if only at a minor level. Actions without consequences exist in a vacuum. They lack meaning, since they have no impact on the world. Most people would agree, however, that we do have an impact on the world around us, and that our actions are therefore meaningful. This is observable on a physical level; see the impact humans have had on nature, as well as on a personal level: for example, in our interaction with family and loved ones. Like it or not, the way we interact with the world around us is meaningful.

Choice

Logically, if our interaction with our surroundings has an impact on them, this automatically leads to the concept of *choice*. If we believe that the outcome of a situation, or the status of our surroundings, can be altered by our actions, it is logical to believe that we have a choice in what actions we take to achieve the outcome we desire.[19]

---

[19] There are people who claim that nothing we do matters at all. This idea is often derived from some extreme form of determinism, but I can only say that I disagree with them on a fundamental level. Which incidentally is a road that leads directly to ethics, but that goes beyond the scope of this book.

This is something that for many people, or even for whole societies, lies at the core of what it means to be human, and of what our place in the world can be. We all have to determine what choices to make in life. It is by making those choices according to whatever personal value or belief system we have adopted that we give our actions meaning.

Meaningful Choices

Let's sum up some of the philosophical material we have covered.

We experience interactivity through feedback from our environment to our senses, which allows us to define ourselves within the context of our surroundings. Our actions within our environment have the potential to change things, and since we have a choice of which actions to perform, those actions can have meaning.

So what it all boils down to is that interaction is all about *meaningful choices*[20]. A conclusion which applies directly to level design, something that will be explored next.

Level Design Application

Many designers claim that what makes our work different, even unique from other art forms, is that it is *interactive*. Because of this, they argue that we must use and emphasize this interactivity as much as we can. This is particularly stressed in level design, where people argue against linear levels, or levels that are on rails, or that are too much directed by the level designer. Some even argue that the more interactive a video game is, the better. There are even alternative terms for videogaming that incorporate this idea. We see this, for example, in the term *interactive entertainment*.

Identifying interactivity as the core of videogaming feels right on the surface. Obviously, interactivity is important, but when placed under closer scrutiny, this does not stand up.

Mega Tetris

Tetris is one of the best and most successful games ever made. It is hard to find any designer who would dispute this. If we try to use interactivity as a yardstick

---

[20] As we have been told by Sid Meier already.

for quality, though, we find that the level of interactivity and choice in the game is surprisingly limited.

In *Tetris*, the player can only shift, rotate and accelerate falling blocks on-screen. The feedback the player is given from these actions is limited to seeing completed lines disappear, or seeing blocks stay where they have been dropped, a score counter counting up, and the game finishing when the blocks stack up too high.

There are some further elements of interaction that are less important, but this is pretty much it. If *more interactivity = a better game*, surely we can improve on this simplistic design? Let's give it a go. Our bigger and better *Tetris* shall be called *Meta Tetris*.

> MEGA TETRIS
>
> Perhaps we can add some enemy AI to the game in the form of *robots* that randomly shift blocks around in ways that are bad for the player. These robots can be defeated by *crushing them* with new special *anti-robot blocks*, added to the regular shapes in the game.
>
> Furthermore, it makes more sense if the blocks come from a *space ship* that is under the player's control, possibly a freighter. The blocks are lowered from the cargo hold, and since the freighter has a mining *laser*, the blocks can be *shot*. Oh, and the robots can be shot too!
>
> The laser uses up *energy*, however, so this needs to be replenished. Perhaps this can be done by using the ship's *grappling hook* to capture the *energy beings* that are released when the robots are destroyed.
>
> The energy beings must be destroyed as well, or they will reach large enough numbers to merge and form a huge *energy cannon* that will try to shoot down the player's *spaceship*.

Okay I'll stop there. *Mega Tetris* is clearly an abomination of a game. (For those of you not familiar with the game industry, some suggestions to make improvements to your game will be just as sensible as those made in *Mega Tetris*. These will often come from publishers, or even from other colleagues.)

Although this admittedly is not a completely honest attempt on my part to improve on the design of *Tetris*, I think it is telling, nonetheless. *Mega Tetris* features a much higher level of interactivity than the original, yet it clearly is a worse game. What, then, has gone wrong?

Game Specific Interactivity

If we look again at our earlier summary of *interactivity*, we may find some answers:

We experience interactivity through feedback from our environment to our senses, which allows us to define ourselves within the context of our surroundings. Our actions within our environment have the potential to change things, and since we have a choice of which actions to perform, those actions can have meaning.

All of these elements can apply to video games:

- Game environments give a player feedback on his or her actions.
- The interplay between this feedback and the player's actions define the player's capabilities within the game world.
- The player's actions have an impact on how the game progresses, and the player's choices within that context can be meaningful.

It is that last bit, "can be meaningful," that we need to focus on.

Sid Meier famously defined[21] games as *a series of interesting choices*[22]. In the context of games, there is much overlap between *interesting* and *meaningful* choices.

This points at the crux of the matter: interactivity only makes sense if it is interesting or meaningful. Otherwise it is completely redundant, or, as in the case of *Mega Tetris*, no more than an irritant. (The trick is of course to determine what choices are meaningful or interesting to the player.)

Meaningful Interactions and Choices in Levels

As we have seen, it is not the amount of interactivity that is important, but the *quality* of the interactivity. Is it appropriate? Does it support the game? Is it *meaningful*? To a degree these concepts will always be subjective, as they often require an individual judgment call to be made. In a way, we are talking about the *quality* of experience, which is a philosophical minefield.[23] I'd rather focus on level design that makes gameplay non-arbitrary and employs interactivity as a tool to attain this.

For example, if a game's gameplay mechanics are geared towards manipulating the physical objects in an environment, it is appropriate to provide interac-

[21] As reported in Andrew Rollings and Dave Morris, *Game Architecture and Design: A New Edition*, New Riders, Berkeley, CA, 2004, p. 61.

[22] Also often quoted as interesting "decisions."

[23] To get an idea of the dangers, read Robert Pirsig's *Zen and the Art of Motorcycle Maintenance*.

tion possibilities that allow for this. Those kinds of actions are meaningful within the context of that particular game and are desirable, since it is our task as level designers to present our audience with a game that provides meaningful choices and interactions.

What follows shows a number of ways in which we can do so.

Interesting Choices

At the most basic level of our level designs lie some very simple choices that we present to the player, often without much thought and without realizing that they are choices. If a room has two exits, the player has to make a choice. If an area features enemy creatures, players can choose to fight them or avoid them. A pickup can ask if the player wants to replenish his or her health. This is almost mundane stuff and as a consequence is often not thought about. But by doing this, level designers miss opportunity after opportunity to make their levels interesting, or at least filled with interesting and meaningful choices.

Let's look at a very basic but typical scenario: a *t-section*.

Figure 13.2 shows a simplified layout that presents the player (P) with the choice of choosing one direction over another. With a bit of investigation, the player learns that both directions are guarded by an enemy creature (E).

Figure 13.3 shows the same setup, but one direction is more heavily guarded than the other, and the player can spot treasure pickups behind the guardians (t).

The first scenario offers an interactive challenge presented as a choice, in this case one based on engagement with enemy AI. But is it an interesting choice? What does it matter in which direction the player chooses to go? All the player knows is what is in front, and in this case the choices are equally good or bad. This means that they aren't interesting, but arbitrary.

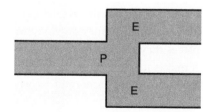

Figure 13.2. T-Junction with two equal enemies.

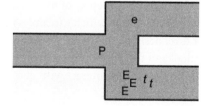

Figure 13.3. T-Junction with unequal enemies.

The second figure shows the same scenario, but with very little effort, it has been made intrinsically interesting. First, the player is shown that there are different enemy encounters to be engaged in, depending on the choice. This is in itself not that interesting; most players would pick the easy enemy. However, the player is also shown an alternative reward that is based on what is chosen.

Now the player has to make a judgment call: risk more for a bigger reward, or risk less for a small one. This IS an interesting choice, and one that ties in to all kinds of considerations that the player has to make. How much health does the player have? How well armed is the player? How did the player fare last time against enemy one, as opposed to enemy two? And so on.

If we always ask the question, "Is this an interesting choice?" we can transform the most basic and mundane gameplay scenarios into interesting ones by providing meaningful interactions.

Meaningful consequences

The above scenario with the two directions shows an example of consequence. Engaging in combat with one enemy over another will yield a different reward, in other words a different consequence. Consequences themselves can be meaningful as well and can therefore greatly add to the quality of the level design.

The interesting choice presented in the second figure shows two awards that the player can earn: one of 100 gold pieces and another of 10. But what if the player already owns 100,000 gold pieces?

Formal Rewards

By formal rewards[24] I mean in-game, tangible rewards, like gold coins or pickups, not abstract rewards like "a sense of achievement," although rewards of that kind are of course essential. What I am talking about is simple interactions leading to direct rewards. Destroying a crate will yield a powerup, killing a baddy makes the baddy drop the loot, opening a chest will give the player treasure. Video games are *littered* with gameplay of this sort. Reward dispensers like this are extremely easy to implement, which explains some of their popularity. They provide a way for level designers to hand out rewards in places they find appropriate. Players understand the convention perfectly, which makes it a favorite tool. Additionally, it is just fun to interact with of one of these reward dispensers and see what you are going to get.

---

[24] Yes, I made that term up, as well.

Intermittent reinforcement and the slot machine effect

There is a lot of scientific data that explains, at least partly, why this is such an effective reward mechanism. Much of this data is in the field of behavioral science.[25] Although there is some controversy associated with the subject, this kind of intermittent reinforcement has been used by the creators of gambling machine; hence it is sometimes referred to as the *slot machine effect*.

The so-called slot machine effect is a well-known psychological phenomenon and is understood well enough that applications of it have become quite sophisticated. There are many recognizable examples of this in the real world. The chocolate eggs of Kinder Surprise have hidden gifts, there's a toy at the bottom of the cereal box, and of course, there are the slot machines themselves. The application of this knowledge in entertainment is not good or bad intrinsically, but there are serious ethical implications that need to be considered, especially when done for commercial gain or when aimed at children.

I am not suggesting that as level designers or game designers we cannot make use of intermittent reinforcement. Nor am I saying that the players of our levels are helpless and without personal responsibility in this regard. However, I do want to make the connection clear that similar processes are at work in activities that are known to be habit forming, like gambling. We need to be aware of our own responsibilities in deciding when and when not to employ this principle.

Exploration

Sometimes the simplest and most rewarding interaction with an environment comes from enjoying it by traveling through it. In other words, exploration can be a meaningful interactive activity. Uncovering the joy of new environments works as a reward in its own right. This hints at certain lessons that need to be learned when one creates levels that have to foster enjoyable exploration. Unlocking a new level area should not be a punishment. Allow the player time and safety to really enjoy and benefit from the exploration. This will make it much more likely that the player will want to keep on exploring.

World Building Conclusion

Seen through the prism of world building, level design touches on almost any aspect of the craft we can think of. It takes notions of gameplay narrative and

---

[25] See, for example, the concept of *operant conditioning*.

classical narrative and asks the designer to construct an experience that is deep and immersive and holds up to scrutiny when thoroughly explored by the player. It deals with the rules of the world, as well as the details in the world. It demands a consistent and intelligent stance on a level's interactive elements and the way in which we populate it with AI inhabitants. Finally, it gives us a framework in which we can explore the exploration of the world we have built, and the way in which this exploration can be enjoyed.

World building overlaps most aspects of level design. While the two are not the same thing, level design can be greatly helped by an understanding of the world building needed to make it effective.

Practice

Example 13.1: Rules of the World— Internal Logic and Consistency

Summary

The rules of the world govern the behavior of the content of the world. This in turn forms a framework in which player actions take place. Since we have to do our level designs based on these parameters, it makes sense to incorporate the rules of the world into the level design at a fundamental level.

Game Genre

This technique is suitable for most games.

Goals to Achieve

- Link the rules of the world to level design scenarios.
- Emphasize the coherence of the levels through internal logic.
- Apply consistency to internal logic so the player can formulate their own mental map of the rules of the world.

Description

(Example type: General)

Level designers can manipulate the player experience by interpreting the game rules that are defined in the game design. This is an essential part of what we do, and something that is required for all levels. We can expand on this, however, by interpreting these mechanical rules by trying to formulate an internal logic that can be interpreted by the player. Indeed, sometimes we can create internal logic by bending the mechanistic game design rules to fit our level design goals.

For example, if the game design rules spell out that the world uses a predictable gravity model, and that falling objects do damage to what they land on, then it is very easy to take that and create an internal logic that the player can have great fun with—especially if we help this along by making sure our levels feature many opportunities for the player to drop things on targets, like enemies or pressure plates, or whatever else would benefit the player.

It is important to make the distinction between mechanistic rules and internal logic as the latter is the one that the player is aware of, while the former is the one that the *level designer* is aware of. Within the framework of world building, this gives us an opportunity to create levels that incorporate and interpret the rules of the world and apply them to, or utilize them alongside, consistent internal logic. The result is a coherent, deep, and detailed gameplay environment for the player.

This principle goes beyond the literal nature of the gravity example I have given.

Fabricated internal logic. I'd like to give an example of internal logic that has to be created by the level designer, which through consistent application in a level becomes part of the rule set of the game in the mind of the player.

In a game based on athletic ability, like a platforming game for example, we often motivate the player by showing them hard to reach areas and enticing him or her to somehow find a way to reach those areas. We can apply a consistent internal logic to these challenges that adds to the understanding of the game for the player. To do this we define our own level-design-based logic rules. Let's take a 2D platform game set in a sci-fi environment:

Internal logic rule 1. If the platform is far away, floating out of reach of everything, the player has to perform a task, possibly locate a switch, for it to float into a position where the player can reach it.

Internal logic rule 2. If the platform is close to other platforms, then the player can get to it by conventional means—possibly by jumping on the heads of enemies in a timed sequence, or by dropping onto an adjacent platform from above.

If we show the player these two rules consistently early on—for example, by making sure that early examples are all solvable within the same screen, and only slowly making the solutions appear further away in subsequent iterations—then the player won't have a hard time learning these rules.

Additionally, further internal logic lessons have been taught in the process:

- obscure platforms feature valuable rewards,
- jumping on enemies is a valid technique to reach areas,
- switches control platforms,
- all platforms with rewards can be reached in one way or another.

All levels do this to some agree, but if we plan these things out beforehand, or at least think about the possibilities this offers to create interesting content, our levels will end up more interesting and coherent.

Further Notes

Internal logic can also be abstract, or surreal, or even humorous. Imagine a running gag in a game, or disturbing visions being the result of specific actions. There is plenty of new ground to be covered in this area.

Example 13.2: Implied Detail

Summary

In level design, implied detail can take on various guises and forms and can be used for various purposes. Aspects of it can be used in a world-building context, specifically by using localized detail to imply a larger and detailed world in which the level is placed.

Game Genre

This technique is suitable for non-abstract games.

Goals to Achieve

- Perform effective world building.
- Maximize the use of art assets in the process.

Description

(Example type: Original)

Implied detail. We can add greatly to the perception of detail in a level by including detail that *implies* further content, without the level designer having to create it. This technique is based on the idea that if we add this detail in strategic ways and places, the players will assume this detail exists throughout the levels and the game in general.

Take, for example, a window that looks out onto an alley. The player can't get to it, but he or she can see a number of details from their viewpoint. These details can be of such a nature that they imply additional content and detail just out of view. Here are some examples:

- a street sign that lists a multitude of other street names,
- an opposite building with a window that can be peered into,
- street sounds,
- posters detailing other events in the game world like concerts or political rallies,
- weather effects.

All these things point at a much more detailed and larger environment, full of variety and life. Yet, the level designer only has to include a few assets to create this perception—parts of a building, signs, sound—and the player will reconcile these hints at other things into a mental image of an environment that is detailed and robust.

Further Notes

These are just some examples but it should be clear that the actual usage depends on the detail that the level designer wants to imply. This will be different for all games, but the principle is clear and easy to reproduce.

Example 13.3: Built-in Meaningful Choices

Summary

We know that an important aspect of level design lies in confronting the player with meaningful gameplay choices. This can be done as part of the level design scenarios that we create piece by piece, but this can also be a goal of the world-building process in a way that is fundamental to the fabric of the level itself.

Game Genre

This technique is suitable for most games.

Goals to Achieve

- Make the likelihood of interesting gameplay choices part of the world building process.
- Do this with a minimum of necessary variables.

Description

(Example type: Existing game/general)

When we create a level, we can ask of every gameplay scenario that we create that it presents a meaningful and interesting gameplay choice to the player. This is the basis of much of our design work. We can, however, also ask this same question of the level environment itself. The structure and fabric of the world we build can ask these questions on its own, if we design it with such goals in mind.

Dyson's built-in, meaningful choices. I have used this principle extensively in the game *Dyson*[26] for which among other things I did most of the design. In *Dyson* the environment consists of asteroids that contain resources and can be conquered by the player or by opposing AI teams. These resources are represented by *energy*, *strength*, and *speed* attributes, and these differ from asteroid to asteroid. These resources are mined and used to create the game's units, which are exploration and conquest entities that the player can use to conquer more territory and attack opponents. A key part is that seedlings produced on asteroids take on the resource attributes of that particular asteroid, which defines their capabilities. So, a seedling produced on an asteroid rich in strength and energy but poor in speed will produce units that are good at fighting and very durable, but are very slow movers. This will have consequences on their chances of success when engaging with opponents or navigating and interacting with the level space. Levels are built in such a way that there is a rich variety of asteroids of varying sizes and consequently of very diverse attribute composition. Within these asteroid fields key details are built in, for example, to do with enemy placement, optimal routes, and asteroid distribution.

Taking these things into account shows us that the level design has incorporated a style of world building that maximizes the chances of meaningful gameplay choices.

We have simple parameters incorporated into the level itself, and they provide constant choices on immediate gameplay consequences and actions:

---

[26] www.dyson-game.com. Developed by Alex May and Rudolf Kremers. Music and audio by Brian Grainger.

- where to send units,
- which asteroids to conquer,
- what units to breed,
- what units to use to engage enemies,
- which asteroids to defend,

and so on.

This is possible because there are only a few basic variables that determine the makeup of a level, but they all affect gameplay in one way or another. There is almost nothing in the fabric of the level that does not contribute to this, and the result leads to interesting complexity, and interesting choices, as the default basis for most gameplay actions.

Further Notes

This is a technique that is extremely useful in games where we would like to encourage emergent gameplay. Sandbox games are especially helped by this, since they need by their very nature to be engaging at a fundamental level. And that means that the world building aspects of sandbox levels are fundamental to the success of such games. The game world *itself* needs to support interesting choices.

Puzzles

14

Why do we enjoy puzzles so much? In almost all cases, puzzles are not real and do not offer a direct benefit. They are often taxing and require a serious amount of concentration. They can cause severe frustration, even anger.[1] You would expect that people have better things to do with their time.

Yet playing with and solving puzzles is a human activity that people are engaged in all over the world. Some puzzle types seem so universal that they pop up and are understood within societies that culturally could not be further apart.

Pretty much all types of puzzles present the player with a challenge. They have a solution or require a certain strategy, or a particular skill, in order to be completed or at least enjoyed.

In many ways they behave exactly like games, in fact, quite often puzzles are classified as games.

Concept

A Monkey, a Termite Hill, Some Salt, and a Bit of Rope

Picture the following puzzle scenario in a game, for example a point-and-click adventure:

The player is located in a desert and has to find water within a certain time frame. The tools to solve this puzzle include

- a monkey,
- some rocks of salt,

---

[1] I wonder how many Rubik's cubes have been destroyed in fits of anger.

307

- a termite hill,
- a length of rope.

All items are to be used to obtain water.

This sounds like a typical non-realistic, arbitrary puzzle scenario. It could have appeared in one of many of the classic point-and-click adventures of the past, like *Escape from Monkey Island* or *Sam and Max Hit the Road.*"

Strangely enough, it is in actuality a real-world puzzle of survival that is faced by the bush people in the Kalahari dessert. I once saw a documentary; I think it may have been called *Animals Are Beautiful People,* which features a scene that has stayed with me all my life. It shows how some Kalahari bushmen have found a solution to the problem of finding enough water to survive.

The documentary includes a scene where one of the bushmen plays with a bit of salt in front of a monkey. The monkey, curious and fond of salt, becomes extremely interested. When the bushman is secure in the knowledge that the monkey is interested, he walks up to a termite hill. He finds a cavity in the hill just large enough for his hand to enter, and drops the salt inside. He then walks off, out of the monkey's view.

The monkey can't contain itself. When it thinks the coast is clear, it quickly runs up to the termite hill. It finds the cavity that holds the salt and grabs it tightly in its paw. But the entry hole is too narrow for the monkey's fist, as long as it is holding the salt. Until it lets go, it is trapped. But stubborn as it is, the monkey will not relinquish its prize. At this point, the bushman comes out of cover and quickly approaches the monkey. Although it could easily escape, it keeps holding onto the salt and is easily captured.

In the next phase of this strange plan, the bushman tie the monkey to a stake, but lets him keep the salt. Sure enough, the monkey starts licking it. Since the monkey has been tied down in the hot sunlight, it soon becomes extremely thirsty. At this point the bushman releases the monkey, who immediately shoots off, closely followed by the man. The monkey runs straight for a hidden reservoir of water.

Problem Solving Skills

The point of this amusing but slightly bewildering anecdote is that there is a correlation between real life challenges and our ability to understand complex and often abstract connections.

Have you ever seen the TV show *MacGyver*? It was an '80s show in which the hero found himself in a jam in every episode and used his knowledge of science to find a solution. If a villain locked him in a cell, he would "simply" combine charcoal and bird droppings to create gunpowder and blow the lock with a small controlled explosion[2] (or some equally fascinating solution).

A certain amount of lateral thinking is needed to come up with the solutions described in the previous section. Although the examples seem far-fetched and irrelevant to most of our lives, it's true that we engage in this kind of puzzle solving. Or at least, we use the same skills and processes, on a very regular basis.

The Kalahari Bushmen and MacGyver examples present exaggerated examples of the use of the problem solving skills I am talking about. Nonetheless, they showcase a very real phenomenon, that human beings are very good at making cross connections and seeing relationships that are not apparent on the surface. This is key to problem solving in general:

> Although all problem solving relies on a largely shared cortical network, the sudden flash of insight occurs when solvers engage distinct neural and cognitive processes that allow them to see connections that previously eluded them.[3]

And if we can use these abilities to solve survival problems, we can also use them in other situations that require problem solving.

Survival skills

As we have seen with the purpose of "play" in general, it is not unreasonable to make a connection between survival and training for difficult challenges through the use of puzzle play. We can greatly improve our chances of survival by training our mental and physical abilities by training our puzzle-solving skills.

Let's look at some typical skills associated with solving puzzles or problems:

- pattern recognition,
- lateral thinking,
- hand-eye coordination,
- abstracting/conceptualizing a problem,
- memory usage.

There are many others.

All of these can come into play even when we are confronted with very mundane or simple puzzles, such as jigsaw puzzles or skill puzzles. Nonetheless, all of

---

[2] Gripping stuff!

[3] Mark Jung-Beeman, Edward M. Bowden, Jason Haberman, Jennifer L. Frymiare, Stella Arambel-Liu, Richard Greenblatt, Paul J. Reber, and John Kounios, "Neural Activity When People Solve Verbal Problems with Insight," *PLoS Biology*, http://biology.plosjournals.org/perlserv/?request=get-document&doi=10.1371%2Fjournal.pbio.0020097&ct=1, 2004.

these are important abilities, and must be trained and sharpened throughout life. Realizing which of our abilities and senses are used the most when we engage in problem solving is very helpful. It can add to our understanding of creating puzzles and is therefore useful within a context of level design.

Concept Summary

Puzzles provide a safe and controlled way of testing one's skills and abilities in very specific and precise ways. They can be started, restarted, or abandoned without serious consequences to the person involved. Because of the playful nature and the fact that they use formal rules, it is fair to say that puzzles provide another form of *gameplay*, or at least are a subset of the "play" family of activities.

They can also be incorporated in the kind of teaching gameplay we talked about in Chapter 2, where we saw that they can provide a number of very important and specific functions.

Theory

The list of puzzle types is endless: block puzzles, pattern puzzles, skill puzzles, mechanical puzzles, door and key puzzles, pressure plate puzzles, and so forth. The level designs of most games littered with different types of puzzles. Some puzzle types are well known outside of video games, while some others are unique to the form. But why are they so ubiquitous? Why are they so useful that level designers keep using puzzles, game after game? Why do people enjoy engaging in puzzles?

It is clear that puzzles provide some very useful functions, or their usage wouldn't be so enormously widespread. This chapter will list a number of reasons why, and ways in which, their useful qualities can be maximized.

Puzzles as Formal Tests

Early in this book, we looked at the concept of games as teaching mechanisms. We concluded that teaching gameplay skills also requires the level designer to test the player's progression in his matter:

> Teaching mechanisms are meaningless unless that which is taught is tested and put into practice. There has to be a way to test the player's knowledge or proficiency within the game, or the game will lack a

purpose. This is another intrinsic goal of level design. If the gameplay is taught well and the player gets tested in an enjoyable manner, the level designer has done a good job.

I believe that one of the reasons we always keep reaching for puzzles in our level design is that puzzles constitute a fantastically practical and enjoyable mechanism for *testing* skill and knowledge. Puzzles can be used as doorways or gatekeepers. Access is granted if the player knows how to solve the puzzle. This applies in a physical sense: we can literally stop progression. Or we can apply it less rigidly: solve this situation (puzzle) and receive a reward. Puzzles are formal tests of the player's gameplay knowledge and skills. And as tests go, puzzles are good ones, because they ask all the right questions.

Gate Keepers or Funnels

A side effect of this function is that puzzles can be used as gate keepers that only allow the player to progress after gaining the necessary skills to solve the puzzle. Alternatively, the game can withhold the means of solving the puzzle unless the player has performed certain other actions. This creates a *funnel* through which the player has to pass before the level opens up further or before progression is allowed.

Game survival skills

A specific *gatekeeper* function is found in puzzles that test for skills that are necessary later in the game. Ideally these puzzles are presented in a non-threatening manner so the player learns important skills in a playful manner, without being under undue pressure. If the puzzle is presented as a progression puzzle, possibly with a secondary reward, the player can be forced to master a skill without realizing that it will play a more vital part later in the game.

Teaching important game survival skills or strategies in this manner is very effective, and it lets the level designer create subsequent challenges with accurate knowledge of the player's skill set.

Dangers

It is very dangerous to make these kinds of *skill gates* absolute. Players may not be able to grasp a certain skill or may be made to feel inadequate if the difficulty of the puzzle is misjudged. If at all possible, allow for multiple ways to solve the progression puzzle, or allow the difficulty level to decrease as time passes.

In addition, we must be careful not to abuse gateway puzzles and create excessive or arbitrary requirements of time investment for the player. There are serious issues in many games with so-called *fetch gameplay,* or what I term *collectathons.*

Fetch gameplay is a situation in which the player's progress is frustrated at a specific physical location in a level and the player is told to go find certain items. Within reason, this kind of gameplay is fine, but often we see that the level duration is padded out excessively by blatant fetch quests that don't add anything to the experience. A clear sign that a level design is weak is when one fetch quest triggers another, with little difference between the two except for the name of the item that must be collected.

Fetch gameplay can turn into a real nightmare when misguided level designers suddenly realize that they can ask their players to fetch not one, but many, items before progressing. Even that is not necessarily wrong if it fits the goals and motivations that are carefully fostered in the player. But this is so easy to misjudge that designers need to be very careful about employing such methods.

Puzzles as Information Conduits

Almost all puzzles stop the player and ask questions. For example, they may ask things like:

- Have you mastered this skill?
- Are you strong enough to perform this task?
- Do you understand this danger?
- Have you encountered and absorbed that earlier lesson?
- Are you ready for the next bit?

Puzzles can be used for all kinds of tests. They can function as benchmarks or bottlenecks or exams, among many other applications.

In some ways, games are like schools, teaching us gameplay (survival) skills, where the level designs are the curriculum, and puzzles are some of the questions being asked in exams and tests. (And the level designers are teachers).

Although this comparison is slightly strained, it is nonetheless a useful one. We need to make sure that we provide a good environment for teaching and learning, and that the curriculum covers the right building blocks for future lessons. It needs to be fun to learn.

We have seen that these properties mean that puzzles can be used as a formal testing device, but it is also good to note that this means that they can convey or receive *information.*

Information for the Level Designer

An often-overlooked aspect of puzzle design and implementation is the opportunity they offer for gathering information about the player. How a player deals with a situation can tell the level designer a great deal, and in the context of a puzzle, that information can be structured and specific. Good examples of his can be found in *data mining* and in reading the outcome of *conditional puzzles*.

In-game data mining

If the game's technology allows for player data to be captured and measured, a designer can find all kinds of useful applications for it. Data mining in this regard is in principle no more than measuring player actions and improving the game experience by interpreting the recorded data and putting it to good use.

Level designers may alter the spawn rate of certain items by reading the player's inventory at certain moments, or they may decide to allow progression in an area of the game when it becomes clear that the player has spent too much time trying to solve a gameplay puzzle.

Conditional level design and puzzles

A level designer can offer multiple outcomes based on the way the puzzle has been solved. Puzzles can be designed to offer diverse progression possibilities, based on certain conditions being met, taking full advantage of this knowledge. For example, if a puzzle is solved by dexterity, the level designer may open up a path that offers a large number of athletic possibilities. The level designer knows that the player can cope with this because of the way that person has manipulated the puzzle. Another possibility lies in testing for certain objects. If the player solves a puzzle by using a certain item, the level designer may opt to remove it from the rest of the level and replace it with something that is still desirable to the player.

Information for the Player

There is also an opportunity to feed information back to the player, often in a very natural way. A puzzle solution may be based on gathering information from the game's environment and putting it to use in the puzzle itself. This can be fairly explicit, like teaching players enough about the backstory of the game for them to answer a specific question.[4]

The application can also be indirect, where information given to players allows them to interact with the game in ways they wouldn't know about before.

---

[4] This kind of application is often seen in survival horror games.

For example, the puzzle may teach the player a new way to use a weapon or a handy item.

Subtle as this technique may be, it can really pay off to have a good look at ways in which you can communicate important information to the player, as this is one of the key tasks that a level designer has.

Puzzles as Reward Mechanisms

To quote Raph Koster again:

> [F]un from games arises out of mastery. It arises out of comprehension.
> It is the act of solving puzzles that makes games fun.
> In other words, with games, learning is the drug.[5]

We know that much enjoyment in gameplay comes from the *learning process*: it is enjoyable to master new skills. Additionally, puzzles can be engineered in such a way that solving them gives the player a tangible award, like delivering a powerup or opening up a new area of the level.

The sky is the limit, really, when it comes to this particular use of puzzles; there are too many examples to name them all. To highlight one, however, a very useful application is found in *exploration gameplay*.

Reward for Exploration

A great way to reward the player for exploration is by placing independent puzzles all through an environment where they can be played with at the player's leisure, without any negative consequences. Because the puzzle would in this context be purely used as a reward dispenser, the player can invest as much time into it as desired.

A note of caution: it is very important in exploration gameplay to not expose the player to time pressure, as this punishes the act of free exploration itself.

Purely self-contained puzzles

The above example acts as a reward for exploration gameplay. However, it is entirely justified to design puzzles as completely independent *reward dispensers*.

A slogan for this might be, "Solve the puzzle, receive a prize."

This may be a simple tactic, but it can be very pleasing indeed for the player, and it gives the level designer a way to teach the player that the game world is equipped

---

[5] Raph Koster, *A Theory of Fun for Game Design*, Paraglyph Press, Scottsdale, AZ, 2005, p. 40.

with these kinds of reward mechanisms. This is an important aspect of rewarding exploration gameplay, or increasing the enjoyment level of the game in general.

Puzzles as Agency Enhancers

It isn't just the learning of skills that is enjoyable: we also revel in that mastery by applying those skills in fun ways. When one learns how to play the guitar, it is fun to actually end up playing songs. We have seen throughout the book that a sense of agency, the ability to act within the game world, is fundamental to a number of level-design goals, such as a deepened sense of immersion and a willingness to engage with the interactive setting of the game.

A certain positive reinforcement can be achieved by making sure that players get to test the gameplay skills that have been taught to them by the level designer, in various ways and settings. It is great fun to try out new abilities and learn to master them, or to feel the thrill of successfully beating a difficult (gameplay) puzzle.

Gameplay Puzzles

Sometimes it is useful to see typical level design tasks in a different light in order to keep their application fresh and inspired. Within this context, I can recommend applying some of the subject matter discussed in this chapter to formally designed gameplay scenarios. Many level designs feature detailed and contained game-play scenarios that have a number of specific ways in which the player can tackle them. It is perfectly reasonable to see these encounters as *puzzles*, and to then try to apply the positive applications of puzzle design to these situations.

Puzzles as Pacing Devices

As already discussed in Chapter 14, puzzles are also very useful as pacing devices. For example, a level's action level can be affected by the placement of more contemplative puzzle gameplay. If the player has just had a long and tense sequence of enemy encounters to contend with, it can be a great relief to be able to take it easy and do some leisurely work to solve a nice rewarding puzzle.

Depending on the type of puzzle employed, the level designer can directly influence the pacing of a level in order to break up the gameplay, for example, so that it isn't all fast action all the time.

> Puzzles are really useful devices to calm down players after an exciting
> part of the game and focus on the details of the world around them. We

build all this detail into the world and in many cases the player whizzes through it at a breakneck pace. Puzzles and "Downtime" are like a sorbet in a multi course meal, in that they allow the player to better appreciate whatever action comes next. Without those pacing contrasts, everything becomes a numbing blur of relentless action, which winds up being fatiguing and not fun after a while.[6]

If used in this way, puzzles become a useful modular gameplay object, where the precise nature of the puzzle is less important than the content of the puzzle itself (within reason, of course.)

Theory Summary

Puzzles are an enormously helpful tool for level designers. Players are already familiar with their use on a fundamental level, including the training and testing of important survival skills or as part of enjoyable activities. In some form or another, we engage in puzzles on a nearly daily basis.

The diverse ways in which they can be used in level design reflects this fact. Puzzles are useful for testing player skills, providing a chance to interact within the game world, influencing the pacing of a level, or providing enjoyment on their own accord.

Puzzle gameplay is fundamental to level design. Indeed, entire games have been based on puzzle gameplay. It is therefore very useful to build up an arsenal of techniques and methods with which to incorporate them into game levels.

The next chapter will show very practical ways in which this can be done.

Practice

Example 14.1: Puzzle as Information Conduit—Investigative Puzzles

Summary

Puzzles can be used as a discreet challenge, where the enjoyment comes from the focus on the puzzle itself. Puzzles can also be used to tie into the game world

---

[6] Josh Weier, *Half Life 2: Raising the Bar*, Valve/Prima Games, Roseville, CA, 2004.

on a wider level, by providing information about the game world to the player in the process of solving the puzzle.

Game Genre

This technique is suitable for games that allow the player to explore a representative game environment and gather information.

Goals to Achieve

- Design and implement an original puzzle.
- Increase the player's knowledge of the game world.
- Deepen immersion and world building.

Description

(Example type: Original)

Investigative puzzles are puzzles that require the player to investigate their environment to solve a puzzle. This can apply in many diverse ways, depending on the specific circumstances of the game.

Examples can be given where the puzzles are part of the challenges incorporated in the actual environment: In an exploration game, the player may need to investigate the behavior of certain creatures to get past them. In a crime adventure game, the player may have to find certain written facts spread through various written accounts located in the game, perhaps to be able to open a safe. A fantasy game may require the player to find a specific mix of herbs in order to create a specific spell that allows the player to proceed.

Other examples can consist of actual *formal* puzzles, encountered in the game. This occurs frequently in survival horror games, as they have become a convention of the genre. With these kinds of games, nobody will bat an eyelid to find a puzzle box that requires a series of passwords to be entered in the correct order, or some other fairly contrived puzzle construct. The correct words and order of words may only become available if the player investigates and learns about the game's back-story.

What matters most in all of these examples is that the process of solving these puzzles is not one that occurs in isolation of the rest of the level. If done well, they are in fact deeply integrated and can be used with great effect to teach the player all kinds of extra information about the level or the game as a whole.

A level designer can construct investigative puzzles in a variety of ways, but it helps if they create a mental map of what it is they are doing. Generally these puzzles are made up of a number of parts:

- Solving the puzzle rewards the player with a consequence.
- The player has to construct a solution from a number of components.
- (Optional) The components need to be manipulated to form the correct solution.
- The player has to go out and investigate the environment in order to find these components.

In the crime adventure game example this process unfolds as follows.

Solving the puzzle rewards the player with a consequence. The player has to unlock a safe to find a suspect's diary.

The player has to construct a solution from a number of components. The safe combination is the birthday of a long lost friend of the suspect. This is broken up into three numbers (day, month, year) that need to be found.

(Optional) The components need to be manipulated to form the correct solution. The date has to be put in the right format (dd/mm/yy).

The player has to go out and investigate the environment in order to find these components. The player needs to go and talk to people who know the suspect, research the suspect's life study and the town's history, and so on, in order to discover the clues that eventually reveal the exact age of the suspect's lost friend.

Further Notes

Investigative puzzles offer much to level designers, because they incorporate the level as a whole. It provides the player with a deep and immersive context from within to explore their skills as well as the level's content, and—despite its constructed nature—it can provide a natural pretext for gameplay.

Example 14.2: Puzzles as Formal Tests— Teaching Mechanic

Summary

Puzzles can be used to test if a player has mastered a certain skill and provide an opportunity to acquire that skill if lacking.

Game Genre

This technique is suitable for all games that employ puzzles.

Goals to Achieve

- Test if a player has acquired a specific skill.
- Teach the player that skill if they haven't acquired it.
- Do this as an optional gameplay encounter.

Description

(Example type: Original)

If a level wants to check if a player has obtained a specific skill, and wants to provide an incentive for the player to lean it if necessary, then the level designer can formalize this into a puzzle design.

The puzzle's solution is only viable by the application of a specific skill, and the puzzle itself provides the teaching mechanism to acquire that skill. Let's take as an example a gameplay scenario where the player can see an award, but is prevented from accessing it unless they solve a puzzle. This can take place by showing the player a locked treasure chest, protected by a complex locking mechanism that consists of words that need to be aligned in an order that spells out a specific sentence. The problem is that the sentence is written in an encrypted language. The player needs to learn how to decrypt the language, and then submit the correct answer in encrypted form.

Let's say that in our example the player once again has to input correct numbers. There are 4 slots, and two of them are already given:

Input: 15 / 16 / – / –

The player may find out through hints that the first two digits stand for O and P, which gives the player the following sequence:

Input: 15 / 16 / – / –
Translation: O / P / – / –

Through logic reasoning, or through trial and error (or both), the player should be able to figure out that the numbers apply to the positions of the letters in the alphabet, and that the correct word/number sequence spells "OPEN":

Input: 15 / 16 / 5 / 14
Translation: O / P / E / N

When successful the player will not only receive the contents of the treasure chest as a reward but will also have acquired the ability to decipher similarly encrypted text throughout the game, which can provide additional gameplay for future level design scenarios.

Further Notes

Please don't use this example literally unless appropriate. It has been used many times in the past and has become a cliché. I only used it as it provides a good demonstration of the principle.

Example 14.3: Puzzle as Pacing Device— Player Controlled Pacing

Summary

Puzzles can be used as a variation to previous gameplay, slowing the pace of the game down and giving the player a chance to do something different, until they solve the puzzle and carry on along the game's path. This can be done in a binary fashion, the puzzle is solved or not, but it can also be done in a slightly different way, one where the player has to decide if they "want" to solve the puzzle.

Game Genre

This technique is suitable for all games that employ puzzles.

Goals to Achieve

- Take control of the pacing in a level.
- Create a puzzle situation within a gameplay scenario.
- Tie various aspects of the puzzle to changes in level pacing.
- Let the player feel like he or she is in control of pacing choices.

Description

(Example type: Original)

Laser fence dilemma. Imagine a situation where the player is in trouble because they are accosted by an ever-larger group of enemies, perhaps an ever-increasing zombie horde. Eventually the player has no choice but to run for safety and ends up racing into an abandoned prison complex. The player is just able to activate its defenses before the zombie horde gains entry. The defenses consist of a fence made up of four laser beams that repel anybody trying to enter or leave the complex. The player is now safe, but also trapped. The same laser defenses also lock a number of zombies within the compound. The player has to figure out how to disable the lasers, yet doing so will unleash the zombies, both in the compound as well as eventually the zombie horde outside. In effect, the player has to solve a puzzle.

We can break this situation down into sections (sub-puzzles) where the player needs to figure out how to disable all four individual lasers one by one. In addition, we show the player a series of weapons lockers with clearly visible, useful weapons or items, protected by individual laser beams that correspond with those in the fence. Disabling one laser means unlocking a new weapon locker, containing weapons or items that allow the player to deal with the unleashed zombies.

It is now up to the player to decide which lasers to disable first and when to do so. In practical terms, the pacing of the setup is in the hands of the player, but with moments of actions when the player has to act and accept the consequences of their actions. Eventually a choice has to be made when to disable the final laser, which makes the entire fence disappear and lets in the zombie horde.

Further Notes

The specific solutions in this scenario don't really matter that much, that will be up to the level designer based on the circumstances of the level or the game he or she is working on. What is key to this setup, however, is that the level designer has a number of great opportunities to affect pacing, while leaving the final choice with the player.

Artificial Intelligence

15

A s noted earlier in this book, it is clear that interaction with artificially intelligent agents in levels is an important factor in level design. This is a statement that is easily made, but the *implications* of that statement are not as easily grasped. What do we actually know about Artificial Intelligence? It is an incredibly rich area of scientific and academic interest, to the point where it has spawned whole new areas of research and application. Before we can talk about formulating theories and techniques for implementing level-design interactions dealing with artificial intelligence, we should have a look at the field as a whole.

Concept

What Is Artificial Intelligence? Some Notes and Concepts

Many a book has been written that tries to answer that question, so I am not going to pretend that this chapter will offer more than the briefest glimpses into the subject matter. First and foremost, I would like to make an important distinction between two types of artificial intelligence: "true" artificial intelligence and *approximated* artificial intelligence. These are not formal definitions from the field, but are rather ways of looking at some of the areas of AI that people are working on.

True AI

First there is the romantic notion of scientists finding the magic spark necessary to create a truly intelligent self-aware artificial life form. This is quite close to the concept of *artificial life*, and it is an attempt to solve all the problems of artificial intelligence in such a way that the outcome is a creature or construct that possesses actual *intelligence*. This kind of AI covers the popular meaning of the term, and as such it frequently pops up in films and books and other popular media. However, it is just a subset of the field as a whole, along with many other areas of AI that are equally relevant to the concept.

Limited AI

Then there are the myriad attempts to create or simulate *aspects* of intelligence or life, and ways to improve on them. This in reality is where most of the focus of current AI work can be found, be it in academic, commercial, or even military terms. This area suggests that perhaps we cannot create true AI at this point in time, but we can work on all the individual requirements that have to be met for it to work in the future. This chapter will show that surprising advances have been made in that respect.

Focus

There are many aspects of AI that are of immediate consequence to the general subject matter of this book. Specifically, there are areas of AI that deal directly with the same issues as those that level designers deal with when implementing AI in their levels. In fact, game AI is a respectable field in its own right, even though others don't always acknowledge that.

So, to avoid getting lost in the immensity of the fields of AI research and application, I want to highlight some specific areas that I feel are most relevant to level design and game AI, starting with the infamous *Turing Test*.

The Turing Test

Alan Turing[1] famously said:

> If a machine acts as intelligently as a human being, then it is as intelligent as a human being.

This statement acknowledges the idea that for a machine to have human-like intelligence, it must be able to reason or behave in such a way that its intelligence is recognizable by other human beings. This assertion is often referred to as the *Turing Test*. Since human beings cannot resist an impossible challenge, the Turing Test has become one of the most popular pursuits in the field of AI. It has

---

[1] The famous British mathematician. See http://www.scienceray.com/Technology/Applied-Science/Artificial-Thought-A-Virtual-Being.514325.

lead many people to an approach where they try to create machines that display behavior that is indistinguishable from that of human beings.

Talking Machines

One of the directions in which to take the Turing Test is to create machines with the ability to *converse* believably with human beings. The best test for this consists in creating a situation where the AI converses with a human being without the person being aware that the conversation partner isn't human. This may seem like science fiction on the surface, and indeed the whole quest for AI has the ring of the impossible to it, but this has never stopped people from trying. It is remarkable, therefore, that with regard to the above version of the Turing test, scientists have achieved very good results relatively easily.

Eliza

To some degree this feat has been performed many times already, sometimes to the dismay[2] of researchers. An early example of this is creation of Eliza by Joseph Weizenbaum at the Michigan Institute of Technology in 1966. Eliza is a computer program that masquerades as a psychotherapist. People can talk to her via a computer interface, typing out and reading questions and answers. I had a chat with "her" myself and this is what came out of it:

> >> Hello.
> How do you do. Please state your problem.
> >> I need to finish writing my book on level design
> Your book on level design ?
> >> Yes, I am currently writing about artificial intelligence
> You seem to be quite positive.
> >> Well, yes. I hope it will be of use to many people.
> You are sure.
> >> I can hope!
> You say you can hope ?
> >> Yeah, one can never be sure with these matters.
> But your book on level design .
> >> Yes sorry I got distracted. I need to know more about you Eliza
> I see.
> >> I hope you don't find it rude if I ask you if you are intelligent?
>
> (From a java applet that faithfully reproduces Eliza's code here: http://www.chayden.net/eliza/Eliza.html)

---

[2] Dismay at the gullibility of human beings.

I won't reproduce our entire conversation, but while playing the role of somebody who could not have known[3] that Eliza was artificial we kept up the conversation for a while. Not bad for a little program that does some simple language parsing based on a parody of a psychotherapist's conversation style.

It is fairly successful because the psychotherapy setting creates patterns of expectation that enhance the validity of certain answers. Normal conversations may not go like this:

> >> Hello.
> How do you do. Please state your problem.
> >> I am anxious.
> Is it because you are anxious that you came to me ?
> >> Yes, I am told you can help me
> You seem to be quite positive.
> >> Well, maybe on the surface, but I am quite sad
> You don't seem quite certain.
> >> Ok, well I am really quite sad.
> I am sorry to hear that you are sad.
> >> Can you help me?
> You believe I can help you don't you ?
> >> Yes, that is why I am here!

As long as the fiction of the session doesn't get too disturbed this seems a remarkable success. It is easy to be fooled by this conversation as the answers conform to the expected response from a real psychotherapist. Now this may not be a very good indication of actual AI, but it is a startling demonstration on the tendency of people to make sensory input fit their patterns of expectation. The brain is quite happy to gloss over discrepancies to a certain degree. It will only go so far however.

> >> Hello.
> How do you do. Please state your problem.
> >> Eliza please explain to me how you work.
> Why do you ask ?
> >> Because I am writing a book about level design and a chapter in it is about the Turing test
> Is that the real reason ?
> >> Yes
> You seem to be quite positive.
> >> That is not relevant
> I'm not sure I understand you fully.

---

[3] Which I think is respectful of the true spirit of the test.

>> Can you explain how you convince people that you are intelligent?
You believe I can explain what I convince people that I are intelligent
don't you ?
>> That sentence makes no sense
Are you saying no just to be negative?
>> What?
Does that question interest you ?
>> You don't seem intelligent to me
Why do you think I don't seem intelligent to you ?

As willing as the brain is to help the illusion along it still doesn't take much for it to shatter completely. Huge improvements have been made however since Eliza was created in 1966. Today's "Chatterbots" are employed with serious levels of success in all kinds of settings.[4]

The original Eliza was still a huge success in its own right, to the point where professor Weizenbaum was so disconcerted by the ease with which it was possible to fool people that he spent a considerable amount of time exploring the subject from different angles. Amongst other things this led to his book *Computer Power and Human Reason: From Judgment to Calculation* in which he further examines the tension between the mechanical and human elements within this field.

Despite Eliza's tendency to fall over fairly quickly when approached outside of its limited area, it is still a shocking success that has led many people to re-examine their relationship towards AI and human beings' reactions to (semi intelligent) machines. The conclusion remains that it is relatively easy to convince people, or rather to *fool* people, to a certain degree, that the entity they are dealing with showcases intelligence it does not actually possess. As we have seen throughout this book, the mind fills in the blanks, which is a phenomenon that can both enthuse and scare, depending on its implementation.

Independence

To avoid the intelligent machine going off the rails completely, a certain amount of *independent reasoning* is required. It has often been argued that for real artificial life to be convincing, it as to have the ability to act independently of its creators. Whatever application or future there would be for an AI construct, it would be much enhanced if it could still function independently, especially if some kind of intelligent reasoning is part of the process. Independence of this kind been approached by some of the most famous thinkers of the last century.

---

[4] See Simon Laven's website dedicated to chatterbots: http://www.simonlaven.com/.

Von Neumann Machines

John von Neumann (1903-1957) was an incredibly influential mathematician whose work has had significant impact on fields as diverse as nuclear power, quantum physics, game theory, economics, computer science, and most applicable to us, artificial life.[5] Von Neumann theorized the concept of *independent self-replicating cellular automata* or, to put it in more easily digestible terms, machines that can create their own offspring independently. Such machines are more popularly known as *Von Neumann machines*. Von Neumann's work was theoretical; he never built self-replicating machines (although Lionel and Roger Penrose later captured the principles of this concept in simple mechanical models made of plywood). However, Von Neumann machines capture two important concepts in artificial intelligence studies: procreation and independence. Most life as we know it is able to make autonomous decisions and is able to safeguard its continued existence through procreation. These are attributes that are hard to achieve in practice.

Freeman's Astrochicken

Another famous thinker and mathematician who has contributed to related areas is Freeman Dyson. Professor Dyson's work has been as influential as von Neumann, and the breadth of the subject matter he has written about is impressive. He is mostly known in popular circles for the concept of Dyson spheres,[6] but the concept most appropriate to this chapter is his imaginary *Astrochicken*. This is a theoretical space exploration robot that takes the concept of von Neumann's self-replicating automaton and places it in the context of space exploration. Astrochicken is a small spacecraft that hatches from an egg laid in space by a regular spacecraft. It then develops extremities that help it gather solar power and uses this to travel to explore planets and other celestial bodies of interest. It would even have the ability to take "nutrients" from any atmosphere it would encounter in order to stay operational.

The point of Astrochicken isn't just that it can act independently of its human creators, but that it can flourish and explore for a reason. It is given a goal, a purpose in life for which to use its intelligent attributes. Were one to observe a colony of space chickens of this type, one would see an *independent society* of at least limited artificial intelligence. This independence matters greatly, as it is needed in situations where the machines have to act autonomously.

---

[5] Specifically, the field of cellular automata.

[6] Dyson Spheres are a theoretical concept. They describe a sphere surrounding a solar system in order to harvest the star's energy in an efficient way.

Mechanical Life

"The incredible adventures of Astrochicken in space!" is a fascinating concept, but, as already noted, it is also purely theoretical. Where are we now then when it comes to the actual construction of artificially intelligent machines? Have we made any serious steps towards this goal?

Vaucanson's Mechanical Duck

There have been some interesting attempts in the past to create convincing mechanical AI's. Jacques Vaucanson created a mechanical duck as early as 1738 that at the time was considered very lifelike (see Figure 15.1). It even had a rudimentary digestive system of sorts. It could be fed and would deposit fake droppings to show that it had "digested" its food. It is important to note that in our technologically sophisticated times the duck may seem primitive, but in the time it was built, it was considered a sensation. Again, we see that an approximation of intelligence elicits strong reactions in people, especially if visually based on biological principles.

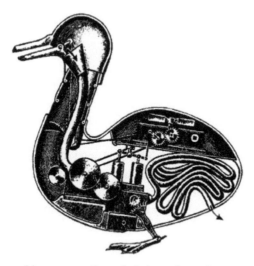

Figure 15.1. Jaques Vaucanson, *Canard digérant*, from *Le monde des automates* (1928).[7]

---

[7] "A postulated interior of the Duck of Vaucanson (1738–1739) by an American observer," *Wikipedia*, http://en.wikipedia.org/wiki/Digesting_Duck, 2009.

Space Exploration Machines

Some of our most successful attempts to create independent mechanical AIs come from necessity. In the case of space exploration, we require probes and such to do our work for us, since we cannot function that well in a vacuum ourselves. Space exploration isn't entirely theoretical after all; we regularly launch space probes and satellites. Some of the machines we launch are expected to be fairly autonomous for long periods of times. The Voyager missions are a good example of space probes whose mission life has been extended due to the fact that they continue to operate with minimal human interference.

Research in this area is very important, as we cannot predict all the challenges that lie ahead when it comes to missions into the unknown.[8] The developers of the failed Mars expedition of the Beagle 2[9] probe are sure to appreciate that.

Robot Toys

Space machines are impressive pieces of engineering, but they are incapable of convincing anyone on a level of human interaction. Surprisingly, we have seen some impressive results in that area in the form of everyday commercial endeavors, namely advances in the toy industry. The clearest example of this can be found in robot toys, which combine sophisticated robotics, rudimentary AI, and human psychology. Much can be learned about human behavior by studying the successes in this area, and the ability of some of these toys to create feelings of empathy in the people who interact with them.

Sony's *AIBO* (Artificial Intelligence Ro*bot*) is quite capable of generating affection, even though it is not convincing as a dog. *Furby* and *Pleo* are two further examples that create serious amounts of empathy, especially from children.

Furbies create a mystique of their own through their non-human language, Furbish, and are cuddly to the touch. They imitate several human emotions and can converse with other Furbies. Pleo is shaped like a dinosaur, is capable of some surprisingly lifelike movement, and reacts to being petted and stroked. Both robotic toys are commercially very successful. Although nobody will mistake them for true life forms, they nonetheless make people react to them as if they were alive.

Having recognizable emotions or shapes that create certain expectations (if it looks like a duck and talks like a duck) has once again shown to be a potent means to convince people of intelligence where there isn't any.

---

[8] It is by definition the unknown; at best, we can expect the unexpected.

[9] See http://www.beagle2.com/index.htm.

As before, however, the visuals or the setting can only take the illusion so far. Eventually, real life will create a scenario that intrudes on the believability of the construct and shatter the illusion of intelligence. And therein lies an interesting proposition: if real life causes the illusion to break, why not remove it as a factor entirely? Why not create *virtual* life?

Virtual Life

There is a way of getting around many of the bothersome engineering problems encountered in the physical construction of artificial life. We can create a world that is predictable and completely controllable by its makers. We can even change the rules of the physical universe and write our own laws that govern our environment. This is done through the creation of computer-based *virtual worlds*, and as a logical extension, *virtual life*.

Evolutionary AI and Virtual Life

Scientists have been creating or capturing elements of virtual life in computer simulations and habitats for a long time. This has been especially important in the field of evolutionary biology, which used to be hampered by the fact that it could only study the effects of evolution, and not evolution itself, since evolution on earth occurs too slowly to notice. This ended in the sixties, when people started to capture and accelerate evolutionary principles in computer models. One of the early pioneers of this approach was John Henry Holland, who wrote a genetic algorithm that allowed a computer to run a program that incorporates basic aspects of artificial life, like self-replication.

Tierra

The field really took off in the early nineties, when people were starting to use similar approaches from different viewpoints, aided by faster and more accessible computers. A notable and influential example is the work done by Thomas Ray, an ecologist who became frustrated with traipsing through rainforests to study evolution and ecological systems. He decided to create a computer program, which acts as an ecosystem for artificial life forms and incorporates enough attributes and environmental data to form a basic Darwinian system. The program he wrote is called *Tierra*,[10] and it can be downloaded and run to this day. *Tierra* is not much more than a program that allows virtual creatures to live, die and replicate, with mutations, in computer memory.

---

[10] See http://life.ou.edu/tierra/.

To quote a *Tierra* webpage:

> Life on Earth is the product of evolution by natural selection operating in the medium of carbon chemistry. However, in theory, the process of evolution is neither limited to occurring on the Earth, nor in carbon chemistry. Just as it may occur on other planets, it may also operate in other media, such as the medium of digital computation. And just as evolution on other planets is not a model of life on Earth, nor is natural evolution in the digital medium.
>
> The Tierra C source code creates a virtual computer and its Darwinian operating system, whose architecture has been designed in such a way that the executable machine codes are evolvable. This means that the machine code can be mutated (by flipping bits at random) or recombined (by swapping segments of code between algorithms), and the resulting code remains functional enough of the time for natural (or presumably artificial) selection to be able to improve the code over time.[11]

Even with these simple parameters, interesting behaviors evolve or develop. Creatures evolved into parasites if their program length was too short to allow procreation (latching on to other longer programs in memory to do so), and hunter-prey cycles between the parasites and host programs began to appear. From an ecology research perspective, this turned out to be very interesting indeed, and the results were accepted as impressive in many ways. The results are easy to study and can be reproduced easily, due to their digital nature.

Karl Sims

Another good example of evolutionary biology and AI meeting in virtual life simulations is to be found in the work of Karl Sims. He has created a number of Darwinian "contests"[12] for virtual creatures, where they are placed in a virtual environment and programmed to compete with each other for certain resources or abilities. For example, two creatures on land (including gravity and friction) have to compete to get to a block of "food" as quickly as possible.[13] The winner gets to evolve to a next generation, thus being rewarded for being fitter than its opponent. Sims' creatures use a virtual brain of sorts, and virtual limbs and muscles that are subject to a process of evolution to define their shape. The resulting creatures are fascinating to behold. Not all evolved creatures end up

---

[11] "What Tierra Is," http://life.ou.edu/tierra/whatis.html, 2004.

[12] See http://www.karlsims.com/papers/alife94.pdf.

[13] An essential text can be downloaded from his website: http://www.karlsims.com/papers/alife94.pdf.

using solutions recognizable in earth's biology, although many do. But almost all the creatures appear lifelike.[14]

Virtual Life in Entertainment

The examples given so far mostly explain the scientific viewpoint with regard to virtual life, but there is just as much to be learned from commercial or entertainment expressions in this field. Throughout the years, we keep seeing virtual life being used in video games and related industries, sometimes with astounding levels of commercial success. Many of these are interesting from a research point of view.

Tamagotchi

Bandai's *Tamagotchis* were at one point some of the most popular pets in the world. Launched in 1996, they sold at ridiculous rates.[15] The "original virtual pet" was so successful partly because it managed to create real empathy in the children who owned one. A *Tamagotchi* is a tiny portable virtual chicken in an egg with an LCD screen. It demands constant nurturing and care or it will die of neglect. Kids have to feed it, play games with it, and in later versions can let it communicate with other *Tamagotchis*.

Nintendogs

The incredible success of the Tamagotchi is no fluke. It has been repeated successfully several times, including more recently in Nintendo's puppy simulator Nintendogs for the Nintendo DS.

Nintendogs quite adroitly manages to portray virtual puppies and give the player several ways of interacting with them in a context of care and responsibility. The adorable puppies can be exposed to voice commands via the handheld's microphone, so they can learn to do tricks or react to their names. You can play with them directly and show affection through "physical" contact. What really makes this a successor to the *Tamagotchi,* though, is that they need regular attention or will suffer negative consequences. They get dirty, for example or feel neglected and get sad. Nobody wants to treat puppies poorly. Just as with *Tamagotchis*, a golden vein of addictive protective gameplay has successfully been mined with the *Nintendogs*.

---

[14] Beautiful examples of his work can be found on his website here: http://www.biota.org/ksims/blockies/#video.

[15] Over 40,000,000 by July 2005, according to some: see http://www.ubergizmo.com/15/archives/2005/07/bandais_tamagot.html.

Little Computer People, The Sims, and Virtual Girlfriends

This principle doesn't only apply to fantastical computer creatures or animals. Not surprisingly, there are many examples of similar games based on the imitation of *human* behavior. This goes all the way back to the exploits of *Little Computer People* in the 1985 Activison game. It was so successful that it was made for several classic formats, including the Commodore 64. It offered a side view of a virtual house in which a computer person moves around and goes about his or her business. Players are approached completely in character as an onlooker, independently from the virtual person, although they can interact with each other in several ways.

This concept was expanded on and taken to dizzying commercial heights by Will Wright and his team through the creation of *The Sims*. At its core, the game provides the same concept as others, but the behavior of the AI entities in the game, and the levels of interaction awarded to the players, are massively enhanced. *The Sims* has become one of the most successful game series ever and has crossed the boundary into mainstream acceptance. Interestingly, there are a lot of female players of the game, without it being specifically targeted at a female demographic.

Having a large female player base is something that cannot be said for the mostly Japanese phenomenon of the *virtual girlfriend*.[16] These appear in dedicated programs in which players try to keep their virtual girlfriend happy, to more elaborate dating SIMs that try to encompass the whole spectrum of the dating experience, from the wooing stage to relationship issues and more. This sub-genre of virtual life may be not as intellectually inspiring as some others, but in its practicalities there are as many lessons to be learned as something like Eliza.

Concept Summary

As this chapter shows, there are many aspects to artificial intelligence and artificial life. All are interesting in their own right, and a surprisingly diverse set of approaches to understanding or even creating artificial life has evolved.

"True artificial intelligence" has not yet been achieved, but there are a large number of projects that have been able to imitate certain aspects of artificial life, and there are myriad examples of largely independent constructs with rudimentary reasoning powers. The elements of imitation and independence may of themselves not provide real AI, but they are instrumental for showing that it

---

[16] Maybe somebody will create a virtual boyfriend soon.

is possible to fool people into believing there are intelligent processes at work. It is especially successful when combined with the ability to create empathy or solicit other strong emotions from the people interacting with the AI. Even when people rationally know that they can't possibly be interacting with an actually intelligent artificial life form, they still react to it as if it were one.

This is a crucial achievement and leads to the creation of believable virtual "life," a concept central to video games and therefore to level design.

Pioneers of this dark art can be found all trough the history of video games. This kind of virtual life may not be driven by scientific goals per se, but it does employ scientific principles. The field has been incredibly successful in learning about and applying psychological principles that allow people to interact and empathize with virtual creatures.

Theory

Artificial intelligence is a big part of almost any video game ever made where the game controls or simulates behavior other than the player's. It is interesting that an activity so much associated with non-serious matters has so much experience dealing with real and practical aspects of successful AI application.

This naturally affects level design in many ways, psychological and gameplay-specific, and leads us to consider the subject from a number of angles.

AI and Level Design

It is probably clear by now that there is much overlap between AI for games and AI in science or other fields. If we take the Turing challenge for example, admittedly a tiny focus, we see huge similarities between the separate fields. This is especially true in its focus on trying to convince participants that they are dealing with real human intelligence. In other areas, the likeness may be less clear. Games don't need to create viable independent spacecraft to be sent away for many years to operate outside of the protection of human guidance. Yet it would be nice if game AI entities could deal with a number of situations like this and convincingly react to diverse player stimuli.

It seems a good idea, then, to identify some of the goals that are specific to level design, as well as to see where they require unique solutions and where we can use ideas from traditional science.

Basic AI Goals for Level Designers

Let's start out by organizing our thoughts around some clear fundamentals. In most cases, AI in level design fulfils two purposes: to *assist gameplay scenarios* and to *enhance immersion*.

The two often feed off each other each other and can be hard to separate.

Assisting Gameplay

There are of course many kinds of AI present in video games. We can have AI opponents in a real-time strategy game, or competing race car drivers in a racing game. Some of these types of AI fall under the category of general AI and aren't necessarily relevant to this book. But there are many instances where the level designer has to take some control over the behavior and/or placement of specific AI entities. When this occurs, we are talking about something of enormous importance to the final success of the levels.

This kind of use of AI agents is what most level designers first think of when discussing AI implementation in level design. AI becomes a useful tool and mechanism for creating all kinds of level design and gameplay scenarios. To do this well, we need to make sure that we have sufficient tools at our disposal and understand the ways in which we can use them.

What is the psychology of creature placement? How do we make AI behavior readable? Or scary? How do we keep AI behavior from becoming too predictable? These are all classic questions that level designers constantly have to deal with.

Enhancing or Protecting Immersion

In tandem with the more practical gameplay aspects of a level, AI also has enormous impact on the overall immersion in the game. This is especially clear in games that require some kind of world building by the level designer, and in games where it really matters that the player be immersed in the game world. If it is important that a player buy into the game world through immersive mechanisms, we will have to take extra care with the implications of our AI usage.

No matter how carefully we have crafted a convincing and immersive experience for our levels, it can all be for naught if the AI presence can't keep up or even sabotages the effort. Imagine a game that is all about employing difficult strategic tactics and maneuvers to get close to a key AI enemy, which is terrible at path finding and gets stuck on every bit of scenery in the level while uttering the same phrase over and over again.

Or imagine something as simple as disturbing a flock of birds perched on a wire when you approach them. The birds settle on a different perch, but return to the original one when you have moved far enough away again for things to be "safe."

When designing levels, the immersive aspects of AI must be taken into account, as well as the play-oriented ones. We have learned from the previous chapter that there are many things that help determine the functionality and human response to AI entities. So, let's see if we can translate these things to level-design considerations. The following sections all discuss techniques or areas of interest that deal with direct gameplay implementation or the perception of the AI by the player. Sometimes they deal with aspects of both.

Believability and Closure in AI

As with the Turing Test, we need our game AI entities to represent some level of believability. They need to be natural inhabitants of the spaces we design and not feel so out of place that they give away the artificiality of the environment. Unsurprisingly, and unfortunately, this is actually quite difficult to achieve, due to the limited level of sophistication that we have reached with regard to creating believable AI behavior. We should not despair, though, since this problem is even worse *outside* of games, and we have some great techniques at our disposal nonetheless.

Allowing the Mind to Fill in the Blanks

Human imagination is a powerful ally to have in the arts, and it is something that can be especially helpful when dealing with the subject of AI. One aspect where this really counts is when the mind engages in *closure*. As mentioned in Chapter 13, closure is a fantastically important aspect of any artistic endeavor where images or concepts need to be resolved among themselves. What I mean by that is that anywhere there are empty spaces to fill in—between the panels in a comic book, between cuts in a film, between chapters in a book and so on—the artist is using his or her skills to tempt the mind of the audience to resolve those spaces into an understanding that fits the artwork. Take for example a scene in a movie that shows a hand holding a match, followed by a scene showing a burnt-out house. The space that has to be filled between those scenes is enormous, yet without any problem, the audience will resolve the two disparate scenes into a logical narrative that leads them to conclude that the match was used to light the fire that burned down the house.

A similar thing can be made to occur in video game AI, and in the way we use AI as level designers. We have already seen in the example of Eliza the virtual therapist that this goal is very much achievable.

Goals and Motivations

In many cases, we attribute the existence of goals and motivations to the existence of some form of intelligence. Non-intelligent entities have no needs and wants; at best, they just react in a rigid, unintelligent way to set parameters. Some of the programming involved in game AI deals with giving the AI entity some simple needs and reasoning ability. So, level designers must choose which needs have to be acted upon and in what way that will be done. This is something the level designer needs to be aware of, as it will tell them how the AI entity will react in specific situations.

Armed with this knowledge, we can enhance these core abilities by setting up situations that showcase them to the player or even exaggerate the existence of these motivations and goals.

Thus, we can set up an event that shows a robot fleeing a fight when it runs out of bullets and retrieving new ammo elsewhere. Or we can engineer a situation where kindness to an animal will make it stick close to the player, while cruelty will make it attack.

Many scenarios can be thought up, but it is helpful to demonstrate to the player that these AI entities have goals and motivations that they act on.

Complexity

Another indicator of intelligence is the ability to deal with complex situations, or the ability to show a complex range of strategies to cope with diverse challenges.

One (low cost) way to present this is by creating scenarios that *hint* at a behavioral complexity that simply doesn't exist. Behavioral complexity is generally seen by the audience as a sign of intelligence: if we convince the audience that the AI behaves in a way that is inherently complex, then we convince the audience that the AI is inherently intelligent. We can also hint at deeper complexity by showing goals and motivations that are completely independent from the player's actions. This hints at an autonomous world in which the AI entity has its own role to play.

We can either show off real complexity in *explicit* ways, or we can simulate complexity by manipulating the player's *perception of the AI* in question.

Explicit complexity

Level designers often do not realize how complex AI code can be, and how hard it is to program entities that can deal convincingly with the challenges they have dreamed up. But once we recognize this, we can show off this depth through our level designs in ways that make the levels much better.

Explicit complexity is the kind of complex behavior that automatically emerges from the AI entity's programming and reactions to outside stimuli. While we have little control over the programming, we can still manipulate the environment and the context and challenges in which gameplay occurs.

For example, sometimes it is possible to dress up a small number of gameplay scenarios in such a way that they keep appearing fresh and original. We can hark back to some of the principles mentioned in the section on "Object-Oriented Level Design" in Chapter 4 and reuse the AI-based challenges in new and complex ways.

In my previous examples of *Tierra* or the Karl Sims "contest" I have shown that sometimes a few simple parameters can lead to incredibly complex results and even lifelike behavior. The simple goals shown in those examples feature situations dealing with basic abilities, terrain or environment rules, a need to eat, adversaries, and so on. These are very similar to factors that we have to deal with in level design:

- Basic abilities become character/entity controls.
- Terrain/environmental rules become the game physics.
- A need to eat becomes resource management.
- Adversaries are game opponents.

Throw these factors in a blender, and we can create very complex scenarios coming out of very basic factors. Even though individual components can be simple, we can make our levels into interestingly complex systems, where small changes in specific parameters can have interesting and even chaotic results.

Perceived complexity

Perceived complexity is the behavior as the player interprets it. This is a very powerful concept that we can play with to enhance the appreciation of apparent sophistication of the AI in question.

As before, we can reuse AI-based level design scenarios, but this time without doing much to actually add complexity to the AI in question. For example, if our AI creature is no good at dealing with diverse types of terrain, we just make sure it is never in a situation where it has to do complex path finding. Instead, we put it on balconies, in towers, on top of a roof, and so forth, but we give it access to different guns and catchphrases.

Again, as long as the player *believes* that the responses are complex, that's good enough.

We can "cheat" by suggesting all kinds of complex reasoning that in fact isn't very complex at all. Here are some ideas on how to do that:

- Give the AI entity knowledge that does not come from its own senses.
- Script it to explain its reasoning in a way that sounds more intelligent than it really is.
- Adjust very simple basic attributes of the entity in a way that changes its abilities drastically, without altering its reasoning.
- Place the entity in areas of the level that make it appear able to cope with all kinds of environments.

Others can be found, as well.

Dangers in seeking complexity

There are a number of things we need to look out for when it comes to seeking complexity.

In many cases, our dealings with in-game AI are based on encounters that provide challenge and adversarial gameplay. The player's skills are often tested against the challenges presented through AI entities. What needs to be remembered, though, is that the AI needs to serve the game's higher goals, and not become a goal in its own right. There isn't much point in seeking to create incredibly sophisticated AI to use against the player if that AI opponent is too smart for the player. The same is true if it has internal workings that are fairly intelligent but unclear to the player, which prevent the player from devising enjoyable play strategies.

We also need to make sure the AI is deemed to be fair. Any time we embark on a path of tricks and smoke and mirrors to make the AI look smarter than it is, we run the risk of the player finding out that we are "cheating." This is something that needs to be avoided, because once the player thinks the game is unfair, he or she will not trust it anymore and the unwritten entertainment contract between game and player is broken.

Imitation

We can also try to create AI behavior that imitates the actions of intelligent entities. This is a valid approach to take and offers all kinds of tools for level designers. If the imitation is good enough to fool the player into believing in a high level of intelligence, we have reached our goal as convincingly as if we had actually created the intelligence we wish to portray.

We can engineer situations where the AI's actions mimic processes that we KNOW to be intelligent. By doing so, we can make the player assume that actual intelligence is being used when it isn't. This is a method that is especially useful in cutscenes and scripted events, where we have more control over circumstances.

Independence

Independence can be hinted at by showing the AI performing autonomous tasks, even mundane ones. After all, if an AI can lead an existence where even the mundane is acted upon, it must surely have a high level of independence. This is often used to great effect in games where we can observe the AI without interference, for example in stealth games where the player spends a lot of time in hiding, studying the behavior of AI entities on patrol.

Most stealth games have the AIs perform quite arbitrary or random independent actions. They stop at a vending machine, chat to another guard, whistle a song, and so on. These actions are not accidental; they are specifically put in to showcase that the AIs have a "life of their own," even though quite often these actions are quite unintelligent and are just hard coded to occur at specific locations. Little touches like these can make a level stand out, sometimes with minimal effort.

Empathy and Antipathy

Alternatively, we can try to create an emotional response in the player that is strong enough for a reaction that makes the player attribute all kinds of mental capabilities to the AI. This can be subtle or brutally direct; the trick is to make the actions emotionally powerful.

An AI enemy is just a bit of code, but say for example we show a human NPC club a seal to death or slap a defenseless person in the face. Chances are that the player will associate all kinds of negative human emotions (and therefore intelligence) to this creature. The opposite principle works equally well; empathy can be just as powerful as antipathy.

Gameplay and Environment Considerations

As much as we can try psychological tricks to make player interaction with game AI as meaningful and convincing as possible, we still need to be able to place the AIs in an environment and use direct gameplay application in a way that works.

The Right Environment (Context)

So how do we achieve all these things? The tips, techniques, and theories mentioned above will certainly help, but it is best to try to put them all into an overall system of logic, a balanced AI ecosystem that performs like clockwork no matter what it encounters.

For AI to work well, it is best to try to create a context that allows for appropriate behavior and that plays to the AI's strengths. To go back to the concept part of this chapter, we can see this principle at work in the Eliza AI. Eliza was very successful because it provided an appropriate context for AI interaction that was conducive to expectations that the AI could easily meet, and that had a setting that played to its strengths.

Appropriateness

In Eliza's case, its framing of a psychotherapy question-and-answer setting immediately creates a situation where vague searching answers and questions don't feel odd. The participant may think some question or answers are a bit strange, but will often ignore these peculiarities because the psycho-probing expected in the session explains it. We assume there are goals and motivations involved that are appropriate due to the setting.

We can do the same thing within our level designs. By creating an environment that makes the actions of the AI look appropriate, we can create a much more believable experience. We can place defensive turrets or robots with limited AI in a damaged factory setting, and suddenly their "glitches" are given a believable context.

Fitting the AI abilities

Eliza's environment is that of the program and another person communicating through a *keyboard and monitor* interface. It fits the AI's limited abilities because it doesn't ask it to show any physical representation of itself and allows it to use the medium it is best suited for: *written* language, without involving the danger of *spoken* language, which it could never pull off well.

In retrospect this is a fairly obvious approach, but isn't everything obvious in retrospect? Sometimes the obvious is worth stating, regardless.

In level design it is often of the utmost importance that we make sure that the AI we employ is used in settings where it operates well and avoids its weaknesses.

- If your game's AI entities are not very good at path finding, don't place them in a complex terrain.
- If they are not very good at dealing with situations up close, don't throw a bunch of them in a cramped environment.
- If they don't have many lines of text to say, don't make them talk constantly.

I am sure you get the picture and are able to add dozens of such cautions of your own.

Scripted Events and Cutscenes

Finally, as mentioned briefly before, when all other things fail, we can use brute force and create prescripted responses that allow us to direct AI the way we want. This is often done in scripted events and cutscenes and can range from subtle actions to taking all power from the player and letting AIs do things they have no business doing.

We can make the AI say things that go beyond its basic vocabulary or traverse environments it can't deal with in-game. Or we can let the AI use its actual capabilities, but we assert control over the circumstances and timing of the scripted event. Either way, due to the potentially intrusive nature of events like these, we should treat this approach with caution.

Theory Summary

It seems that we can spend as much time dealing with the actual capabilities of game AI as on managing the perceptions of these capabilities. Both aspects are indeed valid, and are rooted in sound principles and ideas that can be taken from existing fields of AI research or implementation. Games also have their own knowledge to contribute. The mixture of these elements makes for a potent set of tools to use to improve our levels.

We can make our levels and the AI used in them stand out by using elements of AI, showing off AI capabilities with the use of *real* or *perceived complexity*. We can demonstrate intelligent independence and showcase the use of goals and motivations. We can direct feelings through imitation, empathy, or antipathy. And we can direct entire gameplay scenarios through cutscenes and scripted sequences.

There are many other examples that could be named, but the previous ones should illustrate the general principle and they should apply to many levels.

Practice

Example 15.1: AI Believability—Imitation of Emotions

Summary

A classic way to make AI believable is to engineer situations where the AI is seen to do seemingly intelligent things. One way to do this in a fairly subtle way is to provide moments when the AI "betrays" an emotionally complex "inner life."

Game Genre

This technique is suitable for games that allow moderate scripting of AI entities.

Goals to Achieve

- Enhance the believability AI characters.
- Achieve this by making them appear to suffer from human weaknesses.
- Put this in a practical level setting.

Description

(Example type: Original)

When dealing with level design it is all too easy to get lost in the practical needs with which the AI will be confronted: pure gameplay requirements like the ability to navigate the environment or its effectiveness as a challenge to the player's skills. These subjects are indeed massively important, but at times it is also vital that the AI contributes to the level's immersive qualities, or instills an emotional bond with the player.

There are, for example, many games that require the player to interact with a helpful sidekick or similar type of friendly AI. It is very helpful if the player is convinced by the AI's behavior that its intelligence is fairly sophisticated. It is even more helpful if the player sees the AI as a creature with a personality, and not just a tool with which to progress through the level. That way, the user is able to form some kind of emotional connection to the AI that leads to a more immersive or interesting level.

We can achieve this outcome by hinting at a sophistication that isn't necessarily there, but imitates sophisticated intelligence to such a degree that the player accepts it's there nonetheless. With some minor scripted touches we can achieve a lot, and there are some excellent existing examples to draw inspiration from.

Emotional outburst. In Bungie's *Halo: Combat Evolved*[17] the player is regularly aided by helpful NPCs that help the player combat enemy alien creatures. The NPCs have many lines of dialogue that portray them as gung-ho marines to firmly establish them within the genre's conventions. There are moments, however, where they go beyond shouting one-liners and perform actions that can't help but provoke a response in the player. One such moment occurs right at the end of a challenging battle, when one of these marines runs up to an already dead alien, and shoots it again, gleefully yelling at it.

Nothing is served by this scripted sequence in gameplay terms but the player is unlikely to forget such a moment, and the general enjoyment of the level as a whole is much enhanced.

Humor/fear. *Alien vs. Predator 2*[18] is a particularly scary first person shooter. In one of the game's sequences, the player and a group of marines investigate an off-world installation. The marines are separated from each other but they can communicate through radio. The radio chatter is used by the level designer to convey NPC dialogue that enhances the sense of personality and intelligence of the NPCs, as well as adding to the level's tension as a whole.

Here is an example of the radio chatter:

> A scared and nervous sounding marine:
> "Is that a boot? Is that a boot!? That better be a boot!!"
> A minute or so of silence....
> "Hey, it's a boot!"

The example is very simple but nonetheless very effective in humanizing the AI in this level.

Further Notes

There are many other human character traits that can be incorporated in a game's AI like nervousness, mischievousness, irritation, and so on.

---

[17] Published by Microsoft Game Studios, developed by Bungie Studios, released November 15, 2001.

[18] Published by Fox Interactive, Inc. – Sierra On-Line Inc., developed by Monolith Productions Inc., released October 22, 2001.

Example 15.2: Appropriate Environments—Ambush Scenario

Summary

To get the most out of AI, it is best to use them within an environment where they are best able to perform to their capabilities. A classic ambush scenario provides an opportunity to take that principle even further.

Game Genre

This technique is suitable for games that allow moderate scripting of AI entities.

Goals to Achieve

- Showcase the use of AI in a way that maximizes their impact and minimizes their apparent weaknesses.

Description

(Example type: Original)

The ambush scenario. All AI entities suffer from weaknesses, and at times that makes it hard to use them in a way that does not endanger player immersion. They may be bad at navigating complex terrain, or have difficulty acquiring targets, or have problems choosing from too many actions, and so on. Generally, that means that we design our levels in such a way that they hide these deficiencies: the AI is not placed in a position where their inefficiencies shine through.

We can, however, take this one step further and place the AI in a position where their inefficiencies are hidden and their capabilities are exaggerated—especially if done in such a way that is not possible in general gameplay circumstances. The idea is to design a level design pretext that allows the player to use the AI in such a way without destroying immersion.

One such method is the classic ambush situation. It gives the designer a number of advantages that don't often occur in regular gameplay:

- The AI movement can be logically restricted to specific locations that maximize their efficiency.
- The AI can be placed in locations that stop the player from direct interaction with them.
- The AI can be scripted to perform specific actions.

Take, for example, an ambush in a mountain pass. AI entities can be placed away from the player, on a higher road, in the mouth of a mountain cave set in a cliff face, on top of a large and steep set of boulders, and so on. None of these locations are reachable by the player, yet within the context of an ambush all these locations are explained. Impact can be maximized through specific scripted actions. A far away AI entity can be restricted to using long range weapons, the AI entity on the higher road can run up and down, evading player attacks while returning fire, and the AI on top of the boulders can throw sticks of dynamite when the player comes too close. All things that can be achieved with limited amounts of scripting, and all showing off the AI as capable of a range of actions requiring intelligence.

This can be made even more effective if we signpost the AI's intentions to the player, even if those intentions are faked by us, for optimal believability.

Further Notes

This example features a static set piece, but variations can include a more dynamic scenario. A player can be stalked by an AI moving along a higher, unreachable, path, and taking specific actions at well-designed intervals.

Example 15.3: AI Believability— Emphasizing Ability

Summary

The more natural and capable an AI behaves within a gameplay context, the more it contributes to the success and immersive qualities of a level. We therefore try to showcase AI in its best light.

Game Genre

This technique is suitable for most games.

Goals to Achieve

- Achieve closure by manufacturing the appearance of
  - complexity,
  - independence,
  - emotions.

Description

(Example type: Original)

It is common sense to try to use AI in a way that does not detract from its believability, for example, by avoiding situations that show up its weaknesses. That kind of solution is valid and we often will end up taking exactly that approach. It is, however, a somewhat passive approach, as it is focused on *not* doing certain things.

An alternative and often more effective approach is to create gameplay scenarios and situations that are built around AI *strengths*. So, rather than avoiding things the AI is bad at, we end up researching those things the AI is great at *and* deliver the most fun for the player. Once we have isolated those strengths, we can construct gameplay sequences that are purely built around those strengths.

We may end up with a list of good and bad points from which we can start to draw inspiration. In this example we will look at a robot cat sidekick in an exploration platformer. Our list may look a bit like this:

AI abilities and noteworthy behavior:

- The AI gets confused by more than five onscreen characters.
- It will always chase mice if they are around.
- It can stand up to small dogs.
- The AI is no good against the game's larger animals .
- The AI is very good at jumping (better than the player).
- It is very bad at swimming.
- It won't go outside in the rain.

From this we may derive a mix of skills and behaviors that make us create a gameplay sequence that involves the following elements:

- few enemies,
- no mice,
- some dog encounters,
- no larger animals,
- a series of platform jumps that the cat can perform but the player can't,
- no water,
- sunny weather.

Simplistic as this may sound, it is nonetheless a good exercise to go through when deciding on what ingredients to use for a specific level design situation.

Further Notes

This approach requires the designer to spend a serious amount of time play testing scenarios and circumstances in feature-rich test levels or test beds to be able to judge the strengths and weaknesses accurately. In a way, it is about "finding the fun" and stress testing the AI to find circumstances under which its abilities and impact is at an optimum. This can only be done in the context of representative gameplay, as gameplay mechanics tend to influence each other and do not occur in a vacuum.

Challenge

16

W̲e have encountered the concept of challenge numerous times now through-out this book. We have spoken of positive and negative challenges in life and how conquering them can lead to a sense of empowerment. We have spoken of the willingness of players to deal with challenges if they form part of a reward system, and we have spoken of formal challenges put on a person in order to test knowledge.

These are three distinct ways of looking at the same word, which is an indication that it may not suffice to think of "challenge" as a single discreet concept. This chapter therefore looks deeper into the various aspects that are important to understanding the concept of challenge as a whole.

Concept

Challenge Revisited

Although we already spent a fair amount of time on the subject of challenge in the "Challenge and Empowerment" section in Chapter 7, I would still like to revisit some aspects of this subject. I think it deserves to be approached from several different angles, since it is so important to level design, and because it is a complex subject that warrants multiple observations.

To recap[1] some of the points made, here is an observation I made earlier:

> *There are positive challenges.* If you go running for an hour every day, you will become very fit. If you study a language diligently for ten years, you will become fluid in its use. If your work is better than that of your colleagues, you will get that promotion. (Well, you *should*, anyway.)

---

[1] I know it is bad form to quote one's own text, but it saves you from having to flip back and forth between chapters.

And there are negative challenges. Stand up to that bully and he will stop harassing you. Deal with the tragedy of a loss for a long enough time and it will hurt less and less. Resist smoking for a year and your cravings will be gone.

These are all good examples where there is a sense of empowerment, a reward for meeting the challenge successfully. There are other well-known uses for challenges as well, for example in an educational context.

Problematic Conceptions of "Challenge for Challenge's Sake"

The conclusion that presents itself from all of the examples previously discussed is that we need challenge in life in order to measure our strength of character or to test our skills at a certain activity, and so forth. There are many applications for challenge that are worthwhile and rewarding. While this can be true in its own right, it often leads to the conclusion that therefore challenge is a desirable goal in itself. *This is dangerous and often untrue.*

If challenge were seen as a goal in its own right, than just inserting one or more new challenges into the equation should increase the value of the experience. Indeed, many people have done so in the past. Unfortunately, this approach can lead to serious problems.

To understand this, let's look at some examples.

Lack of Meaning

When an artist challenges his or her audience, it generally is expected that there is a reason to do so. If the audience is presented with challenge for challenge's sake, it will eventually come to realize that there is no meaning behind the act. This is a very dangerous thing to court, because once an audience realizes that it has been put through its paces for no good reason, it loses its motivation to stick around for the ride. This problem can occur across the spectrum of creative expression. Challenging but pointless dissonance in a composition will be experienced as off-key or cacophonous. Harsh and disorientating edits in a film without serving the content of the shot will just dizzy and upset an audience.

Creating Resentment

A similar problem with challenge for challenge's sake lies in the likelihood that it will build up *resentment* in the audience. If you were to poke somebody in the chest for no good reason, that person would probably object. Maybe not the first time, but do it a lot and even your best friend will start to resent the action. It has to be understood that if challenge is not placed within a context, it is just hardship. And who wants to be subjected to arbitrary hardship?

An artist and their audience have an unwritten contract. The artist presents creative output and invites the audience to experience it, even if the experience can become unpleasant or challenging. The audience will go along with this, based on this unwritten contract, which states that there is some value or payoff in doing so. If it turns out that there is no good reason for the audience's discomfort, that contract has been broken.

Desensitization and Boredom

Additionally, there is the danger of just overloading the audience. If there is no particularly good reason for being harassed by the artwork and the audience catches on to this, it will either stop taking it seriously or just stop feeling an emotional connection to the work. Both are clearly disastrous results.

Concept Summary

If challenge is to be incorporated into art and entertainment, it needs to serve a higher goal.

This is just as true for video games as it is for other art forms. Generally, this kind of artistic challenge exists to eventually reach a positive outcome. In video games, challenge is used more than in almost any other artistic medium, because challenges are a great way to test the player's skill level, which is an intrinsic part of level design. In video games, much enjoyment comes from learning how to use the gameplay mechanics and from being confronted with new and enjoyable ways to test one's ability.

Challenge is a formal invitation to the player to overcome adversity through applying his or her gameplay skills.

Theory

Few words are used so freely, but misunderstood so much in discussions about level or game design as *challenge*. Worse yet, people always think that everybody agrees on the exact meaning, or even worse, that they agree on the right application of it in level design. The reality of the situation is that almost nothing does more harm to players' enjoyment of games than the misuse of the concept of challenge.

Challenge and Difficulty levels

Challenge as a concept is often used in conjunction with *difficulty levels*. While the two can have a relationship, they are not the same thing. *Challenge is a formal invitation or demand on the player to overcome adversity. Difficulty,* on the other hand, is much more subjective and simply describes *how well the player is equipped to do so.* In other words, a level can offer the same challenge to different players, and they may have a completely different appreciation of the difficulty level of that challenge.

Frustration and Boredom

One of the biggest dangers in level design is misjudging the abilities of the player in such a way that a level becomes too hard or too easy. The emotions that come into play when we get this wrong are frustration and boredom, and both of them can severely damage a player's enjoyment of the game.

For one last time, let's go back to the diagram of Csiksczentmihalyi's flow theory. (See Figure 16.1.)

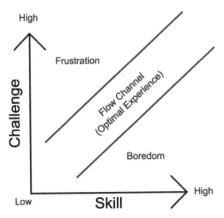

Figure 16.1. Flow theory diagram.

The main danger in the implementation of challenge is spelled out right in front of us. If challenge and skill are not appropriately balanced, the player leaves the zone of optimal experience and becomes either *anxious* (frustrated) when the game is too hard, or *bored* when the game is too easy.

Frustration

Of the two, this emotion is potentially lethal to the success of a game. Anywhere in life where an activity is beyond the skill level of participants, they will be literally frustrated in their ability to enjoy it. If that frustration is too fundamental and cannot be overcome, participants will become so unhappy that they will cease the activity.

The same thing occurs in video games. A player who becomes frustrated with the difficulty level of a game will eventually give up playing all together, likely for good. Why would someone want to spend time on an activity that frustrates the desired outcome, such as an enjoyable or worthwhile or rewarding experience? Challenges are often used to affect the game's difficulty level and learning curve. This can be appropriate in many cases, but when the difficulty level is too challenging, and the player has no prospect of this changing, the game will have gone too far.

Boredom

Boredom has its own unique problems and can lead to the same negative result. Interestingly, one of the justifications for harsh challenges in a level is to stave off boredom. The argument often goes something like "The game has to be challenging or the player will become bored. Therefore, we must make the game more challenging over time or the player will lose interest." This is a subtle but serious mistake. As we already established, challenge is simply a tool, no more than a means to an end. In this case the tool helps avoid boredom. So far so good, but *boredom is not necessarily avoided by escalating difficulty levels*. Just upping the difficulty will not automatically push the player back into the flow channel, the *zone* of an optimal game experience. If an activity doesn't require the use of new skills or refine the use of current skill sets, its activity will become less interesting and certainly less rewarding.

Apparent Exceptions

In some rare cases, games actually provide frustration as a gameplay goal. There are games that propose an almost masochistic test to the player, where it is a given that although harsh and unforgiving treatment will be doled out, in exchange the player receives a very particular kind of satisfaction that comes from successfully overcoming the extreme challenges of such games. This kind of gameplay often occurs in specific taste niches or areas of specialization and is typically some kind of challenge-based game.

Bullet Hell

An amusing example of this kind of specialized, challenge-based game is a phenomenon found in some types of classical shootemups. The level or mission design for these games boils down to the player trying to maneuver into ever decreasing areas of the screen where there are no enemy bullets. This is entirely acceptable, even expected, in these kinds of shootemups. It becomes an endurance test to players who are already used to being tested by these conventions of gameplay.

Unfortunately, this also often occurs in inappropriate places. One example is in third-person action games where the player literally cannot set a foot down wrong without being shot to pieces or otherwise hindered from playing the game.

Unfairness and humor

There is a case to be made for recognizing these principles and using extremely unfair challenges for comedic appeal. This works well to varying degrees. If the whole game is based on that premise, players will be forewarned and may take on the challenges with a good sense of humor. A recent example of this can be found in the indie game *I Want to Be the Guy*, which prides itself on providing unfair and frustrating gameplay in a series of brutally hard and challenging levels.

The game maker says the following in the "how to play" section of its website[2]:

> This game is very hard. You could find that getting past the very first few screens is taking you the better part of an hour, or more. Do not be deterred. It's supposed to be unfair. Realize this before all else; any and all situations can kill without warning. Take nothing for granted. If it appears safe; you can be nearly certain that it is a trap. Understand that you can only get hit once before you die in a particularly gruesome manner. Be careful!

The player has certainly been forewarned in this particular case!

---

[2] "I Wanna Be the Guy! Manual!" *IWBTG!*, http://kayin.pyoko.org/iwbtg/manual.php, 2007.

Narrow flow channel

It can be argued that these are *exceptions to the rule* that too high a challenge leads to anxiety, as these games openly *court* frustration. On closer inspection one could come to a different conclusion. These games don't present a challenge level that is *too* high, but one that is appropriate to the game genre itself.

The *zone* in these kinds of games is a very *narrow* flow channel, but the same principles still apply that we saw before. It is just that the intended audience is willing to deal with much higher and more specific challenge levels than players of more accessible games.

Appropriate Challenges

There are two major aspects of challenges in level design that should never be ignored. As already shown in the flow diagram[3], *skill* needs to be in balance with *challenge*. Additionally, the balance definition itself, the *positioning* of the flow channel, is subject to considerations of *context*.

Skill

Skill issues in level design are the easiest to recognize, yet also the most frequently misjudged. We have already discussed the potential dangers of challenging the player too much by requiring unreasonable skills. Let's look at ways that this danger can be avoided.

Dynamic Difficulty Adjustment

Dynamic difficulty adjustment is the practice of allowing the game to react to the apparent skill level of the player and adjust difficulty levels accordingly. A classic example of this would be measuring player death at specific locations in levels. If a player dies too many times in a conflict area, for example a shootout scenario, the difficulty of the encounter can be adjusted downwards, perhaps by making enemy AI shooting less accurate. There are many ways of implementing this principle, and if done without the player being overly conscious of getting a helping hand, this can yield good results. However, there are some real dangers and disadvantages attached to this kind of difficulty adjustment.

---

[3] See Figure 16.1.

Data limitations

To make the decision to change the difficulty level of the game, the *dynamic difficulty adjustment (DDA)* system needs some way of evaluating the *need* to do so. Performance data needs to be gathered and interpreted before any change can be made. For example, the player's ability to hit targets in a first person shooter or the number of hit points left after specific encounters, need to be known.

The problem with collecting this kind of data is that it gives us very limited information on which to base important decisions. What if the player enjoys a playing style that results in being very close to death most of the time? What if the player enjoys shooting the scenery as well as shooting at enemies? Since we cannot gather data that objectively tells us the player's real emotions and experiences directly, this kind of reactive or passive difficulty adjustment will always be based on subjective guesses. And that means that the interpretation of the data can yield incorrect conclusions, resulting in inappropriate adjustments.

Passivity

However, let's assume that the DDA system gets it right. Take a series of jumps to reach the exit in one of our levels in a platforming game. The system is alerted that the player keeps failing the last jump; in response, it may lower the difficulty level by allowing a collapsing tree to create a bridge between the two jump points.[4] To a degree, the DDA has worked correctly, and the resulting intervention has allowed the player to progress through the game. This is all true, but it did not happen until *after* the player has left the flow channel and had to be guided back into it. Because the system can only *react* to data, actions always occur after the fact. And levels that constantly have to correct themselves in order to make an unhappy player happy again are far from ideal.

Jenova Chen–Flow In Games

Thankfully, there are ways in which these problems can be avoided or minimized. Jenova Chen has done great work in this field by taking the basic principles of Csikszentmihalyi's flow theory and incorporating it into a specific flow theory for games. His thesis, "Flow in Games," is a must read for all serious students of level and game design theory. He has much to say on the subject of flow and what he calls *"player centric* dynamic difficulty adjustment."

> So why don't we give the players choices in a video game and let them navigate their Flow experience? In order to create a game like this, …[5],

---

[4] Yes, I realize this is a very silly example.

[5] I removed a redundant reference to an image in the original thesis.

the game needs to offer a pool with a wide spectrum of activities and dif-ficulties for different types of players to swim inside. Based on players' tastes, each individual will choose different choices and work at a dif-ferent pace to navigate through the game. Once a network of choices is applied, the Flow experience is very much customizable by the players. If they start feeling bored, they can choose to play harder, vice versa.[6]

What Jenova Chen is proposing here is proactive difficulty adjustment con-trolled by the players themselves. This is an intriguing concept that is worth ex-amining in more detail.

Player controlled difficulty adjustment

As opposed to trying to design a self regulating difficulty system that tries to read player behavior or preempt player actions, Chen argues for a system that puts these choices in the player's hands. Who else is better able to judge what is too hard or frustrating or fun? A logical consequence of this philosophy is a game that has based its core game mechanics on player-controlled difficulty adjust-ment. This is what Chen and Nicholas Clarke have done with *flOw*. This game has incorporated these choices seamlessly into the core gameplay, and this has led to a remarkably successful project.[7]

FlOw is based on a simple premise: the player controls a primitive marine organism that has to find food in order to evolve to more evolved states. To do this, the creature has to dive to depths that are more dangerous than shallower water. The game therefore allows the player to find a gameplay space that he or she is the most comfortable with.

Context

Challenge has been shown to not only be subject to personal skill levels, but also to context. This context comes from the multifaceted dimension of the whole notion of *challenge*. We can challenge players to test their shooting skills, or to affect pacing, or we can give them something by which they can measure their own strength. All of these add a unique contextual dimension to the challenge in question, and therefore to the experience of the player. The last boss in the game presents a different context and experience than an idle puzzle along the way.

---

[6] Jenova Chen, "Flow in Games Thesis," *Flow in Games*, http://www.jenovachen.com/flowingames/Flow_in_games_final.pdf, 2004, p. 13.

[7] The flash version of the game downloads numbers in the hundreds of thousands. There are a PS3 version and a PSP version, and other games based on the same principles are in development.

Challenge as a Level Design Tool

What these aspects of appropriateness highlight is that we should never forget that challenge is a tool for achieving something specific. It is meaningless as a goal in its own right, and level designers who claim that all gameplay needs to be challenging completely misunderstand this basic principle. It is those level designers who implement challenge for challenge's sake who commit some of the worst offenses to be found in gameplay implementation.

Arbitrary Difficulty

One of the common dangers that creeps into designs is *arbitrary difficulty* that provides pointless challenge. A good analogy is a lopsided bicycle tire. Once in a while you see these contraptions at carnivals or in similar places. Sometimes there is a bicycle with a very lopsided tire, and an obstacle course to be traversed. In the right context (a few minutes of silly fun), this can work okay; but for most uses, a bicycle is not improved by making the wheel lopsided. In fact, when you want to go somewhere, it is incredibly annoying to have a lopsided wheel. Yet there are plenty of games out there that insist on taking a useful game mechanic and making it awkward without any good reason whatsoever.

Prohibitive Difficulty

Some games are just too hard for most people to enjoy. They require a commitment unlikely to be deemed enjoyable. Some surpass the skill level of most players, who will never be able to do certain things in the game. Unless a game is made specifically for people who seek a challenge like that, this is a serious problem.

In level design this problem often occurs because level designers have spent so much time playing a game that they have reached an atypical skill level, and are trying to entertain themselves in their level design. This is a fatal error since their job is to entertain their audience, not themselves.

Unfair Challenges

This is a very strange one to understand, but it keeps occurring on a regular basis. Some level designers seem to think of the player as the enemy, and feel their job is to kill the player as harshly as possible. If you are one of those people, stop that immediately please!

Gameplay situations can test a player's skills. No issues there, as that is what gameplay learning is all about. It is enjoyable to use new skills in interesting ways, and good level designs provide players with fun ways to test their skills. Challenges can also be fun if there is an interesting or enjoyable sense of achievement to be had, especially if it ties in contextually to the game's overall objectives.

What is not appropriate to players, though, is to be challenged to do tasks or overcome obstacles that are presented in an unfair way. This can include situations like

- instant death (unannounced),
- requiring payers to do something extremely hard without training them first,
- obscure nonsensical puzzles,
- extended memory-based gameplay,
- overly harsh restrictions (impossibly short time trials),
- lack of save points,
- one-way doors that close behind the player without warning.

There are many, many more.

Theory Summary

At the beginning of the book, we established that if we are to teach players how to enjoy a game through our level designs, we also have to test their skills and progress on occasion. To truly enjoy the fruits of their gameplay journey, players need to be able to put their gameplay skills into practice and enjoy their mastery of the abilities required to solve the problems set up by the game.

One of the ways this can be done is by devising gameplay challenges to the player, against which they can measure their skills. This is something they will be happy to engage in if the challenge is appropriate and there is some kind of decent reward. A challenge without a purpose or reward is very adversarial, and while this can be okay once in a while, it can become quite off-putting to people who want to enjoy their gameplay time and not be punished for trying to progress.

Practice

Example 16.1: Player Controlled Challenge Levels—Varying Skills

Summary

A different way of allowing the player to control the challenge level they face is by catering to different play styles and skills. This allows the player to choose those styles and skills he or she is most comfortable with.

Game Genre

The technique is suitable for games that allow for multiple solutions to gameplay challenges.

Goals to Achieve

- Define challenge by skill type and play style.
- Set up a scenario that incorporates several play styles and skills.
- Allow the player to make a choice between them.

Description

(Example type: Original)

Laser fence dilemma 1. In the practice section in Chapter 14 ("Puzzles"), I gave an example where puzzles can work as a pacing device and introduced a hypothetical gameplay scenario based on the player being locked in a fenced-off prison compound. The scenario was called the "laser fence dilemma," and it can easily be adjusted to provide player controlled challenge levels.

The basic setup of the scenario was as follows:

> Imagine a situation where the player is in trouble because they are accosted by an ever-larger group of enemies, perhaps an ever-increasing zombie horde. Eventually the player has no choice but to run for safety and ends up racing into an abandoned prison complex. The player is just able to activate its defenses before the zombie horde gains entry. The defenses consist of a fence made up of four laser beams that repel anybody trying to enter or leave the complex. The player is now safe, but also trapped. The same laser defenses also lock a number of zombies within the compound. The player has to figure out how to disable the lasers, yet doing so will unleash the zombies, both in the compound as well as eventually the zombie horde outside.

> We can break this situation down into sections (sub-puzzles) where the player needs to figure out how to disable all four individual lasers one by one. In addition, we show the player a series of weapons lockers with clearly visible, useful weapons or items, protected by individual laser beams that correspond with those in the fence. Disabling one laser means unlocking a new weapon locker, containing weapons or items that allow the player to deal with the unleashed zombies.

Laser fence dilemma 2. We can adjust this scenario slightly to fit the context of player controlled challenge levels. In this second scenario the player can find two weapons spread out across the compound: a sniper rifle and a flamethrower. Both have a limited amount of ammunition, so the player can try them out, potentially on a few wandering groups of zombies already in the compound, but they will soon run out of ammunition.

The weapons lockers from the original scenario are now more frequent, and they house ammunition for the two new weapons, rather than the weapons themselves. This means that the player can disable the four defensive lasers and in doing so effectively choose which ammunition type becomes available.

In effect, the player can choose a preferred play style:

- Ammunition for the sniper rifle may allow for a play style that emphasizes slow and deliberate play. The rifle is only effective at a large distance, is slow and unwieldy to use, but it is devastatingly powerful. This will suit players who like careful, deliberate strategies.

- Ammunition for the flame thrower requires players to run in amongst the zombies, and affect whole groups of them at once, but the player is then exposed to them at close range. This requires different skills and playing styles, which will suit other players.

This provides an elegant and completely integrated way of allowing the player to choose their preferred challenge level.

Further Notes

Again, the specific solutions in this scenario don't really matter that much, just that catering to different player abilities can provide an effective dynamic challenge environment, under full control of the player.

Example 16.2: Player Controlled Challenge Levels

Summary

Dynamically adjusted difficulty levels are generally an outcome of a game's core design, and not so much the domain of the level design, which just interprets the game design parameters. There are ways, however, in which we can set the levels themselves up in such a way that the players can actively choose the challenge they are comfortable with.

Game Genre

This technique is suitable for most games but works best in games with open environments.

Goals to Achieve

- Allow players to choose the challenge level they are comfortable with in certain scenarios.

Description

(Example type: Original)

We can create a straightforward way of letting the player decide how much challenge they are comfortable with by providing a level *environment* that features challenge or danger gradients. That is to say that the levels are open enough that the player can traverse the level areas at will, but that progress is tempered by escalating levels of challenge, for example, through increased danger.

Imagine a level that gets more challenging (or dangerous) the further the player strays from the main path. This can be set in a valley, for example, where progress becomes harder due to natural obstacles or in a forest where the deeper forest hides more dangerous creatures.

This technique works especially well if the player is given proportional awards when facing these challenges. The player can keep going further away from the minimal challenge path until he or she finds that the awards are no longer worth the difficulty in obtaining them. In effect, this is a physical level design representation of the optimal flow channel discussed before, one where the player can balance skill versus challenge.

Example 16.3: Skill Gates and Challenges

Summary

There are times when we don't want the player to decide where to go unless we are sure they are able to handle the challenges. To address this we can use skill gates, which act as a hard barrier against unwarranted progress, while leaving the choice aspect largely intact.

Game Genre

The technique is suitable for most games that feature skill-based progression.

Goals to Achieve

- Prohibit the player from progressing beyond their skill level.
- Make this feel like it is under the player's control.
- Balance skill and challenge within the level design rather than the game design.

Description

(Example type: Original)

Similar to the previous example but less forgiving is the use of skill gates. The same principle applies: the player decides which path to attempt through an area with varying difficulty levels, but in this case the player needs to possess certain skills to be able to enter the high-challenge area. A higher path through a level may, for example, only be accessed if the player can execute a tricky athletic maneuver, or is able to displace a guard of certain strength. In some ways this is a *lock-and-key* situation: the key is, in fact, the player's skill level and if high enough it gives access to high-challenge areas in a level.

Think of it as a series of walkways each with a skill exam at the entrance to the walkway. If the player passes the exam they can explore that particular route and reap the rewards as well as face the higher challenge levels. If the player fails the exam, it shows that the player is not yet ready for the level of challenges that follow.

The advantage of this technique is that players are not able to end up in situations they are not ready for, and therefore avoid excessive frustration. Additionally, it gives the player something to aim for, especially if the skill gate is clearly signposted. Few things are as motivating as locked-off areas that contain rewards.

Further Notes

This technique also works with other factors prohibiting premature progress. It can be the possession of certain inventory items, player hitpoint levels, or specific weapons. Other options can easily be found depending on the game.

Final Thoughts

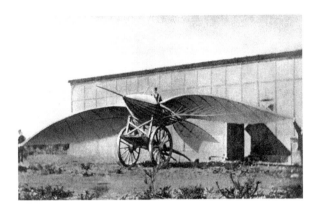

"Le Bris Flying machine", *Wikipedia*, http://commons.wikimedia.org/wiki/File:LeBris 1868.jpg, 2009.

Considering the Future 17

A while ago I bought the first eight years of the popular science and science fiction magazine *Omni* and have been marveling ever since at some of the incredibly fun content it contains. Omni started in the late 70s and had attracted a number of great thinkers and scientists to contribute to its pages since the very first issues. Some of the most fun to be had with such a retro chic magazine is to examine their views on the future, and sure enough, Omni published several futurist articles early on. They make entertaining sci-fi reading material now, but not much of what was predicted has come to pass. Reading those predictions of the future is a rather sobering experience actually as even the greatest scientists and thinkers have very limited success in predicting the future[1].

With that realization in mind I made sure that one of the goals I had with this book was to provide a text that ages as little as possible. Something that is useful even in 20 years time. As a consequence of that goal I have left out speculative topics and I have minimized technology specific subjects. The latter because I wanted to write a book about *design* fundamentals, not about *production*, but also because technology in games move so rapidly that it would have aged the book faster than I could have written it.

Nonetheless, probably to the amusement of readers that pick up this book when it is a bit older, I would like to point at some areas where I think improvements to our craft and exciting new directions can come from.

Tools and Technology

Development tools and technology are some amongst a number of tools available to us to create levels and games. They are not the only tool, nor the most important ones, yet at the time of writing this book there is still an excessive focus on technology, especially as a means to produce photo realistic visuals. Much time is spent in game engines and tools on rendering capacity and visual

---

[1] Notable examples like Arthur C. Clarke buck the trend.

tricks and special effects, almost always aiming for "Hollywood style" graphics, as if that should be the main goal of game development.

Yet, within the tools and technology there is almost no evolution towards techniques that make game levels play better, or to fundamentally improve the way levels are made. Quite often they are based on the same style of content creation as 3D art packages, event though the content created by level designers is completely different from that.

What we really need are tools that set designers free to try out level design ideas rapidly and independently. Tools that allow scripted sequences to be mapped out coherently. We need technology that makes it easy to create environments that can be adjusted to play testing results.

In other words, tools that focus on the improvement of the actual work a level designer does.

Resources

Now that the information age has truly established itself it is becoming clear that society as a whole has to reexamine its ways in which knowledge is created, stored, and made available to others. Projects like Wikipedia have shown that there are large gains to be made by pooling resources and information and making this process open and transparent, even cooperative. Many subjects are now starting to find their way to the public in ever increasing efficiency and volume.

Yet apart from a limited number of books and websites there is very little in the way of resources for level designers. With tremendous effort and patience one can compile a good list of helpful data resources and programs but it is a disparate affair that every individual level designer is forced to go through. I think there are two major areas of improvement that can yield better future results.

Education

Most people working in games are too busy to make games and learn the ropes to be able to teach the subject to others. And consequently there is a real issue with finding people of real experience to be able to teach level design or game design classes. As the profession is still very young I suspect it is just a matter of time for this to improve. Eventually current professionals will reach an age and a level of accumulated wisdom that academic careers will become enticing. This will take a while however and before this can really be an effectively taught subject we will need to reach a broader consensus on many of the field's often-controversial subjects.

Online Resources

As professionals and enthusiasts we should also be able to collect and distribute knowledge ourselves. One way in which this can be done is to start a level design knowledge database, similar to Wikipedia, but based on level and game design knowledge. This can be of immense use as a practical resource and source of reference because game development is such a wide-ranging affair. It would allow specialist knowledge to be collected into a central location, made available for general use. There are level and game designers who are in possession of vital knowledge on the most diverse subjects: How to balance unit types in turn based fantasy role playing games. Somebody else may know a lot about the use of camera techniques in survival horror games or ambush scenario templates for third person action games.

Once a project like this reaches critical mass I suspect it can become a priceless aide to game developers all over the world.

Corporate vs. Independent Development

Most people think of game development through the prism of big console platform holders like Nintendo or Sony, or big corporations like Electronic Arts. The mainstream game industry model sees video games get developed by studios that sign publishing deals with big companies to fund the production of the games that everybody knows and loves. The reality of this model is that most game development is fuelled by commercial goals, and decisions are made within a business model that is not always that suitable to individual artistic intent.

There is another area of future growth and excitement that has started to assert itself quietly but clearly nonetheless. Independent game creators are starting to make games based on their own personal desires and goals, and although these games are not made by teams of a 100 developers with multi million dollar budgets, they have something to offer that the big boys often can't touch: freedom from focus groups, financial dogma, shareholders, and so on. They can, and often do, differentiate themselves from mainstream games with ideas and concepts that are genuinely original and progressive to the art of making games.

I myself have recently snuck over to that way of working and I find it a very exciting place to be. Hopefully I can take the things I have learned while writing this book and use them to make a positive contribution to the grass on this side of the fence.

Recommended Reading & Materials

In the process of writing this book, and in the years preceding it, I have been exposed to an enormous amount of worthwhile reading material and other inspirational content. Many extracts from this material have found their way into this book as quotes or in footnotes. I encourage the reader to follow up on the material referenced within the main body of text, but I would also like to highlight some extra useful resources—not as an attempt to create an exhaustive list, but to provide a good starting point to examine some of the things I found useful while writing the book or while creating levels and games.

This section will therefore showcase some examples of what I found to be inspirational or that I kept going back to on multiple occasions. I created some loose categories, within which books appear in alphabetical order; publication dates come from the editions I own or have read.

Architecture

Architecture: Form, Space and Order, Second Edition
Francis D. K. Ching
Published by John Wiley & Sons, Inc., 1996

This wonderful book demonstrates architectural principles from high-level concepts to nitty-gritty architectural details and brings it to life in clear and informative examples. The book features hundreds of handmade drawings by the author himself, and it is a joy to read as a reference work as well as an art book. It is one of those rare books that will never grow old.

Fantasy Architecture: 1500–2036
Neal Bingham, Clare Carolin, Peter Cook, and Rob Wilson
Published by Hayward Gallery Publishing, 2004

This is a thin but remarkably rich little book that takes a look at fantastical architecture through the ages. It is rich with inspirational concepts, ranging from the farcical to the truly majestic. If you want to be inspired by something a bit different in architecture try this book.

In addition, I recommend works by Syd Mead and Lebbeus Wood.

Game Development/Level Design

A Theory of Fun for Game Design
Raph Koster
Published by Paragryph Press, 2004

This quirky little book combines concepts from flow theory with aspects of neurology and couples that with the author's own personal experiences with loved ones and game design. The book may not necessarily present much new material, but it is all useful and extremely readable and likeable.

Designing Virtual Worlds
Richard Bartle
Published by New Riders Publishing, 2004

This big beast of a book is a must-have with regards to creating virtual worlds and multiuser game environments. Professor Bartle not only provides a thorough and incredibly enlightening book, but it has since its original release been accepted as a foundation from which to build further knowledge. The book introduces language and concepts that have become the state of the art, which makes it a book that you can't do without when interested in this subject.

Creating Emotion in Games
David Freeman
Published by New Riders Publishing, 2004

This book is a bit of a tour de force. It attempts to create a practical reference work on how to apply the author's self-coined methods of "emotioneering." The techniques are meant to create deeper emotional experiences in the games we develop, not the least in areas of narrative and story. The book has been grumbled at by some people because of its somewhat exuberant and confident tone, but it succeeds largely in providing the reader with a huge amount of inspirational content.

Half-Life 2: Raising the Bar
Valve
Published by Prima Games, 2004

Raising the Bar is sometimes mistaken for a coffee table book filled with nice concept art, and indeed the art is wonderful. That misses the true worth of the book, though: it is a fantastically honest and insightful account of the design process, including level design, that Valve went through to create its masterful *Half Life* games. The book is filled to the brim with great insights, practical anecdotes, and examples, and no level designer should do without it. Unfortunately, it is currently out of print and most copies, once tracked down, are rather expensive.

Various

Flow: The Psychology of Optimal Experience
Mihaly Csikszentmihalyi
Published by Harper-Collins Publishers, 1991

This is a groundbreaking work that combines years of exacting academic research into the subject of happiness. The results are of massive importance to game developers as they so easily translate to our work

Making Movies
Sidney Lumet
Published by Vintage Books, 1996

Sidney Lumet shares in a clear and insightful way many of the things he has learned and practiced in his extinguished career.

On Writing: A Memoir of the Craft
Stephen King
Published by Pocket Books, 2000

A brush with mortality led Stephen King to write this engrossing hybrid between biography and reference work. It works well on both levels.

The Design of Everyday Things
Donald A. Norman
Published by Basic Books, 2002

Last but certainly not least, this is a book that every level designer must own. The design of everyday things is one of the best books on product design, usability, and other key areas of interest to level designers. Out of all the books in this section I would recommend this one the most.

Glossary

L evel design is at times a highly specialized and often technical field. This naturally leads to a certain amount of jargon and field-specific terminology. Although I have tried to keep the language used in this book as transparent and accessible as possible, some notes on terminology are needed. The glossary provided here can be used as a handy dictionary of level design terms. Please check this section any time a word's usage seems ambiguous or unclear.

2D games: Games that make use of a two-dimensional representation of the game world.

3D games: Games that make use of a three-dimensional representation of the game world.

agency: The ability of an "agent" to act in (and make an impact on) the world.

AI: Artificial intelligence.

ARG: Alternate reality gaming.

bots: Robots; AI player characters that simulate human opponents.

bullet hell: Describes shoot-em-up games that drown the playing field with bullets.

catharsis: The (rewarding) release of pent-up emotions.

chatterbots: AI constructs that are created to try to converse with humans.

cognitive dissonance: Tension that comes from holding contradictory beliefs.

CGI: Computer graphic imaging.

concept art: Artwork intended to visualize concepts, rather than illustrate actual subjects.

COOP: Cooperative play; a game mode where players band together to play a level.

cutscene: Sequence, often cinematic, where the player has no control over the onscreen events.

deathmatch: Multiplayer game mode where players compete against each other.

double think: The ability to hold two contradictory beliefs.

experience points: Points awarded to players of role playing games for engaging with the game's content; the points are used to gain higher character stats.

fantabulate: Entertaining an audience through fantastical content (admittedly a made-up word).

FPS: First person shooter.

graphic novel: Comic book that tells a story of substantial length.

hitpoints: Health points of a game character.

level up: Advance a character to a higher level of experience, typically by being awarded experience points; higher levels bestow higher character stats on the player.

MMO: Massively multiplayer online game.

MMORPG: Massively multiplayer online role playing game.

mechanic (gameplay): Planned gameplay aspect. For example the wall-jump in a platform game.

mod: Modification. The ability to edit existing game content in order to create new content. The result is also referred to as a "mod".

multiplayer: Game mode where multiple players co-exist.

on rails gameplay: Completely linear gameplay.

OOLD: Object-oriented level design.

OOP: Object-oriented programming.

playtest: Testing the integrity of a level or a game through playing it.

point-and-click adventure: Classic adventure game genre that requires the player to use the mouse pointer and click on onscreen objects to interact with them.

prop: Decorative scenery.

retro games: Games that have received classical status.

RPG: Role playing game.

RTS: Real-time strategy game.

sandbox games: Game type or play style that allows players to come up with many of their own solutions or challenges within the gameworld.

sense of wonder: Feeling that describes a sense of awe or indeed a sense of wonder in science fiction or fantasy entertainment.

serious games: Games that have a goal that goes beyond entertainment, typically education or information delivery.

SHMUP: Shoot-em-up.

shoot-em-up: Game type that has shooting as its central gameplay mechanic.

single player: Game type enjoyed by a single player.

survival horror: Horror game genre that pitches the player against an adversarial environment.

suspension of disbelief: The ability to accept impossibilities in art and entertainment to better enjoy the work itself.

units: Controlled entities in strategy games.

world building: The creation of a virtual world.

Index